EFFECTIVE PROGRAMS FOR STUDENTS AT RISK

Robert E. Slavin

Nancy L. Karweit

Nancy A. Madden

Center for Research on Elementary and Middle Schools
The Johns Hopkins University

ALLYN AND BACON
Boston London Sydney Toronto

Copyright © 1989 by Allyn and Bacon
A Division of Simon & Schuster
160 Gould Street
Needham Heights, Massachusetts 02194

Library of Congress Cataloging-in-Publication Data
Slavin, Robert E.
  Effective programs for students at risk.
  Bibliography: p.
  Includes index.
  1. Socially handicapped children—Education
—United States.   2. Compensatory education
—United States.   3. Special education—
United States.   I. Karweit, Nancy L.
II. Madden, Nancy A.   II. Title.
LC4091.S55   1989   371.96'7   88-34281
ISBN 0-205-11953-0

Printed in the United States of America
10 9 8 7 6 5 4 3 2 1   93 92 91 90 89

CONTENTS

iii

PREFACE

In June 1986, a remarkable conference was held in Washington, DC. This conference, organized by the U.S. Department of Education's Office of Educational Research and Improvement, was intended to bring together the most influential researchers in regular as well as compensatory education to consider what was known about effective instruction that would be of use in the design of programs for students at risk of school failure. After two full days of paper presentations and lively discussion, a most disheartening consensus was reached. First, there was widespread agreement that existing Chapter 1 programs were having only marginal effects on the achievement of students at risk. Second, there was equally wide consensus that educational research had few if any sure answers to the question of how compensatory education might be changed to make a substantial difference in the educational success of students at risk.

Since that conference, it has become increasingly apparent that almost a quarter-century after President Johnson launched Title I (now Chapter 1) as part of his War on Poverty, researchers and practitioners familiar with compensatory education are questioning long-established policies and practices, yet have few clear conceptions about what alternatives will be more effective than current practice. Part of the problem is that the federal investment in research and development of programs specifically designed for compensatory education has been near zero for more than a decade. Another is that simplistic beliefs about what is required to reform compensatory education have taken some time to die. For example, much of the discussion about design of Chapter 1 programs has had to do with the *location* of the services (pullout versus in-class); it has taken more than ten years to discover that pullout and in-class Chapter 1 models are equally effective, or more accurately, equally ineffective (see Chapter 8). Experimentation and reform in Chapter 1 have also been constrained by regulatory limits and by overly restrictive readings of federal regulations by state and local administrators. Finally, real progress in design of compensatory education has been impeded by a false sense of complacency. School districts' Chapter 1 evaluations usually show healthy fall-to-spring gains in standardized test scores. The fact that comparable gains are made by similar students *not* served by Chapter 1 programs has only recently been widely acknowledged.

Paralleling the sense of a need for new directions in compensatory education is a similar feeling in special education. As with the pullout versus in-class debate in compensatory education, special education has also been engaged in a debate about the *location* of services for students with mild academic handicaps, a debate which has diverted attention from the *quality* of services handicapped children receive. At the same time, special educators are becoming concerned about the 260 percent increase since 1976 in the number of students being served under the label *learning disabled* or its equivalent—students who would never have come to the attention of special education fifteen years ago.

Both compensatory and special education are at a watershed. Both are dissatisfied with current practice and are ready for change, yet neither has a clear direction for the future.

This book was written to provide the best available information on what is known now about effective programs for students at risk of school failure, particularly those who are currently served in compensatory and special education programs. The message of this book is that we know much more than we are currently using in programs for students at risk, and that while much more remains to be learned, we know how to proceed to discover how best to prevent and remediate learning deficits. We know that the tragic progression of events that begins with poor achievement in the elementary grades is not an inevitable consequence of low socioeconomic background, poor socialization, or inadequate skills at school entry; we know that well-designed school programs can keep students from starting in that descending spiral. Reform of compensatory and special education to ensure all students an adequate level of basic skills in the early grades will require a major restructuring, not fine-tuning, of existing programs. As much as the need for restructuring is becoming apparent to educators, the discussion of how to proceed is only beginning. This book helps to lay the empirical and intellectual groundwork for the changes that must come in programs for students at risk of school failure.

Preparation of this volume was supported by a grant from the Office of Educational Research and Improvement, U.S. Department of Education, to the Center for Research on Elementary and Middle Schools at Johns Hopkins University (No. OERI-G-86-0006). In particular, we would like to thank Rene Gonzales, our project monitor, for suggesting and then encouraging this work. However, the opinions expressed are those of the authors, and do not necessarily represent OERI positions or policy.

___PART ONE___

INTRODUCTION

1

STUDENTS AT RISK
OF SCHOOL FAILURE:
THE PROBLEM
AND ITS DIMENSIONS

Robert E. Slavin

Center for Research on Elementary and Middle Schools
The Johns Hopkins University

Virtually every child is capable of attaining an adequate level of basic skills. The recognition of this fact is an essential starting point for a discussion on education for students at risk of school failure. For example, there is little doubt that if students had highly skilled one-to-one tutors as long as they needed them, all but the most seriously dyslexic or mentally handicapped children (no more than 1 to 2 percent of the population) would learn enough reading and mathematics in the elementary grades to serve as a basis for success in the later grades. Yet, according to the National Assessment of Educational Progress (1985), almost a quarter of all seventeen-year-olds *in school* read below a level considered necessary to read simple popular magazines. Add to this percentage the approximately 14 percent of students who have dropped out by age seventeen and it becomes apparent that the problem of functional illiteracy is enormous in scope.

The fact that a substantial proportion of students fail to attain an adequate level of basic skills says nothing at all about the capacity of these children to learn; rather, it says that given the level of resources we are able or willing to commit to the education of all students and the way in which these resources are used in practice, a certain proportion of students will not succeed. While it is certain that virtually all students can learn, instructional methods and materials now in use are failing large numbers of students. Even under optimal instructional conditions, some students will require more resources, more time, or both to achieve an acceptable level of achievement.

The problem of low achievement among large numbers of students is hardly new, and in some ways it is improving. For example, although the high school dropout rate has remained at about 14 percent for whites over

3

the period from 1970 to 1985, for blacks it has diminished from 31 percent to 19 percent (U.S. Department of Commerce, 1986). The National Assessment of Educational Progress shows improvements in the reading scores of blacks and Hispanics over the past decade (Carroll, 1987). Yet there is still a long way to go. International comparisons consistently find U.S. students to rank among the lowest in literacy and mathematical skills among industrialized nations, and minority students still perform substantially below their white classmates.

While the problems of low achievement are not new, the consequences of this problem are becoming more serious. The U.S. economy no longer has large numbers of jobs for workers lacking basic skills. Recent studies of cities experiencing very high growth rates find that even when entry-level jobs (such as fast-food jobs) are plentiful, there is a substantial core of workers who cannot qualify for them because of poor basic skills. Allowing large numbers of disadvantaged students to leave school with minimal skills ensures them a life of poverty and dependence—the consequences of which are disastrous to the social cohesiveness and well-being of our nation. Yet the problem of low achievement is by no means restricted to poor or minority students; more than 10 percent of *advantaged* students lack the ability to read popular magazines, and only half have the reading skills considered necessary to read most newspaper stories or popular novels (NAEP, 1985).

As many economists have pointed out, if the United States is to compete successfully in the world market, we must work smarter, not just harder. Real and lasting improvements in the standards of living of nations only come about through increases in the productivity of the workforce. As a nation, we cannot afford to continue to allow our school systems to turn out students lacking in the skills necessary to becoming productive citizens. We cannot afford to allow children to start out on a path that begins with poor achievement and leads to truancy, behavior problems, delinquency, early pregnancy, and dropout. The economic costs, not to mention the social costs, of allowing this progression to unfold for so many students are intolerable. The negative spiral that begins with poor achievement in the early grades can be reversed. We know we can guarantee virtually all children adequate basic skills in the elementary school, and if we choose to do so, there is every likelihood that we could dramatically increase the school success of large numbers of students and consequently the quality of life of our society.

DEFINING "AT RISK"

Recently, educators have begun to use the term *at risk* to describe a certain category of students. The meaning of this term is never very precise, and varies considerably in practice. One possible definition is that students who are at risk are those who, on the basis of several risk factors, are unlikely to graduate from high school. Among these risk factors would be low achievement, retention in grade, behavior problems, poor attendance, low socioeconomic status, and attendance at schools with large numbers of poor students. All of these factors are closely associated with dropping out of school, and research has found by the time students are in the third grade, we can fairly reliably predict which students will ultimately drop out and which will complete their schooling (Howard and Anderson, 1978; Lloyd, 1978; Kelly, Veldman, and McGuire, 1964). In practice, however, different factors have different predictive value depending on student age and other variables. For example, in looking at preschool students, the best predictors of dropout and other school problems are socioeconomic status indicators (Schreiber, 1968). As students move through the grades, their actual performance in school becomes a much better predictor; grades, attendance, and retentions of sixth graders, for example, are very highly predictive of dropout (Lloyd, 1974).

The probability that a student will complete high school is not the only rational criterion for designating students as being at risk. For instance, we might define as *at risk* those students who are unlikely to leave school (at whatever age) with an adequate level of basic skills. With the increasing use of competency-based graduation requirements, we might define as *at risk* those students who are unlikely to pass criterion-referenced graduation tests. And, as still another possibility, we might use criteria such as being at risk for failing one or more grades, or being assigned to special education.

Each of these definitions would produce a somewhat different set of students held to be at risk, but there would be considerable overlap among them. The group we are focusing on is those students whose intelligence is within normal limits but who are failing to achieve the basic skills necessary for success in school and in life. A practical definition of *at risk* might be those students who are presently eligible for special or compensatory education.

This book focuses on programs for students who are at risk by any of the definitions discussed above, with one major exception: students who might be considered at risk solely on the grounds that they speak a language other than English. (For discussions of issues related to the education of students with limited English proficiency, see Carter and Segura, 1979; Ramirez, 1986; Willig, 1985; Wong-Fillmore and Valadez, 1986).

What do we know now about effective programs for students who are at risk for school failure? What do we need to know to better serve these students? These are the central questions posed in this book and addressed by the various chapters.

TYPES OF PROGRAMS FOR STUDENTS
AT RISK

There are three major types of programs for students at risk: compensatory or other remedial programs, special education programs, and general education programs. Each of these has its own history, legal requirements, and practical constraints.

Chapter 1/Title I

Compensatory education refers primarily to federal programs targeted toward low-achieving, disadvantaged students. The largest compensatory program by far is Chapter 1 (formerly Title I), currently budgeted at $4.3 billion per year. One in every nine students receives Chapter 1 services—a total of almost five million children (Guttman and Henderson, 1987). More than 90 percent of school districts receive Chapter 1 funds (Kennedy, Jung, and Orland, 1986). Chapter 1 funds are given to schools on the basis of the number of low-income students they serve, but within schools they are used to serve students according to their educational needs, not their poverty level. Because of this, and because nonpoor students so outnumber poor ones, the majority (58 percent) of students receiving Chapter 1 services are not themselves from families in poverty (see Figure 1–1, from Kennedy, Jung, and Orland, 1986). However, poor students are disproportionate recipients of Chapter 1 services, as are black and Hispanic students. Figure 1–1 also shows that the great bulk of Chapter 1 services go toward elementary schools (grades K–8). Most Chapter 1 funds provide instructional services to students in reading, mathematics, and/or language, as illustrated in Figure 1–2 (from Kennedy, Birman, and Demaline, 1986).

For further discussion of the history and purpose of Chapter 1/Title I, see Chapter 6.

Models of Chapter 1 Service Delivery. Two guiding principles of delivery of Chapter 1 services are that only eligible low-achieving students may benefit from these services, and that the services must supplement, not supplant, local educational efforts. The first of these, which typically limits the use of Chapter 1 funds to students who score below a certain cutoff score on standardized tests (e.g., below the 40th percentile), keeps most schools from using Chapter 1 funds to improve the school overall, for example by reducing class size or implementing more effective practices in the school as a whole (the exception is schoolwide projects, described below). The "supplement, not supplant" requirement generally keeps schools from using Chapter 1 funds to provide services that non-Chapter 1 students receive out of local funds. For instance, a district could not provide preschool or summer school programs for low-achieving or disadvantaged students out of

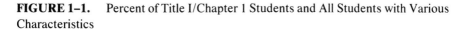

FIGURE 1–1.   Percent of Title I/Chapter 1 Students and All Students with Various Characteristics

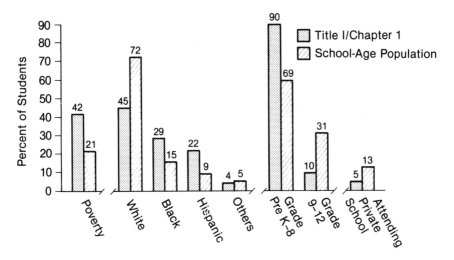

Figure reads: "Among Title I students in 1976–77, 42 percent were poor. Among the student population in general in 1976–77, 21 percent were poor."

Source: M. M. Kennedy, R. K. Jung, and M. E. Orland, *Poverty, achievement, and the distribution of compensatory education services* (Washington, DC: Office of Educational Research and Improvement, U.S. Department of Education, 1986), p. 71.

Chapter 1 funds if it also provided similar programs for non-Chapter 1 students out of local funds. A small army of state regulators audit Chapter 1 programs to make sure that funds are spent only on eligible students and that they supplement local efforts.

There are five principal models of service delivery used under Chapter 1 funding: pullout, in-class, add-on, replacement, and schoolwide. In pullout, students are taken out of their homeroom classes for thirty- to forty-minute periods, during which time they receive remedial instruction in a subject with which they are having difficulty, usually from a certified Chapter 1 teacher and usually in a class of eight or fewer pupils. In in-class models, the teacher (or, more commonly, an instructional aide) works with eligible students within the regular classroom setting. Add-on programs provide services outside of the regular classroom, as in summer school or after-school programs. (An increasingly popular option, using Chapter 1 funds to provide pre-kindergarten programs or to extend kindergarten to a full day, might also be considered an add-on model.) Replacement models involve placing Chapter 1 students in self-contained classes in which they receive most or all of their instruction. These programs require school districts to provide additional local resources to supplement Chapter 1 funds. Schoolwide projects are those in which all students in a high-poverty

FIGURE 1–2. Percent of Chapter 1 Students Receiving Instructional and Non-instructional Services,* 1983–84

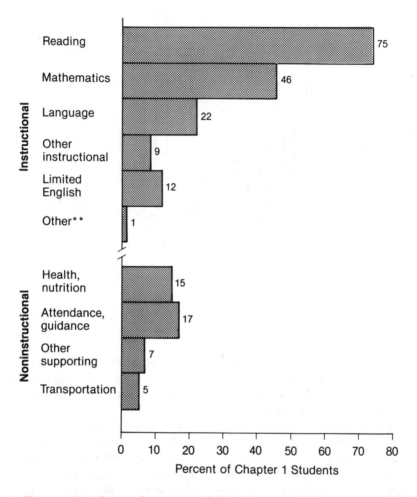

Figure reads: "Seventy-five percent of all students enrolled in Chapter 1 programs received supplementary reading instruction during the 1983–84 school year; 46 percent received supplementary mathematics instruction."

* Total number of students = 4.85 million. If children receive more than one service, they are counted in each subject in which they are enrolled.
** Includes vocational instruction and special services for handicapped students.

Source: M. M. Kennedy, B. F. Birman, and R. E. Demaline, *The effectiveness of Chapter 1 services* (Washington, DC: Office of Educational Research and Improvement, U.S. Department of Education, 1986), p. 2.

school can benefit from Chapter 1 funds. To date, schoolwide projects have been rare, as they could be used only in schools in which at least 75 percent of students were in poverty and in which the district was willing to provide matching funds to supplement the Chapter 1 allocations. New federal legislation has removed the matching fund requirement, so schoolwide projects may become more common among high-poverty schools.

Although use of in-class, add-on, and replacement models has increased in recent years, Chapter 1 funds still overwhelmingly provide pullout programs. Figure 1–3 shows that in elementary schools, pullout designs are used in 84 percent of all Chapter 1 reading programs and 76 percent of math programs—more than all other models combined. Part of the reason for this is that pullout models most clearly fulfill the "supplement, not supplant" requirement of Chapter 1 regulations; in in-class models in particular, there is always concern about the possibility that teachers or aides present in the regular classroom will be helping ineligible as well as eligible students (see Chapters 7, 8, and 11).

How Effective Is Chapter 1?

Chapter 1 has a very well defined purpose: to increase the reading and mathematics achievement of low-achieving students within schools with concentrations of students from families of low socioeconomic status. Measurement of the outcomes of Chapter 1 services would appear to be straightforward, but in practice this is not the case.

One major problem is that the overwhelming majority of school districts evaluate their own Chapter 1 programs by comparing standardized achievement test scores obtained from program participants in the fall to those obtained in the spring. If the average percentile score or Normal Curve Equivalent (NCE)* score increases, then the program is held to be successful, because the students have gained relative to the norming sample used by the test publishers. There is nothing wrong with this evaluation design in theory, but in practice it has turned out that fall-to-spring evaluation designs greatly overestimate true gains, for reasons that are only dimly understood. One indication of this is that nationally, Chapter 1 students show fall-to-spring gains of 7 to 8 percentile points, but these gains are essentially wiped out over the summer; fall-to-fall or spring-to-spring gains average 1 to 2 percentile points at most (see Gabriel, Anderson, Benson, Gordon, Hill, Pfannenstiel, and Stonehill, 1985). Even these gains may be overstated, as annual gains can be influenced by such factors as entry and exit from

---

* A Normal Curve Equivalent is a standard score that has a mean of 50 and a standard deviation of about 21. NCEs resemble percentile scores but are on an equal-interval scale.

FIGURE 1-3. Settings in Which Chapter 1 Reading and Mathematics Are Provided by Public Schools, as Reported by School Principals, 1985–86

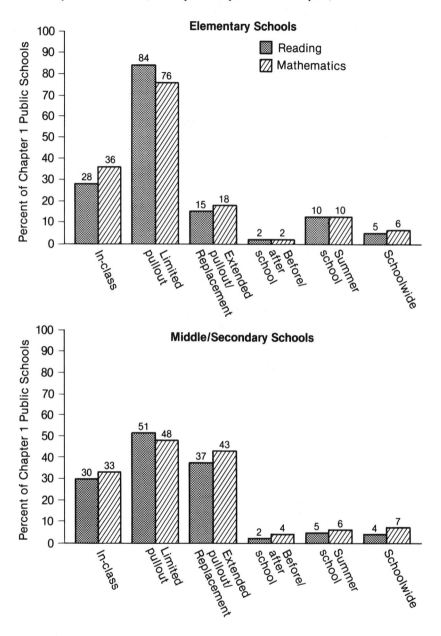

Figure reads: "Of all public elementary schools that offer Chapter 1 reading instruction, principals in 28 percent report use of an in-class setting to teach Chapter 1 reading."

Source: B. F. Birman, M. E. Orland, R. K. Jung, R. J. Anson, G. N. Garcia, M. T. Moore, J. E. Funkhouser, D. R. Morrison, B. J. Turnbull, and E. R. Reisner, *The current operation of the Chapter 1 program* (Washington, DC: Office of Educational Research and Improvement, U.S. Department of Education, 1987), p. 63.

Chapter 1, district promotion/retention policies, and other district practices such as increasing alignment of curriculum with the objectives assessed on the standardized tests.

Since random assignment to Chapter 1 programs would probably be illegal, the best permissible research design for evaluating Chapter 1 is to compare students receiving Chapter 1 services to matched students who did not receive services. This design, which is rarely used in practice, has one major drawback, namely that there may be systematic reasons that certain students do not receive services. For example, a student scoring at the 20th percentile in reading who does not receive services may be located in a non-Chapter 1 school, whereas a matched Chapter 1 student scoring at the same level is in a school with many poor classmates. However, the control group design does not suffer from the fall-to-spring inflation or from confounding with the district policies, so it is the most objectively meaningful evaluation.

The differences in conclusions depending on the type of evaluation design are starkly illustrated by the results of an evaluation of the Oklahoma City Chapter 1 program (Kimball, Crawford, and Raia, 1985). This evaluation presented the data three different ways, as shown in Table 1–1. The table shows that different evaluation designs lead to different conclusions. The fall-to-spring and spring-to-spring gains indicate an extraordinarily effective Chapter 1 program, as these gains are considerably greater than the national seven- to eight-point fall-to-spring gain and one- to two-point spring-to-spring gain. Yet comparing Chapter 1 students to matched control students, the difference is less than two NCE points in reading and less than three in math. Similarly, an evaluation in Baltimore found that Chapter 1 students gained about eight NCE points from fall-to-spring, but so did matched students who received no services (Granick, Quigley, Katzenellenbogen, and Richardson, 1984). A later comparison of served and unserved students in Baltimore also found negligible differences (Pinderhughes, Richardson, Granick, and Katzenellenbogen, 1986).

The best national assessment of the effects of Title I is the now rather dated Sustaining Effects Study (Carter, 1984), which compared achievement gains made by Title I students in 1976–77 to matched "needy" students and

TABLE 1–1. Oklahoma City Chapter 1 Evaluation, Grades 1–6: NCEs Computed Three Ways

	Reading	Math
Fall-to-spring NCE gain	13.0	17.1
Spring-to-spring NCE gain	5.9	8.0
Experimental-control difference	1.9	2.8

FIGURE 1-4.   Reading and Mathematics Achievement of Students Receiving and Not Receiving Compensatory Education, Sustaining Effects Study, 1976–77

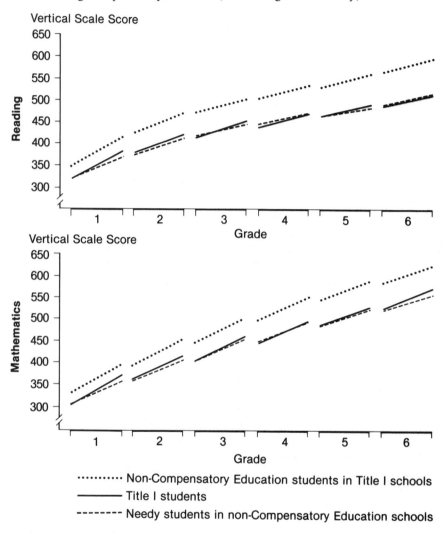

Figure reads: "The vertical scale scores of Title I first-grade students for reading and mathematics increased more from the fall to the spring than did those of similar students not enrolled in Title I schools, yet Title I first graders started behind regular first graders in Title I schools who did not receive Chapter I and failed to catch up by the spring."

Source: M. M. Kennedy, B. F. Birman, and R. E. Demaline, *The effectiveness of Chapter I services* (Washington, DC: Office of Educational Research and Improvement, U.S. Department of Education, 1986), p. 34.

to a representative sample of non-needy students. Figure 1–4 shows that Title 1 students did generally make greater gains in reading and math than other needy students, but these gains were not adequate to close the gap between Title 1 and non-needy students. Table 1–2 summarizes the same data in standard deviation units. Note that in comparing Title 1 and matched needy students, only in first grade did differences exceed 15 percent of a standard deviation (roughly three NCE or percentile points).

The Sustaining Effects Study has been criticized on the basis that the comparison group of needy students may not have been truly equivalent. However, a recent reanalysis correcting for selection bias found essentially the same differences (Myers, 1986).

It is of course possible that in the years since the Sustaining Effects data were collected (1976–77), improved practices within Chapter 1 may have led to markedly improved outcomes. However, in light of the Oklahoma City and Baltimore experimental-control comparisons this seems unlikely. These and other data point to a conclusion that Chapter 1/Title I

TABLE 1–2.   Growth of Three Groups of Students Participating in the Sustaining Effects Study, 1976–77 (Expressed in Standard Deviation Units*)

	Representative Sample	Title I Students	Needy Students With No CE
Reading			
Grade 1	1.98	1.79	1.60
2	.87	.85	.77
3	.61	.64	.53
4	.46	.50	.49
5	.42	.38	.34
6	.37	.37	.37
Math			
Grade 1	1.75	1.76	1.40
2	1.24	1.19	1.04
3	1.21	1.13	1.03
4	.84	.90	.79
5	.70	.68	.55
6	.58	.64	.49

* All gains are converted to standard deviation units, using the standard deviation of the fall scores of the representative samples.

Source: M. M. Kennedy, B. F. Birman, and R. E. Demaline, *The effectiveness of Chapter 1 services* (Washington, DC: Office of Educational Research and Improvement, U.S. Department of Education, 1986), p. 31.

may be effective in the early grades, but if so, the effects are small, on the order of two to three percentile points. Perhaps this is as much as we should expect from an expenditure of only about $500 per student per year, but it is clear that a few more sight words or a little more speed doing arithmetic problems will hardly change the chances that a disadvantaged youngster will ultimately succeed in school or in life.

Because of the importance of Chapter 1 for large numbers of students at risk for school failure, most of the chapters in this book discuss Chapter 1, and all of the chapters have direct bearing on the design of instructional or remedial programs that could in principle be funded by Chapter 1. In particular, Chapter 1 programs, as they exist today, are described in Chapter 7, and effective teaching behaviors within Chapter 1 pullout programs are discussed in Chapter 9. Chapter 8 reviews research on design features of Chapter 1 programs, and Chapters 2 and 3 present information on effective classroom and pullout programs, respectively, which could be used to provide compensatory services.

Head Start

Head Start is a federal compensatory program for students from age three to school entry. Head Start programs provide a half-day preschool setting for children from low-income families with activities designed to enhance their socioemotional and cognitive growth, and most programs also provide health, nutrition, and/or family support services (see Zigler and Valentine, 1979; McKey, Condelli, Ganson, Barrett, McConkey, and Plantz, 1985). Head Start and other compensatory preschool programs are discussed in Chapters 4 and 6.

Follow Through

Follow Through refers to a federal funding program originally meant to maintain the successes of students in Head Start by building in special services for low-income students in the early elementary grades. However, in part because of limited funding, Follow Through soon became a source of funding for model programs designed to help the children of the poor. During the 1970s, Follow Through funded a massive Planned Variation Experiment, in which various innovative programs were developed, implemented, and compared to control groups and to one another in terms of effects on student achievement. Planned Variation is discussed in Chapters 2 and 6. Cutbacks in funding have reduced Follow Through to a minor role in federal compensatory efforts.

Special Education

Special education services have long been provided to students who have identified handicaps. Since the passage of Public Law 94–142 in 1975, school districts have provided a continuum of services for handicapped students, ranging from special schools to special classes within regular schools to various part-time placements. In these programs, students typically receive instruction in very small groups from teachers with certification in special education. Eligibility for special education depends on assessments of individual students' levels of functioning, and a variety of procedural and legal safeguards provided for in PL 94–142 are intended to ensure that students receive appropriate services in the "least restrictive environment" (see Chapter 6).

One of the most important trends in recent years relating to the subject of this book is a substantial increase in the number of students with mild academic handicaps who are receiving special education services. Table 1–3 shows that although the percentage of students categorized as physically disabled and mentally retarded has stayed at about the same level over the period 1976–1985, the number of students categorized as learning disabled increased by about 260 percent. Almost 90 percent of this increase represents the entry into the special education system of low achievers who would not have been served in special education in the past. In other words, special education has assumed a substantial burden in trying to meet the needs of students at risk of school failure. Yet research comparing students with mild academic handicaps in special education to similar students left in

TABLE 1–3.   Percent of Children Served in Educational Programs for the Handicapped

Type of Handicap	Percent of Children Aged 3–21 Served		
	1976–77	*1980–81*	*1984–85*
All conditions	8.33	10.11	11.08
Learning disabled	1.80	3.57	4.67
Mentally retarded	2.16	2.02	1.82
Emotionally disturbed	0.64	0.85	0.95
Speech impaired	2.94	2.85	2.87
Other (deaf, blind, health impaired)	0.81	0.83	0.78

Source: Adapted from U.S. Department of Education, Office of Special Education and Rehabilitative Services, *Eighth Annual Report on Congress on the Implementation of the Education of the Handicapped Act,* 1986.

regular classrooms finds few if any benefits for this very expensive service (see Leinhardt and Pallay, 1982; Madden and Slavin, 1983). Special education for students at risk is discussed in Chapter 6, and effective instructional practices in the regular classroom for mainstreamed academically handicapped students are discussed in Chapter 10.

General Education Programs for Students at Risk

Often ignored in discussions of programs for students at risk is the fact that many programs and practices typical of general education have important consequences for students who are at risk of school failure. For example, tracking and other forms of between-class ability grouping are often held to be beneficial for low achievers by putting success within their reach (although research generally fails to support this; see Slavin, 1987a). Most successful innovations in classroom practices or school organization have positive effects on low- as well as average- and high-achieving students. A major goal of education is to bring all students to an acceptable level of achievement. Therefore, if certain instructional methods had important positive effects on the achievement of *all* students, including low achievers, these methods could be justified for use as means of serving the needs of students at risk. For example, continuous-progress programs and cooperative learning programs tend to be beneficial for all students, not just low achievers (see Chapter 2). Research generally finds that teacher behaviors that are successful with low achievers tend to be very similar to those successful with all students (see Chapters 6, 9, and 10). Thus it is likely that if programs focusing on improving teachers' general instructional skills are successful with low achievers, they will also be effective with other students.

On the other hand, there are general instructional strategies that may differentially affect high and low achievers. For instance, there has been much discussion of the potential "Robin Hood" effect of group-based mastery learning (see Arlin, 1984; Slavin, 1987b), in which instructional time is taken away from high achievers to be used to provide corrective instruction to students who initially fail to master a given set of objectives. Another example of differential effects is departmentalization. Becker (1987) found that having sixth-grade teachers specialize in one subject (so that students had different teachers for each subject) had a somewhat positive effect on the achievement of students from families high in socioeconomic status, but had a marked negative effect on low-SES students.

Discussions of potentially effective practices for students at risk have often been limited in that they focus on only one form of service, such as Chapter 1, special education, preschool, or effective classroom programs for low achievers. However, rather than focusing entirely on pieces of the solution, we need clearly to keep in mind that there is only one problem to be solved—the problem of low achievement. Although it is true that this one problem has many facets, it is critical to step back from current practice to ask what *should* be the response of the educational system overall to ensuring all students an adequate level of basic skills in the elementary grades. To restate the assertion made at the beginning of this chapter, it is certain that virtually all students can learn. But what kinds of programs and what allocations of resources will most effectively bring about a state in which far more students will be successful in their early schooling? To answer this, we must think beyond the confines of current practice. We must learn what we can from the programs that exist today, but never forget that these programs are products of the prevailing conditions when they were formulated, and can in principle be altered if we find other programs or patterns of resource allocation to be more effective. It is certain that if we continue to do what we are doing now, we will continue to experience the same results, and it is equally certain that the results we are obtaining now are not enough. If we are to use the schools to make a significant change in the lives of students who are on a path leading toward school failure, we need to make substantial changes in regular, compensatory, and special education. This book is intended to provide an empirical and conceptual basis for the changes that must come in programs for students at risk.

REFERENCES

Advanced Technology (1983). *Local operation of Title I, ESEA 1976–1982: A resource book.* McLean, VA: Author.

Arlin, M. (1984). Time, equality, and mastery learning. *Review of Educational Research, 54,* 65–68.

Becker, H. J. (1987). *Addressing the needs of different groups of early adolescents: Effects of varying school and classroom organizational practices on students from different social backgrounds and abilities* (Tech. Rep. No. 16). Baltimore, MD: Johns Hopkins University, Center for Research on Elementary and Middle Schools.

Birman, B. F.; Orland, M. E.; Jung, R. K.; Anson, R. J.; Garcia, G. N.; Moore, M. T.; Funkhouser, J. E.; Morrison, D. R.; Turnbull, B. J.; and Reisner, E. R. (1987). *The current operation of the Chapter 1 program.* Washington, DC: Office of Educational Research and Improvement, U.S. Department of Education

Bureau of the Census (1985). *School enrollment: Social and economic characteristics of students.* Washington, DC: U.S. Department of Commerce.

Carroll, J. B. (1987). The national assessments in reading: Are we misreading the findings? *Phi Delta Kappan, 68,* 424–428.

Carter, L. F. (1984). The Sustaining Effects study of compensatory and elementary education. *Educational Researcher, 13*(7), 4–13.

Carter, T. P., and Segura, R. D. (1979). *Mexican Americans in school: A decade of change.* Princeton, NJ: College Entrance Examination Board.

Gabriel, R. M.; Anderson, B. L.; Benson, G.; Gordon, S.; Hill, R.; Pfannenstiel, J.; and Stonehill, R. M. (1985). *Studying the sustained achievement of Chapter 1 students.* Washington, DC: U.S. Department of Education.

Granick, L.; Quigley, M. M.; Katzenellenbogen, R.; and Richardson, L. H. (1984). *Optimizing Chapter 1 program effectiveness.* Baltimore, MD: Baltimore City Public Schools.

Guttmann, B., and Henderson, A. (1987). *A summary of state Chapter I participation and achievement information for 1984–85.* Washington, DC: Decision Resources Corporation.

Howard, M. A. P., and Anderson, R. J. (1978). Early identification of potential school dropouts: A literature review. *Child Welfare, 52,* 221–231.

Kelly, F. J.; Veldman, D. J.; and McGuire, C. (1964). Multiple discriminant prediction of delinquency and school dropouts. *Educational and Psychological Measurement, 24,* 535–544.

Kennedy, M. M.; Birman, B. F.; and Demaline, R. E. (1986). *The effectiveness of Chapter 1 services.* Washington, DC: Office of Educational Research and Improvement, U.S. Department of Education.

Kennedy, M. M.; Jung, R. K.; and Orland, M. E. (1986). *Poverty, achievement, and the distribution of compensatory education services.* Washington, DC: Office of Educational Research and Improvement, U.S. Department of Education.

Kimball, G. H.; Crawford, J.; and Raia, F. (1985). *Evaluation of the 1984–85 Oklahoma City Public Schools Chapter 1 program.* Oklahoma City, OK: Oklahoma City Public Schools.

Leinhardt, G., and Pallay, A. (1982). Restrictive educational settings: Exile or haven? *Review of Educational Research, 52,* 557–578.

Lloyd, D. N. (1974). Analysis of sixth grade characteristics predicting high school dropout or graduation. *JSAS Catalog of Selected Documents in Psychology, 4,* 90.

Lloyd, D. N. (1978). Prediction of school failure from third-grade data. *Educational and Psychological Measurement, 38,* 1193–1200.

Madden, N., and Slavin, R. E. (1983). Mainstreaming students with mild handicaps: Academic and social outcomes. *Review of Educational Research, 53,* 519–569.

McKey, R.; Condelli, L.; Ganson, H.; Barrett, B.; McConkey, C.; and Plantz, M. (1985). *The impact of Head Start on children, families, and communities.* (DHHS No. (OHDS) 85-31193). Washington, DC: Department of Health and Human Services.

Myers, D. E. (1986). *An analysis of the impact of Title I on reading and math achievement of elementary school aged children.* Washington, DC: Office of Educational Research and Improvement, U.S. Department of Education.

National Assessment of Educational Progress (1985). *The reading report card: Progress toward excellence in our schools; trends in reading over four national assessments, 1971–1984.* Princeton, NJ: NAEP.

National Commission on Excellence in Education (1983). *A nation at risk.* Washington, DC: U.S. Department of Education.

Pinderhughes, A. G.; Richardson, L. H.; Granick, L.; and Katzenellenbogen, R. (1986). *Chapter 1 services report FY'86.* Baltimore, MD: Baltimore City Public Schools.

Ramirez, J. D. (1986). Comparing structured English immersion and bilingual education: First-year results of a national study. *American Journal of Education, 95,* 122–148.

Schreiber, D. (1968). 700,000 dropouts. *American Education, 4,* 17–21.

Slavin, R. E. (1987a). Ability grouping: A best-evidence synthesis. *Review of Educational Research, 57,* 293–336.

Slavin, R. E. (1987b). Mastery learning reconsidered. *Review of Educational Research, 57,* 175–213.

U.S. Department of Commerce (1986). *Current population reports,* series P-20, Nos. 222, 303, 362, Md. 409.

Willig, A. C. (1985). A meta-analysis of selected studies on the effectiveness of bilingual education. *Review of Educational Research, 55,* 269–317.

Wong-Fillmore, L., and Valadez, C. (1986). Teaching bilingual learners. In M. C. Wittrock (Ed.), *Handbook of research on teaching* (3rd ed.). New York: Macmillan.

Zigler, E., and Valentine, J. (1979). *Project Head Start: A legacy of the War on Poverty.* New York: Free Press.

PART TWO

ELEMENTARY PROGRAMS

2

EFFECTIVE CLASSROOM PROGRAMS FOR STUDENTS AT RISK

Robert E. Slavin

Nancy A. Madden

Center for Research on Elementary and Middle Schools
Johns Hopkins University

In recent years, there has developed a growing dissatisfaction with the educational services provided to students who are at risk for developing learning problems or school failure. Much of this dissatisfaction has centered on the practice of pulling low-achieving students out of class for remedial instruction, usually provided as part of the federal Chapter 1 (formerly Title I) program (see Chapters 6–8). Some researchers have found that the more time students spent in pullout programs, the *less* they learned (Coulson, Hanes, Ozenne, Bradford, Doherty, Duck, and Hemenway, 1977; Glass and Smith, 1977). Chapter 1 pullouts have been criticized on the basis that instruction in the pullout program is rarely well integrated with that provided by the regular classroom teacher (Kaestle and Smith, 1982; Johnston, Allington, and Afflerbach, 1985). Also, much time is lost in transitions between regular and pullout settings, and pullouts rarely increase the total instruction provided to students (Vanecko, Ames, and Archambault, 1980; Kimbrough and Hill, 1981). Similar problems of coordination and supplanting of regular classroom instruction have been noted for special education pullouts (Sargent, 1981) and when students qualify for special education *and* remedial services, these problems multiply (Birman, 1981).

Although the problems of pullouts are well recognized, *alternatives* to pullouts have their own drawbacks. Having the remedial teacher work in a corner of the regular classroom, as is typical in in-class Chapter 1 models, provides no guarantee that coordination with the regular program will be enhanced (see Lee and Rowan, 1986). In-class models are often structurally identical to pullout programs except that the remedial services are provided in a different location. Research comparing pullout and in-class Chapter

1/Title I models has found few differences in achievement effects (see Chapter 8).

One point on which there is agreement among virtually all reviewers of research on Chapter 1 and special education programs for students at risk is that *program quality* is far more important than the setting in which the program is implemented (see Chapters 6 and 8; Leinhardt and Pallay, 1982; Madden and Slavin, 1983; Archambault, 1987). Clearly, there can be effective pullout programs and effective in-class programs to meet the needs of at-risk students. This chapter examines research on classroom programs for elementary school students who are at risk for learning problems. The full range of alternative classroom organization models designed to meet the needs of low-achieving or heterogeneous classes is explored; the principal question this chapter asks is: How can the educational needs of all students be met by fundamentally restructuring the regular classroom, as opposed to adding on services outside of the regular classroom?

SCOPE OF REVIEW

This chapter focuses on a review of specific, comprehensive programs that may be beneficial for the achievement of students who are at risk for learning problems. A *program* is defined here as a set of procedures intended to be implemented as a total package and capable of being replicated by others. These features distinguish a program from a set of variables. For example, there is evidence that such variables as strong principal leadership, high expectations, and high time-on-task are related to student achievement gains (e.g., see Brophy and Good, 1986). However, these variables do not in themselves constitute a program; a program would lay out a specific set of procedures that might incorporate these variables (and others) but would do so in a structured and replicable format. The word *replicable* is particularly important in the definition of a program. It is often the case that a particular school or district has considerable success with at-risk students, but the success is due to the unusual skill or devotion of a set of individual principals or teachers rather than to any particular set of practices that can be easily transmitted to others.

PROCEDURES

This review used a set of procedures adapted from best-evidence synthesis (Slavin, 1986), a review method that combines features of meta-analytic and traditional narrative reviews. In essence, a priori inclusion criteria relating to internal and external validity were established and a broad literature search was conducted to identify studies that met those criteria. When possible, achievement effects of the qualifying studies were characterized in terms of effect size, the difference between experimental and control means divided by the control groups' standard deviation (Glass, McGaw, and Smith, 1981). However, the strengths and weaknesses of the individual evaluations are described to set the effects in context. These procedures are described in more detail in the following sections.

Literature Search

Every effort was made to search the literature on instructional programs for elementary-aged students (grades 1–6) as broadly as possible. Academic journals yielded a few relevant studies, but research on comprehensive instructional programs is rarely reported in these journals. The most fruitful source of information by far was reports submitted to the Joint Dissemination Review Panel (JDRP), a U.S. Department of Education panel that reviews evaluations of programs originally supported by federal funds. Programs whose effects are certified as valid by the JDRP are eligible for funding and dissemination through the National Diffusion Network (NDN). What makes the JDRP submissions such a rich source of information for identifying effective programs is that, with few exceptions, the programs submitted to the JDRP were designed to be replicable. The main reason for a school district or research and development organization to go through JDRP review is to obtain funds to disseminate a program nationally. Thus data on programs that could not be easily transported to a new location would be unlikely to be submitted to the JDRP. Also, the JDRP review process demands enough data to enable reviewers to determine program effects. The submissions for more than 300 programs which successfully passed JDRP review were obtained from the Department of Education. Also, the Northwest Regional Education Laboratory recently published an *Effective Compensatory Education Sourcebook* (Griswold, Cotton, and Hansen, 1986) which listed 116 district Chapter 1 programs nominated and selected as being particularly effective. Data and program descriptions were requested from these districts. Finally, ERIC documents, journal articles, and other reports were obtained in a general literature search relying in particular on references from other reviews (e.g., Ellson, 1986).

Substantive Inclusion Criteria

In order to be considered germane to the scope of this review, studies had to conform to a broad set of criteria:

1. The programs evaluated had to be directed toward increasing the reading and/or mathematics achievement of students in grades 1–6.

Programs that were designed primarily for use in kindergarten are discussed in Chapter 5, whereas those that overlapped the elementary grades (e.g., K–2, K–6, K–12) are included here.

2. The programs had to be implemented in regular classrooms. This excludes self-contained special education programs. Pullout and tutoring programs are reviewed in Chapter 3.

3. The programs had to be applicable to the education of at-risk students. This criterion was interpreted very broadly. Even if programs did not present evidence that they had been successfully evaluated in schools containing disproportionate numbers of at-risk students, they were included if they could, *in principle*, be applied to such students. However, a lack of data on effects for at-risk students is noted as a drawback in descriptions of effective programs.

4. Programs specifically designed for non-English speakers are not included in this review.

Methodological Inclusion Criteria

Unfortunately, the methodological quality of most evaluations of instructional programs is very low. Many evaluations compare the achievement of students in experimental programs to that of students in "comparable" schools, with no evidence given that the comparison schools were in fact comparable before the treatments were administered. Others lack even this much control, claiming that since students achieved above "grade level expectations," the program must be successful.

Perhaps the most common reason for invalid evaluation design is the use of fall-to-spring gains in percentiles or, more commonly, normal curve equivalents (NCEs). A normal curve equivalent is a standard score with a mean of 50, a standard deviation of about 21, and a range of 1 to 99. Thus NCEs are similar to percentile scores, but they are preferable because they use an equal-interval scale. In recent years, districts receiving Chapter 1 funds have been encouraged to report fall-to-spring gains in NCEs for their Chapter 1 recipients, which helps explain the popularity of this design.

The rationale behind the fall-to-spring design is sensible in theory. If students score at, say, a mean NCE of 40 in the fall and 50 in the spring, then they have apparently gained relative to the national norming group, which should have remained at the same level on average. However, in recent years it has become apparent that this assumption is incorrect. Among Chapter 1 populations, NCE gains of about eight points are routinely made from fall to spring (see Gabriel, Anderson, Benson, Gordon, Hill, Pfannenstiel, and Stonehill, 1985; Keesling, 1984). However, by the following fall, these differences have generally disappeared. The fall-to-spring gain is probably a statistical artifact, not a true effect of Chapter 1. For example,

Chapter 1-eligible students who do not actually receive Chapter 1 services make similar gains (Carter, 1984; Granick, Quigley, Katzenellenbogen, and Richardson, 1984). Almost all of the "exemplary" Chapter 1 programs cited by Griswold, Cotton, and Hansen (1986) that provided multiyear data showed a pattern of fall-to-spring gains followed by equal spring-to-fall declines; the fall-to-fall or spring-to-spring gains were essentially nil over as many as five years. National data reported by Gabriel et al. (1985) indicate that the fall-to-spring effect is largest in the younger grades, diminishing from almost 9 NCEs in grade 2 to 4.5 in grade 12.

Unfortunately, the cause of the fall-to-spring artifact is unknown (see Kennedy, Birman, and Demaline, 1986), and it is unlikely that the gains are equal across tests, types of students, or other factors. Therefore, it is not even possible to assume that because a particular district reports gains much more than 8 NCEs that this is evidence of an effective program. There are examples of school districts in which fall-to-spring gains of 16 NCEs or more are reported each year, yet no growth from fall-to-fall or spring-to-spring is evident.

Program evaluations that use fall-to-fall or spring-to-spring NCE or percentile gains as a criterion for program effects are better than fall-to-spring studies, because the expected gains for annual testing are much smaller, in the range of 1–3 NCEs (Gabriel et al. 1985). Yet these have serious drawbacks as well. Some evaluations report annual gains for successive cohorts of students at a particular grade level (e.g., third graders in 1978–80 versus third graders in 1980–81). Cohort differences can be affected by many extraneous factors, such as changes in district testing or promotion procedures. However, this design is preferable to a comparison of this year's gain to last year's for the same students (e.g., comparing the gains made by this year's fourth graders compared to those made by last year's third graders). Such designs confound programs' effects with retention/promotion, selection into or out of Chapter 1 or other special programs, and other factors. Comparing last year's gains to this year's for *promoted* students only is a much better procedure, but is rarely used; including nonpromoted students inflates estimates of annual gain because these students are being compared again to the same grade-level norms after a year of instruction and growth.

The inclusion criteria applied in the present review follow from the above discussion. The purpose of these criteria is to extract from a large, diverse, and messy literature the most convincing evidence available at present on effective classroom programs for students at risk. The criteria are as follows:

1. Convincing evidence of effectiveness had to be presented. Unfortunately, the nature of existing program evaluation data and of the sources of reports on such data precludes identification of programs that are *not*

effective. The JDRP and exemplary Chapter 1 programs come to our attention only because they were felt to be outstanding. A pattern of fall-to-spring gains and spring-to-fall losses cannot be used as evidence of *effectiveness,* but neither is it convincing evidence of *ineffectiveness.* In a usual review of the literature on experimental programs, effective and ineffective programs would be compared in an attempt to identify consistent characteristics of the more effective ones (see Cooper, 1984; Light and Pillemer, 1984; Slavin, 1986). However, in the present case, the review focuses on those programs with convincing evidence of effectiveness, as distinct from others that may or may not be equally effective but do not present convincing data. A discussion of programs considered for inclusion but not included and reasons for exclusion is presented later in this chapter.

The remaining methodological inclusion criteria define what is meant by "convincing evidence of effectiveness."

2. Evaluations had to use control group designs with random assignment to groups and/or convincing evidence that comparison groups were initially equivalent in achievement. Studies that showed spring-to-spring gains of at least 7 NCEs were also included, but in a separate category. This is about one-third of a population standard deviation (approximately 21), but more like half of the standard deviation typical of Chapter 1 students, who have a more restricted range of scores. One important category of programs excluded from the set of effective models is those that were involved in the Follow-Through Planned Variation evaluation (Kennedy, 1978) and were found to be no more effective than control groups *overall,* even though they were found to be effective in one or more sites. In many cases, data from the successful sites passed JDRP review, as the JDRP procedures do not require that data from all sites be submitted or considered.

3. Evaluations had to use standardized, broadly based measures of reading and/or mathematics achievement. This excluded a small number of studies that used experimenter-made measures or only assessed a narrow set of reading or mathematics skills.

4. The duration of evaluations had to be at least one semester (sixteen weeks). Almost all JDRP and Chapter 1 evaluations cover at least a one-year period, but many evaluations of promising programs that have appeared in academic journals have involved much shorter treatment durations. To be considered a practical evaluation of a replicable program, a duration of one semester is a minimal requirement.

CATEGORIES OF EFFECTIVE MODELS

The principal results of the search for instructional methods with convincing evidence of positive effects are summarized in Tables 2–1 through 2–3. In each table, those programs that evaluated studies that employed matched or (rarely) randomized control groups are listed first, with associated effect sizes. These effect sizes should be interpreted very cautiously and should not be compared across methods, but are included to characterize the relative magnitudes of effects on different outcomes or for different sub-populations within programs.

The effective models are discussed according to catagories of programs. Surprisingly, among the dozens of programs evaluated for possible inclusion, programs that presented convincing data fell into only three categories: continuous progress, individualized instruction, and cooperative learning.

Continuous Progress

The largest number of programs with convincing evidence of effectiveness are those falling in the category labeled *continuous progress*. The individual programs in this category vary in many particulars, but features common to all include the following:

1. Students proceed through a well-specified hierarchy of skills. They are tested at each level to determine their readiness to move on to the next skill. Special procedures are established to assist students who fail to pass regular mastery assessments. These may include corrective instruction in small groups, tutoring, assignment to different groups, or special materials or activities. In these respects, continuous progress programs resemble mastery learning and they are often described as such. However, continuous progress programs are fundamentally different from the group-based mastery learning programs more commonly seen in elementary and secondary schools (see Slavin, 1987a). (Group-based mastery learning is discussed later in this chapter.)

2. Careful records are kept of each student's progress through the curriculum. These data are used to make grouping, remediation, and other decisions.

3. Most instruction is delivered by teachers to *groups* of students at the same instructional level. This is primarily what differentiates continuous progress from individualized models. In continuous progress models, students progress at their own rates, but are primarily instructed by teachers rather than by programmed or other individualized materials. In these methods, students are constantly grouped and regrouped according to their levels of reading and/or math skills; this grouping is often done across grade lines, as in nongraded programs (see Goodlad and Anderson, 1963).

Individualized Instruction

Although there are many individualized programs that have been approved by the JDRP, only a few qualified as effective by the criteria applied in this chapter. The characteristics common to these programs are as follows:

1. Students work primarily on programmed or other individualized materials, with teachers working mostly with individuals rather than groups of students. This is the primary difference between continuous progress and individualized models; many continuous progress models describe themselves as "individualized," but do not rely on self-instructional materials.
2. As in continuous progress programs, individualized models keep careful records of student progress through a structured, hierarchical set of learning objectives.

Cooperative Learning

Although there are many methods based on principles of cooperative learning (Slavin, 1983a, b; 1988), only two have been evaluated over periods of at least one semester in terms of effects on standardized tests of reading and math: Team Assisted Individualization (TAI) (Slavin, 1985) and Cooperative Integrated Reading and Composition (CIRC) (Stevens, Madden, Slavin, and Farnish, 1987). In addition to structuring cooperation among students, both methods also incorporate elements of continuous progress. The elements in common to TAI and CIRC are as follows:

1. Students work in four- to five-member mixed ability learning teams and receive certificates or other recognition based on the learning of all group members. Students both help one another learn and assess one another's skills in preparing for tests or teacher assessments, which will be taken without teammate help.
2. Teachers instruct students (drawn from the different teams) who are at the same level in a hierarchy of skills. Most information comes from the teachers, not from peers or materials; teammates help one another *master* skills, but they do not provide initial instruction to each other.
3. Students are frequently assessed, first by teammates and then by the teacher. Specific corrective procedures are provided for students who do not meet a preset level of mastery.

CHARACTERISTICS AND OUTCOMES OF EFFECTIVE MODELS

Continuous Progress

Table 2–1 lists a total of eleven programs that were categorized as continuous-progress models with convincing evidence of effectiveness. Seven of these used control group designs.

Distar.   Distar (Becker and Carnine, 1980) is a program developed at the University of Oregon. Distar is unusual, even within the range of continuous-progress programs. It provides teachers with very specific scripts to use in teaching reading and math and trains teachers in very specific methods, down to the level of how to use hand signals to elicit student responses and how to call on students. In describing the program, Distar's developers tend to emphasize the sequential, hierarchical curriculum design, direct instruction and rapid pace, and high frequency of student responses (Becker and Carnine, 1980). However, what defines Distar as a continuous progress model is that students are taught in small groups that are homogeneous in skill level, are assessed frequently on their progress through a well-defined skill hierarchy, and are regrouped if necessary according to the results of these assessments.

The evidence supporting the effectiveness of Distar for increasing student performance in certain skill areas is strong. Distar was the only one of the nine major programs evaluated in the national Planned Variation Follow Through studies conducted by Abt Associates (Stebbins, St. Pierre, Proper, Anderson, and Cerva, 1977) to have consistently positive effects on the achievement of disadvantaged students. The effect size estimates that appear in Table 2–1 are from the Abt evaluation, pooling across cohorts (see Kennedy, 1978). As the table indicates, however, the effects of Distar appeared primarily on language and math computations tests, not on such higher-order skills as reading comprehension or math problem solving. Even on these scales, though, Distar students scored higher than all other Follow Through models. Note that these effects were brought about over three or four years of implementation, as the Abt evaluation focused on students who were in their respective programs from kindergarten or first to third grade.

What makes the Abt evaluation results particularly impressive is that this evaluation involved many sites, matched control groups, and consistent measurement across non-Follow Through and various Follow Through treatments. In reviewing instructional programs for this chapter, there was always a nagging question of whether reports of successful evaluations sent to the JDRP or published in a journal are anomalies, perhaps one or two sites out of dozens in which the program was evaluated. In fact, in several cases, sites that had positive results successfully passed JDRP review even though

TABLE 2–1. Continuous-Progress Programs

Program and Source	Grades/ Subjects	Description	Evaluation		Effect Sizes	
I. Programs Evaluated Using Control Group Designs						
DISTAR (Becker & Carnine, 1980; Stebbins et al., 1977; JDRP #77–122, JDRP #80–50)	K–6 Reading Math	Teacher instructs small groups using highly structured, scripted lessons. Students frequently assessed, regrouped.	Abt evaluation found positive effects in reading and math in most sites; JDRP-approved sites include Flint, MI; Dayton, OH; Flippin, AK; E. Las Vegas, NM; Uvalde, TX; Kingstree, SC; Cherokee, NC; Washington, DC.	Gr. K–3 (4 yrs.)	Rdg. Comp Language Math Comp. Math P.S.	+.07 +.84 +.57 +.17
U-SAIL (JDRP #76–95)	1–9 Reading Math	Combines continuous progress, individualized activities. Adapts to existing curriculum, materials.	Both time series and control group comparisons show clear effects in reading and math in suburban school near Salt Lake City. *Not disadvantaged.*	Gr. 3–5 (2 yrs.)	Reading Math	+.45 +.27
PEGASUS-PACE (JDRP #1, JDRP #79–1)	K–8 Reading	Students proceed through 17 reading levels, gr. K–8; frequently assessed, regrouped.	Matched control group design found convincing effects in reading in rural Princeton, IL; some students were Title I, but mostly *not disadvantaged.*	Gr. 2 +.72 Gr. 3 +.80 Gr. 4 +.50 Gr. 5 +.39 Gr. 6 +.43	Rdg. Voc. Rdg. Comp.	+.53 +.61
ECRI (JDRP #74–48)	1–6 Reading	Teacher instructs small groups; frequent mastery checks	Most evaluations fall-spring or spring-spring. One control group evaluation in suburban Chapter 1 school near Cincinnati found convincing effects.	Gr. 4	Rdg. Voc. Rdg. Comp.	+.51 +.39
Project INSTRUCT (JDRP #75–37)	K–3 Reading	Cross-grade grouping according to reading skills; students proceed through skills at own rate.	Compared students in Lincoln, NE, schools that had successfully implemented program to matched schools. *Not disadvantaged.*	Gr. 2	Word Knwl. Reading	+.30 +.23

Program	Grades/Subject	Description	Comparison	Results
GEMS (JDRP #79–2)	K–12 Reading	Students work in small groups or individually on materials at their own level. Frequent assessment, mastery tests, corrective instruction.	Compared project schools with matched controls in suburb of Salt Lake City. *Not disadvantaged.*	Gr. 1 +.11, Gr. 2 +.00, Gr. 3 +.41, Gr. 4 +.23, Gr. 5 +.44, Gr. 6 +.39; Rdg. Voc. +.39, Rdg. Comp. +.14
Early Childhood Preventative Curriculum (JDRP #74–57)	1 only Reading	Students identified as high risk given intensive continuous progress, diagnostic-prescriptive program with small group and individualized activities.	Compared project schools to matched controls in Miami, FL.	Gr. 1; Par. Mng. +.95, WRAT +.28

II. *Programs Evaluated Using Year-to-Year Gains*

Program	Grades/Subject	Description	Comparison
WILASD (JDRP #83–2)	1–3 Reading	Combines continuous progress, whole class, and individualized instruction.	Compared cohorts in mostly Hispanic, low-income school in Weslaco, TX, before program begun and then several years after. Clear differences in scores.
COMP (JDRP #74–114)	1–8 Math	Students taught in small groups, progress through 25 levels in 8 yrs.	Fall-to-fall trends in NCEs show clear gains in math. Columbia, MO. *Not disadvantaged.*
CLIMB (JDRP #81–44)	1–12 Reading Math	Diagnostic-prescriptive, continuous progress. Title I teachers mostly consult, do some pullout.	Grades 4–6 Title I students in suburban Middlesex, NJ, gained significantly in fall-to-fall reading and math NCEs.
Outcomes-Driven Developmental Model (Mamary and Rowe, 1985; JDRP #85–7)	1–8 Reading Math	Students grouped across grades according to skills. Frequent mastery assessments, corrective instruction. Uses cooperative learning during independent practice.	Gains over several years in percent of students scoring above grade level, Johnson City, NY. Mostly *not disadvantaged.*

they were using methods that were unsuccessful at most other sites. The effects for Distar summarized in Table 2–1 are averaged across all sites that used the program, successfully or not.

Recent research on Distar has found that the program's effects can be long-lasting. Following up students from an inner-city New York elementary school, Distar students exceeded control in high school graduation; about 55 percent of the former Distar students graduated, compared to 34 percent of control students (Meyer, 1984).

Despite the well-documented and widely acknowledged positive effects of Distar, there has also been much criticism of this approach, principally on the basis of its use of scripted lessons and a perceived focus on rote skills rather than higher-order, learning-to-learn skills (e.g., see Calfee, 1986). Many teachers and administrators resist Distar for similar reasons. Given this reality, it is important to note that Distar is only one of several successful continuous progress models, is the only one to use scripted lessons, and is one of only two (with ECRI) to emphasize the highly organized, teacher-centered classroom organization that many teachers find offensive.

U-SAIL.   The Utah System Approach to Individualized Learning (U-SAIL) was developed and evaluated in Utah. It is a continous progress program quite different from Distar. In it, students proceed through a hierarchical sequence of objectives at their own rates. Most instruction is given to small groups, but some individual work is included. While the teacher is instructing skill-level groups, other students are given independent, exploratory activities, with a particular emphasis on independent reading (see Hales, 1983a, b).

The JDRP submission for U-SAIL presents data from only one elementary school in suburban Davis County, Utah. Evidence is provided to show that the school was similar to the control school for three years before U-SAIL was begun, but gained more than the control school afterwards. The data in Table 2–1 represent the degree to which U-SAIL students outperformed control students in reading and math from grades 3–5. Unfortunately, we have no idea how successful the program has been in other schools, or whether the active involvement of the developer is needed to make the program successful. Also, no evidence is given that U-SAIL can be effective with disadvantaged or low-achieving students.

PEGASUS.   This program was apparently the first to pass JDRP review, as it was given the first JDRP number. PEGASUS is a classic continuous-progress program. It organizes the reading program into seventeen levels, spanning grades K–8. Students progress through these levels at their own rates, but are taught in groups appropriate to their current levels. Within each of the levels is a continuum of skills that students must master.

PEGASUS was originally developed in Tuscaloosa, Alabama, but data could be obtained for evaluation only from a "turnkey" site in rural Illinois. In this evaluation, schools in Bureau County were matched with similar schools in La Salle County for a one-year study. Results indicated significantly greater growth in reading for PEGASUS students at most grade levels on vocabulary as well as reading comprehension measures. However, although some of the students were poor, results for these students were not separately reported, so generalization to disadvantaged groups may not be warranted.

ECRI. The Exemplary Center for Reading Instruction (ECRI), like U-SAIL, originally developed in Utah. However, it is quite unlike U-SAIL in procedures, more resembling Distar in classroom organization, rapid instructional pace, detailed and specific instructions for teachers, and frequent assessment of student progress. In ECRI, students are usually assigned to three reading groups. They receive instruction in their groups, and then work on materials at their own rates. ECRI emphasizes teaching specific word attack skills and proceeding through large numbers of words in a short time.

Most evaluations of ECRI presented as part of the JDRP submission used fall-to-spring designs. One study, in a relatively low-SES school in a suburb of Cincinnati, used a control group design, and the results of this study were used to compute the effect sizes shown in Table 2–1. Also, spring-to-spring data from a mostly low-SES, all-black school in rural Louisiana and from a Chapter 1 school in suburban Englewood, Ohio, suggest that ECRI can be effective with disadvantaged and low-achieving students.

Project INSTRUCT. Like PEGASUS, Project INSTRUCT is a classic continuous-progress program. It was developed and evaluated in Lincoln, Nebraska. In the program, students are grouped according to skill levels, and may proceed through a hierarchy of skills at their rates. An evaluation of the program by Novak (1975) compared schools that successfully implemented Project INSTRUCT to matched control schools, and found small positive effects in reading and math.

GEMS. Goal-Based Educational Management System (GEMS) is a diagnostic-prescriptive reading program developed in Utah. In this program, students proceed at their own rates through 200 skill levels covering grades K–12. Each unit has a pretest and a posttest. According to placement tests or pretests, students are placed in appropriate instructional groups. Teachers use a variety of teaching strategies, following which students must attain a score of at least 80 percent to exit the unit. Those who do not achieve this score are given alternate materials and enough time as they need to ultimately pass. A computer management system helps teachers keep track of student progress.

An evaluation in rural Jordan, Utah, found that GEMS students generally exceeded control in vocabulary, although differences in reading comprehension were small and were not found in grades 1 and 2. No evidence is given to suggest that the program might be effective with disadvantaged students.

Early Childhood Preventative Curriculum.   This program is quite different from the others in Table 2–1 in that it is intended to be used intensively with high-risk first graders. These students are put into a special class during first grade and experience an individualized diagnostic-prescriptive program, in which students' individual strengths and weaknesses are identified and students are allowed to proceed at their own rates. Most instruction is given in small, skill-level groups.

ECPC was developed and evaluated in Miami, Florida. The evaluation compared the program to matched as well as random controls. Overall, positive effects were found on the Paragraph Meaning scale of the Stanford Achievement Test and (to a lesser extent) on the WRAT.

Continuous-Progress Programs Evaluated Using Year-to-Year Gains.   In addition to the programs listed above, four additional continous-progress models presented convincing evidence for year-to-year gains: Weslaco Individualized Reading/Language Arts Instruction and Staff Development Process (WILASD), Conceptually Oriented Mathematics Curriculum (COMP), Coordinated Learning Integration—Middlesex Basics (CLIMB), and Outcomes-Driven Developmental Model (ODDM). The ODDM model, developed and evaluated in Johnson City, New York, has received much attention in the educational literature (e.g., Mamary and Rowe, 1985). The procedures used in these models generally fall within the range represented among the other continous-progress programs.

A few additional continuous-progress programs passed by the JDRP might also be effective, but did not present adequate evidence. For example, Intensive Reading Instructional Teams (IRIT; JDRP No. 74-11) presented only fall-to-spring percentile gains. The Cranston Comprehensive Reading Program (JDRP No. 82-28) used a regression-discontinuity evaluation design that showed an increase in student scores the year the program was begun, but the district also changed test forms at the same time, making the gains difficult to ascribe to the program with any confidence.

Individualized Instruction

Table 2–2 lists individualized instruction programs that presented convincing evidence of effectiveness. Only three programs fall into this category and of these, only one used a control group design.

TABLE 2–2. Individualized Instruction Programs

Program and Source	Grades/Subject	Description	Evaluation	Effect Sizes
I. Programs Evaluated Using Control Group Designs				
Matteson Four-Dimensional Reading Program (JDRP 77-109)	3–8 Reading	Students work on individualized learning packets 40–60% of reading time.	Compared project classes to matched control classes in suburban Chicago. *Not disadvantaged.*	Gr. 3–6 Reading +.57 (3 yrs.)
II. Programs Evaluated Using Year-to-Year Gains				
AIRS (JDRP 74-25)	1–6 Reading	Students mostly work on individualized materials, some small-group work.	Comparison of spring testing shows cohort gains in suburban Andover, MA. *Not disadvantaged.*	
STAMM (JDRP 76-87)	K–8 Math	Structured, individualized program with programmed materials.	Evaluations in suburban Denver and suburban Atlanta show gains in spring NCEs. *Not disadvantaged.*	

Matteson Four-Dimensional Reading Program.   This program, developed and evaluated in a Chicago suburb, provides students with individualized learning packets through which students proceed at their own rates. Some small- and large-group activities are used, and the individualized work occupies only 40–60 percent of the total reading period, so the Matteson model cannot be called a "pure" individualized program. An evaluation comparing matched schools found that fourth graders in the Matteson program gained more than control students in Stanford Achievement Test scores over a three-year period. However, no evidence is given that would suggest that this program could be successfully applied to at-risk students.

AIRS.   Andover's Individualized Reading System (AIRS) is another self-paced instructional model developed and evaluated in a well-to-do school district, Andover, Massachusetts. AIRS is a classic, comprehensive individualized approach that uses programmed self-instructional materials. Almost all language arts instruction is delivered through the materials with teachers, aides, and parent volunteers giving one-to-one assistance as needed. Comparisons of Stanford Achievement Test scores in student cohorts before and after the AIRS program was introduced show clear gains that were maintained over several years. An AIRS evaluation in rural Rhode Island also found achievement gains each year after the program was installed. Again, no evidence is given to suggest that AIRS would be effective with disadvantaged or low-achieving students.

STAMM.   Systematic Teaching and Measuring Mathematics (STAMM) was developed and initially evaluated in Jefferson County, Colorado, a Denver suburb. Like AIRS, STAMM is a fully individualized instructional program, relying primarily on self-instructional materials and one-to-one instruction by teachers and aides. Evaluations in Jefferson County and in an Atlanta suburb showed that students who experienced STAMM scored higher on the CTBS than did students in earlier cohorts. Special forms of STAMM exist for use with Chapter 1 and learning-disabled students, but evaluations with these or other at-risk students are not known to exist.

Other Individualized Programs.   What is noteworthy about Table 2–2 is not so much the programs listed there as the programs *not* listed. A large number of JDRP-approved programs used individualized models, and the broader educational literature has many studies of such methods. Yet very few of these present convincing evidence of effectiveness.

One individualized program that was carefully considered for inclusion in Table 2–2 is the University of Kansas Behavior Analysis Program (Ramp and Rhine, 1981). This program is generally acknowledged to have been the second most effective of the Planned Variation Follow Through models, after Distar. Also, two Behavior Analysis sites, Trenton, New Jersey (JDRP No. 77-139) and Waukegan, Illinois (JDRP No. 77-126), passed JDRP review with convincing control-group evaluations (conducted as part of the overall Abt evaluation). However, site variability for Behavior Analysis was extreme; in some locations, especially New York City, Behavior Analysis students scored significantly worse than non-Follow Through students. Overall, Kennedy (1978) reports effect sizes of $-.12$ for reading comprehension and $+.02$ for language. Only in math computations is there positive evidence (ES $= +.28$), but math problem-solving scores slightly favored the control group (ES $= -.06$).

Another individualized model, the Responsive Early Childhood Education Program (RECEP; JDRP No. 77-154) also presents a paradox in that data submitted to the JDRP show some positive effects but the overall combined results from all Planned Variation sites did not. Several other individualized programs compared experimental to "matched" control groups without establishing that the control groups were initially equivalent (e.g., Randolph County Follow Through, JDRP No. 77-149), or presented only minimal spring-to-spring gains (e.g., Personalized Classroom Management System, JDRP No. 78-170).

The JDRP programs that were excluded from Table 2–2 rarely provide data that could indicate that the programs are *not* effective, as such programs would be unlikely to pass JDRP review. However, in the broader education literature there have been several good-quality evaluations of individualized programs that have indicated few positive effects (see Horak, 1981; Miller, 1976; Thompson, 1975). When positive effects of individualized programs have been found, they are often in studies with poor methodological characteristics. For example, Wang and Walberg (1983) claimed positive effects of the University of Pittsburgh's Adaptive Learning Environments Model (ALEM) presenting comparisons of "expected" scores based on national norms to scores of students in the ALEM program. However, the one study of this method to use a control group found no achievement differences (Wang and Birch, 1984).

Cooperative Learning

Table 2–3 lists two cooperative learning programs, TAI and CIRC, both of which were developed and evaluated at the Johns Hopkins University Center for Research on Elementary and Middle Schools. All four of the studies that evaluated these models (plus four additional studies that had durations of less than a semester) used control group designs.

TAI.   Team Accelerated Instruction or TAI (Slavin, 1985) combines cooperative learning with a continuous progress approach to mathematics instruction. In this model, students are assigned to four- to five-member,

TABLE 2-3. Cooperative Learning Programs

I. Programs Evaluated Using Control Group Designs

Program and Source	Grades/ Subjects	Description	Evaluation	Effect Sizes	
Team Accelerated Instruction (Slavin et al., 1984; Slavin & Karweit, 1985; JDRP #84-5)	3–6 Math	Students work on programmed materials in mixed-ability teams while teachers teach same-ability teaching groups.	In three studies, two with random assignment, one matched, TAI classes exceeded control. One study in rural MD, one in suburban MD, one in urban DE.	Full Sample (Gr. 3–6)	Math Comp. +.50 Math C&A +.06
				Mainstreamed Students	Math Comp. +.38 Math C&A +.47
Cooperative Integrated Reading & Composition (Stevens et al., 1987)	3–5 Reading Writing	Students work in mixed-ability teams while teacher teaches reading groups.	CIRC classes exceeded matched control classes in study in suburbs of Baltimore.	Full Sample (Gr. 3–4)	Rdg. Voc. +.12 Rdg. Comp. +.35 Oral Rdg. +.54 Language +.30
				Remedial Students	Rdg. Voc. +.26 Rdg. Comp. +.40 Oral Rdg. +.71 Language +.37
				Mainstreamed Students	Rdg. Voc. +.90 Rdg. Comp. +.99 Language .00

mixed-ability learning teams, and they are also assigned to skill-level groups on the basis of a placement test. Teachers instruct the skill-level groups on the concepts of mathematics, after which students return to their teams and work on self-instructional materials. Teammates frequently check one another's work against answer sheets, assist one another with difficult problems, and prepare one another for quizzes. Quizzes are taken apart from the team area, and achieving mastery score on quizzes adds points to students' team scores. At the end of each week, teams that exceed a preestablished criterion in terms of numbers of units mastered may earn certificates or other rewards. Specific procedures and parallel assessments are provided for students who do not achieve at a mastery level.

TAI has been evaluated in six field experiments, but only three of these met the one-semester duration requirement for inclusion in Table 2–3. Two of the three studies (Slavin and Karweit, 1985) are the only studies listed in Tables 2–1 through 2–3 that randomly assigned teachers to treatments. One of these took place in and around Hagerstown, Maryland, and the other in inner-city Wilmington, Delaware. The Hagerstown study compared TAI to a control group and to the Missouri Mathematics Program (Good, Grouws, and Ebmeier, 1983), a whole-class instructional method that incorporates teaching behaviors derived from process-product research. The Wilmington study compared TAI to the Missouri Mathematics Program only; and a study in a Baltimore suburb (Slavin, Madden, and Leavey, 1984) compared TAI to an untreated control group.

Results of all three studies favored the TAI classes, with the largest effects in the Wilmington study. Separate analyses for mainstreamed academically handicapped students in the suburban study also found positive effects for these students.

CIRC.   Cooperative Integrated Reading and Composition (Madden, Slavin, and Stevens, 1986; Stevens, Madden, Slavin, and Farnish, 1987) uses a combination of mixed-ability, cooperative work groups and skill-based reading groups to teach reading, language arts, and writing in the upper elementary grades. In CIRC, students are assigned to pairs within their reading groups, and then the pairs are assigned to four- to five-member teams, so that the teams are heterogeneous. During reading periods, teachers work with reading groups over the course of each week to set a purpose for reading, introduce vocabulary, discuss the characters, setting, problems, and problem solutions in narrative stories, and so on. Students back in their team areas work in pairs on a prescribed series of activities, including reading basal stories to one another, identifying elements of story structure, predicting story outcomes, practicing vocabulary, word lists, and spelling, and writing in response to stories. Each week teachers provide instruction in such reading comprehension skills as finding the main idea. Students earn points for their teams based on the sum of their individual performances on regular quizzes. The CIRC language arts program is based on a writing process model, with students working together in their teams to plan, draft, revise, edit, and ultimately publish compositions. Language mechanics instruction is provided in the context of students' writing.

The semester-long study that evaluated CIRC found positive effects in comparison to matched control classes on CTBS reading comprehension, reading vocabulary, language expression, and language mechanics scales. Separate analyses for mainstreamed academically handicapped students found strong effects on both reading scales but not on the language measures; for remedial reading students (mostly Chapter 1), effects were similar to those in the full sample.

Other Research on Cooperative Learning.   Although the four studies cited above are the only ones to use standardized reading and math measures at the elementary level in studies of at least a semester, several additional studies support the achievement effects of cooperative learning. Two shorter studies of TAI found positive effects on math computations measures (Slavin, Leavey, and Madden, 1984), though a third found no differences (Oishi, Slavin, and Madden, 1983). A twelve-week study of CIRC (Madden, Stevens, and Slavin, 1986) found positive effects on CTBS reading comprehension, reading vocabulary, language expression, and spelling scales. Other cooperative learning methods, such as Student Teams-Achievement Divisions (STAD) and Teams-Games-Tournaments (TGT), have had positive effects in mathematics, language arts, and other subjects at the elementary and secondary levels (Slavin, 1983a, b; 1988). In addition, all of the cooperative learning methods have had positive effects on such outcomes as race relations, acceptance of mainstreamed students, and self-esteem (Slavin, 1983a).

Other Classroom Models

Considering that there are more than 400 programs passed by the JDRP, plus many others evaluated and reported in the educational literature, how is it that only sixteen programs in three categories are emphasized here?

Essentially, this chapter took a conservative approach in identifying effective programs. Only programs with convincing evidence of effectiveness were listed, and even those are not all certain, as there is always the possibility that data submitted to JDRP or published in journals is taken from one or more selected sites and is not representative of all program sites. Yet it seems certain that there are more than sixteen effective classroom programs.

This section discusses the state of the evidence on well-known or widely used models not represented among those listed in Tables 2–1 through 2–3.

Developmental/Humanistic Models. One major category of programs not listed in this review is models that might be categorized as "developmental/humanistic." This includes the open classroom, Piagetian-based models, and other types of programs in which students are given choices of activities appropriate to their developmental levels, and are encouraged to discover and experience language and mathematical concepts rather than to master a preestablished series of skills.

One important example of the developmental/humanistic approach is the program developed by the Bank Street College of Education (Gilkeson, Smithberg, Bowman, and Rhine, 1981). Several sites using the Bank Street Program passed JDRP review (JDRP No. 77-156). However, the overall effects of this program in the Planned Variation evaluation were about zero in reading and language and negative in math. The High Scope/Cognitively Oriented Curriculum (Weikart, Hohmann, and Rhine, 1981), a child-centered, Piagetian model that extends into the elementary grades many of the elements of the Perry Preschool Program (Weikart, 1974), also has several JDRP-approved sites (JDRP No. 77-123), but came out near the bottom of the list in the overall Abt evaluations (Kennedy, 1978). What these findings may imply is that the developmental/humanistic models *can* be effective, as evidenced by their apparent success in several sites, but the evidence for this or evidence of what is required to ensure their success are essentially lacking. Also, it should be noted that critics of the Abt evaluation (e.g., House, Glass, McLean, and Walker, 1978) have argued that the use of standardized achievement tests may have biased the evaluation in favor of such highly structured programs as Distar and Behavior Analysis. However, the Abt evaluations focused on children who had been in their respective models three or four years. If the programs had any important effects on students' cognitive performance, a standardized test should have registered some (if not all) of those effects.

Group-Based Mastery Learning. Another widely used approach to school improvement is group-based mastery learning (Block and Anderson, 1975; Guskey and Gates, 1985). The teacher assesses student learning at the end of a series of lessons. Those who achieve at a preestablished level of mastery (e.g., 80 percent) are given enrichment activities, while others are given corrective instruction designed to bring them up to the mastery criterion. Claims of substantial positive effects of group-based mastery learning on student achievement are based largely on very brief experiments. In a review of research on group-based mastery learning, Slavin (1987a) found that in studies of at least four weeks' duration there were no significant positive effects of mastery learning on standardized measures, and modest effects (median ES = +.25) on experimenter-made measures. However, it is important to note that the concepts of mastery assessment and corrective instruction are central to all three categories of effective programs emphasized in this review, and some of the continuous-progress programs, such as GEMS and the Outcomes-Driven Developmental model, identify themselves as mastery learning models (see Levine, 1985).

PRINCIPLES OF EFFECTIVE CLASSROOM PROGRAMS FOR STUDENTS AT RISK

The purpose of this chapter is not only to identify individual programs, but also to discover *principles* that underlie effective models for students at risk. The effective programs identified as an extensive review of the literature fell into three categories: continuous progress, individualized instruction, and cooperative learning. However, the three effective individualized instruction models were all developed and evaluated in middle-class, nondisadvantaged areas in which few students could be categoriezed as ''at risk'' for learning problems. Also, the broader literature has not tended to support the use of individualized, programmed instructional models. AIRS, STAMM, and the Matteson 4-D models may have unique features that could make them effective with at-risk students, but given the past history of research on individualized programs, this remains to be seen.

It is in the remaining two categories that the greatest confidence can be placed. In the case of the continuous progress models, it is important to note not only the quality of the individual studies but also the number of successful models that began from very different theoretical bases and ended up with similar programs. Some of these models describe themselves as ''individualized'' (e.g., U-SAIL), but in order to provide adequate instruction to all students, incorporated groupings of students according to skill levels. Others (e.g., GEMS, ODDM) describe themselves as ''mastery learning,'' but incorporated subgrouping of students to accommodate instruction to individual needs. Developers of Distar describe the model as ''direct instruction,'' yet the skill-level grouping, frequent assessment, and progress through a structured hierarchy of skills have little in common with more recent class-paced forms of ''direct instruction'' such as the Missouri Mathematics Program (Good, Grouws, and Ebmeier, 1983).

Although very different in many respects, the effective cooperative learning programs listed in Table 2–3 have many features in common with the continuous progress models. First, even though students do most of their work in mixed-ability, cooperative learning teams, instruction in TAI and CIRC is directed toward small, homogeneous groups of students, so instruction is at a level appropriate to student needs. Second, instruction comes from the teacher, not from written materials or peers. Third, students' progress is constantly assessed and specific procedures exist to remediate any small problems before they become large ones. Finally, in TAI and in the reading comprehension component of CIRC, there is a structured hierarchy of skills that students must master. Cooperative learning methods add to these the opportunity for students to explain concepts to one another and help one another study, team incentives based on the learning of team members, and student responsibility for many elements of classroom management. This last feature may be particularly important in today's lean times; TAI and CIRC have always been evaluated in classrooms in which there were no aides or volunteers, whereas continuous-progress and individualized models have almost always had additional personnel.

What emerges from an examination of the effective classroom programs is the following characterization: *Consistently effective classroom programs accommodate instruction to individual needs while maximizing direct instruction, and they frequently assess student progress through a structured hierarchy of skills.*

The first part of this statement, the need to accommodate instruction to individual needs while maximizing direct instruction, is also supported by research on ability grouping in elementary schools, recently reviewed by Slavin (1987b). This review found that while assigning students to self-contained classes on the basis of general ability was ineffective, two forms of ability grouping did have considerable support in good-quality experimental studies. One was the Joplin Plan, in which students are regrouped for reading across grade lines into reading classes all operating at one reading level. This plan obviates the need for grouping within the reading class, giving teachers the opportunity to spend all of the reading period in direct instruction. Studies of the Joplin Plan and closely related forms of nongraded plans found consistent positive effects on standardized reading measures (median ES = +.44).

The second form of ability grouping found in the Slavin (1987b) review to be instructionally effective was within-class ability grouping in math (median ES = +.34). Use of math groups, especially if the number of groups is kept to two or three, strikes a balance between accommodating instruction to individual needs and providing adequate direct instruction. Since there is a need for independent seatwork in math, grouping within the class to meet students' diverse needs and having the teacher present two or three lessons at different levels may be the most efficient use of instructional time.

Slavin (1987c) has argued that to make a meaningful difference in student achievement, four elements of classroom organization must be simultaneously addressed: quality of instruction, appropriate level of instruction, incentive, and time. The continuous programs and cooperative learning methods address most of these elements, in particular in providing appropriate levels of instruction (by grouping students according to skill level) while maintaining an adequate quality of instruction (by having the teacher be responsible for direct instruction and by having a well thought out sequence of instructional objectives). Cooperative learning adds to the incentive element the use of team rewards based on team members' learning, and both types of programs emphasize effective use of time through careful structuring of classroom activities.

The importance of accommodating student needs while maintaining adequate direct instruction is perhaps greatest for at-risk students. Students who begin to experience difficulties in their early years in school are unlikely to be able to keep up with the class pace or grade-level expectations. In response to this, schools provide remedial and special education for students who are falling behind. Yet these programs rarely accelerate students enough to enable them to catch up with their classmates (Kennedy, Birman, and Demaline, 1986; Madden and Slavin, 1983; Slavin, 1987d; Carter, 1984). Building classroom models able to meet diverse needs would seem to be a better approach to the problems of at-risk students than creating a parallel instructional system, which creates a large set of new problems in terms of coordination with the regular program, transitions, and so on (Johnston, Allington, and Afflerbach, 1985).

CONCLUSIONS

This chapter reviewed all sources of evidence concerning classroom programs that have been or could be applied to accelerating the reading and math achievement of at-risk students. Among programs whose evaluations used control group designs with good evidence of initial experimental-control equivalence, study durations of at least a semester, and standardized measures of reading and math, two categories of programs emerged as particularly effective: continuous progress and cooperative learning. These approaches have in common the use of instruction to small, skill-based groups; instruction from the teacher rather than from materials or peers; and frequent assessment of student progress through a hierarchical curriculum.

However, while this review is based on the best evidence currently available concerning the achievement effects of practical classroom instructional models, it is important to reiterate that this evidence is far from definitive. Even the carefully selected programs emphasized in this review could prove to be ineffective in later research; as noted previously, it is always possible that data submitted to the JDRP or to journals is from the *best* sites, not from a representative sample of implementations. It is also likely that many programs excluded from this review will prove to be effective or could be modified to be effective. Further, while it is of some use to know that Program X is effective in comparison to traditional methods, there is much more we must understand to make this information useful in informing us about program design and classroom instruction in general. What elements of Program X account for its effects? For whom is it effective? Does it have important side effects?

We are still at a primitive state in understanding effective instruction for students at risk. What is needed is a renewed focus on development, evaluation, and component analyses of programs based on many models of teaching and learning.

One approach to identifying effective, transportable instructional models for students at risk would be learning from the mistakes of the Planned Variation Follow Through evaluation but trying again to accomplish its objectives. A very small proportion of the enormous Chapter 1 budget, for example, could fund development of promising models, evaluation and component analyses of such models, and ultimately evaluation of the models in new sites with multiple measures (not only standardized tests), with random assignment of programs to schools (see Slavin, 1987d). In this way, we could finally achieve the ambitious goals of Chapter 1 to make a meaningful difference in the lives of disadvantaged students.

While we cannot conclude that the search for effective classroom programs for at-risk students is over, the findings of this review do have important implications for current practice. It identified several programs that have demonstrated potential for increasing the achievement of disadvantaged and low-achieving students and identified program elements that seem to characterize effective models. All the identified programs are designed to be replicable and transportable; in most cases the developers have training staffs who work to help school districts successfully implement the models. However, there are two notes of caution that practitioners should bear in mind. First, all of the effective models identified in this review are complex and are quite different from usual practice. Adequate provisions for training, followup, and monitoring of project implementations are imperative. Any of these programs can fail (and most have failed) when inadequate resources have been devoted to implementation. Program implementations should start on a small scale, beginning with volunteers and only gradually expanding from a solid base of success. Second, districts should conduct their own evaluations of new programs, using random assignment or careful matching to compare program users and nonusers. The fact that a program was effective elsewhere suggests but does not guarantee that it will be successful in any particular district.

The study for reliably effective programs for students who are at risk for school failure is a task of great importance. This chapter and others in this book are intended to sum up where we are now, in the hope that we can learn from the past in helping direct future research, development, and evaluation into effective instruction for our neediest students.

REFERENCES

Archambault, F. X. (1987, April). *Pullout versus inclass instruction in compensatory instruction*. Paper presented at the Annual Convention of the American Educational Association, Washington, DC.

Becker, W. C., and Carnine, D. (1980). Direct instruction: An effective approach for educational intervention with the disadvantaged and low performers. In B. J. Lahey and A. E. Kazdin (Eds.), *Advances in child clinical psychology.* New York: Plenum, pp. 429–473.

Becker, W. C.; Engelmann, S.; Carnine, D. W.; and Rhine, W. R. (1981). Direct instruction model. In W. R. Rhine (Ed.), *Making schools more effective: New directions from Follow Through.* New York: Academic Press, pp. 95–154.

Birman, B. F. (1981). Problems of overlap between Title I and P.L. 94-142: Implications for the federal role in education. *Educational Evaluation and Policy Analysis, 3,* 5–19.

Block, J. H., and Anderson, L. W. (1975). *Mastery learning in classroom instruction.* New York: Macmillan.

Bloom, B. S. (1984). The 2 sigma problem: The search for methods of instruction as effective as one-to-one tutoring. *Educational Research, 13,* 4–16.

Brophy, J. E., and Good, T. L. (1986). Teacher behavior and student achievement. In M. C. Wittrock (Ed.), *Handbook of research on teaching,* 3rd ed. New York: Macmillan, pp. 328–375.

Calfee, R. (1986, May). *Compensatory reading.* Paper presented at the OERI Conference on Effects of Alternative Designs in Compensatory Education, Washington, DC.

Carter, L. F. (1984). The sustaining effects study of compensatory and elementry education. *Educational Researcher, 13(7),* 4–13.

Cooper, H. M. (1984). *The integrative research review: A systematic approach.* Beverly Hills, CA: Sage.

Coulson, J. E.; Hanes, S. C.; Ozenne, D. G.; Bradford, C.; Doherty, W. J.; Duck, G. A.; and Hemenway, J. A. (1977). *The third year of Emergency School Aid Act (ESAA) implementation.* Santa Monica, CA: System Development Corporation.

Ellson, D. G. (1986). *Improving the productivity of teaching: 125 exhibits.* Bloomington, IN: Phi Delta Kappa.

Gabriel, R. M.; Anderson, B. L.; Benson, G.; Gordon, S.; Hill, R.; Pfannenstiel, J.; and Stonehill, R. M. (1985). *Studying the sustained achievement of Chapter 1 students.* Washington, DC: U.S. Department of Education.

Gilkeson, E. C.; Smithberg, L. M.; Bowman, G. W.; and Rhine, W. R. (1981). Bank Street Model: A developmental-interaction approach. In W. R. Rhine (Ed.), *Making schools more effective: New directions from follow through.* New York: Academic Press, pp. 249–290.

Glass, G.; McGaw, B.; and Smith, M. L. (1981). *Meta-analysis in social research.* Beverly Hills, CA: Sage.

Glass, G. V., and Smith, M. L. (1977). *Pull out in compensatory education.* Washington, DC: Department of Health, Education, and Welfare.

Good, T.; Grouws, D.; and Ebmeier, H. (1983). *Active mathematics teaching.* New York: Longman.

Goodlad, J. I., and Anderson, R. H. (1963). *The nongraded elementary school,* rev. ed. New York: Harcourt, Brace, & World.

Granick, L.; Quigley, M. M.; Katzenellenbogen, R.; and Richardson, L. H. (1984). *Optimizing Chapter 1 program effectiveness.* Baltimore, MD: Baltimore City Public Schools.

Griswold, P. A.; Cotton, K. J.; and Hansen, J. B. (1986). *Effective compensatory education sourcebook.* Washington, DC: U.S. Government Printing Office.

Guskey, T. R., and Gates, S. L. (1985, April). *A synthesis of research on group-based mastery learning programs.* Paper presented at the Annual Convention of the American Educational Research Association, Chicago.

Hales, C. (1983a). *A teacher's guide to individualizing reading.* Salt Lake City, UT: U-SAIL Project.

Hales,C. (1983b). *Teaching for mastery in mathematics.* Salt Lake City, UT: U-SAIL Project.

Horak, V. M. (1981). A meta-analysis of research findings on individualized instruction in mathematics. *Journal of Educational Research, 74,* 249–253.

House, E.; Glass, G.; McLean, L. D.; and Walker, D. (1978). No simple answer: Critique of the Follow Through evaluation. *Harvard Educational Review, 48,* 128–160.

Johnston, P.; Allington, R.; and Afflerbach, P. (1985). Curriculum confluence in classroom and clinic. *Elementary School Journal, 85,* 465–477.

Kaestle, C. F., and Smith, M. S. (1982). The historical context of the federal role in education. *Harvard Educational Review, 52,* 383–408.

Karweit, N. L. (1987, April). *Effective early childhood education and kindergarten programs for children at risk of academic failure.* Paper presented at the Annual Convention of the American Educational Research Association, Washington, DC.

Keesling, J. W. (1984). *Diferences between fall to spring and annual gains in evaluation of Chapter 1 programs.* McLean, VA: Advanced Technology, Inc.

Kelly, F. J.; Veldman, D. J.; and McGuire, C. (1964). Multiple discriminant prediction of deliquency and school dropouts. *Educational and Psychological Measurement, 24,* 535–544.

Kennedy, M. (1978). Findings from the Follow Through planned variation study. *Educational Researcher, 7,* 3–11.

Kennedy, M. M.; Birman, B. F.; and Demaline, R. (1986). *The effectiveness of Chapter 1 services.* Washington, DC: Office of Educational Research and Improvement, U.S. Department of Education.

Kimbrough, J., and Hill, P. T. (1981). *The aggregate effects of federal education programs.* Santa Monica, CA: Rand Corp.

Lee, G. V., and Rowan, B. (1986). *The management and delivery of instructional services to Chapter 1 students: Case studies of twelve schools.* San Francisco: Far West Laboratory for Educational Research and Development.

Leinhardt, G., and Pallay, A. (1982). Restrictive educational settings: Exile or haven? *Review of Educational Research, 52,* 557–578.

Levine, D. U. (Ed.) (1985). *Improving student achievement through mastery learning programs.* San Francisco: Jossey-Bass.

Light, R. J., and Pillemer, D. B. (1984). *Summing up: The science of reviewing research.* Cambridge, MA: Harvard University Press.

Madden, N. A., and Slavin, R. E. (1983). Mainstreaming students with mild academic handicaps: Academic and social outcomes. *Review of Educational Research, 53,* 519–569.

Madden, N. A., and Slavin, R. E. (1987, April). *Effective pull-out programs for students at risk.* Paper presented at the Annual Convention of the American Educational Research Association, Washington, DC.

Madden, N. A.; Slavin, R. E.; and Stevens, R. J. (1986). *Cooperative Integrated Reading and Composition: Teacher's manual.* Baltimore, MD: Johns Hopkins University Center for Research on Elementary and Middle Schools.

Mamary, A., and Rowe, L. A. (1985). Flexible and heterogeneous instructional arrangements to facilitate mastery learning. In D. U. Levine (Ed.), *Improving student achievement through mastery learning programs.* San Francisco: Jossey-Bass.

Meyer, L. A. (1984). Long-term academic effects of the direct instruction Project Follow Through. *Elementary School Journal, 84,* 380–394.

Miller, R. L. (1976). Individualized instruction in mathematics: A review of research. *The Mathematics Teacher, 69,* 345–351.

Novak, C. D. (1975, April). *An unobtrusive experimental evaluation of a systems approach for teaching reading.* Paper presented at the annual convention of the American Educational Research Association, Washington, DC.

Oishi, S.; Slavin, R. E.; and Madden, N. A. (1983, April). *Effects of student terms and individualized instruction on cross-race and cross-sex relationships.* Paper presented at the annual convention of the American Educational Research Association, Montreal, Canada.

Ramp, E. A., and Rhine, W. R. (1981). Behavior analysis model. In W. R. Rhine (Ed.), *Making schools more effective: New directions from Follow Through.* New York: Academic Press. pp. 155–200.

Rowan, B.; Guthrie, L. F.; Lee, G. V.; and Guthrie, G. P. (1986). *The design and implementation of Chapter 1 services: A study of 24 schools.* San Francisco: Far West Laboratory for Educational Research and Developent.

Sargent, L. R. (1981). Resource teacher time utilization: An observational study. *Exceptional Children, 47,* 410–425.

Savage, D. G. (1987). Why Chapter 1 hasn't made much difference. *Phi Delta Kappan, 68,(8),* 581–584.

Slavin, R. E. (1983a). *Cooperative learning.* New York: Longman.

Slavin, R. E. (1983b). When does cooperative learning increase student achievement? *Psychological Bulletin, 94,* 429–445.

Slavin, R. E. (1985). Team-assisted individualization: Combining cooperative learning and individualized instruction in mathematics. In R. E. Slavin, S. Sharan, S. Kagan, R. Hertz-Lazarowitz, C. Webb, and R. Schmuck (Eds.), *Learning to cooperate, cooperating to learn.* New York: Plenum, pp. 177–209.

Slavin, R. E. (1986). Best-evidence synthesis: An alternative to meta-analytic and traditional reviews. *Educational Research, 15(9),* 5–11.

Slavin, R. E. (1987a). Mastery learning reconsidered. *Review of Educational Research, 57,* 175–213.

Slavin, R. E. (1987b). Ability grouping and student achievement in elementary schools: A best-evidence synthesis. *Review of Educational Research, 57,* 347–350.

Slavin, R. E. (1987c). A theory of school and classroom organization. *Educational Psychologist, 22,* 89–108.

Slavin, R. E. (1987d). Making Chapter 1 make a difference. *Phi Delta Kappan, 22,* 110–119.

Slavin, R. E. (1988). Cooperative learning and student achievement. In R. E. Slavin (Ed.), *School and classroom organization.* Hillsdale, NJ: Erlbaum.

Slavin, R. E., and Karweit, N. L. (1985). Effects of whole-class, ability grouped, and individualized instruction on mathematics achievement. *American Educational Research Journal, 22,* 351–367.

Slavin, R. E.; Leavey, M.; and Madden, N. A. (1984). Combining cooperative learning and individualized instruction: Effects on student mathematics achievement, attitudes, and behaviors. *Elementary School Journal, 84,* 409–422.

Slavin, R. E.; Leavey, M. B.; and Madden, N. A. (1986). *Team accelerated instruction—Mathematics.* Watertown, MA: Mastery Education Corporation.

Slavin, R. E.; Madden, N. A.; and Leavey, M. (1984). Effects of team assisted individualization on the mathematics achievement of academically handicapped and nonhandicapped students. *Journal of Educational Psychology, 76,* 813–819.

Stebbins, L. B.; St. Pierre, R. G.; Proper, E. C.; Anderson, R. B.; and Cerva, T. R. (1977). *Education as experimentation: A planned variation model,* vols. IV A-D. Cambridge, MA: Abt Associates.

Stevens, R. J.; Madden, N. A.; Slavin, R. E.; and Farnish, A. M. (1987). Cooperative Integrated Reading and Composition: Two field experiments. *Reading Research Quarterly, 22,* 433–454.

Stroup, A. L., and Robins, L. N. (1972). Elementary-school predictors of school dropout among black males. *Sociology of Education, 45,* 212–222.

Thompson, R. (1975). Individualized reading: A summary of research. *Educational Leadership, 32,* 57–63.

Vanecko, J.; Ames, N.; and Archambault, F. (1980). *Who benefits from federal education dollars?* Cambridge, MA: Abt Books.

Wang, M. C., and Birch, J. W. (1984). Comparisons of a full-time mainstreaming program and a resource room approach. *Exceptional Children, 51,* 33–40.

Wang, M. C., and Walberg, H. J. (1983). Adaptive instruction and classroom time. *American Educational Research Journal, 20,* 601–626.

Weikart, D. P. (1974). Curriculum for early childhood education. *Focus on Exceptional Children, 6,* 1–8.

Weikart, D. P.; Hohmann, C. F.; and Rhine, W. R. (1981). High/scope cognitively oriented curriculum model. In W. R. Rhine (Ed.), *Making schools more effective: New directions from Follow Through.* New York: Academic Press, pp. 201–248.

Ysseldike, J., and Algozzine, B. (1982). *Critical issues in special and remedial education.* Boston, MA: Houghton Mifflin.

3

EFFECTIVE PULLOUT PROGRAMS FOR STUDENTS AT RISK

Nancy A. Madden
Robert E. Slavin

Center for Research on Elementary and Middle Schools
Johns Hopkins University

From the beginning, one of the guiding principles of compensatory education has been that compensatory services must supplement, not supplant, the educational programs provided to eligible students. Low-achieving students in schools that are eligible for Chapter 1 (formerly Title I) services must receive something identifiably "extra." Evaluators located in every state check to see that Chapter 1 services are in fact supplementing rather than supplanting regular education programs.

Partly because of the "supplement, not supplant" regulations, schools have overwhelmingly relied on pullout models as a means of providing Chapter 1 or Title I services. Most often, students who qualify for compensatory services are taken out of their regular classrooms for thirty to forty minutes of remedial instruction in reading and/or mathematics. This arrangement has the advantage of making it clear that Chapter 1 services are supplementary, as special personnel and materials are clearly allocated only to identified students. In in-class alternatives to pullout, maintaining the distinction between who is served and who is not served is more difficult. At least partly for this reason, Chapter 1 programs have overwhelmingly chosen pullout as the mode of service delivery. A study conducted during the 1981–82 school year found that pullout outnumbered in-class models by nine to one (Advanced Technology, 1983), and in a more recent study of schools specially chosen to represent a variety of service delivery models, fifteen of seventeen elementary schools used pullout in reading and/or math (Rowan, Guthrie, Lee, and Guthrie, 1986).

Despite the many criticisms of pullout (e.g., see Glass and Smith, 1977; Johnston, Allington, and Afflerbach, 1985; Archambault, 1987), pullout is likely to remain as a widely used means of providing compensatory education services. In any case, as many have noted previously (e.g.,

Archambault, 1987; Kennedy, Birman, and Demaline 1986), the important issue is not the setting in which compensatory services are provided, but the quality of the programs provided in the setting. This chapter reviews research on effective pullout programs for elementary students who are at risk for school failure.

SCOPE OF REVIEW

The focus of this chapter is on programs provided to students who have been identified as being in need of remedial services that are implemented outside of the regular classroom. This excludes programs implemented in the regular class (which are reviewed in Chapter 2) and self-contained "replacement" or special education programs in which students are assigned to a remedial class for most or all of their school day. The emphasis of this review is on programs that could be (or have been) readily replicated by schools other than those that developed them. For example, many school districts have developed exemplary Chapter 1 programs (see Griswold, Cotton, and Hansen, 1986), but the features of these programs are often uniquely adapted to the situations, personnel, and students of the district and were not designed to be replicated as such in other districts. Also, a few studies have identified variables related to effective Chapter 1 programs (see Chapter 9; Cooley and Leinhardt, 1980). In contrast to these, the programs emphasized in this review are models that have well-specified manuals, materials, training procedures, and other features that characterize programs intended for replication by others.

PROCEDURES

The procedures used in this review are the same as those described in Chapter 2. Essentially, the review procedure was an adaptation of best-evidence synthesis (Slavin, 1986)—a method that combines the features of meta-analytic and traditional narrative reviews. The initial literature search examined many sources, including published and unpublished articles, school district reports, and government documents. Requests for information were sent to all of the 116 exemplary compensatory education programs identified by Griswold, Cotton, and Hansen (1986). However, as in Chapter 2, the most useful sources of information were reports submitted to the Joint Dissemination Review Panel (JDRP), a U.S. Department of Education panel that reviews evaluations of programs supported by federal funds.

The same set of substantive and methodological inclusion criteria as were used in Chapter 2 were applied in deciding which programs to emphasize in this review. In brief, programs had to assess effects on standardized reading and/or math scales in studies of at least a semester's duration. Programs had to be compared to matched or randomized control groups, or year-to-year gains of at least 7 NCEs had to be reported (fall-to-spring NCE gains, which have been found to have serious methodological problems, were not considered adequate evidence of program effects; see Gabriel, Anderson, Benson, Gordon, Hill, Pfannenstiel, and Stonehill, 1985). All programs presented data to indicate that they were effective with students eligible for Chapter 1 services or other at-risk students.

CATEGORIES OF EFFECTIVE PULLOUT MODELS

The effective pullout programs for students at risk of school failure fell into three broad categories. One, *diagnostic-prescriptive programs,* covers the great majority of existing Chapter 1 programs. In this model, students identified as being in need of remedial services are carefully assessed and then instruction appropriate to their needs is given by a teacher in a location separate from the regular classroom (or occasionally within the classroom setting). Instruction may be given to individuals or to small groups within a pullout class of roughly three to eight students. The second category is *tutoring programs,* in which tutors work one-on-one with identified tutees. Tutors may be teachers, paraprofessionals, volunteers, or older students. In the third category, *computer-assisted instruction* (CAI), students work on computers for at least part of their remedial reading or math time. It should be noted that many diagnostic-prescriptive programs use computers for management (as opposed to instructional) purposes, but these are not categorized as CAI.

CHARACTERISTICS AND OUTCOMES OF EFFECTIVE PULLOUT MODELS

Diagnostic-Prescriptive Programs

Because of the widespread use of diagnostic-prescriptive pullout programs, the data available on such programs is extensive. Almost all of the exemplary Chapter 1 programs identified by Griswold, Cotton, and Hansen (1986) used diagnostic-prescriptive models, as did many of the programs certified by the JDRP. However, very few of these presented convincing evidence of effectiveness. In most cases, these programs were identified as exemplary on the basis of fall-to-spring gains in normal curve equivalent scores (NCEs). However, most districts presented fall and spring scores for several years, and with few exceptions these indicate little or no growth in fall scores or spring scores over time. The typical pattern is a fall-to-spring gain of eight to twelve points, followed by a decline over the summer of the same magnitude. This cannot be seen as convincing evidence that the programs are *not* effective; it could be that the lack of year-to-year growth in scores is due to dropping of students with high scores from the Chapter 1 lists, or that scores increased when new programs were introduced but then remained stable during the years for which data were provided, or there may be other methodological or substantive factors involved.

However, there are a few diagnostic-prescriptive programs that do present more convincing evidence of effectiveness. Information on these programs is provided in Table 3–1.

Only two of the successful diagnostic-prescriptive programs used control group designs. One of these, Project Conquest (JDRP No. 74-12) mostly provides remedial services to groups of six students. However, early in the year, students receive one-to-one tutoring until they acquire word perception skills. Students are carefully assessed by special "reading clinicians" and given individual prescriptions.

An evaluation of Project Conquest was conducted in low-income, mostly black schools in East St. Louis, Illinois. Project Conquest students made greater gains than control students at grade levels from 1–6 on many standardized leading measures. However, these data are difficult to interpret because no evidence is given that the experimental and control classes were initially equivalent. A more sophisticated analysis was conducted using fifth-grade data and correcting for pretest differences, and this also showed a clear advantage for the program.

One of the exemplary Chapter 1 programs identified by Griswold, Cotton, and Hansen (1986) used a control group design to evaluate its diagnostic-prescriptive pullout model. This is the Oklahoma City, Oklahoma, Chapter 1 program, a classic diagnostic-prescriptive pullout model. In this program, students are assessed in terms of skills and learning styles and then given instruction appropriate to their needs, individually or in small groups. Some use is made of computer-assisted instruction; the evaluation of this component is discussed later in the section on CAI.

The evaluation of the Oklahoma City diagnostic-prescriptive pullout program (Kimball, Crawford, and Raia, 1985) involved careful matching on prescores of students who received Chapter 1 services with those who did not. The same procedures were followed in two successive years. Results indicated that Chapter 1 students gained an average of 3 NCEs more in math than their counterparts who did not receive Chapter 1 services. Using the standard deviation of NCEs of about 12 (estimated by Gabriel, Cotton, and Hansen, 1985), this is equivalent to an effect size of +0.25. However, gains in reading were much smaller and, in one year, were not statistically significant (ES = +.12).

TABLE 3–1. Diagnostic-Prescriptive Pullout Programs

Program and Source	Grades/ Subjects	Description	Evaluation		Effect Sizes
I. Programs Evaluated Using Control Group Designs					
Project Conquest (JDRP # 74-12)	1–6 Reading	Individual and small-group instruction provided outside of class to remediate specific deficits identified by individual assessment. Extensive inservice.	Students in East St. Louis, IL, compared to "comparable" group. Gains significantly higher in Conquest schools.	Gr. 1–6	Cannot be estimated
Oklahoma City, OK Chapter 1 Program (Kimball, Crawford, and Raia, 1985)	1–6 Reading Math	District-wide management objectives used to coordinate regular class and Chapter 1 objectives.	Chapter 1 students compared to matched unserved students.	Gr. 2–6	CAT (reading) +.25 MAT (math) +.12

II. Programs Evaluated Using Year-to-Year Gains

Program	Grade/Subject	Description	Gains	Grade
Lincoln, NE Chapter 1 Management and Coordination Project	K–6 Reading Math	District-level objectives and monitoring system managed by computer, emphasis on day-to-day coordination between Chapter 1 and regular class.	Spring-to-spring gains of 4-5 NCEs in reading, 5-9 NCEs in math.	Gr. 1–6
Diagnostic-Prescriptive Arithmetic Program	3–5 Math	Math lab approach emphasizes hands-on experience, manipulatives.	Spring-to-spring gains of 10.4 NCEs on Stanford Diagnostic Arithmetic Test.	Gr. 3–5 (students 2 yr. or more below grade level)
Columbia, MO Chapter 1 Math Program	2–6 Math	Program emphasizes coordination between Chapter 1 and regular class, use of manipulatives.	Fall-to-fall gains of 8.7 NCEs on Iowa Test of Basic Skills.	Gr. 2–6

The Baltimore, Maryland, school system also conducted a comparison of students served by Chapter 1 pullout programs and matched students eligible for Chapter 1 but not served. This evaluation found that served and unserved students made about the same fall-to-spring gains in reading and math scores (Granick, Quigley, Katzenellenbogen, and Richardson, 1984).

Other than Project Conquest, only one JDRP-approved program appears in Table 3–1: the Diagnostic-Prescriptive Arithmetic Program (JDRP No. 74-68). This model, developed and evaluated in Staten Island, New York, uses a math lab approach to remediation of deficits in mathematics. Individualized and small-group activities keyed to problem areas identified by the Stanford Diagnostic Mathematics Test are provided to students. Spring-to-spring gains of approximately 10.4 NCEs were made; however, since the Stanford Diagnostic Mathematics Test was also used as the posttest, there is a possibility that this program was essentially teaching the test.

Two additional programs from the list of effective Chapter 1 programs also presented evidence of effectiveness based on outstanding year-to-year gains. One of these is the Lincoln, Nebraska, Chapter 1 program. In this program, a computer management system was introduced to help handle diagnostic tests, assign students to the program, maintain coordination between the regular teacher and the Chapter 1 teacher, monitor student progress, and evaluate student success. During the years when the program was implemented, Chapter 1 students showed steady gains in spring scores in reading and math, which appear to be due to the addition of the computer management system rather than to the diagnostic-prescriptive pullout model already in use in the district (Weatherl, 1986).

Another apparently effective Chapter 1 model cited by Griswold, Cotton, and Hansen (1986) is the Columbia, Missouri, Public Schools' Chapter 1 mathematics program. This model places considerable emphasis on coordination of instruction between Chapter 1 and regular classroom teachers; forms indicating specific objectives students are working on are passed back and forth between Chapter 1 pullout teachers and regular classroom teachers, and time is set aside for Chapter 1 and regular teachers to meet. Program data indicate fall-to-fall gains of 8.7 NCEs in math.

The evidence from the Chapter 1 programs listed in Table 3–1 indicates that diagnostic-prescriptive programs *can* be effective, but their effects do not generally appear to be large. However, the almost universal use of fall-to-spring gains (or year-to-year gains at best) as the criteria of program effects means that we really know little about which programs (or components of programs) are having important effects on the students they serve.

Tutoring Programs

A wide variety of tutorial programs using tutors ranging from experienced, specially trained teachers to paraprofessional aides to older, often low-achieving students have demonstrated considerable effectiveness in improving students' achievement in reading and math in grades 1–6. These effective programs fall essentially into two groups: those that were designed as remedial programs and those that were designed as preventative programs.

Remedial Tutorial Programs.   Three models of remedial uses of tutoring were identified. Descriptions of them appear in Table 3–2. The two strongest models, Training for Turnabout Volunteers (TTV) and School Volunteer Development Project (SVDP), were developed in Dade County, Florida. TTV used volunteer junior high school students who took tutoring as an elective class to tutor low-achieving first through sixth graders in reading and math. Tutors were required to be able to read and compute at the fifth-grade level, which allowed underachieving students to act as tutors. Tutors received considerable training involving a specified structured curriculum before they began to tutor, and spent one day out of five in group supervision, receiving continuing training in the specific subject matter being taught as well as in tutoring skills such as rewarding the tutees' successes, refraining from criticizing failures, organizing the work to be presented, and so on. The tutorial materials were not programmed. Tutors drew from a wide variety of materials deemed to be useful for teaching the needed skills. The gains made by students working with the well-trained tutors were compared to the gains made by students working with tutors who did not receive continuing supervision, but otherwise worked for similar amounts of time with similar students using the same kinds of materials. Students worked together four days a week for sixteen weeks for forty minutes a day.

Gains were significantly greater for both tutors and tutees when the tutors received continuing training. Students tutored by trained tutors in math gained 0.93 standard deviations more than those tutored by untrained tutors on the Metropolitan Achievement Test. In reading, the tutees of trained tutors gained 0.51 standard deviations more on the Metropolitan than their comparison group. Trained tutors gained 0.49 standard deviations more than their untrained counterparts in math, but did not gain significantly more in reading.

One difficulty with the TTV program was that it required that an elementary and junior high school be physically close to one another so that students could travel back and forth in the time allotted for one class period and still have time to tutor. The second program developed in Dade County avoided this difficulty by focusing on the recruitment and training of adult volunteers as tutors. In the School Volunteer Development Project, adult

TABLE 3-2. Remedial Tutoring Programs

Program and Source	Grades/Subjects	Description	Evaluation	Effect Sizes	
I. Programs Evaluated Using Control Group Designs					
Training for Turnabout Volunteers (JDRP # 81-11)	Tutors 7-9 Tutees 1-6 Reading Math	Cross-age tutoring. Tutors trained with preservice and inservice classes. Not programmed material. Tutored 40 min/day, 4 days/week. Inservice training on fifth day.	One-year study in Miami, FL, compared trained vs. untrained tutors. Nonequivalent but unbiased groups. Five schools in study.	Tutees 1-6	Tutees: MAT (math) +.93, MAT (reading) +.51; Tutors 7-9	Tutors: MAT (math) +.49, MAT (reading) +.08
School Volunteer Development Project (JDRP # 75-79)	2-6 Reading Math	Community volunteer tutors. 2-4 hrs/week/volunteer. Each student tutored 1/2 hr. 4 days/week minimum.	Students in Miami, FL, randomly assigned to tutored or nontutored conditions for one school year.	Gr. 2-6	MAT (reading) +.50, MAT (math) +1.1
Success Controlled Optimal Reading Experience (SCORE) (JDRP # 80-42)	1-6 Reading Math	Each student tutored 15 min/day by older students or adult volunteers.	Students in San Francisco, CA, randomly assigned to tutored, control conditions—2 controls replicated over 3 yrs. No tests of reading comprehension—effects are on word recognition only.	Gr. 1-6	WRAT +.5-.7, Gilmore +.5

volunteers tutored underachieving first through sixth graders for a half hour a day four or five days a week. Tutors were trained prior to tutoring in a variety of tutoring skills and use of multimedia materials, and worked with the reading specialist on the skills they were tutoring. Again, a variety of materials pertaining to the skills being developed were used. Students were randomly assigned to tutored or untutored groups. Those who received tutoring gained 0.50 standard deviations more in reading and 1.1 standard deviations more in math than the untutored control students.

In contrast to these two programs, Success Controlled Optimal Reading Experience (SCORE), the third successful remedial model identified, uses highly programmed materials and a very specifically structured tutoring session. SCORE uses rapid drill and practice in lists of words grouped to teach specific decoding skills (short and long vowel sounds, sound blending, word patterns such as *night, light, fight,* and so on). Students who are deficient in decoding skills are tutored for fifteen minutes a day until they complete the program, usually a period from four to six months.

In the original evaluation of the program, educationally handicapped students were randomly assigned to a special class for learning-disabled students, to regular class placement with no support, or to regular class placement with fifteen minutes of tutoring by students in grades 6 to 12. The SCORE treatment group exceeded both control groups on measures of word recognition and oral reading accuracy. Effect size estimates ranged from 0.5 to 0.7 standard deviations. The results were replicated over three successive years. The program has been implemented in a wide variety of settings with lower middle- and upper-class populations in urban and rural settings using older students, parent volunteers, and aides as tutors. Gains in these settings have exceeded the gains in the original study in almost every case.

A limitation of these data lies in the fact that no reading comprehension data are provided. The gains seen in word recognition and oral reading accuracy are large and important, and would be expected to enable readers to pay more attention to comprehending their reading, but there is no guarantee that this generalization occurs. Comprehension gains would have to be assessed in any implementation of this program. It may be that SCORE would provide a strong first step in a more complete program that explicitly addressed comprehension as well.

Preventative Tutoring Programs.   Four different programs have addressed the problem of reading failure by attempting to prevent failure at the first-grade level. Descriptions of these programs appear in Table 3–3. Programmed Tutorial Reading (PTR) provides one-to-one tutoring by paraprofessionals to first graders in the bottom quartile in reading. The tutoring process is highly structured. The tutor uses programmed materials based on the basal series used in the school that instruct the tutor in where to start,

TABLE 3–3. Preventative Tutoring Programs

Program and Source	Grades/ Subjects	Description	Evaluation	Effect Sizes
I. Programs Evaluated Using Control Group Designs				
Programmed Tutorial Reading (JDRP #74–17)	1 only Reading	Each student tutored 15 min/day by paraprofessionals or older students.	Evaluation contained matched pairs of tutored/nontutored students in Farmington, UT. No pretest differences. Effects replicated using nonstandardized tests in several other districts.	Gr. 1, reading, bottom quartile Vocabulary +.65 Comprehension +.41 Basal comprehension measure +.50
Prevention of Learning Disabilities— New York (JDRP #79-33)	1–2 Reading	Each student tutored 3–5 times/week for 30 min. by a resource teacher.	Students randomly assigned to tutoring or control treatments. Achievement measured 2nd grades.	Gr. 1 and 2, students with low readiness scores. Gr. 1 Gr. 2 WRAT + .86 +1.06 Word Attack +1.41 +1.67 Word Recog. + .95 + .91

Program	Subjects	Description	Sample	Measures / Effect Size
Wallach Tutorial Program (Dorval, Wallach, & Wallach, 1978)	1 only Reading	Students turored 30 min/day, 28 hrs. total. Tutored by paraprofessionals.	Unclear how students were assigned to treatments but groups were equivalent at pretest. Compared tutoring to no tutoring to time with aide.	Gr. 1, students below 40% on MAT	Spache Word Recognition 1.3 GE CTBS Total Reading .75
Reading Recovery (Pinnell et al., 1986).	1 only Reading	Students tutored by specially trained teachers 30 min/day, at least 60 days.	Study 1 compared lowest readers in 14 Columbus, OH, classes to similar students in comparison classes. Study 2 randomly assigned low readers to exp., control.	Grade 1 Low readers	CTBS Rdg. Vocabulary .70 CTBS Rdg. Comprehension .92

what to say, when to praise, how to respond to a failure in word recognition, and so on. Students are essentially taught the words in the basal using a sight word approach, and in addition are taught word analysis and passage comprehension skills using the same vocabulary in separate series of lessons.

Programmed Tutorial Reading has been evaluated against a control group in two studies. In the first (Ellson, Harris, and Barber, 1968), students were randomly assigned to receive PTR, directed tutoring, or no tutoring. Directed tutoring involved having paraprofessionals tutor students using specific materials provided by the teacher that were designed to correspond to the instruction going on in the classroom. Tutors in both PTR and directed tutoring were trained for about eighteen hours prior to the beginning tutoring. Results indicated that PTR was more effective than directed tutoring and control, but the differences were not large.

In the second study of PTR (JDRP No. 74-17), students receiving fifteen minutes of tutoring a day were compared to students receiving no tutoring over a one-year period. In this study, substantial differences were seen between the two groups in favor of the tutored group.

Two other prevention models used programs designed to improve students' skills in specific reading or prereading areas. The Wallach Tutorial Program (Dorval, Wallach, and Wallach, 1978) used paraprofessionals to tutor children identified as low in readiness skills for one-half hour per day on phoneme identification skills. This training focused the students on breaking up the sounds in words so that, for instance, beginning sounds could be heard, sounded, and represented separately from the rest of the word. Wallach and Wallach based their program on research showing that disadvantaged children were drastically deficient in recognizing phonemes in heard words—such as knowing whether *house* or *man* starts with the sound "mmmmmmm." The tutored children performed at the 56th percentile on the California Test of Basic Skills at posttest after having begun at the 17th percentile. The control group moved from the 19th percentile to the 35th. The effect size for the comparison is 0.75 standard deviations.

Prevention of Learning Disabilities, a program developed by the New York University Medical Center, takes an approach that is somewhat similiar to the Wallach and Wallach approach. Students are screened for deficits in sensory skills related to reading at the kindergarten or beginning first-grade level, and those found to be deficient are tutored in those areas in which they are low. Auditory discrimination exercises similar to those used by Wallach and Wallach form a significant part of this instruction. Students were assigned to work on a tutorial basis or in small groups (two to three students) with a resource teacher three to five times a week. The program is designed as a two-year program, but evaluations after both one and two years showed significant gains for the treated group on word recognition scales and on a word attack measure. No standardized tests of reading comprehension were used.

The most recently developed of the preventative tutoring models is Reading Recovery, a program originally developed in New Zealand by Clay (1985), and currently being adapted and evaluated in the United States by a group at Ohio State University. In this model, first graders who are diagnosed as having difficulties in reading work one-on-one with specially trained tutors for thirty minutes a day. Students are released from tutoring when they achieve a certain level on diagnostic tests that are part of the program. Some proportion of children are released from tutoring at the end of first grade without having reached the required level. On the average, Reading Recovery children receive sixty to eighty lessons (Pinnell, Short, Lyons, and Young, 1986). Reading Recovery instruction emphasizes having students read aloud from minibooks and write their own stories. No particular attempt is made to integrate tutoring with instruction students may be receiving in their regular classes. Tutors, who are certified teachers, are trained over the course of a full school year, with trainers observing tutoring sessions from behind one-way mirrors and providing detailed feedback.

Two cohorts of first graders have been compared to control groups. The 1984–85 cohort originally consisted of fifty-five Reading Recovery and fifty-five matched control students, the eight lowest-achieving first graders in seven experimental and seven control classes, respectively.

As of this writing, these students have been followed through the end of the third grade (DeFord, Pinnell, Lyons, and Young, 1987). At the end of the first grade, the Reading Recovery students scored considerably higher than control students on the Stanford Reading Test (ES = +.605). Unfortunately, the standardized tests were not repeated in subsequent years. What was used longitudinally was an assessment of "text reading level" from the diagnostic test used in the Reading Recovery Program itself. On this test, effect sizes separating experimental and control students were as follows:

Text Reading Level:

Comparison	Effect size
Pretest (Dec. '84)	+.16
End of Gr. 1 (May '85)	+.87
Fall, Gr. 2 (Oct. '85)	+.75
End of Gr. 2 (May '86)	+.45
End of Gr. 3 (May '87)	+.29

Clearly, Reading Recovery had a substantial positive effect on reading performance at the end of grade 1, and this effect is still detectable (and statistically significant) two years later. Not surprisingly, though, the effects diminished over time. In addition to the achievement effects, it is important to note that Reading Recovery students were significantly less likely than control students to fail a grade; 66 percent of Reading Recovery students were in third grade in 1986–87, compared to only 51 percent of control students.

A similiar pattern of results was found for the 1985–86 cohort. By the end of first grade, these students exceeded control on CTBS Reading Vocabulary (ES = 0.67) and Reading Comprehension (ES = 0.61). In text reading level, the longitudinal results were as follows:

Text Reading Level:

Comparison	Effect size
Pretest (Oct. '85)	+.19
End of Gr. 1 (May '86)	+.97
End of Gr. 2 (May '87)	+.65

A total of 81 percent of Reading Recovery students were promoted to the second grade, in comparison to 73 percent of control students.

The results of the Reading Recovery studies indicate that this model can have substantial effects on the reading achievement of the first graders. Although the effects diminish over time, they are still important at the end of third grade, even in the absence of any special programs in grades 2 and 3.

Overall, the preventative tutoring programs have great potential for giving students a good start in reading. Combined with less intensive instructional improvements in the later grades, these programs may provide a means of obviating the need for remedial or special education for all but the most retarded or disabled students (see Chapter 12).

Computer-Assisted Instruction

Computer-assisted instruction (CAI) can be seen as another form of tutoring in which the tutor is a machine rather than a person. Like a human tutor, computers can determine students' needs, provide instruction appropriate to those needs, recognize and reinforce student success, and keep records of student progress. However, computers are usually less able to explain concepts to students, and for this reason CAI programs invariably have teachers available to students while they are working on their computer lessons. Descriptions of effective CAI models appear in Table 3–4.

Several studies of CAI as a pullout program for students in need of remediation have been conducted, but both the largest number of evaluations and the highest quality evaluations have involved the reading and math programs developed at Stanford University in the early 1970s and currently disseminated by the Computer Curriculum Corporation (CCC) (Jamison, Fletcher, Suppes, and Atkinson, 1976). Unlike most current CAI programs which operate on microcomputers, CCC uses a mainframe with terminals linked to a central processing unit by telephone. The computer keeps records of student performance levels and progress, and provides students with exercises appropriate to their needs.

The most important evaluation of the CCC curriculum itself was conducted in the Los Angeles Public Schools by the Educational Testing Service (Ragosta, 1983). In this four-year longitudinal study, students were randomly assigned to receive ten minutes per day of CAI in mathematics, reading, or language, as part of a thirty-minute Chapter 1 pullout period. Results on the CTBS indicated substantial effects of CAI on math computations, which increased from an effect size of 0.36 in the first year to 0.72 by the third year of intervention. Effects on concepts and applications scales were smaller and nonsignificant. In reading, positive effects were found for vocabulary and comprehension scales after one year (ES = +.25 and +.23, respectively), but while the vocabulary effects increased to +.59 by the third year, comprehension effects actually favored the control group by that time (ES = −.24). Effects in language mechanics were at about one-quarter of a standard deviation all three years, but were small and generally nonsignificant on language expression and spelling scales.

The JDRP-approved projects that used the CCC curriculum also present convincing evidence of effectiveness. One, a program evaluated in Lafayette Parish, Louisiana, called Title I Mathematics Laboratory with Computer Assisted Instruction (JDRP No. 82-46), randomly assigned students to regular Title I pullout or to a combination of the regular pullout model with ten minutes of CAI in mathematics. Effects on the CTBS Total Math Scale were modest, only +.19, but the extraordinary quality of the experiment makes the effect credible. Another JDRP program based on the CCC reading materials is the Merrimack (Massachusetts) Education Center (JDRP No. 82-34), a program that supplements ten minutes per day of CAI with tutorial and small-group instruction from the teacher. A study with random assignment of students to CAI and control treatments found positive effects averaging 40 percent of a standard deviation on the MAT reading scale.

One interesting CAI program that does not use CCC materials is Basic Literacy through Microcomputers, a model developed and evaluated in Salt Lake City, Utah. This program uses either electric typewriters or computers to supplement the teacher's instruction by giving students opportunities to practice and apply phonics skills by typing words, sentences, and stories. The evaluation of this program involved comparison classes in gains on standardized tests. Differences at grades 1 and 3 favored the experimental group, but substantial pretest differences at grade 3 make these results inconclusive. Ironically, the grade 1 experiment, which found substantial positive effects on California Achievement Test Total Reading scores (ES = +.58), used typewriters rather than computers.

Overall, results for the CAI programs (especially CCC) are well-

TABLE 3–4. Computer Assisted Instruction Programs

Program and Source	Grades/ Subjects	Description	Evaluation	Effect Sizes			
					Yr1	Yr2	Yr3
I. Programs Evaluated Using Control Group Designs							
Computer Curriculum Corp.		Students engage in drill and practice activities on computers 10 min/day in addition to regular instruction.					
Study 1 (Ragosta, 1983)	1–6 Math 3–6 Reading, Language		Comparison with randomly selected controls. Groups studied longitudinally over four years in Los Angeles Unified School District—4 schools.	Gr. 1–6 Math 3–6 Rdg. 3–6 Lang.			
				CTBS			
				Math			
				Comp	+.36	+.56	
				Conc	−.02	+.12	+.09
				Appl	+.03	+.12	+.26
				Rdg			
				Voc	+.25	+.17	+.58
				Comp	+.23	−.01	−.24
				Spel	+.14	+.05	+.14
				Lang			
				Mech	+.22	+.27	+.25
				Expr	+.11	+.05	+.23

Study	Subject (Chapter 1)	Description	Grade/Subject	Test	Effect
Study 2 Lafayette Parish Title I Math (JDRP #82-46)	3–6 Math (Chapter 1)	Compared to students receiving Chapter 1 pullout. Students randomly assigned in Lafayette Parish, LA.	Gr. 3–6 Math	CTBS Total Math	+.19
Study 3 Merrimack Education Center (JDRP #82-34)	2–9 Reading (Chapter 1)	Students randomly assigned in Merrimack, MA. Compared to students receiving Chapter 1 pullout.	Gr. 2–9 Rdg.	MAT Reading	+.40
Basic Literacy Through Microcomputers (JDRP #84-14)	1–3 Reading (Chapter 1)	Microcomputers or typewriters used to practice phonics and writing skills in addition to regular instruction. Students randomly assigned. Compared to students receiving no additional time.	Gr. 1 CAT Reading		+.58

established and positive, though in the best-controlled studies they are usually modest in magnitude and appear more frequently on basic skills than on higher-order skills. Since the costs of CIA can be very high (see Ragosta, 1983), this approach can be compared to adult tutoring, which tends to have larger effects in studies of similar methodological quality.

CONCLUSIONS

Chapter 2 reviewed research on effective classroom programs for students at risk for school failure. The review concludes that the most consistently successful classroom models were continuous-progress programs in which students are taught in skill-level groups and proceed through a hierarchical set of skills, and cooperative learning programs in which students also receive instruction at their appropriate levels but then practice skills in mixed-ability learning teams. On the basis of this and other evidence, Chapter 2 concluded that effective programs for students at risk balanced adjustment of instructional approaches to meet students' unique needs with provision of adequate direct instruction. In addition, effective classroom programs provide frequent assessment of student progress through a well-specified, hierarchical set of skills.

The examination of effective pullout programs conducted in this chapter provided further support for these conclusions. The most successful models, tutoring and CAI, completely adapt instruction to students' unique needs and provide plentiful direct instruction appropriate to students' levels of readiness. Diagnostic-prescriptive pullout models, which have generally been less successful than tutoring or CAI, also carefully assess students' needs and adapt instruction to these needs, but often suffer from one of two problems. Chapter 1 pullout teachers often work with individual students, leaving others in the group to spend much time working on worksheets, which may be of relatively little value. Alternatively, Chapter 1 teachers may present lessons to heterogeneous groups of students that are poorly adapted to their individual needs, and may be poorly integrated with instruction being provided in the regular class (see Chapter 11). In either case, the instruction provided in traditional diagnostic-prescriptive pullout programs may not be markedly better than that provided in the regular classroom. If so, it is unrealistic to expect that thirty to forty-five extra minutes of instruction will make a substantial difference in achievement. Both the tutoring and the CAI studies suggest that *intensive* interventions are needed to make a substantial difference in a pullout program.

Taken together, the conclusions of this chapter and Chapter 2 suggest that the achievement of at-risk students can be significantly increased, either by making relatively inexpensive but extensive modifications in the regular instructional program or by implementing relatively expensive but intensive interventions as pullout programs. It is possible that a combination of these strategies would be more effective than either one by itself.

There is much more we need to know about effective programs for students at risk. Research on diagnostic-prescriptive models is generally of low quality; it may be that certain forms of diagnostic-prescriptive models would be highly effective in well-designed experiments, but much research and development is needed to establish what these forms might be and how much difference they could make in student achievement. The tutoring and CAI studies are of much higher methodological quality, but except in cases where peer tutoring or volunteer programs are practical, these are expensive interventions. For practical as well as theoretical reasons, then, there is a need to identify the *elements* of tutoring and CAI that account for their effects, so that perhaps these same principles could be applied in a less expensive form. In addition, the cost-effectiveness of alternative approaches to prevention and remediation remains to be determined. For example, it is possible that very expensive but very effective preventative tutoring models may, by reducing retentions, remedial needs, and special education referrals, be cost-effective. Even if these preventative programs could not completely justify themselves on a dollar basis, however, they could help avoid the human cost of retention and special education.

REFERENCES

Advanced Technology (1983). *Local operation of Title I, ESEA 1976–1982: A resource book*. McLean, VA: Author.

Archambault, F. X. (1987, April). *Pullout versus inclass instruction in compensatory instruction*. Paper presented at the Annual Convention of the American Educational Association, Washington, DC.

Clay, M. M. (1985). *The early detection of reading difficulties*. Exeter, NH: Heinemann.

Cooley, W. W., and Leinhardt, G. (1980). The instructional dimensions study. *Educational Evaluation and Policy Analysis, 2*, 7–26.

DeFord, D. E.; Pinnell, G. S.; Lyons, C. A.; and Young, P. (1987). *Report of the followup studies, Columbus, Ohio. Reading Recovery Project, 1985–1986 and 1986–1987*. Columbus: Ohio State University.

Dorval, B.; Wallach, L.; and Wallach, M. A. (1978, April). Field evaluation of a tutorial reading program emphasizing phoneme identification skills. *The Reading Teacher*, 784–790.

Ellson, D. G.; Harris, P.; and Barber, L. (1968). A field test of programmed and directed tutoring. *Reading Research Quarterly, 3(3)*, 307–368.

Gabriel, R. M.; Anderson, B. L.; Benson, G.; Gordon, S.; Hill, R.; Pfannenstiel, J.; and Stonehill, R. M. (1985). *Studying the sustained achievement of Chapter 1 students*. Washington, DC: U.S. Department of Education.

Glass, G.; McGaw, B.; and Smith, M. L. (1981). *Meta-analysis in social research*. Beverly Hills, CA: Sage.

Glass, G. V., and Smith, M. L. (1977). *Pull-out in compensatory education.* Washington, DC: Department of Health, Education, and Welfare.

Granick, L.; Quigley, M. M.; Katzenellenbogen, R.; and Richardson, L. H. (1984). *Optimizing Chapter 1 program effectiveness.* Baltimore, MD: Baltimore City Public Schools.

Griswold, P. A.; Cotton, K. J.; and Hansen, J. B. (1986). *Effective compensatory education sourcebook.* Washington, DC: U.S. Government Printing Office.

Jamison, D.; Fletcher, J. D.; Suppes, P.; and Atkinson, R. C. (1976). Costs and performance of computer-assisted instruction for education of disadvantaged children. In J. Froomkin, D. Jamison, and R. Radner (Eds.), *Education is an industry.* Cambridge, MA: Ballinger.

Johnston, P.; Allington, R.; and Afflerbach, P. (1985). Curriculum confluence in classroom and clinic. *Elementary School Journal, 85,* 465–477.

Kennedy, M. (1978). Findings from the Follow Through planned variation study. *Educational Researcher, 7,* 3–11.

Kennedy, M. M.; Birman, B. F.; and Demaline, R. (1986). *The effectiveness of Chapter 1 services.* Washington, DC: Office of Educational Research and Improvement, U.S. Department of Education.

Kimball, G. H.; Crawford, J.; and Raia, F. (1985). *Evaluation of the 1984–85 Oklahoma City Public Schools Chapter 1 Program.* Oklahoma City, OK: Oklahoma City Public Schools.

Pinnell, G. S.; Short, K. G.; Lyons, C. A.; and Young, P. (1986). *The reading recovery project in Columbus, Ohio. Year 1: 1985–1986.* Columbus, Ohio State University.

Ragosta, M. (1983). Computer-assisted instruction and compensatory education: A longitudinal analysis. *Machine-Mediated Learning, 1,* 97–127.

Rowan, B.; Guthrie, L. F.; Lee, G. V.; and Guthrie, G. P. (1986). *The design and implementation of Chapter 1 services: A study of 24 schools.* San Francisco: Far West Laboratory for Educational Research and Development.

Slavin, R. E. (1986). Best-evidence synthesis: An alternative to meta-analytic and traditional reviews. *Educational Research, 15*(9), 5–11.

Weaterl, R. (1986). *Lincoln Public Schools Chapter 1.* Lincoln, NE: Lincoln Public Schools.

PART THREE

EARLY CHILDHOOD PROGRAMS

4

EFFECTIVE PRESCHOOL PROGRAMS FOR STUDENTS AT RISK

Nancy Karweit

Center for Research on Elementary and Middle Schools
The Johns Hopkins University

Early childhood education has traditionally been aligned with social and educational reform efforts (Lazar and Darlington, 1982). From the first pioneers who championed early education for the poor (e.g., Comenius, Pestalozia, and Montessori) to present-day advocates of quality preschool programs for students "at risk," the connection between early education and social intervention has clearly been made. For example, in the United States the early efforts of the Peabody sisters in Massachusetts to provide early education for children of poverty were motivated by the desire to better the future lives of these children. More recently, the establishment of the Head Start program as a part of President Johnson's War on Poverty provides evidence of the connection between early education and social reform.

Despite the existence of this long-term connection between preschool and social reform, actual support for preschool has been intermittent, being picked up and abandoned as a function of economic, social, and political forces. For example, during the depression and World War II, the federal government sponsored nursery schools, but had little other involvement until the mid-1960s. The spotty history is in part due to the fact that preschools are operated by multiple sponsors, including churches, public schools, private schools, and profit and not-for-profit day care centers. Given the different auspices, regulations and governing agencies vary widely. Consequently, no regularized, institutionalized system guarantees preschool for the disadvantaged or for any other group. Head Start, and programs run under Chapter 1 funds, have existed for more than twenty years, but are constantly in jeopardy and have never served a large proportion of the eligible students. (See Chapter 6 for a discussion of the history of Head Start.) At present, preschool has no legal, provisional, or guaranteed financial foundation. Part of the issue surrounding preschool is the question of its legal and financial status within the education system. Although such questions are inherently political and social, issues of educational benefit are clearly relevant in this debate.

It is therefore important and especially timely for a discussion of the evidence regarding the short-term and long-term effects of preschool. What does research indicate about the effectiveness of preschool as an intervention strategy? What is the evidence about the effects of particular programs for students at risk? Finally, what are some of the larger issues that need to be considered as states and locales move to include preschools in their elementary schools?

This chapter reviews the major literature on the effects of preschool. Particular attention is given to the question of the effects of specific curricular models and programs, including programs that have been certified as effective by the U.S. Department of Education's Joint Dissemination Review Panel (JDRP).

THE CHANGING FACE OF PRESCHOOL

The term *preschool* covers a wide variety of early educational experiences. It may mean a half-day nursery school program that emphasizes play and socialization, or it may mean a full-day academic program where the intention is to teach reading and math readiness skills. It may mean programs for four-year-olds, three-year-olds, or even earlier intervention efforts. In this chapter, we focus primarily on prekindergarten programs for four-year-olds, although a few studies included three- and five-year-olds as well.

The first important change in preschool programs is the very rapid rate of growth over the last twenty years. While only 15 percent of all four-year-olds were enrolled in 1964, almost half of all four-year-olds are presently enrolled in preschool (Center for Education Statistics, 1986, fig. 1).

A second important change is the auspices for preschool. There is a growing involvement of public schools in the provision of preschool programs. State education agencies in fifteen states and the District of Columbia currently fund prekindergarten programs for four-year-olds (Morado, 1985). State-funded programs are operated either by permissive language in the state's school code or by special legislative provision for programs. One example of permissive language is the provision for preschool in Texas where the legislation reads "Any school district may offer prekindergarten classes, but a district shall offer prekindergarten classes if the district identifies 15 or more eligible children." The bill defines as eligible those four-year-olds who are either "unable to speak and comprehend the English language" or are "from a family whose income . . . is at or below subsistence level" (Schweinhart, 1986, p. 35).

   The increase in provision of public preschool will most likely result in different attendance patterns for different income and ethnic groups. Recent statistics on preschool enrollment indicate that of the four-year-olds enrolled in preschool in 1984, there are already differences in patterns of enrollment by race and income. Whites are more likely to be enrolled in private preschools than are blacks (32.9 versus 16.2 percent). Income level is an important determiner of enrollment patterns. For families with incomes less than $20,000, a greater proportion of black four-year-olds are enrolled in preschool than are white, and this difference is primarily due to differences in public school enrollment. For families with incomes greater than $20,000, a greater percentage of white children participate in preschool than do black, and this again comes about primarily due to differences in auspices, with 43.6 percent of the whites attending private preschool.

   Between 1975 and 1984, the greatest growth in preschool attendance was among high-income white children with mothers not in the labor force. In 1975, 53.4 percent of white four-year-olds in families with income of $15,000 and over were in preschool. In 1984, 65.9 percent of white four-year-olds in families with income over $30,000 were in preschool. The percent of enrolled four-year-olds of nonworking mothers rose from 37.5 percent in 1975 to 48.2 percent in 1984.

   These figures suggest that there may be two very different trends developing in the expansion of early education. One force is the continuing demand for compensatory programs, as witnessed by the state efforts at programs for the disadvantaged. The other growth is in the private sector for programs that primarily serve high-income families with nonworking mothers and mothers who are employed part-time. Private preschool appears to be growing at a more rapid pace than public preschool. This uneven growth in preschool opportunities creates greater inequality in preparation for school.

   A third area of change is the singular view of the significance of early childhood experiences for later development. The empirical groundwork suggesting the importance of environment on development was started by studies of the Iowa schools in the 1930s and 40s. Although the studies lacked adequate controls and experimental designs, the publication of results helped contribute to a sense that intervention strategies aimed at early ages were particularly effective in overcoming effects of deprivation.

   Kirk (1958) carried out the first properly controlled experiments on the effectiveness of early intervention. He conducted a two-year intervention in which the IQ of the treatment group was significantly raised. Eventually, however, these IQ gains washed out, and students who had benefitted from the early intervention program were indistinguishable from those who had not.

   Longitudinal studies of orphans/adoptees (Skeels, 1966) were also influential in building the view of the critical importance of early life experiences. Twenty-five infant residents of Iowa Soldier's Orphan Homes who were previously not offered for early adoption because of adverse social histories were divided into treatment and control conditions. Thirteen treatment children were transferred to an institution where active, stimulating efforts were made to make them more adoptable (i.e., to increase their apparent IQ). Twelve stayed at Orphan's Home without intervention.

In adult life the contrasts between these two groups were stark. The experimental group on the whole were normal, well-adjusted members whereas the control group was not. This study reinforced the notion that early intervention could have an important impact on adult social and educational status.

The early 1960s saw an increased focus on early childhood as a prime time for intervention. Part of the reasoning was that because infancy is a period of unusually rapid maturation and sensitivity, intervention at this point was particularly critical. Bloom (1964), in *Stability and Change in Human Characteristics,* states the prevailing beliefs about early development and intervention as:

> In terms of intelligence measured at age 17, about 50% of the development takes place between conception and age 4, 30% between 4 and 8, 20% between 8 and 17. . . . The evidence so far available suggests that marked changes in environment in the early years can produce greater changes in intelligence than will equally marked changes in the environment at later periods of development.

Thus the prevailing belief in the mid-1960s was that a single, restricted, and essentially modest intervention could have life-long consequences. As Elkind states, "Great expectations and promises were based on the view that the young child was plastic material to be molded quickly and permanently by the proper school environment." The early childhood intervention programs of this era were conceived in a period of great optimism and equally great naivete about the possibility of the strength of early intervention.

Some of the enthusiasm was diminished by early evaluations of Head Start and by statements that "we have tried compensatory education and it has failed" (Jensen, 1969). Yet, of the interventions born in this era, the long-term positive effects recently documented are altering this gloomy picture (Berrueta-Clement, Schweinhart, Barnett, Epstein, and Weikart, 1984).

Accompanying this shift in the view of environment on development was an important redefinition of the role of early cognitive experiences. Prior to the 1960s, there was actually very little concern with the issue of early intellectual functioning. Instead, the concern was with the development of the healthy personality of the child, which if properly taken care of would automatically include intellectual maturity as well.

When this "normative maturational" view of early development was in vogue, there was little interest or concern over providing appropriate learning environments, since satisfactory intellectual development was seen as primarily maturational, not environmental. After the late 1960s and into the present, this view of childhood has given way to what Elkind (1986) calls the "competent infant" point of view.

The competent infant movement has two important asssumptions: (1) malleability of traits such as IQ and (2) singular importance of early intervention to prevent later impoverishment in intellectual functioning. The latter issue points directly to the need for appropriate early childhood education programs both as an intervention strategy for the disadvantaged and as an appropriate educational step for advantaged students as well.

With these changes in the views of children and with ever increasing numbers of women in the labor force, it is not surprising that the area of early education has become an area of great interest in the 1980s. Many states and local districts are buying into the idea, but there are some concerns being voiced. For example, some black citizens note that the school system has failed them already and question why the public schools should have any better a record in early education than they do in elementary and secondary education. Others note the difficulty in funding programs at a sufficiently high level to duplicate the quality programs that served as an impetus for implementing preschool programs in the first place (Grubb, 1987). Still others are concerned that the preschools are being implemented to help alleviate the need for child care and question why the public schools should foot the bill for these services. Therefore, many social, political, and educational issues are involved in present discussions about preschool. Nonetheless, the educational benefits of preschool programs should be a primary consideration and understanding the short- and long-term educational benefits of such programs is central to the current debate. The discussion here focuses first on those studies that have examined the effects on students of attendance at preschool in comparison to students who did not attend preschool. Next, the discussion considers the results of participation in particular types of preschool curricula.

PARTICIPATION IN PRESCHOOL PROGRAMS

The first set of studies we consider addresses the issue of the effects of participation in preschool programs. An important body of studies, collectively known as *The Consortium for Longitudinal Studies* (1982), provides critical evidence of the long- and short-term effects of early intervention efforts. The Consortium came about in response to the findings of an influential Westinghouse (1969) evaluation of Head Start, which concluded that the program was not having long-term effects on success in school. Recognizing the need for true longitudinal studies to assess effects of early intervention, Lazar and Grotberg proposed in 1974 finding well-designed earlier studies that could be used as a base for followup efforts. Fifteen such studies, authored by twelve developers, were located. The studies differed in many respects—sample size, age of student, approach to intervention— but they all had in common the intention to assist the future chances of low-income children, primarily from minority homes. The Consortium then examined the long- and short-term benefits of enrollment in these programs.

For our purposes, we are primarily interested in programs whose effectiveness was determined by an adequate experimental design and which focused on programs for four-year-olds. We focus on four-year-olds because most programs being implemented today are specific to this age child.

From the fifteen projects in the Consortium studies, six projects were located that focused on four-year-olds (those developed by Bellar, Deutsch, Gray, Karnes, and Weikart). From this list of six, two studies (Gray and Weikart) randomly assigned students to treatment and control groups. Following Slavin's (1986) best-evidence synthesis methodology, these two studies are therefore given the greatest attention here.

Gray (Early Training Project)

Gray's Early Training Project (Gray, Ramsey, and Klous, 1982) consisted of a ten-week summer program in which students met for four hours daily, five days per week. Students participated in a class of twenty, served by one teacher and four assistants. During the school year, home visitors also worked with each family once a week for a period of one hour.

The Early Training Project focused on perceptual/cognitive and language development using a traditional nursery school format, but with activities sequenced to become increasingly complex and carefully focused on increasing language use. The first entry in Table 4–1 summarizes the major features and effects of Gray's study.

Sixty-one students were randomly assigned to one of three conditions: two groups that entered the program just described at different ages, and an untreated control group. An additional control group in another city was also used. The two different treatment conditions differed only in the age at which they started the program.

The pretest IQ scores for the treatment and control groups were 89.4 and 87.3, respectively. At age five, after participation in the program, the IQ scores were 96.05 and 86.3. By age 17, the IQs were once again very similar: 78.7 and 76.4.

Gray determined that 2.4 percent of the program children were placed in special education and 23.8 percent of the control children were so placed. The program children also showed a greater likelihood of not being retained in grade. Nearly 56 percent of the program children were retained in grade, whereas the figure was closer to 69 percent for the control children. About

TABLE 4–1. Effects of Preschool Attendance on Achievement and Other Outcomes

Project	Program/Focus	Strategy/Treatments	Population	Study Design	Measures/Effects			
					IQ	TRT	CTL	ES
Early Training Project (Gray)	Intervention program to change attitudes/aptitudes needed for school success.	Morning (4 hrs) summer session for 10 wks and weekly 1-hr home visits with parent/child to emphasize parental role in education of child. Small staff ratio (5:1).	88 black children in Murfrees-boro, TN, aged 3 1/2– 4 1/2 in 1962. Grp A = 61 children in same town; Grp B = 27	Group A (67 students) randomly assigned to T1 (3 yrs treatment), T2 (2 yrs), or T3 (no trt). Group B was second control group (T4).	End of yr	89.4	87.3	.15
					+ 1 yr	96.1	86.3	.81
					+ 2 yrs	94.9	81.9	1.09
					+ 3 yrs	97.7	89.6	.63
					+ 4 yrs	93.6	86.1	.51
					+ 6 yrs	88.4	81.2	.54
					Spec. ed.	2.4	23.8	.50
					Repeat	47.5	55.6	.16
					Drop out	22.0	43.0	.14

(continued)

TABLE 4–1. (continued)

Project	Program/Focus	Strategy/Treatments	Population	Study Design	Measures/Effects
Perry Preschool (Berreuta-Clement et al., 1984)	Examination of effect of preschool on disadvantaged children. Longitudinal study followed students up through age 19.	Curricular approach based on developmentally appropriate activities stressing role of planning and active learning of child.	123 disadvantaged 3- to 4-yr-olds from Ypsilanti, MI, with IQs between 60–90, not otherwise handicapped.	Five waves, 1962–67. Students in each wave randomly assigned to experimental or control condition.	*Cognitive/Scholastic*

Study Design:

Wave	PS	No PS
0	13	15
1	8	9
2	12	14
3	13	14
4	12	13
Total	58	65

Measures/Effects:

Cognitive/Scholastic

Age	PS	No PS	ES
Pre	79.6	78.6	.17
5	94.1	83.2	1.01
6	91.3	86.3	.45
7	91.7	87.1	.44
8	88.1	86.9	.11
10	84.9	84.6	.03
14	82.3	82.0	.04

CAT (percent correct)

Age	PS	No PS	ES
7	37%	32%	.11
8	53	47	.12
9	46	38	.14
10	60	54	.12
11	67	65	.05
14	36	28	.17

School Success

	PS	No PS	ES
HS grad	67%	49%	+.72
Retain	15	13	−.22
Special	31	45	+.27

Social/Behavioral

	PS	No PS	ES
Arrest	22%	43%	+.85
Employ	48	29	.92

NY State Experimental preK Program (Irvine, 1982)

Individualized program emphasizing total environment and student choice.

Parent involvement. Health srvs. Social srvs.

Longitudinal preK–3 5000 disadvantaged in program, selected into pgm on low-economic status.

Control grp was "waiting-list control group" eligibles without space; and other-district control grp, similar but not operating preK.

Two waves, 1975, 1976.

		Wave I WL/CTL	Wave II WL/CTL
Walker Readiness	PK	+	+
	Start K	+	+
	End K	0	0
	1	0	0
	2	0	0
	3	0	0
Peabody	PK	+	+
	Start K	+	0
	End K	+	+
(Longitud. analysis)	1	+	0
	2	+	0
	3	+	0
Grade Repetition		+	
Special Education		+	

22 percent of the program children dropped out of high school prior to completion; the corresponding figure for control children was about 43 percent. Thus the program had significant effects on important variables of grade repetition, special education status, and high school completion. The effect sizes are in the range of 0.14 to 1.09 (see Table 4–1, far right-hand column).

Concerning the effects on reading and mathematics achievement in elementary schools, the Gray study provides little reason to expect continued effects of program participation. The performance of students in the program was not significantly different from that of control students in math or reading at grades 4 and 6. Thus the study does not lend support to long-term effects of this type of early intervention effort on achievement.

When the effects are analyzed separately by sex, a somewhat different picture emerges. There are pronounced sex differences. In particular, the Gray program appears to have been beneficial for girls, but not for boys. Table 4–2 summarizes these results by sex. It is not clear what factors or processes created these sex differences in the Gray study.

Weikart (Perry Preschool)

The other study included in the longitudinal followup that focused on four-year-olds and used random assignment in its design is the Perry Preschool Project (Berrueta-Clement et al., 1984). There are two parts to the Perry Preschool data that will be discussed. The first considers the effect of participation in preschool versus no preschool. The second considers the effect of participation in a particular preschool curricula.

The sample consisted of 123 disadvantaged, low-IQ children from Ypsilanti, Michigan. The subjects were recruited by locating all families with three-year-old children and interviewing the parents to determine their

TABLE 4–2. Comparison of Experimental and Control Groups by Sex in Gray's Early Training Project

Factor	Males			Females		
	EXP	CTL	ES	EXP	CTL	ES
Repeat grade	.76	.53	−.33	.35	.50	.30
Complete HS	.24	.36	.10	.75	.20	.80
EMR placement	.09	.36	.41	.00	.30	.65
WISC-R	79.2	76.8	.18	78.2	76.1	.11
Task: Reading	33.1	32.2	.06	40.7	37.4	.18
English	31.1	33.9	−.21	46.1	39.6	.46
Math	22.1	22.4	.02	23.3	20.6	.25

occupation, education, and household density. Children from low-SES families were administered an IQ test and those who scored in the 70–85 range were selected. Students were randomly assigned to treatment and control groups.

There were five waves of this study, beginning in 1962 and continuing through 1967. Across the five waves, fifty-eight students were assigned to the preschool condition and sixty-five to the no preschool condition.

In contrast to the Gray project, the Perry Preschool Project took place during the academic year as a regular school program. The curricular approach was based on the theories of development of Piaget. The "theoretical framework emphasized the interplay of content (e.g., classification and spatial relationship), three levels of representation (e.g., index, symbol and sign), and two levels of operation (motor and verbal)" (Lazar and Darlington, 1982). The approach emphasized developmentally appropriate activities and stressed the role of students' planning and initiation in their own learning.

Children entered the program at age three and attended the program for two years, mid-October to May. The sessions were half-day, five days per week. In addition, the teachers visited the home of the students for ninety minutes weekly.

The short-term benefit of the Perry Preschool program is evident in the eleven-point differences in IQ scores between program and control students. The percent enrolled in special education is also appreciably lower for the preschool enrollees (45 percent versus 31 percent). The differences between those repeating and not repeating a grade were 2 percent. The largest differences were in the percent who graduated from high school, with 67 percent of the experimental students completing high school and only 49 percent of the students in control classes. Similar differences in the percent employed and arrested were found, favoring the Perry Preschool Program.

The differences in the percent correct on the CAT, taken at ages 7, 8, 9, 10, 11, and 14, favored the Perry preschool children but were not statistically significant and ranged from only 2 percent to 8 percent. The second entry in Table 4–1 summarizes the findings from the Perry Preschool.

Both the Gray and the Perry Preschool programs support the conclusion that preschool programs can have strong immediate effects on cognitive functioning, as measured by IQ tests. These effects are apparent at the onset of treatment and continue several years afterward. In the case of Perry Preschool, the experimental group is 44 percent of a standard deviation above the control at age seven. In the case of Gray's study, the effects are still detectable six years after the initial treatment (effect size = .51).

Both studies also showed similar patterns of effects on reduced referral to special education and lower rates of dropping out of high school. In the case of the Perry Preschool Program, the effect size was 0.72 for high school graduation. In the case of Gray, the effect size was 0.80 for females and 0.10 for males.

Both studies showed minimal long-term effects on achievement as measured by standardized tests. Gray's study measured achievement at grades 4 and 6 and showed no significant effect on achievement scores at either grade. Weikart's study also shows only modest achievement effects (effect sizes of 0.05 to 0.17).

Head Start Evaluations

Head Start programs were begun in 1965 as a national effort to "improve children's intellectual skills, to foster their social and emotional growth, and to help meet their health and nutritional needs." The importance of early intervention was based on the belief that infancy was an especially critical time for intervention. It was believed that intervention of a short duration during this critical time could provide a life-long developmental boost.

Perhaps the most publicized evaluation of Head Start was the Westinghouse Evaluation (1969), which concluded that Head Start was not satisfactorally meeting its objectives. However, many methodological and philosophical issues were leveled against the report and its conclusions.

The study used a posttest-only research design, comparing the achievement of Head Start attendees with a sample of students matched on age and sex. The Head Start sample included children who attended summer school only and children who attended full-year Head Start programs.

The posttest-only comparisons indicated no measurable advantage of Head Start children in summer programs over comparison children. The full-year program was more effective than the summer program, but the lack of robust effects led the authors to conclude that "the benefits cannot be described as satisfactory."

A major criticism of the report was the expectation that success would be measured as positive effects not only immediately after the program, but also several years later. Other criticisms of the report cited the insensitivity of the research design to differences in programs and the nonequivalence of the control and experimental groups.

More recent and methodologically rigorous evaluations (McKey, Condelli, Ganson, Barrett, McConkey, and Plantz, 1985) have emphasized that Head Start was apparently successful in meeting many of its objectives. Studies using random assignment or matched control groups in the McKey review provide very strong evidence of the immediate effects of Head Start on cognitive functioning (average effect sizes = 0.52), but little evidence for long-term effects (effect size = 0.10 after first year, 0.08 after second year, and 0.02 after 3+ years). A more positive picture of the long-term effects emerges if grade retention and special education placement are used as the criteria. Here, the three studies of the long-term effects indicate median effect sizes of 0.31 for retention and 0.29 for special education placement (McKey et al., 1985, p. 19).

New York Experimental Prekindergarten Study

New York state began an experimental prekindergarten program in 1966, designed to serve children from low-economic homes (Irvine, 1982). The prekindergarten program had four components: classroom experience, health services, social services, and parent involvement.

The effects of the program were assessed by comparison of the prekindergarten group with two control groups. One group was comprised of students who were on a waiting list for the program. The other group was comprised of eligible but not participating students.

The effects of the program were assessed by a comparison of these groups at the end of the prekindergarten year and at the beginning and end of kindergarten and at the end of grades one, two, three, and six.

The comparisons suggest that the prekindergarten program had immediate effects and some sustained effects in terms of achievement, grade retention, and rates of referral to special education. With the available technical and published reports, it was not possible to compute effect sizes for all relevant comparisons. Thus Table 4–1 indicates only the direction of the effect without its magnitude.

These four studies collectively suggest that there is an immediate and sizeable cognitive effect for participation in preschool that is diminished but still detectable in the elementary grades. The effect sizes diminish from a range of around 1.00 standard deviation at the end of the prekindergarten year, to around 0.20 by the end of the third grade.

EFFECT OF PARTICIPATION IN PARTICULAR PROGRAMS

Curriculum Comparison Studies

We now consider studies that have examined the effect of participation in particular preschool curricula. Two types of studies are considered—those that make direct comparisons among particular curricular models (Table 4–3), and those that provide evidence of effectiveness of a particular model, in particular JDRP programs (Table 4–4).

The first study contrasted the immediate and long-term effects of three different preschool curricula. The three models were a language training approach based on the work of Bereiter and Engelman (1966), a cognitively oriented approach based on the Perry Preschool model, and a unit-based approach which followed a traditional nursery school model. These models represent a wide range of approaches to preschool education.

The structural features of the programs were identical. The programs

TABLE 4–3. Comparison of the Effectiveness of Particular Curricular Approaches

Project	Program/Focus	Treatment	Population	Study Design	Effects
Perry Preschool CD Project	Comparison of effects of 3 distinct preschool curricular approaches on short- & long-term factors.	Half-day preschool sessions and home visits 1½ hr/wk. T1 = Academic preschool program (N = 23). T2 = Cognitively oriented curriculum (N = 22). T3 = Traditional Nursery School (N = 23). N = 68 Perry. N = 65 Control group	Disadvantaged black 3-yr-olds in Ypsilanti, MI, who scored between 62–90 on Stanford Binet test.	Four waves of children entered the project from 1967–70. Students randomly assigned to one of three treatment conditions and then reassigned to balance on IQ. (Control grp was Perry preschool grp from wave 0–4 in previous study)	*(see below)*

Effects

Cognitive Effects—IQ

Age	DSTR	H/S	NS	CTL	DSTR HS	NS HS
3	79	77	79	79	HS	HS
4	107	106	102	83	+.06	-.26
5	104	97	92	84	+.46	-.35
6	99	97	93	87	+.13	-.26
7	97	92	95	87	+.35	-.33
8	91	92	90	87	-.06	-.13
10	97	92	90	85	+.35	-.13

School Achievement (CAT + APL)

Age	DSTR	H/S	NS	D/HS	NS/HS
7	100	102	106	-.05	+.10
8	160	167	154	-.14	-.14
15	15.1	17.7	18.4	-.29	+.07

School Success

	DSTR	H/S	NS
Repeat Grade	20%	18%	20%

Social/Behavior (Age 15)

	DSTR	H/S	NS
Delinquent	12.8%	5.4%	6.9%

Louisville (Miller & Bizzel, 1983)

To compare the effects of 4 distinct preschool curricular approaches. Longitudinal study K–10. Program had demonstrated effectiveness and represented different philosophies.

Followup sample in 9th and 10th grade.

Random assignment to groups.

All 4 treatments attended preK classes 6.5 hrs/day for one academic year.

T1 = B-E (Bereiter Engelman)
T2 = Darcee (Gray)
T3 = Montessori
T4 = Traditional
C = Regular Head Start.

B-E—Academic preschool carefully structured, highly verbal, patterned drill and practice in small groups.

DARCEE— Gray's pgm focused on lang. development and motivation in teacher-directed format.

14 preK classes in Louisville, KY. Students assigned to
T1 = 64
T2 = 64
T3 = 33
T4 = 53
N = 214

Students in program for 1 yr.

Kindergarten yr they were in different program.

Random assignment to T/C.

IQ	T1 BE	T2 DAR	T3 MONT	T4 TRAD	C CTL
PPK	94.7	96.7	90.9	91.8	89.0
EPK	99.8	96.4	96.8	98.2	90.8
K	94.7	93.2	93.3	95.0	95.0
1	91.4	93.4	93.8	93.4	93.0
2	86.6	89.3	92.5	90.8	92.8
7	82.9	84.8	87.4	86.0	ND
8	86.7	85.3	88.9	86.6	ND

Males

IQ	T1 BE	T2 DAR	T3 MONT	T4 TRAD
PPK	97.1	94.3	89.1	91.3
EPK	100.5	95.8	91.7	96.0
K	93.2	93.8	91.3	97.9
1	93.1	94.2	92.8	97.5
2	90.2	89.4	96.6	94.3
8	90.0	83.5	92.7	88.1
10	84.5	78.0	93.3	83.9

Females

IQ	T1 BE	T2 DAR	T3 MONT	T4 TRAD
PreK	92.9	100.0	92.4	92.1
endK	99.2	97.5	101.1	99.4
K	95.8	92.2	94.8	93.4
1	90.1	92.2	94.6	91.1
2	83.8	89.1	89.2	88.8
8	84.1	88.3	85.7	85.7
10	82.1	88.5	77.4	87.1

(continued)

TABLE 4–3. (continued)

Project	Program/Focus	Treatment	Population	Study Design	Effects
		MONTESSORI— Emphasis on use of self-corrected materials and discovery focus on relation development of mind and senses. Structured curriculum in which sequence of activities controlled.			
		TRADITIONAL— Traditional nursery school program focusing on social and emotional development.			

	T1	T2	T3	T4	T5
	94.5	93.3	94.1	96.0	93.5
	102.6	98.4	99.6	110.3	109.2

T4 and T5 > T1, T2, T3   .39

Comparison post hoc control group

				Percent	
Referred		spec ed		21.6	33.3
Retained				12.9	35.7

| Karnes (comparison of five approaches) | Comparative evaluation of 5 preschool programs for children from low-income families.

Programs varied on extent of structure and program emphasis.

Differential program effectiveness favored T4 and T5 on immediate cognitive effects, but T3 on long-term effects.

No IQ effects by age 16. | T1 = Traditional Nursery
T2 = Community/Integrated
T3 = Montessori
T4 = GOAL (Karnes)
T5 = Direct Verbal (B-E)

T4 = emphasis on sensory motor with concurrent emphases on exp. lang.

T5 = direct instruction in preskills.

Low parental involvement in these projects

Half-day program for 1 yr.

Second year:
T1, T2, T3 -> regular K
T4 -> regular K + 1 hr
T5 -> intensive lang. not regular K. | Low-income families from Champaign/Urbana. 123 students in original sample, 45 in post hoc comparison grp.

Aged 4 at entry. Duration 1 hr and some treatment in second yr. | Random assignment to treatment, no control grp at the time, post hoc group constructed later 15-yr study. |

TABLE 4–4. Description of Evaluated Preschool Programs

| | Home-Based Programs | | |
Name	Program Description	Staffing/Components	Study Design
Verbal Interact Project (Levenstein)	Home-based early intervention program for ages 2–4 based on view that conceptual growth built on language of mother/child in home.	Toy Demonstrator (High school ed.). Half-hour home sessions twice/week for 7 months over two years.	Comparison with randomly assigned control group.
Compensatory Early Education Home-Based Program	Identification of students who are significantly deficient in language development, gross and fine motor and readiness skills. Treatment is to provide instructional activities, instruct parents in home in 1½ hr/wk training session.		Pre-post gains over 10-month period.

Program	Description	Method	Evaluation
Parent Child Early Education Program (PCEE) Ferguson, MO	Primary focus on early identification and treatment of educationally disadvantaged child; focus on improving parent competencies IDENTIFICATION: Comprehensive diagnosis includes initial evaluation by parents and teachers and diagnosis by staff specialist as needed. TREATMENT: Home teaching visits to provide individualized instruction Saturday school-home activity guides	Saturday school-parent home visits/teaching carried out by specialist in learning disabilities.	Comparison of preK participants with control with no preK at entry to kindergarten. No evidence of initial equivalence of groups.
Portage Project Portage, WI	Home teaching program for multicategorically handicapped birth to 6 yrs and for nonhandicapped with developmental delays. Individualized curriculum, parents as teachers, weekly data collection on progress in home.	Individual assessment. Individual planning. Home teaching/visits monitoring progress.	Comparison of Portage Project with local preschool program for disadvantaged. Original certification by JDRP on basis of pre-post growth scores of 1.3 to 2.3 months in areas of physical, cognitive, language.

(continued)

TABLE 4-4. (continued)

Center-Based Programs

Name	Program Description	Staffing/Components	Study Design
Child Parent Centers (CPC)	Individualized, highly structured half-day program, parent participation emphasized, general readiness objectives.	Support services by nurse, social worker, speech therapist, and curriculum specialist 17:1 staff.	Comparison with control group of children living in comparable conditions.
Seton Hall	Parent-child visit school weekly 2-hr session for structured learning activities/parent discussion group, home activities to take away.	Parent educator.	Pre-post design.

Diagnostic/Prescriptive/Supplemental

Reading Improvement and Preschool	Students are selected to participate on basis of developmental delays, using Denver Developmental Screening Test. Program consists of balance of activities taken from guidebook. Children attend 3 hrs/day 4 day/wk for 160 days/yr. Training session with parents on fifth day.	One teacher, one aide and volunteers to make ratio 5:1.	Pre-post NE gain.
Communication Program	Supplemental 30-min period/week in which teaching focuses primarily on communication.	Speech/language clinician works with classroom teacher.	Pre-post design monthly gain.

General Academic Programs

COPE Cognitively Oriented Pre-Primary Experience	General and academic curriculum for preschool children, focuses on provisions of cognitively appropriate curriculum.		Pre-post design monthly gain.
Cognitively Oriented Preschool Curriculum	Open framework curriculum based on Piaget, Plan-do-review sequence.	Teaching team: two adults/classroom.	Pre-post design.

met for half days and had a low adult/child ratio. Home visits of 1½ hours were made every two weeks with an emphasis on training the parents as teachers in a method consistent with the model.

Students were randomly assigned to treatment groups. Eligible students lived within the Ypsilanti public school attendance area, were from low-SES homes, were three years old, and were below average in IQ. (The average IQ range was 62–90).

Four waves of children participated in the CD project from 1967–1970. These waves were called waves 5 through 8, following waves 0 through 4 in the original study.

Wave 5 ($n = 27$) contained children who had been in the Perry Preschool program the previous year either as controls or as program participants, as well as new enrollees. Control group children went to the language program, new enrollees to the unit-based, and Perry Preschool program continued in the cognitively oriented group. In the original report of the CD project, these twenty-seven children were not included. "Since children in Wave 5 experienced different educational programs as three year olds and were not enrolled for two consecutive years in one of the three CD project programs, they are not included in the longitudinal sample." However, we note that these students were included in later reports and analyses.

Siblings were assigned to the same programs. Some reassignment of children was necessary to maintain equivalence along IQ lines. Of the various background features, the only one that was significantly different across the three groups was "years of mother's education" (the language group had 9.7, the cognitively oriented curriculum group had 9.3, and the nursery school had 10.9).

Cognitive measures of the three different preschool groups were taken at ages three through eight and ten. The most striking pattern is the large jump in IQ for all three groups after entry into the program and a steady decline after the initial jump. However, many factors influence the validity of these results. First, the predictive validity of IQ scores before age five is minimal (McCall, Applebaum, and Hogarty, 1973). Second, students were selected on the basis of low IQ scores, ensuring that the means would tend to rise over time due to statistical regression. These difficulties and the fact that the means are based on a small number of cases suggest a great deal of caution in interpreting these results. We do note that, in most cases, the mean IQ for students in the language group exceeded that of the cognitively oriented group, by as much as nearly half of a standard deviation (at age five) and by a third of a standard deviation (ages seven and ten). These results are not statistically significant given the small sample size, but are suggestive that the language program did have more positive impact on cognitive measures than did the cognitive curriculum.

The recent major finding from this study, which has received a great deal of attention, is the claim that there is a connection between type of preschool experience and delinquency at age fifteen. Schweinhart and Weikart (1986) followed fifty-four of the original sixty-eight children in the study at age fifteen and obtained self-reports of delinquent acts for these groups. They found that the cognitively oriented and nursery groups reported engaging in half as many delinquent acts as the direct instruction group—5 for the high/scope, 7 for the nursery school, and 13 for the direct instruction group. From this finding, the authors (Schweinhart, Weikart, and Larner, 1986) have suggested that enrollment in academic preschool programs is linked to delinquency. In particular, the lack of autonomy and self-direction in direct instruction models is suggested to be related to the emergence of different rates of juvenile delinquency.

How credible are these claims of different effects by preschool program type? Bereiter (1986) and Gersten (1986) point out several difficulties with the study design and methodology.

First, there is the problem that sample attrition from the original sample to the fifteen-year-old sample resulted in an uneven distribution of females across the three groups. In the original sample ($n = 68$), the female proportion was 59, 52, and 59 for direct instruction, cognitively oriented curriculum, and nursery school; in the age-fifteen sample, the respective female proportion was 44, 61, and 55. These differences, although not statistically significant, are important because the differences between self-reported incidents of juvenile delinquency vary by sex, with males reporting far more and more serious delinquent behaviors than females (Gottfredson, 1987). As Bereiter (1986) points out, this difference in the sex composition of the sample could account for the difference between the treatments. Schweinhart and Weikart, however, replied that the "delinquency scale showed no gender bias, with study males reporting an average of 9 offenses and study females an average of 8." They go on to note that direct instruction males averaged twelve offenses whereas females averaged fourteen offenses. Unfortunately, separate results by sex are not presented to assess the role that differential attrition by sex may have contributed, although the authors report that a series of two-way analyses of variance that controlled for sex, race, and mother's education found the same pattern of results.

Second, some of the children in the nursery and direct instruction models had only one year of preschool experience, but all the cognitively oriented children were enrolled two years. Again, it is not clear the extent to which these duration differences is of consequence.

A third concern is that observational data collected at the time of the study (Seifert, 1969) do not suggest that the operating environments in the classrooms were in fact all that different in terms of the major intervening theoretical variable—opportunities for self-direction and child-initiated activities.

Finally, the conclusions of this study seem to be at odds with the conclusions of other longitudinal studies of the effects of different curricula.

Two other longitudinal studies that have made curricular comparisons similar to the ones made by the Curriculum Demonstration project (Karnes, Shwedel, and Williams, 1983; and Miller and Bizzel, 1983) do not find differences by curricula. The results of these two studies are summarized in Table 4–3. The Karnes studies contrasted five treatments: traditional nursery school, community/integrated, Montessori, GOAL (Karnes), and direct verbal (Bereiter-Engelman). The authors conclude that no one method demonstrated superiority over the others. They also conclude that the effects of preschool fade out after about the middle of the elementary years. It does appear that the initial scores for students in the GOAL and the direct verbal treatment were greater than the other treatments, although these results do not appear to be long lasting.

Miller and Bizell (1983) found an interesting pattern of treatment by sex interaction effects in their comparison of the short- and long-term effects of participation in four distinct preschool curricula. The four treatments were Bereiter-Engelman, Gray, Montessori, and a traditional nursery school. They found minimal evidence of effects until the results were analyzed separately by sex. The Montessori males had achievement and IQ scores in the range of 0.25 to 0.50 of a standard deviation higher than the other treatments. The Montessori males also had higher achievement at kindergarten and through the eighth grade.

Taken together, the three studies do not present a consistent picture of the greater effectiveness of a particular preschool model. On the basis of these data, it would be difficult to justify or condemn a particular approach. This suggests that many competing programs may be worthwhile and not injurious to children and that other considerations may therefore be more important in deciding how to organize and deliver prekindergarten instruction. This finding is also consistent with evidence for the kindergarten year (see Chapter 5 of this book).

PARTICIPATION IN PARTICULAR PROGRAMS

JDRP Studies

In addition to these three studies that contrast specific programs, evidence of program effectiveness is provided by evaluations submitted to the JDRP, from the Compensatory Education Source Book and from other published literature. We wrote to the developers of the programs listed by the JDRP and by the Compensatory Education Source Book for details of program design, operation, and evaluation. Many of the evaluations provide only a limited description of the evaluation or did not use a strong evaluation design. Virtually none of the studies in the two compilations used random assignment to treatment or control or used a matched control group. Therefore, many of these studies should be viewed as illustrative of possible effective strategies and be candidates for a more thorough evaluation.

The studies listed in Table 4–3 are illustrative of the programs found in these sourcebooks. They cover a wide range of approaches to early childhood education. There are parent involvement programs centered in the home (Levenstein and Compensatory Early Education Home Based Program) and in the school (Child Parent Centers and Seton Hall), diagnostic prescriptive programs (Reading Improvement and Preschool, Early Prevention of School Failure), supplemental programs (Communication Program), general curricular models (COPE and Cognitively Oriented Curriculum), and languge enrichment (Peabody Language Development Kit evaluations).

We list these studies to give a flavor of the variety of approaches and to make a plea for evaluations with adequate control groups so that effectiveness might be better judged. Of the studies listed here, typical of the ones listed by JDRP and the other sourcebook, effectiveness was judged primarily by comparing pre-post gains with expected pre-post score gains. But such an approach does not control for the operation of other factors that influence the growth as well. The two exceptions to this are the evaluations by Levenstein and the evaluations of the Peabody Language Development Kit. In Levenstein's case (1970), individuals were randomly assigned to a treatment and control group for comparisons on maternal interactive behavior (the major intervening variable) and to a matched control group on cognitive and school success measures. In the case of the PLDK, although the findings of various meta-analyses have been disputed, the original evaluation of the pilot materials (Dunn, Horton, and Smith, 1981) does provide evidence of its effectiveness.

SUMMARY AND CONCLUSION

This chapter has examined the short- and long-term effects of participation in preschool programs for disadvantaged students. Two types of studies were examined—those that contrasted the effect of preschool versus no preschool and those that examined the effect of participation in particular types of preschool programs.

These studies suggest that there are short-term and long-term benefits for children from participation in preschool programs. The benefits are most pronounced immediately after participation and exhibit the familiar wash-out effect as students progress through elementary school.

The examination of program effectiveness does not suggest the superiority of one particular approach. However, this conclusion does not imply that schools can therefore open up their doors to four-year-olds and automatically expect the same types of effects as demonstrated by the curriculum studies. The curriculum studies all used well-conceptualized, highly integrated, very structured, and coherent approaches to preschool education. They were quality versions of a particular philosophical approach. We actually know very little about the effectiveness of programs as they are currently being implemented, which often fall far short of the quality programs discussed here. We do not know, for example, how far programs can deviate from the conditions in these studies in terms of class size, teacher training, and physical environment before the effects disappear. It is important to learn if programs, as implemented, are indeed as effective as the research on which they are based indicates they might be.

Our knowledge base on which we can form decisions about early childhood programs is limited in four important regards. First, we are lacking empirical studies of the relative costs/merits of alternative ways of combining preschool and other services for young children. There are pressing child care needs for young children that are only partially addressed by the availability of preschool. We need studies of the costs and the effects of alternative arrangements to meet the child care, educational, and emotional needs of young children and their families. What workable combinations of day care, before and after school care, and preschool education might there be? Under what conditions is preschool a good investment? For everyone? In what type of program? Would home-based models, which are considerably cheaper to operate, have the same type of effectiveness?

Second, we lack sufficient empirical studies of the effects of major approaches to preschool curricula. The review conducted here of this issue was based on *three studies!* As important a topic as the curriculum of the preschool is certainly deserving of more intense research scrutiny.

A third limitation is the nature of the methodology used in many of the evaluations of program effectiveness. By and large these evaluations based their judgment of effectiveness on pre-post gain scores. Of course, this procedure does not control for other factors, beside the program, which may have contributed to the gain. More rigorous evaluations are needed to inform the question of the usefulness of most of the curriculum used today.

A fourth limitation in the available studies is that they often fail to consider how preschool is connected to the kindergarten and elementary grades. Given that resources for education are constrained, it is important to assess whether placing resources into preschool is more effective than adding these same resources into kindergarten or elementary grades. Would a student benefit more from attending a preschool program or from attending an all-day kindergarten and tutorial program in the first grade? Simply distributing a small amount of resources around to provide more services is probably not going to benefit very many children—at risk or otherwise. The critical question is how the demand for preschool can be balanced against the urgent need for so many other educational services for at-risk students.

To address this issue fairly, we need more than rhetoric or a handful of studies. We need to carry our experimental contrasts of interesting combinations of services to provide an empirical base for future decisions among educational alternatives for young children.

REFERENCES

Bereiter, C. (1986). Does direct instruction cause delinquency? *Early Childhood—Research Quarterly, 1 (3)*, 289–292.

Bereiter, C., and Engelman, S. (1966). *Teaching disadvantaged children in the preschool.* Englewood Cliffs, NJ: Prentice-Hall, 1966.

Berrueta-Clement, J. R.; Schweinhart, L. J.; Barnett, W. S.; Epstein, A. S.; and Weikart, D. P. (1984). Changed lives: The effects of the Perry Preschool program on youths through age 19. *Monographs of the High/Scope Educational Research Foundation, 8.*

Bloom, B. (1964). *Stability and change in human characteristics.* New York: Wiley.

Center for Education Statistics (1986). Pre-School Enrollment Trends and Implications Issue Paper.

Dunn, L. M.; Horton, K.; and Smith, J. (1981). *Peabody Language Development Kits—Revised Teacher's Guide Level P.* American Guidance Service, Circle Pines, MN 56014.

Elkind, D. (1986). Formal education and early childhood education: An essential difference. *Phi Delta Kappan,* April, 631–636.

Gersten, R. (1986). Response to Consequences of three preschool curriculum models through age 15. *Early Childhood Research Quarterly, 1(3)*, 303–312.

Gottfredson, G. (1987). American education—American delinquency, Technical Report No. 22. Baltimore, MD: Center for Research on Elementary and Middle Schools, The Johns Hopkins University.

Gray, S.; Ramsey, B.; and Klous, R. (1982). *From 3 to 20: The Early Training Project.* Baltimore: The University Park Press.

Grubb, N. (1987). *Young children face the states: Issues and options for early childhood programs.* New Brunswick, NJ: Center for Policy Research in Education, Eagleton Institute of Politics, Rutgers University.

Irvine, D. J. (1982). *Evaluation of the New York State Experimental Prekindergarten Program.* Paper presented at the annual meeting of American Educational Research Association, New York.

Jensen, A. R. (1969). How much can we boost IQ and scholastic achievement? *Harvard Educational Review,* 1–23.

Karnes, M. B.; Shwedel, A. M.; and Williams, M. B. (1983). A comparison of five approaches for educating young children from low-income homes. From *As the Twig is Bent . . . Lasting Effects of Preschool Programs.* Hillsdale, NJ: Lawrence Erlbaum Associates.

Kirk, S. (1958). *Early education of the mentally retarded.* Urbana, IL: University of Illinois Press.

Lazar, I., and Darlington, R. (1982). Lasting effects of early education. *Monographs of the Society for Research in Child Development, 47* (2–3, Serial No. 195).

Levenstein, P. (1970). Cognitive growth in preschoolers through verbal interaction with mothers. *American Journal of Orthopsychiatry, 40(3)*, 426–432.

McCall, R. B.; Applebaum, M. I.; and Hogarty, P. S. (1973). Developmental changes in mental performance. *Monographs of the Society for Research in Child Development, 38(3)*.

McKey, R.; Condelli, L.; Ganson, H.; Barrett, B.; McConkey, C.; and Plantz, M. (1985). *The impact of Head Start on children, families and communities*. DHHS Publication No. (OHDS) 85-31193. Washington, DC.

Miller, L. B., and Bizzel, R. P. (1983). The Louiseville experiment: A comparison of four programs. From *As the Twig is Bent . . . Lasting effects of preschool programs*. Hillsdale, NJ: Lawrence Erlbaum Associates.

Morado, C. (1985). *Pre-kindergarten programs for four year olds*. State Education Agency Initiatives. National Association for the Education of Young Children, Washington, DC.

Schweinhart, L. J. (1986). *Early childhood development programs in the eighties: The national picture*. High/Scope Educational Research Foundation, 600 N. River Street, Ypsilanti, MI 48197.

Schweinhart, L. J.; Weikart, D. P.; and Larner, M. B. (1986). Consequences of the preschool curriculum models through age 15. *Early Childhood Research Quarterly, 1*, 15–45.

Seifert, K. (1969). Comparison of verbal interaction in two preschool programs. *Young Children, 24*, 350–355.

Skeels, H. (1966). Some preliminary findings of three follow-up studies of the effects of adoption of children from institutions. *Children, 12*, 33–34.

Slavin, R. (1986). Best evidence synthesis: An alternative to meta-analytic and traditional reviews. *Educational Researcher, 15*, 9.

Westinghouse Learning Corporation (1969). *The impact of Head Start: An evaluation of the effects of Head Start on children's cognitive and affective development*. ERIC (ED 036 321).

5

EFFECTIVE KINDERGARTEN PROGRAMS AND PRACTICES FOR STUDENTS AT RISK

Nancy Karweit

Center for Research on Elementary and Middle Schools
The Johns Hopkins University

Kindergarten attendance is nearly universal in the United States today. About 93 percent of all five-year-olds are presently enrolled in school, primarily in kindergarten programs. However, the kindergarten experience itself is far from uniform. Kindergartens may be operated by public or private schools, may be academic or developmental in focus, may be in session for a full-day every day, a half-day every day, or, more rarely, for a full-day every other day. As the first introduction to the formal apparatus of schooling for many children, kindergarten is an important experience, but one that clearly takes on different meaning for different children.

It is especially important to understand how these different kindergarten experiences affect students at risk of future academic difficulty. Do these students enter first grade adequately prepared to succeed in elementary school or do they enter already behind and on their way to failure? What alternatives are there for students who are not successful in the kindergarten year? And finally, what arrangements of kindergarten seem most likely to increase the chance of academic success for these students?

The purpose of this chapter is to describe effective kindergarten programs and practices for students at risk of future academic failure. *Program* is defined as a set of procedures intended to be implemented as a total package (including curriculum materials, inservice training, and strong evidence of effectiveness) and capable of being replicated by others. In order to be included in this review, evaluations had to present convincing evidence of effectiveness based on rigorous methodology. Alterable features of kindergarten, such as class size, length of day, and staffing patterns, are also highlighted.

What students are at risk of later failure? Is there a single diagnostic procedure or a series of procedures to identify such students? The definition and assessment of *at risk* is both a political and methodological issue that cannot be addressed in detail here. Instead, we leave the definition of *at risk* purposely vague. Students may be at risk because they enter school with specific auditory, visual, or other developmental lags. Students may be at risk because the linguistic opportunities in their daily lives are very limited and they lack the necessary background and experience in receptive and expressive language. Students may be at risk because they lack the necessary social/emotional skills to function semi-independently in a group setting such as a kindergarten classroom. Lastly, students may be at risk because the school program is inappropriate for them either in its approach or in its difficulty level.

The kindergarten year is pivotal for students who may encounter later academic difficulties—it provides the basis for their success in the elementary curriculum that follows. Once viewed primarily as a year of transition and outside the realm of the elementary program, today the kindergarten year is primarily viewed as an academic/preparatory year (ERS, 1986) with clear connections to the elementary curriculum. Most of the programs in the public schools are focused either directly on academics (22 percent) or on academic preparation (63 percent).

These changes in the focus of kindergarten have gone along with changes in enrollment patterns and governance structure of kindergartens. Kindergarten enrollment has soared from about 5 percent of five-year-olds in 1901 to the present 93 percent. At the same time, more and more of the kindergarten programs (84 percent) are provided by public schools. There is also increasing activity by states to make the kindergarten year mandatory. Finally, kindergarten programs, which started as full-day programs but were reduced to half-day programs during the baby boom era, are moving to full-day programs again.

These changes in enrollment, provision, and length of the kindergarten day are occurring concurrently with great pressures to increase the academic standards of schools, and a renewed optimism about the efficacy of early programs for disadvantaged youths. Also, the movement against social promotions has had a general effect on escalation of the curriculum for those who are promoted (Shephard and Smith, 1985), and this has produced increasing demands for accountability for the performance of kindergarten students. In the past, when kindergartens were mainly in private schools, were attended by only some students, and were mainly focused on socialization and adjustment, questions of program effectiveness and accountability were of little interest.

Today, kindergarten teachers need to send the first grade teacher "prepared students." If children need to be ready to read in the first grade, then the kindergarten is held responsible for that preparation. If children need to be ready to add and subtract in first grade, then the kindergarten needs to teach them the necessary prerequisite number skills and concepts.

Some commentators are concerned that the push to early academics is harmful rather than beneficial to children (Elkind, 1986). The stress created by the demands of the formal learning situation, rather than benefitting students, may well place them at risk of future academic failure. Despite these concerns, the pressures for an academic kindergarten continue. In a recent survey, 61 percent of public school principals and about the same number of kindergarten teachers said the primary focus of their kindergarten program was "academic and social preparation" for first grade. About 22 percent of the principals said the primary focus was on academics. The kindergartens in urban areas were most likely to focus on academics.

PREPARATION FOR FIRST GRADE

If the major task of the kindergarten is to get students ready to read and compute, we need to know what readiness in these areas means. Many school districts are specific about the intended outcomes of the kindergarten year. For example, Figure 5-1 shows the twenty-three objectives given by one school district. The kindergarten report card for this district indicates that kindergarten students are formally evaluated on these stated objectives.

Another way to examine the academic requirements for kindergarten is to look at the typical readiness tests given children in the kindergarten year. For example, consider the Metropolitan Readiness Test, a widely used test whose validation centered on an analysis of the beginning reading process.

FIGURE 5-1.   Expected Student Outcomes: Kindergarten

1. Recognize and print name
2. Name colors and letters
3. Distinguish beginning sounds
4. Tell a picture story in sequence
5. Name six shapes
6. Name and count objects 0–10
7. Sequence numerals 0–10
8. Match numerals with objects 0–10
9. Color within boundaries
10. Know personal data
11. Fasten and tie shoes and coat
12. Use scissors with ease
13. Express ideas and take part in group discussion
14. Listen attentively
15. Recognize likenesses and differences
16. Practice self-control
17. Work and play cooperatively
18. Follow directions
19. Complete projects promptly
20. Obey safety rules
21. Practice good health habits
22. Work independently
23. Participate in organized activities

Level I (early kindergarten) and Level II (late kindergarten) assess the following areas:

Level I	*Level II*
Auditory Skill Area	Auditory Skill Area
1. Auditory Memory	1. Beginning Consonants
2. Rhyming	2. Sound-Letter Correspondence
Visual Skill Area	Visual Skill Area
3. Letter Recognition	3. Visual Matching
4. Visual Matching	4. Finding Patterns
Language Skill Area	Language Skill Area
5. School Language and Listening	5. School Language
6. Quantitative Language	6. Listening
	Quantitative Skill Area
	7. Quantitative Concepts
	8. Quantitative Operations

Some of the skills, such as auditory memory and rhyming, may not seem directly related to reading. But learning to read requires calling upon a complex combination of visual, auditory, and kinesthetic skills. Visual perception is required in order to differentiate different letters, such as *w* versus *m* and *b* versus *d*. Auditory discrimination of similar sounds, such as *t* versus *d,* is needed to link the visual to the language known orally. The sound-sight correspondence of letters (phonemes) must also be mastered. The child needs to understand the concept of a word and syllable and how blending of phonemes creates words. Short-term memory is important— children need to be able to recall accurately the syllables they have blended, such as *an-i-mal,* not *am-i-nal,* a common occurrence. Thus the kindergarten goal of preparing children for reading and arithmetic instruction in the first grade involves activities and tasks that may have little obvious resemblance to first-grade activities. Prerequisite skills are not necessarily the same skills in smaller dosages or of less difficulty. Mastering prequisite skills does not mean working on smaller ditto sheets. Instead, readiness for reading and math involves conquering many visual, auditory, and fine and gross motor skills that are necessary in the process of reading, but may not seem to be obviously connected to reading.

KINDERGARTEN SCHEDULE AND ACTIVITIES

In the recent ERS (1986) study of public kindergartens, about three-fifths of all teachers stated that they followed "definite time allotments and sequence for each activity.'' A fairly typical half-day kindergarten schedule might be:

8:30–8:35	Arrival/Get Together
8:35–9:25	Reading
9:25–9:45	Exploration (free time)
9:45–10:10	Math
10:10–10:25	Movement/Music
10:25–10:55	Social Living/Art
10:55–11:00	Dismissal

Reading or reading readiness instruction is typically based on a commercial reading readiness series (75 percent of all teachers in the ERS survey said they used the readiness series), and the teacher typically provides formal structured instruction during reading and math periods.

Objectives for the kindergarten year may be explicitly stated. For instance, detailed objectives for minimum, average, and above-average students may be formulated for comprehension skills (e.g., noting details, main idea, sequence, drawing conclusions), and vocabulary (e.g., phonetic analyses, short vowel, word meaning, final consonant, and consonant blends). As an example, the kindergarten objectives for the Baltimore City Public Schools covering phonetic analyses of initial consonant sounds states that ''given a picture of an object or an action and several words, one with the same beginning sound as the pictured object, the student will select the word that begins the same as the pictured object or action.''

WHEN STUDENTS ARE UNSUCCESSFUL

One of the major problems facing the transition from kindergarten to first grade is how to assess readiness for first grade and what to do with and for students who are deemed not ready to go on to first grade. There are varied practices for assessing student readiness for first grade work. These include teacher recommendation and judgment, results of standardized screening and assessment devices, and evaluations by specialized personnel. For example, the state of Georgia just passed legislation specifying peformance on the CAT as a basis of promotion from kindergarten (*Education Week,* February, 1988). Bases for nonpromotion include student immaturity, low attention span, small size for kindergarten, inability to sit still, and retarded large/fine motor or language development. Concerning who is most likely to experience difficulty in kindergarten, we know that males far outnumber females, and that low-SES and minority students also outnumber their advantaged peers. The specific reasons for these referrals are quite different, however. For example, the males may be retained more often because of immaturity, whereas low-SES or disadvantaged students are more often retained because of language or other developmental lags.

Actions taken as a result of the failure to thrive in kindergarten generally fall into three categories: repetition of the kindergarten program, additional time within the kindergarten year, and alternative programs. By far, the most common practice is repetition of the kindergarten year, either in the guise of pre-first, transition, or junior first-grade classes. This approach is based on the belief that children who fail to prosper in the kindergarten year are simply "young" for their age, and by letting them mature, they will be able to perform adequately and even blossom. However, the evidence on student grade repetition (discussed later) offers no support for this view.

A second approach has been to provide more time within the same year for kindergarten students, usually by extending the kindergarten day. There are several variations on this approach. One is to screen children and give only some students additional remedial or enrichment instruction. Another way is to add time for an entire school system that has a high percentage of at-risk students. Finally, many school systems that do not have a high percentage of at-risk students are extending the school day for kindergarten students anyway. We discuss the effectiveness of the increased time approach in the next section (see Karweit, 1987).

The third approach involves screening and assessment of children for learning problems prior to entry to kindergarten and the delivery of a specialized curriculum to suit their needs. This approach differs from the other two in its assumptions about learners and the role of the school and the personnel needed. It assumes that children learn in different ways and through different modalities and styles and that intervention strategies are needed to address these distinct areas of strength and weakness. This is not just individualizing instruction according to the level of difficulty of the material or rate of learning, but according to the learning avenues best suited for a particular child (e.g., visual, auditory, kinesthetic).

We will now examine the effects of these approaches.

PROMOTIONAL PRACTICES

One of the outgrowths of the 1983 reform movement has been a renewed focus on standards and a renewed interest in nonpromotion as a way to achieve these standards. However, nonpromotion has not been supported as an effective policy (Holmes and Matthews, 1984; Jackson, 1975; Niklason, 1984; Shephard and Smith, 1985). Gredler (1984), after examining the effects of transition rooms for students deemed unready for first grade, concludes:

> Analysis of the research studies of transition rooms raises questions about the degree of educational "payoff" obtained with such programs. Research indicates that transition room children either do not perform as well or at most are equal in achievement levels to transition room eligible children placed in regular classrooms" (p. 469).

Research findings notwithstanding, schools continue to retain students as a remediation strategy, especially at the early grades. Part of the reason for continuation of the practice may be that schools cannot locate other alternatives. Also, teachers may view the practice as effective—retained students do make some gain during the retained year, and teachers are unable to compare this gain during the retained year to gains the students would have made had they been promoted.

Shephard and Smith (1985) took advantage of the existing variation in school kindergarten retention rates to address this issue. They noted that many previous studies were flawed methodologically because the comparisons were not of equivalent students under different policies, so they sampled same-sex students with similar birthdates, family backgrounds, and entering test score data from schools with contrasting retention rates. They compared retained students with nonretained students. The results were striking. Students who had spent an additional year in kindergarten were basically identical to those control students who had been promoted. The only notable difference was that the repeaters scored one month higher (1.9 versus 1.8) on the CTBS reading comprehension test taken at the end of the first grade. One month gain for one year does not seem like a very economical practice.*

EXTENDING THE KINDERGARTEN DAY

Karweit (1987) examines the effects of full-day versus half-day kindergarten in detail. Table 5–1 summarizes the individual studies reviewed in that paper. Figure 5–2 provides an indication of the direction of effects by the adequacy of the study design and the population served.

Figure 5–2 suggests where the effects of all-day kindergarten programs are located. Disadvantaged students who receive additional instruction are the primary source of the positive effects. Nine studies focused on the effect of full-day kindergarten for underachieving and disadvantaged students. Of the two strongest studies (using random assignment), one showed significant effects for the full-day kindergarten treatment. The other seven studies fell

---

* One may take issue with the equivalence of these groups. Many referrals to repeat kindergarten are based on behavioral indicators that were not equated. Also children grow at very different rates during the kindergarten year. The entering test score may not be a very good proxy for where the students were at the end of the year when the assessment for promotion was made. Finally, there may be school level differences that drive the differences in retention rates which may also affect performance of the students. Policies such as providing students special help in the summer or after-school tutors, rather than retaining them, might have given the nonretainees additional resources as well.

TABLE 5-1.   Summary of Effects of Full-Day versus Half-Day Kindergarten Programs

			Random Assignment/Matched Control Group Studies		
Study	_Sample_	_Treatment_	_Effects_	_Effect Size_	_Notes_
Johnson (1974) Pre-post Random assignment Replicated Longitudinal effects	Princess Anne, MD. 20 students matched on age, race, SES, sex, and ability assigned to TRT (full-day) or CTL (half-day). 3 experiments: 1970, 1971, & 1972	EXP=full-day (5'15") CTL=half-day (2'30") Same curriculum. Enrichment given full-day. Measures: Walker Readiness Stanford Achievement Reading group grade 1	Walker Cohort 1 2 3 Stanford Cohort 1 2 3 Reading Grp Cohort 1 2 3	.66p < .05 .58 ns .08 ns .13 ns .28 ns .59 ns .00 ns .06 ns .57 ns	
Winter and Klein (1970) Screened; then random assignment to treatment/ control	Two studies: 1) Disadvantaged. Treatment and control selected from lowest 10% of class. TRT: _n_=6 CTL: _n_=7	CTL=attendance am/pm TRT=regular+90 minutes academic pgm No pretest difference.	Metropolitan at end of K Stanford at end of K Stanford at end of 1st	+3.01 p<.005 .62 ns .62 ns	

Study	Sample	Treatment	Measure	Effect size	Comments
2) Advantaged. Selected trt & control from those most able to benefit. TRT: $n=26$ CTL: $n=29$		CTL=attendance regular TRT=regular+90 minutes academic pgm Significant pretest differences favoring TRT	Pretest Peabody Picture Metropolitan at end of K (adj post) Stanford at end of K (adj post) Stanford at end of 1st (adj post)	1.28 p<.05 – ns – ns 1.03 p<.05	
Oliver (1980) Pre-post ANCOVA No pretest differences Comparable program	Cambridge, MA. 61 students in 4 classes half-day. 98 students in 6 classes full-day.	EXP=full-day with structured curric. 117 minutes/day CTL=half-day with same structured curriculum 83.8 minutes/day	Clymer-Barrett Prereading Inventory Murphy-Durrell Prereading	2.84 p<.05 1.16 p<.05	Effect size inflated by use of class means

Nonmatched Groups/Pre-Post Studies

Study	Sample	Treatment	Measure	Effect size	Comments
Carapella and Loveridge (1978) ANCOVA Both groups eligible: control group of nonparticipants who were eligible	St. Louis public schools. 507 students who scored below 50th percentile on CPI who were eligible for attendance at extended day kindergarten. 273 enrolled 234 control	Supplementary instruction for kindergarten pupils using small-group and individual instruction in extended day.	Comprehensive Test of Basic Skills Mathematics Reading	.43 p<.001 .32 p<.001	

(continued)

TABLE 5–1. (continued)

Nonmatched Groups/Pre-Post Studies

Study	Sample	Treatment	Effects	Effect Size	Notes
Nieman & Gastright (1981) Existing sample Longitudinal Post only, with evidence of initial equivalence	551 kindergarten students in 16 Cincinnati schools receiving Title I. Full-day students had preschool experience, half-day did not.	EXP=full-day K (n=410) CTL=half-day K (n=141) EXP also had preschool	Pretest (Sept. Kinder "Goal card") Boehm (Dec. Kinder) Metropolitan (April Kinder) Metropolitan (4th grade—70% sample) Metropolitan (8th grade—50% sample) Grade retention Special education	NS .35 p<.001 .35 p<.001 .25 p<.01 .25 p<.01 .13 p<.01 .25 p<.001	
Hatcher (1980) ANCOVA Ad hoc sample	4 school districts in Texas, 2 having half-day K and 2 having full-day K. 60 students selected at random.	Half-day vs. full-day. No information on curriculum or on differences in treatments.	Metropolitan Readiness California Test of Personality Valett Developmental Survey Basic	ns ns ns	

Adcock (1980)	189 urban and rural kindergarten children in 5 Maryland local ed. agencies. Comparison of existing full-day and half-day Ks.	EXP=full-day(n=131) CTL=half-day(n=58) Measures: Metropolitan (pre and post)	Results ANCOVA Post = pre + K type .56 $p<.001$ Estimated setting t=3.09, minimum value for $p<.001$
Jarvis and Molnar (1986)	New York City. 1807 full-day K 223 half-day K Citywide conversion to full-day K. Half-day were ones unable to convert.	Contrasts: Half-day/ language Full-day/ language Measures: Brigance Pre/Post LAB Pre/Post	Results ANCOVA Brigance English speakers .09 ns Non-English speakers .45 $p<.05$ LAB .38 $p<.05$
Evans and Marken (1984)	Metropolitan school district in Wash. state. Mostly white, middle-class. 174 1st, 2nd, 3rd in 2 diff. elem. schools who had different kindergarten pgms.	Contrasts: Full-day(n=87) Half-day(n=87) Measures: Ability test (K) CAT (1,2, or 3) Early Chd School Sentiment Teacher ratings Reading attitude	Results ANCOVA CAT – ns Reading attitudes + Referral special education –.26 $p<.05$

(continued)

TABLE 5-1. (continued)

Nonmatched Groups/Pre-Post Studies

Study	Sample	Treatment	Effects	Effect Size	Notes
Derosia (1980)	Jefferson City, CO. 384 students in kindergarten. 1st and 2nd grades having full or half-day kindergarten.	Full-day ($n=67$) Half-day ($n=93$)	Boehm (adjusted for pretest, SES, age) CTBS (Grade 1) CTBS (Grade 2)	.36 $p<.05$ ns ns	
Warjanka (1982)	30 students who scored < 65 on Metropolitan Readiness Test and 40 students who were in same K classes with scores >65.	Six-month treatment, regular kindergarten + extended day Curriculum based on participant's ability	At pretest, FDK group 1 standard deviation lower than other group (37.8 vs. 20.5) on Metropolitan Readiness Test After 6 months of treatment, EKD group and regular group were same (54.3)	(+)	

Slaughter (1983)	96 students who were indentified as at risk and 191 other K students	Additional instruction (119 to 242 hours). Smaller classes (15 : 1). Curricular change—whole language approach	Pre-post design. At pretest, FDK group signif-cantly lower than reg. group on CAT listening skills subtest in NCEs (24 vs. 45). At posttest, FDK made significant gains; reg. group de-clined (36 NCE to 42 NCE).	(+)
Lysiak and Evans (1976) Convenience sample Replicated two years	Fort Worth, TX. 916 students in 111 K classes	Comparison of 6 curricular models, for students of differing SES, ethnicity, and for full- & 1/2-day	Full-day > half-day for low SES and for high SES.	(+)
Alper and Wright (1979)	Phoenix, AZ. 98 students in kindergartens in extended day and regular	Full-day had longer day (5 vs. 2 1/2) and smaller classes (12–25). Teacher visits to homes. Three-month study.	Metropol. Readi-ness Test Extended day > regular No report of significance level	(+) ? No significance levels computed

(continued)

TABLE 5-1. (continued)

Nonmatched Groups/Pre-Post Studies

Study	Sample	Treatment	Effects	Effect Size	Notes
Humphrey (1983)	Evansville-Vanderburg School District	Contrasts: 2 cohorts 78–79 full = 81 half=108 79–80 full=115 half=114	Reading Gates MacGintie CTBS Grade Retention	78–79 (+) 79–80 (+) 78–79 (+) 78–79 (+) 19% Half (+) 9 Full	Significance not reported
McClinton and Topping (1984) Post only No evidence of initial equivalence	80 1st graders in 10 public schs randomly selected. EXP= enrolled EKD CTL= enrolled reg	EXP=4'15" CTL=2'40" Major difference was amount of time, not curriculum.	CAT at end of K CAT at end of 1st Teacher ratings academic ability EXP>CTL $F(1.9) = 5.15$ $p<.05$	$-$ ns $-$ ns 1.42 $p<.05$	
Harman (1982) Convenience sample	55 half-day, 66 full-day in K classes in same school and matched on ethnicity, mobility, & SES	Posttest-only design. Comparison of CAT reading and math at end of year.	CAT: reading math	+.27 ns .40 $p<.05$	

	Contrasts:	Percent scoring in first quartile ITBS
Chicago's Govt Funded Kindergarten Programs	Funding source:	HDK, chpt 1, size 16 = 26%
	Chapter 1	ADK, chpt 2, size 23 = 39%
110 schools. Comparison of existing programs	Chapter 2	ADK size 26 = 46%
	OEEO	OEEO size 28 = 51%
Convenience sample	Board Funded	HDK, board, size 28 = 73%
	Format:	
	all-day	
	half-day	
	No pretests	

FIGURE 5–2.   Summary of Effects for Full-day Kindergarten by Quality of Study, Immediacy of Effect, and Population Studied

	Regular or Advantaged Students		Disadvantaged Students	
	Kindergarten	Long term	Kindergarten	Long term
Random Assign or Matched	Johnson + Oliver + Winter 0	Johnson 0 Winter 0	Johnson 0 Winter +	Johnson 0 Winter 0
Nonmatched	Hatcher 0 Adcock + Jarvis 0 Derosia +	Evans 0 Derosia 0	Carapella + Niemann + Jarvis + Warjanka + Slaughter + Lysiak + Entwisle +	Niemann +

into the less methodologically rigorous category, and all of these found positive effects for all-day kindergarten.

There are no long-term effects demonstrated for attendance at full-day kindergarten. Only one study (Nieman and Gastright, 1981) found significant long-term effects, but limitations of this study limit the credibility of the results. First, the study compared students who had preschool and all-day kindergarten to those in half-day programs, a somewhat different comparison than in the other studies. Second, their test for equivalence of the two groups at entry into kindergarten was of unknown validity and reliability. Finally, the long-term results in grades 4 and 8 included only 70 and 50 percent of their initial samples. Sample attrition may have been differentially important.

Other studies focusing on the effects of compensatory efforts (Lazar, Hubbell, Murray, Rosche, and Royce, 1977; McKey, Condelli, Ganson, Barrett, McConkey, and Plantz, 1985) have found that the results of the extended day/year are primarily immediate and not long-term, and our findings support this conclusion concerning the effects of full-day kindergarten.

The finding that full-day kindergarten programs seem most effective on short-term measures for disadvantaged populations raises many new questions. To what extent is this finding due to differences in the sheer amount of time in school or due to differences in program emphasis and focus? It seems possible that a combination of more time and greater emphasis on academic preparation is important. Studies linking the allocation of time to differences in achievement results typically find only modest results (Karweit, 1983). One primary reason is that the same allocated time can have quite varied actual usages in different classrooms, depending on the grouping patterns, the curriculum, the teacher, and the students.

An observational study of kindergarten instruction in three school districts by Meyer (1985) illustrates this point. Contrasting the use of time in districts that have half-day and full-day programs, Meyer showed that the actual amount of time on academic matters was not all that different in the full- and half-day programs observed. The total minutes allocated to instruction in the half-day classes (150-minute sessions) was 78 minutes, whereas in the full-day classes (330 minutes) the total instructional time allocated was 103 minutes. In general, the students in the full-day programs had more total minutes allocated to instruction, but some teachers in the half-day schedule actually exceeded the allocated time of some teachers in the full-day schedule. Again, individual teacher practices and curricula seemed to be important elements in determining how the school day was spent.

This suggests the importance of understanding more than the effects of the length of the kindergarten day. What instructional programs are effective for kindergarten students? What difficulties are there in operating these programs in a full-day or half-day setting? Is it possible to have effective half-day programs and thus save the considerable expense in expanding the kindergarten? And if districts decide to extend their kindergarten day, what programs have been demonstrated to be effective? Do they require a full day for successful implementation?

The major conclusion from examining the effects of full-day kindergarten is that attendance at full-day programs appears to be beneficial for disadvantaged students. The source of this effect—whether it is simply more time in school or a change in the focus of the kindergarten program that accompanied a full day—is not clear. In the next section, we focus on the nature of the programs that seem to be effective for disadvantaged kindergarten students.

EFFECTS OF PROGRAMS OF INSTRUCTION

There are two major sources for the programs reviewed here: programs approved by the U.S. Department of Education's Joint Dissemination Review Panel (JDRP), and programs listed in the Office of Educational Research and Improvement's Effective Compensatory Education Sourcebook (Griswold, Cotton, and Hansen, 1986). The studies/programs are classified and presented (see Table 5–2) by the adequacy of the research design. Programs that used random assignment to treatment and control groups were weighted most heavily, followed by studies that used a matched/experimental control group design. Cohort, or before- and after-implementation designs, are discussed next. Given the least weight are studies that base their evidence of effectiveness on comparisons of expected fall-to-spring growth, or on posttest-only effects.

Assessments of effective early childhood programs not only suffer from all the methodological difficulties discussed for elementary studies (see Madden and Slavin, 1987), but include a few of their own. One, it is much less clear what the goals of kindergarten programs may be, and there are fewer reliable measures of the goals. Measures are often homegrown tests of unknown reliability. When tests of known reliability are used, there is little consensus about which to use. For example, the twenty JDRP-approved programs for kindergarten used twelve different standardized tests.

Furthermore, the test selected may not match the objectives of the program. For example, in a school with an outstanding prekindergarten program, the principal was asked her primary goal for the prekindergarten students. She was very quick to respond, "To make them articulate." Yet no test or measure of the children's expressive language was used in evaluating the program's effectiveness. Instead, the program effects were measured using standard paper and pencil instruments.

Also, the evaluations can render false positive effects if they measure skills that improve test-taking performance on narrow educational goals, but not skills that lay the foundation for future learning. For example, children can be taught to recognize numbers and count to fifty without having the necessary skills to master addition. Or children can learn at an early age to recognize letters, but still not possess the necessary language skills to learn how to read. An evaluation that shows mastery of discrete components related to reading and the separate skills related to math comprehension does not show competency in reading and math. There needs to be integration of the skills and the necessary linguistic and numeric background for the skills to be applied.

Finally, kindergarten programs may have very different goals, so that comparison of treatment and control groups can be misleading. Comparing an academic kindergarten program to a traditional control group that is basically nonacademic in orientation, one should not be surprised to find large effects on readiness activities for the academic program, since the traditional program did not intend to teach these objectives. This problem of program goal is particularly at issue for kindergarten programs because the purpose of kindergarten has been changing over time and evaluations indicate very little about the curriculum for the control group.

Table 5–2 provides a synopsis of the kindergarten programs for which we have evaluation data. As noted, these programs are presented by the adequacy of the research design in the following order:

1. Random assignment
2. Matched control group
3. Cohort comparison
4. Spring-to-spring growth (no control)
5. Fall-to-spring growth (no control)

We consider studies that used random assignment, matched control groups, or cohort comparison groups to be methodologically adequate studies. Effect sizes are presented for these more adequate studies. The less rigorous methodological studies/programs are presented along with the general direction of effect.

Alphaphonics/Astra's Magic Math

Alphaphonics/Astra's Magic Math are two widely used and successful beginning readiness programs. Combining systematic, sequenced lessons into a game-like format, both programs are motivating and fun yet still provide abundant practice and repetition of presentation. Friendly visitors from outer space (Astro for reading; Astra for math) leave a bag of lesson materials daily for the teacher and children. The suspense and anticipation derived from the magic bag appear to sustain student interest and motivation.

In the Alphaphonics program, the letters of the alphabet are introduced sequentially one at a time, in a twenty-six-week sequence. Astro's bag contains items that start with the letter the class is studying, such as apple, (plastic) alligator, alarm clock, and an abacus for the letter *A*. Badges, stickers, and letters to parents are also in the bag.

There are six lessons for each letter of the alphabet. The student learns to name a letter, then to write it, and then to locate the upper- and lower-case example of the letter. Astro manages to create and keep a fantasy and fun-like atmosphere for the children while getting them to practice and review. Astro also brings ditto sheets or other tools for independent practice.

Astra's Magic Math uses a similar outer space theme for the introduction of twenty-two math concepts in a sequenced manner. The units are introduced to the whole class. The twenty-two units cover shapes, matching, size comparison, counting and recognition of the numbers 0 to 30, number sequences, addition and subtraction of the numerals 0 to 5, and time in hours.

The Alphaphonics program takes about an hour each day. A typical schedule would be

1. Sing alphabet song
2. Sing poem song (for particular letter group)
3. Class discussion
4. Individual work
5. Sing poem song

The evaluation of the program used a posttest-only analysis of variance. The treatment classrooms were compared with twelve control schools

TABLE 5–2.   Effective Kindergarten Programs

	Programs Evaluated with Random Assignment or Matched Control Group Design				
JDRP	*Name*	*Developer*	*Grade*	*Content*	*Instructional Strategy*
74-15	Alphaphonics	So. San Francisco U.S.C.	K	Reading Readiness	Readiness phonics program focusing on sequential learning, immediate correction, feedback, & game-like presentation for about 1 hr/day.
83-54	Astra Math	So. San Francisco U.S.C.	K	Math Readiness	Comprehensive, structured, & sequenced curriculum with 22 self-contained units. Uses multisensory approach & behavior modification & high-interest materials.
77-116	MECCA	Trumbull Public Schools (CT)	K		Development & implementation of early identification procedures & prescriptive educational programs for children entering K with specific potential handicaps.

Evaluation Design	Measures	Effects	Costs & Training	Adoptions & Activity
Post ANOVA on treatment sch. & remaining 12 in district. Stated that IQ & background of T & C equivalent.	Metropolitan Ach. readiness ach. G1 ach. G2 ach. G3	.89 1.14 .90 1.07	$135 for materials classroom 1-day trng; pay trnr honorarium & travel	6000 cities 50 states
All students there for K–3.				
Pre-post random assignment to treatment—control 3 classes each.	CTBS fall-sprg	.45 (adj) .30 (not adj)	$112 for materials classroom 1-day trng	4000 cities 30 states
Pre-post random assignment to trtmt & control.	JANSKY Metropol. Monroe	.67 .57 .88 .96	No data	No data

(continued)

TABLE 5–2.   (*continued*)

Programs Evaluated with Random Assignment or
Matched Control Group Design

JDRP	Name	Developer	Grade	Content	Instructional Strategy
78-189	TALK	Rockford, IL, school system	K–3	Lang.	Lang. specialist in class instruction in listening skills 4 wk 1/2 hour for 6 mos then classroom tchr continues lessons.
79-7	MARC	Wakulla City, Crawford-ville, FL	K–1	Rdg.	Continuous progress using multisensory activities & systematic instruction. Diagnostic & recordkeeping instrument, skill sheets provided.
75-37R	INSTRUCT	Lincoln Public Schools	K–3	Rdg.	Individual placement & progress through multiunit model
79-38	PLAY	Bristol, VA	K–1 and 3/4 years	Motor/ Cogni-tive	Diagnostic/ prescriptive direct instruction in perceptual/ motor monthly home reinforcement & activities.

Evaluation Design	Measures	Effects		Costs & Training	Adoptions & Activity
Pre-post ANCOVA on treatment & matched local control. Original study: (75–76) Replication: (76–77)	PPVT 75; 76 WISC 75 76 PPVT 75 76 (K) 75 76	.25 .42 .38 .46 .26 (K) .74 .38 (K) .55		$50 manual tchr & sub time for tchr to attend 1/2-day trng	572 dists. 33 states 6 int'l Currently active
Post ANOVA on treatment & matched local control at end of K & end of 1st. Pre ANOVA to ensure equivalence.	SESAT (II) letters word rdg sent rdg BOEHM KUHLMAN ANDER-SON SESAT (I)	#1 1.12 .88 .25 ns ns ns	#2 .55 na na	3/5 day trng or self-trng manual	No exact data (FL&SC) Not active at present
ANCOVA on trmt & comparable schs. chosen on similar SES, school org & #s compensatory students.	Metropolitan word know rdg. spelling	.35** .25*[1] ns		5 days trng materials $100/class	No data
ANOVA on treatment and control. Control were eligibles (score below cut off) not enrolled because positions filled.	BOEHM 75-76 76-77 77-78	1.77 .23 1.33		na	Not active

(continued)

TABLE 5–2.   (continued)

Programs Evaluated by Comparison with
Expected Growth, National Norms, or Fall-to-Spring Growth

JDRP	Name	Developer	Grade	Content	Instructional Strategy
81-44	CLIMB	Middlesex, NJ	K–12	Rdg. Math	Diagnostic/ prescription approach in acquisition of rdg & math skills providing a mngmt design for coordinating & integrating classroom & support personnel.
76-87	STAMM	Lakewood, CO	K–8	Math	Continuous progress math with mngmt system.
78-184	Education assessmt. & Inst. for the Educationally Deprived	Kenosha, WI	K–10	Lang.	Extended-day K 2–3 hrs in afternoon, additional time for remedial instruction.
78-198	Every Student Every Day	St. Mary Parish Sch. Bd.	K–4 K–6	Math Rdg.	Daily diagnosis, evaluation & prescription, computer scoring for coordination. Pullot design using 40 mins each day.

Evaluation Design	Measures	Effects	Costs & Training	Adoptions & Activity
Spring-to-spring achievement compared to nat'l norms & compensatory growth.	CTBS	+		781 (1982–6) from sponsor
Pre-post implementation scores for district & adoption site.	CAI	+	# stdts × 7, avg startup, # stdts × c if wkbks used as consumables	41 states; 1500 adoptions
Pre-post design. Fall-to-spring.	PPVT	+		
Pre-post design changing %tile fall-to-spring 7 52 (76) 7 59 (77) 7 32 (82) 2 40 (83)	TOBE (presch. & K)	+		

(continued)

TABLE 5–2.   (continued)

	Programs Evaluated by Comparison with Expected Growth, National Norms, or Fall-to-Spring Growth				
JDRP	*Name*	*Developer*	*Grade*	*Content*	*Instructional Strategy*
74-102	Baptist Hill K	Baptist Hill K, Greenville, AL	K	Rdg. Math	Full-day K, lrng ctrs, diagnoses individual lrng needs on continuous basis with appropriate learning activities.
74-46R	Early Prevention of School Failure	Peotone District Illinois	4, 5, 6 year olds		Early identification of developmental needs & lrng styles of 4, 5, & 6 yr olds. Screening, planning, & pullout 20–30 min instruction in different modalities in lrng ctrs.

Evaluation Design	Measures	Effects	Costs & Training	Adoptions & Activity
Pre-post design.	TOBE	+		No data
Fall-to-spring.				
3rd 6th stanine stanine				
Improvement per month on different scales—no comparison data either w/ a control grp or preimplementation	getting data	+	2-day trng $127/clsrm teacher materials	6000 (from sponsor)

(continued)

TABLE 5–2.   (continued)

		Programs Evaluated by Comparison with Expected Growth, National Norms, or Fall-to-Spring Growth			
JDRP	*Name*	*Developer*	*Grade*	*Content*	*Instructional Strategy*
84-1	First Level Math	PRIMAK Educational Fndt.	K or 1	Math	Sequential curriculum & mngmt system which is diagnostic/ prescriptive. Instructional grps formed on basis of pretests. Instruction in 3–4 grps for about 20–30 mins.
74-71	New Adventure in Learning	Moore Elem. Sch., Tallahassee, FL	K		Individually determined instruction with positive behavior mngmt.
74-75	Strategies in Early Childhood Education	Waupun, WI	preK and K		Developmental & screening model. Self-instructional, individually paced, learning ctrs, develop-mentally sequenced materials.

Evaluation Design	Measures	Effects	Costs & Training	Adoptions & Activity
Pre-post design	CIRCUS	+	$35/kit	
Fall-to-spring.		not possible to compute		
Pre-post nat'l norm comparison using expected growth.	PPVT—mean imprvmt 1.67/math Gilmore oral rdg test—10% on grade level at pre, 57% at post		No curr. data	No curr. data
Ad hoc comparison of trtmt children with another grp.			10 sessions inservice	
No evidence of prior comparability				

(continued)

TABLE 5–2.   (continued)

		Programs Evaluated by Comparison with Expected Growth, National Norms, or Fall-to-Spring Growth			
JDRP	*Name*	*Location*	*Serves*	*Area*	*Description*
74-93	Right to Read	Glassboro, NJ	K–3	Reading	Diagnostic, prescriptive, indiv. progress model. ungraded.
	Project Catch Up	Newport Mesa, CA	K–6	Reading Math	Remedial instruction in rdg & math to underachieving students using diagnoses, prescription
					Positive contacts with family.
	Amphitheater School District KIP	Tucson, AZ	K		Parent involvement once a wk training of parents in game or activity that gives practice in basic skills with followup practice with students who need practice in that skill & monitoring of student progress.
	VIP	Spokane, WA	K	Develop Skills	Develop friendly feeling parents & school, provide training for parents in how to help children at home, to send home games which reinforce skills learned at school.

Evaluation	Test	Effects	Cost	Adoption
No control 325 children pre-post	CRI Classrm Rdg. Inv.	avg gain 1.52 yrs	20 hrs inser- vice + 1 hr/ wk	No data
Mean gain by grade on CTBS from fall to spring	CTBS Fall- spring			
No data on K				
Comparison to comparable school on percent scoring above 50 %tile 1 year after	CAT	66% vs. 38%	No data	No data
Santa Clara Inv. gain 2.32 mos. in dev. age/month	Santa Clara Inv.			
No control grp	Note problem with fall-spg			

[1] Effect sizes were computed by determining the t value to generate p<.01 and .05 respectively.

in the same district, which did not differ with respect to entering IQ or SES. The achievements of treatment classes and control classes were measured at the end of kindergarten, first, second, and third grade using the Metropolitan Achievement Test. The effect sizes were 0.89, 1.14, 0.90 and 1.1 respectively for these grades. Data for the equivalence of control/experimental classes and method of assignment to treatment were not detailed.

The evaluation of Astra's Magic Math used random assignment to treatment and control classes. The effectiveness of the program was gauged by performance on the CTBS. The effect size computed here was 0.45 at the end of kindergarten.

The evaluations do not indicate very much about the goals and practices of the comparison group. It is likely that the comparison classrooms may have been traditional kindergarten programs that include readiness activities, but not in a systematic fashion that assures coverage, practice of skills, and teacher feedback.

There is no evidence supplied that the program is equally effective for all students or, on the other hand, that it is not effective for students at risk of failure. The general orientation of the program is that of a whole class, direct instruction model with individual assistance and remediation provided as can be accommodated. That is, remediation efforts are not structured in any specific way in these programs.

MECCA

MECCA (Make Every Child Capable of Achieving) is a diagnostic/prescriptive program that provides daily observation, assessment, and planning for specialized teaching depending on children's needs. Additional instruction within the classroom is provided based on students' learning profiles. The additional activities are based on a task analysis of the learning activity with which the student is having difficulty. Task analysis is the process of breaking down a learning activity into the steps necessary for its successful completion, such as breaking down the activity into its auditory, visual, and gross and fine motor components. Specialized instruction, prescribed by a team composed of classroom aide, learning disabilities specialist, and classroom teacher, is provided either individually or in small groups in the classroom.

The target group of children is identified by a preschool screening with the school psychologist and a speech and language clinician. High-risk children are those who do not attain age appropriate scores on three/four areas on the DIAL taken in the spring. In September, further assessment is done on marginal and high-risk students and an individual programming survey is administered to identify particular strengths and weaknesses. From this profile, an educational plan is devised.

For example, a child who has a very limited use of expressive language—such as single-word responses to questions or no usage of pronouns or adverbs—might be placed in a speech and language program. In the beginning of the program, the child would be rewarded continuously with praise or with tokens. The basic structure of each lesson is:

1. *Auditory Reception:* The instructor gives verbal directions to which the student responds with a gross motor or fine motor action ("Pick up the tomato").
2. *Verbalization:* The child uses the language she or he has responded to in step 1 ("Here is the tomato").
3. Reading readiness activities are combined with a lesson using the words and sounds from the first two parts.

The lessons are structured to give the child practice in increasingly more difficult auditory reception, memory, and other readiness skills.

Eligible students were randomly assigned to the MECCA treatment or a control group. The Jansky Predictive Screening Index, an individually administered twenty-minute test, was used as the pretest and one of the posttest measures. There are five predicting tests: letter naming, picture naming, Gates word matching, Bender motor Gestalt, and Binet Sentence Memory. The posttests used were the Jansky and the Metropolitan Readiness Test.

The comparisons found no significant differences in pretest scores between the thirty-seven students in the MECCA program and the thirty-three in the control classes. At the posttest, the MECCA group outperformed the comparison group by about seven points (effect size = +.67). Similar effects were found on the Metropolitan Readiness Posttest, where the effect size was 0.88.

Another comparison between students randomly assigned to MECCA and a "multidisciplinary" comparison group shows similar results (Jansky effect size = .57, Monroe Reading Aptitude Test effect size = .96). In the comparison classrooms, the children were taught by an LD teacher and three other specialists.

The replication of effects under the multidisciplinary comparison is significant, for it suggests that the power of MECCA arises from more than its use of specialized personnel. It suggests that the curriculum, materials, and approach are important factors in MECCA's effectiveness. Screening, diagnoses, and task analysis of learning activities target the time and resources within the school in a productive way, especially for students very much at risk of future failure.

TALK

The focus of Project TALK is to improve expressive and receptive language skills in children in grades K–3. This is accomplished by structured activities that foster language growth. A language specialist teaches specific expressive and receptive language lessons to the class twice a week for half an hour over a six-month period. The classroom teacher watches and then participates in the demonstration lessons, and conducts followup lessons twice each week.

The following sample indicates the type of lesson used in TALK.

Lesson 92

TITLE:
Describe All

PURPOSE:
To encourage use of descriptive words of color, size, shape, and quantity.

MATERIALS:
List of simple descriptive words—descriptive word list

PROCEDURE:
The teacher walks through the class, stopping here and there by a child. The teacher describes the child with one word. For instance, "Blond John," "Listening Susan," "Tired Billy," and so on. The teacher may build from this by continuing and adding more descriptive words like "Pretty, blonde Sherry," "Clever, old Johnny," and so on.

Now the teacher asks the class what has been happening. A short discussion of descriptions and descriptive words should follow. How do you describe things? What kinds of words do you use to describe things? You use words that tell size, shape, color, smell, taste, feelings, and so on.

The teacher will begin by standing and telling one word about herself or himself such as: *tall, big, teacher, woman,* and so on. Now each child must stand one at a time and think of one word or a phrase to tell about him or her, such as: *little, red hair, freckles, braids,* and so on. When everyone has had a chance to tell a word then everyone can have another turn and think of still another word that tells about him or her. When a child gives a self-descriptive word that might fit another child in the room, stop and discuss it—How many people fit Mark's word?—this will broaden the lesson.

Younger children may want to pick a favorite self-descriptive word. The teacher can make a card for the child to wear pinned on all day that describes him or her. This will give the child a chance to explain his or her word to people who ask about it.

MORE IDEAS:
The teacher picks a simple descriptive word, such as *hard,* and each child in the class must find an object in the room that fits the descriptive word, such as "hard floor," "hard desk," "hard pencil," "hard window pane," and so on. The teacher chooses one word from a box of slips with simple descriptive words written on them. Each student finds an item in the classroom that fits the descriptive word. Now the children take turns drawing a descriptive word and finding objects that fit on his or her own. For a more difficult twist, especially in the upper grades, have children draw two or three descriptive words and place them in the proper sentence order, such as a *big, red* _____, and not a *red, big* _____, or *two small* _____, and not *small two* _____.

Three experimental and control schools were compared. Target groups of twenty-six students were randomly selected for pretesting from each grade level (K–3). In Table 5–2, we provide two sets of results: for overall (K–3) and for K alone.

The Peabody Picture Vocabulary Test (PPVT) was used to measure receptive oral vocabulary. The expressive measure used was the vocabulary subtest of the Wechsler Intelligence Scale (WISC).

Results for the original experiment and a replication the following year gave effect sizes (across all grades) around 0.38. Results presented for the separate grades indicate that the program was as effective or more effective for kindergarten students as for first- through third-grade students.

The amount of actual time spent on the Project TALK activities is small compared to the results obtained. Only two hours per week are actually spent on the program. If the results are generally replicable, this program seems to be particularly powerful in its effects. Additional evaluations need to be conducted to learn if these effect sizes are generalizable.

MARC

Multisensory Approach to Reading and Reading Readiness Curriculum, or MARC, is a continuous-progress K–1 reading program. It combines activities that emphasize knowledge through the senses with a systematic instructional delivery and management system. It is designed to enhance the likelihood of success in the beginning reading task for students from low-income and/or rural backgrounds. The major goal of the program for kindergarten students is to increase their readiness skills, especially in the area of letter recognition and auditory perception of beginning sounds.

For example, introduction of a letter of the alphabet involves the use of visual, auditory, and kinesthetic avenues of learning. The MARC program specifies the steps to be followed when introducing letters. These steps are called *linkages* because they link the visual, auditory, and kinesthetic approaches. For example, the steps in this program in teaching the letter *a* are:

1. Teacher shows children the letter from the drill pack and says, "This is the letter *a*." (VISUAL)
2. The teacher asks the children to give the letter name. (AUDITORY)
3. Children repeat the letter name. (AUDITORY)
4. Teacher presents the key word (*apple*) and introduces the sound by the key word: "*A* is for *apple*." (AUDITORY, VISUAL)
5. The children repeat the key word and sound while the teacher describes how it feels in the mouth and throat. (AUDITORY)

6. The teacher asks the children to place their hands on their throat while repeating the letter name, sound, and key word to "feel" the sound. (KINESTHETIC)

The project was evaluated by comparing an experimental group with a matched control group. The MARC and control classes did not differ significantly on pretests given in September of the kindergarten year (Boehm, Kulhman-Anderson IQ; SESAT I—Letters and Sounds or Aural Comprehension). At the beginning of the next school year, the MARC students scored significantly higher than the control on tests of letters and sounds and word reading. The effect sizes obtained were $+1.12$ for letters and $+0.88$ for word recognition. Because these effects were obtained for students in a fall-to-fall testing, they are not as likely to have resulted solely from short-term acquisition of test-taking skills or from artifacts of the test themselves, as in fall-to-spring testing. A replication study also produced significant effects for the MARC group, although the effect size was smaller ($+0.55$).

The MARC program is not currently funded by the National Diffusion Network, although materials are still available through the Florida Educational Resource for a nominal fee. The program has been successfully used in Florida in about one-third of the counties and is still being used actively in South Carolina. Project MARC has been used as a remedial program for older students as well as a regular readiness program. The inservice guide provides thorough coverage of the instructional program, assessments, grouping, and program philosophy.

First Level Mathematics

First Level Mathematics is a continuous-progress, developmentally oriented entering mathematics program. It provides a sequential curriculum and management system that provides for individual developmental growth. It is a diagnostic/prescriptive program. Children take a placement test to determine where they will be placed for instruction. Instruction may take place in small groups or individually.

The program recognizes that many early math programs require fine motor (write numerals) and visual skills that have little to do with mathematics skill development. First Level Math does not require these fine motor skills. It teaches the children the universal language of math with concrete objects and actual physical operations, and progress is made in small steps as the child's concepts are formed.

Evaluation data are based on norm expectancy comparisons only, which unfortunately do not provide very strong evidence of success.

Early Prevention of School Failure

This program provides developmental screening, diagnosis, and training based on identified learning styles and modalities. Screening of four-, five-, and six-year-olds is carried out in fine and gross motor auditory, visual, and language areas using a variety of instruments: the Preschool Language Scale (PLS, developed in conjunction with the program), the Peabody Picture Vocabulary Test (PPVT), and the Developmental test of visual motor integration. On the basis of these tests, a profile is created for each child which identifies his or her strengths and weaknesses. Students who are two years or more below expectancy on two modalities are classified as high risk; one year or more below are classified as medium risk.

Students are given additional instruction in their weak areas in a pullout setting. The program presents guides for direct modality instruction in the areas of language, auditory, visual, and fine and gross motor. Student profiles indicate their performance in these areas on a scale from 1 to 5.

Guides for modality instruction include correlation with major texts and breaking down a specific skill into a sequenced set of prerequisite skills. For example, if the skill is to tell stories in sequence with/without the aid of pictures, nine distinct skill performance areas are checked:

1. Child arranges picture stories in sequence.
2. Child tells story using sequence cards.
3. Child tells story in parts before retelling entire story.
4. Child uses felt pieces or fingerplay to tell story.
5. Child uses pictures to tell story.
6. Child uses assorted toys and objects to tell story.
7. Child unscrambles story.
8. Child gives a narrative to the series of drawn pictures.
9. Child uses puppet to help tell a story.

EFFECTIVE PROGRAMS AND STUDENTS AT RISK

The JDRP evaluations do not in general address the issue of a program's effectiveness for special populations. Data are not routinely presented that detail the progress of students by race, sex, SES, or entering ability/achievement level. Thus these JDRP data are not ideally suited for addressing the question with which we began this chapter.

However, as a basis for improving practices for students at risk in the kindergarten years, this data base is a worthwhile place to start. It seems likely that sound instructional programs, with demonstrated effectiveness across several sites, will be effective for most students. Analyses of aptitude-by-treatment interactions from studies of later grades do not find many interaction effects; programs effective for one subgroup tend to be effective for others (see Slavin and Madden, 1987). On the other hand, it may be that the nature of differences between the backgrounds of disadvantaged and advantaged children as they enter school would make programs differentially effective for different subgroups at the kindergarten level.

There is some evidence (Lysiak and Evans, 1976) of interaction effects for program and SES background. In this examination of the effectiveness of different kindergarten programs, they found that the lower SES students benefitted in particular from a structured curricular approach. This finding is consistent with the common wisdom about the need for structure for disadvantaged students, although it is really not clear what *structure* means. On one hand, structure is conceived of as the opposite of the open classroom, itself an ill-defined intervention. On the other hand, structure is thought of as rigid and heavily prescribed. Semantics aside, structure in the sense of a systematic approach to instructional delivery is a vital ingredient for any effective program. What is striking about the kindergarten approaches here—which encompass a wide variety of philosophies—is the extent of the specificity of activities, planning, and goals. Effective programs are ones that are detailed and specific.

The systematic aspects of programs may be more important in effectiveness than are the philosophical aspects. Is this a program that can be implemented on a day-to-day basis by a regular teacher facing thirty students? We do find successful systematic approaches that encompass quite different philosophies. For example, with respect to the degree of individualization and attention to individual differences, there are effective programs that focus basically on providing whole-class instruction (that is, that do not differentiate instructional pace, delivery, or content), and there are effective programs that have as their basic premise the need to focus on individual strengths and weaknesses.

This contrast is seen in the approaches taken by Early Prevention of School Failure and MARC. Early Prevention of School Failure diagnoses modality strengths and weaknesses and tailors instruction to these modalities. MARC underscores the significance of different avenues of learning but does not differentiate instruction for students based on their modality profiles. Both programs assume that an appropriate kindergarten program is multisensory in its approach: EPSF customizes instruction or provides modality training for those below a certain cutoff point; MARC structures every lesson to include linkages among the different avenues of learning. Not only are these programs quite different in their philosophical approach to learning style differences, they require quite different staff and support personnel as well. A team of specialists including a psychologist and speech clinician is required to evaluate and screen all students in the EPSF model. Instruction is then provided in a pullout format to address modality weaknesses, such as practice in fine motor coordination.

Thus, although different approaches may be effective, effective kindergarten practices incorporate specific materials, management plans, activities, and structures. The teachers have an instructional plan that they follow and specific activities that make sense in the context of that plan. The programs are not overly rigid, nor do they reduce teachers to automatons—but they are specific. Such specificity is needed to ensure a faithful implementation of a program.

PROGRAM EFFECTIVENESS AND ALTERNATIVES

We have evaluations of reasonable adequacy that compare programs to control classes. However, we do not have data about the relative effectiveness of these different approaches or their effectiveness for different students. Is a program of screening and instruction in specific modalities more effective than a regular class-paced approach? What are the relative costs and implementation difficulties of the different approaches? These basic data are needed to make intelligent decisions about approaches to the kindergarten year—to build on our collective past experiences in a systematic way. Otherwise, the present practice of individual districts building their individual curriculum without benefitting from the successes and failures of other locations seems likely to continue. Improving educational practice can be a cumulative effort, but it requires sustained and systematic evaluations. As the kindergarten has become the first formal academic experience for most students, the need to understand effective practices for this critical stage in students' schooling is great.

REFERENCES

Educational Research Service Report (1986). *Kindergarten programs and practices in public schools.* Study conducted and reported by Randolyn Gardner.

Elkind, D. (1986). Formal education and early childhood education: An essential difference. *Phi Delta Kappan, April,* 631–636.

Gredler, G. (1984). Transition rooms: A viable alternative for the at-risk child? *Psychology in the Schools, 21,* 463–470.

Griswold, P. A.; Cotton, K. J.; and Hansen, J. B. (1986). *Effectice education sourcebook.* Washington, DC: U.S. Government Printing Office.

Holmes, C. T., and Matthews, K. M. (1984). The effects of nonpromotion on elementary and junior high school pupils: A meta-analysis. *Review of Educational Research, 54*(2), 225–236.

Jackson, G. B. (1975). The research evidence on the effect of grade retention. *Review of Educational Research, 45*, 438–460.

Karweit, N. (1983). *Time-on-task: A research review* (Technical Report No. 322). Baltimore: Center for Social Organization of Schools, The Johns Hopkins University.

Karweit, N. (1987). *Full day or half day kindergarten: Does it matter?* (Technical Report No. 11). Baltimore: Center for Research on Elementary and Middle Schools, The Johns Hopkins University.

Lazar, I.; Hubbell, V.; Murray, H.; Rosche, M.; and Royce, J. (1977). *The resistance of preschool effects.* DHEW Publication No. (OHDS) 78-30129.

Lysiak, F., and Evans, C. (1976). *Kindergarten—Fun and games or readiness for first grade: A comparison of seven kindergarten curricula.* Presented to AERA, San Francisco, CA, ERIC (ED 121 803).

Madden, N., and Slavin, R. (1987). *Effective programs for students at risk of academic failure.* Paper presented at the annual meeting of the American Educational Research Association, Washington, DC.

McKey, R.; Condelli, L.; Ganson, H.; Barrett, B.; McConkey, C.; and Plantz, M. (1985). *The impact of Head Start on children, families, and communities.* DHHS Publication No. (OHDS) 85-31193.

Meyer, L. (1985) *A look at instruction in kindergarten: Observations of interactions in three school districts.* ED 268 489.

Nieman, R., and Gastright, J. (1981). The long-term effects of Title I preschool and all-day kindergarten. *Phi Delta Kappan, November,* 184–185.

Niklason, L. B. (1984). Nonpromotion: A pseudoscientific solution. *Psychology in the Schools, 21,* 485–499.

Shephard, L., and Smith, M. (1985). *Boulder Valley kindergarten study: Retention practices and retention effects.* Laboratory of Educational Research, University of Colorado, Boulder, Boulder Valley Public Schools.

Slavin, R., and Madden, N. (1987). *Effective classroom programs for students at risk* (Technical Report No. 19). Baltimore: Center for Research on Elementary and Middle Schools, The Johns Hopkins University.

PART FOUR

EFFECTIVE PRACTICES IN REMEDIAL AND SPECIAL EDUCATION

6

INSTRUCTIONAL ISSUES FOR TEACHING STUDENTS AT RISK

Mary Kay Stein
Gaea Leinhardt
William Bickel

University of Pittsburgh
Learning Research and Development Center

Over the past decade, the U.S. educational system has been the focus of intense scrutiny. By the end of 1984, thirty national reports had been written and over 300 state task forces had been organized to examine issues of public education (Cross, 1984). The "parent" report, "A Nation at Risk," has become both an ubiquitous reference in opening paragraphs of current educational literature as well as a household phrase.

This exposure has spawned numerous calls for reform. Plans to reform our schools have come from all levels of government—local, state, and federal—and from a variety of stakeholders in the educational process—educational researchers, teacher educators, and teachers themselves. An underlying assumption of many of the reform plans is that the central problem is one of standards—standards that many critics claim are unacceptably low. Hence, suggested remedies often focus on raising standards and on making instruction more demanding and more uniform for all students. The danger in this focus is that, unchecked, it may result in

The research reported herein was supported by the Learning Research and Development Center, supported in part by funds from the Office of Educational Research and Improvement (OERI), United States Department of Education. The opinions expressed do not necessarily reflect the position or policy of OERI, and no official endorsement should be inferred.

increased failures of those least able to meet the new standards, and may provide a rationale for the funneling of a disproportionate amount of future resources toward the more gifted students—those who will likely rise to the occasion of higher standards. What is needed is a parallel focus on the provision of quality and equitable schooling experiences on which higher expectations for *all* students could justifiably be based.

A significant percentage of our nation's school-age population continues to fail to learn the most basic literacy skills necessary for informed and responsible participation in our society. Furthermore, without the prerequisite reading and math skills, such individuals find it difficult to master the relatively higher-level skills necessary for the increasing number of technological jobs available in our society. Given the predicted demise of unskilled occupations, such individuals are doomed to become economic prisoners of their low educational achievement. Moreover, evidence suggests that the number of such imprisoned individuals will steadily increase. Relatively high proportions of low-SES and minority children in today's schools have academic deficits in need of remediation. An analysis of demographic data, reported by Reynolds and Lakin (1987), projects that the number of children under age eighteen who are nonwhite and who are poor will grow at a disproportionately fast rate over the next two decades. The predicted remedial needs of these children, of course, will be reflective of social and economic factors beyond their control. Nevertheless, the needs are no less pressing. The schools must accept the responsibility to provide these children with the most effective academic education possible, yet the increasing number of children likely to be in need of such remediation can be expected to put additional strain on an already overburdened special and compensatory educational system.

This problem demands a response. Our response can be reactive or proactive; it can be driven by political, economic, and/or demographic factors, or it can be driven by an educational knowledge base gleaned from reflections upon practice and research. A proactive, educationally informed response requires taking stock of what we know and what we still need to know about educating children for whom traditional forms of schooling have been less than satisfactory. Hopefully, the chapters in this book make strides in that direction.

This chapter also sets out to explore that territory. It does so with a focus on variables related to instruction and learning. Through this lens, we will review the changing responses to low-achieving children already in practice as well as promising research findings upon which we might base future instructional practices. The chapter is organized into three major sections: (1) a brief overview of the historical responses to low achievement, (2) a description of current practice, and (3) a discussion and analysis of the instructional knowledge base that is needed to inform more effective responses to low achievement.

The perspective from which this chapter is written builds upon past analyses (Leinhardt, Bickel, and Pallay, 1982) and includes two assumptions. First, what is effective instructionally with one type of low-achieving student tends to be effective with other types; hence, the distinctions between compensatory education and the various categories of special education for the mildly handicapped are not driven by educational necessities. Second, due to lack of evidence that restrictive settings promote higher student achievement than regular classrooms, and the moral and social problems associated with those restrictive settings, students should be educated in the least restrictive environment possible. We take this as *both* a moral imperative and a legal one (in light of PL 94–142). In this chapter, we are concerned with the educational conditions that will most effectively promote positive academic outcomes for compensatory education students, for those categories of special education students traditionally referred to as mildly handicapped (learning disabled [LD], socio-emotionally disturbed [SED], and educably mentally retarded [EMR]), and for unidentified "slow learners" (the bottom 20–25 percent of the achievement distribution).

HISTORICAL RESPONSES TO LOW ACHIEVEMENT

Large-scale problems in learning have been recognized since the turn of the century when the passage of compulsory education laws drew children with extremely diverse ability and motivational levels into the public schools. Initially it was felt that the provision of equal educational exposure was sufficient, and that early school exit was an individual decision or failure. Gradually, this position changed. The next prominent strategy was to identify children for whom learning in traditional classrooms was difficult and remove them to sheltered special education settings. This strategy was reflective of a concern (manifested by parents and educators alike) that participation in regular schools was harmful to these children. The belief and evidence was that handicapped children suffered rejection from their peers, experienced frustration due to failure on routine academic tasks, and built up expectations of future school failure. Instruction provided in a warm, nurturing environment by specially trained teachers, it was thought, would be much more beneficial to both their academic and emotional welfare.

Beginning in the early 1960s, individuals began to exhibit concern over the educational problems encountered by yet another group of students—children from impoverished backgrounds. Unlike the handicapped children first identified earlier in the century, these students' poor academic performance was seen as due to the social and economic conditions in their homes and communities rather than due to organic deficits. Therefore, several programs were established by the federal government in which poor children were to receive supplemental instruction by specially trained teachers using innovative techniques before, during, and after school. It was hoped that the provision of this enriched educational experience would remediate the students' academic difficulties which, in turn, would help to free them from a future of poverty.

In the 1970s, the segregation of low-achieving students was challenged by several court cases. The cases established the constitutional right to equal access to an appropriate education and upheld the principle of integration. The mainstreaming movement is based on the belief that both special needs and regular children need to learn to participate side by side in a multifaceted, integrated society. Ironically, many of our educational programs for low-achieving students, although well intentioned, have failed to promote such integration; in many cases, they have increased separation of children by race and achievement levels. The following sections provide a brief overview of the history and current structure of both the compensatory and special education systems.

Compensatory Education

Our current system of compensatory education began as part of President Johnson's "War on Poverty." During the 1960s, there was increasing concern about the educational prospects of children who came from poor families. The attention of educators, politicians, and parents was focused on two interrelated concepts: "cumulative deficit" and the "vicious cycle of poverty." Essentially, these phrases refer to the belief that children who begin school performing behind their peers remain so and fall continuously further behind. The belief is that these students are likely to exit from school at a point when they are still ill-prepared, like their parents before them, to compete successfully in society. Compensatory education is the major component in the system of social programs designed to break this cycle by "compensating" for initial deficits.

Compensatory education provides services to schools with a significant percentage of children whose families are below the poverty line. Within qualifying schools, students are then identified to receive compensatory services based on some measure of achievement (e.g., more than one-half grade equivalent below grade level). Both the selection of schools and the administration of programs are based on federal guidelines as interpreted by state educational agencies. Local educational agencies (LEAs) carry out the federal and state directives and generally spend money on remedial teachers, instructional aides, and equipment.

Federally supported compensatory education has its functional bases in two legislative acts: the Economic Opportunity Act (EOA) passed in 1964 (and amendments to it), and the Elementary and Secondary Education Act (ESEA) passed in 1965. EOA established Head Start; ESEA established

Title I and Follow Through programs. With the passage of the Education Consolidation and Improvement Act (ECIA) in 1981, the programs provided by ESEA Title I were transferred to Chapter 1 of the new legislation.

Head Start

Head Start, as its name implies, is a preschool program servicing children from age 3 to school entry. If a family meets low-income requirements, and if the community has a Head Start program available, then a child can gain access to Head Start. The fundamental goals of the program are to guarantee children's physical well being, to aid their social-emotional development, to improve their mental processes and skills, to establish patterns of success, to improve family relationships, to develop social responsibility, and to increase children's sense of self-worth and dignity (Richmond, Stipek, and Zigler, 1979; Zigler and Anderson, 1979).

To answer the often-asked question, "Has Head Start been successful?" is not easy. Over time, evaluations of the effectiveness of Head Start have been mixed; there have been many individual success stories as well as many examples of unproductive efforts (Wolff and Stein, 1966). One of the impediments to consistent findings is the fact that Head Start is the label of a program and not an identifier of a particular instructional (or other) treatment. Under the heading of Head Start, many very different instructional programs have been implemented, some more successful than others. Another problem in evaluations of Head Start has been lack of agreement over when and what criterion measures should be adopted. A major finding with many of the Head Start programs has been that when participating students are tested in kindergarten and first grade, they show few, if any, lasting academic gains (McKey, Condelli, Ganson, Barrett, McConkey, and Plantz, 1985). It has been pointed out, however, that the initial Head Start goals also included medical and social features, which have sometimes been lost in the storms surrounding this apparent academic "failure."

The Perry Preschool Program is an example of one of the most notable and well-documented successes (Barnett, 1985; Berrueta-Clement, Schweinhart, Barnett, Epstein, and Weikart, 1984; Schweinhart and Weikart, 1980, 1985; see Chapter 4). In this program, it was precisely the medical and social goals that were met, and when they were met, they had a powerful impact on life chances. Findings from a series of well-designed longitudinal studies show that by age nineteen, those students who attended the Perry Preschool Program were more likely to have finished high school, were dramatically less likely to have committed a crime, were less likely to be on welfare, and were earning more money (Barnett, 1985). Convergent findings have resulted from the research of Lazar and Darlington (1982) in their estimates of the reduction of special education assignments which is attributable to participation in Head Start. In summary, it is important to note that individual programs under Head Start have been successful even if the total collection of initiatives demonstrates mixed results.

Over the years, Head Start has maintained its base of financial support with a current annual budget of approximately one billion dollars (ECIA, 1981; HSAA, 1984; Schweinhart and Weikart, 1985). Head Start serves more than 400,000 children each year (White and Castro, 1985).

Follow Through

In 1967, President Johnson recommended the establishment of a "follow through" program that would systematically build upon preschool Head Start programs by extending educational support from kindergarten through the third grade. Due to budget cuts (from a recommended $200 million to an appropriated $15 million), however, a new conception of Follow Through surfaced: the so-called planned variation approach (Haney, 1977). In short, Follow Through dollars would not be used to extend services to former Head Start students but rather would be used to develop demonstration projects around the country designed to identify promising instructional treatments.

One important finding of the planned variation studies was that program membership *per se* made little difference in children's learning. For example, studies that contrasted Follow Through with non-Follow Through students showed little consistent advantage for program participation because, like Head Start, the Follow Through programs were quite different across sponsors. In addition, the characteristics of students assigned to Follow Through programs varied. However, the Follow Through programs that engaged in elaborate programmatic descriptions and data collection were valuable in developing our understanding of what worked and why (Gersten, Carnine, and White, 1984).

Evaluations were essentially of two types: very large-scale national evaluation such as the controversial but often insightful studies conducted by Abt Associates (Stebbins, St. Pierre, Proper, Anderson, and Cerva, 1977), and smaller project-level studies that focused on implementation evaluation and the impact of program features (Becker and Gersten, 1982; Bereiter and Kurland, 1981–1982; Gersten, 1984; Gersten, Carnine, Zoref, and Cronin, 1986; Leinhardt, 1976, 1977). Glossing over many of the important methodological and policy issues that were raised by these studies, it seems the findings point in similar directions. They tend to suggest that of the models available, the most effective were behaviorally focused, emphasized learning math and reading, had systems for monitoring student progress, provided performance-based feedback, and had mechanisms that ensured reasonable levels of implementation. The individual studies carried out by the program designers and developers or by their evaluation staffs found results similar to the national evaluations and smaller project-level studies. Students learned more in those classrooms where much of the available time was spent on highly directed learning of basic skills and in which the progress of individuals or groups of students was monitored and in which some type of reinforcement was available (Stebbins et al., 1977). In recent years, annual allocations for Follow Through programs have decreased substantially.

Title I/Chapter 1

Title I was launched in 1965 as part of the Elementary and Secondary Education Act. It was a massive program that aimed to provide support to school districts that were heavily impacted by high numbers of disadvantaged and low-achieving students. Maximum flexibility was given to LEAs to develop programs to help educationally deprived children catch up with their peers. In 1981, the enactment of Reagan's Education and Consolidation and Improvement Act modified the way former Title I resources were distributed and monitored. Although the educational goal of Title I (hereafter called Chapter 1) funds remained the same (i.e., the provision of support to states and districts heavily populated with low-income and low-achieving students), constraints were put on the ways in which the funds were used. For example, there were increased efforts to monitor funding flows in order to assure that only Chapter 1 eligible students received services and that those services were clearly supplemental to the regular classroom instruction (Dougherty, 1985).

Like Head Start and Follow Through, Chapter 1 programs vary considerably from district to district. Evaluations of Chapter 1 programs that carefully describe the instructional features of the program as well as the academic progress of students have produced the most useful data. For example, the Instructional Dimensions Study (IDS) (Cooley and Leinhardt, 1980) showed that, after adjusting for initial student ability, the time available for learning subject matter coupled with the coverage and focus of that subject matter (overlap) was more important than any program style or instructional organization. In addition, the Sustaining Effects Study (SES) (Carter, 1984) also found that the opportunity to learn was very important and that other valued strategies (such as grouping and better teacher/student ratios) were related to increases in opportunity, although themselves not directly influential on student learning. These two studies (IDS and SES) and another large study, the Beginning Teacher Evaluation Study (BTES) (Fisher, Filby, Marliave, Cahen, Dishaw, Moore, and Berliner, 1978), again emphasized the need to look at specific instructional practices rather than at programmatic labels.

Special Education

Unlike compensatory education, which arose as a response to a perceived social and economic problem, special education arose as a response to problems that were perceived to reside within the individual. Before the turn of the century, such problems were largely ignored by public institutions; a handicapped child was seen as an individual and private family concern, not as a societal responsibility (Lazerson, 1983). With the influx of a much wider range of students into the schools brought on by compulsory education laws, these students could not so easily be ignored. Special programs and schools were designed and teachers were trained who would be especially sensitive and skilled in dealing with children possessing the various handicapping conditions. Parents of handicapped children formed strong advocacy groups and successfully lobbied Congress for funds to support a wide array of categorical programs for the handicapped. It should be noted that, although this time period witnessed an upsurge of interest in handicapped children, the predominant remedial strategy was to segregate them from their nonhandicapped peers and place them into isolated settings that offered little or no opportunity for interaction with their nonhandicapped peers. As mentioned earlier, the rationale behind this strategy was to protect and nurture vulnerable children and to avoid exposing them to ridicule and failure.

The segregated nature of special education was directly challenged by what has come to be known as the mainstreaming movement. Mainstreaming is based on the principle of the least restrictive environment as expressed in court decisions (*Pennsylvania Association for Retarded Children [PARC] v. Pennsylvania,* 1972) and in law (PL 94–142, 1975). Currently, the United States is dedicated, in principle, to the maximum integration of all students. In fact, as we shall soon see, the present situation reflects the long history of special programs still operating quite separately.

From the outset, special education was presumed to be beneficial. It was widely held that an accepting environment, modified instructional goals and techniques, and teachers with special training in specific areas of exceptionality would lead to more effective programs for handicapped individuals. Hence, special education programs initially received little systematic scrutiny (Sheehan and Keogh, 1984). Recently, however, a number of political, economic, and professional pressures have made evaluating and demonstrating program impact a high priority. Unfortunately, evaluation studies in special education have been plagued by a variety of conceptual and methodological problems, some of which parallel evaluation research in compensatory and regular education and some of which are unique to special education.

A problem already noted with respect to many compensatory education studies is the failure to adequately specify instructional features (independent variables). The special education literature shares this neglect of treatment definition and measurement. Although groups of students in different types of programs are often compared on various outcome measures, the components of these programs typically are not explicated or analyzed.

The failure to provide descriptive—as well as analytical—information about instructional features may be related to a second issue in special education research: its authorship. Program developers or designers are the most frequent evaluators of special education programs. Because they most often evaluate their own programs, their most pressing question has been "Does it work?" This often results in pre-post designs that leave program content unmeasured. Hence, even after significant differences have been found in favor of the treatment group, one is still left with the unanswered question: "What was it about the program that led to its success?" There has been a trend toward the use of "degree of implementation" measures by program designers to specify the extent to which the program is being implemented as intended, the so-called fidelity approach (Fullan and Pomfret, 1977). This degree of implementation information is then used to attempt to explain various outcome measures and to inform the developer as to revisions required to bring the program closer to the ideal. Although a step closer to unveiling the "black box" of treatment variables, degree of implementation measures, it has been argued, often fail to adequately unmask program features (Leinhardt, 1980).

Inadequate specification and imprecise measurement has also plagued dependent variables in special education research. As noted earlier, the most frequently stated goal or desired outcome for special education is to help each individual child reach his or her maximum potential, a goal shared by regular education. Although philosophically sound, this goal cannot be easily operationalized. Traditionally, the IQ has been the most common outcome measure for early intervention and the standard achievement test for special education. The inadequacies of these measures for special education populations, however, have been well documented. They include: the lack of growth norms for handicapped learners, possible cultural bias of item content, and little overlap between the content of special education curriculum and the content of test items (MacMillan, Keogh, and Jones, 1986). Recently, there has been a call for broader definitions of outcome variables in special education research (e.g., the social goals that were achieved in the Perry Preschool Project—high school graduation, success in later life, etc.). It must be recognized, however, that such reconceptualization of outcome domains carries with it new demands for the development of adequate and sound designs and instrumentation.

Finally, interpretation of the results of special education research is limited because of the variability over time in definition of various mildly handicapped categories and programs. This limitation on interpretation of findings stems from both historical and present-day practices. Historically, the changing criteria for membership in the various mildly handicapping categories has led to the unfortunate situation where the results of research are valid only for the period of time for which the definition parameters for a category remained unchanged. Results from present-day studies also are questionable due to inconsistencies about both definitional and placement criteria for subject selection. For example, many studies use system-identified children, but criteria for access to various special education programs can vary from district to district. A child classified as LD in one district may possess different characteristics from a child classified as LD in another district (see Ysseldyke and Algozzine, 1983).

Given the many limitations of special education research, findings on effective practices must be treated with caution. Nevertheless, some findings seem strong and robust enough to appear with a fair amount of consistency. Furthermore, those findings that are consistent seem to emerge from studies that are focused on the details of instructional practice as opposed to more global programmatic variables.

One such set of effective practices can be grouped under the label of teacher-directed instruction, also referred to as direct instruction (Rosenshine, 1983). This refers to instruction that is planned and presented by the teacher and that can be characterized as systematic and academically focused. Concepts are presented in sequential order of difficulty and are related to what students already know. Teachers model correct performance, closely monitor student performance, and provide corrective feedback during recitation, drill, practice, or application activities. Active academic responding by students is encouraged. Recently, direct instruction has been scrutinized regarding its efficacy in promoting higher-order thinking. Although direct instruction approaches tend to be associated with high student scores on achievement tests, it has been suggested that direct instruction may not be the best method for encouraging the development of critical thinking and problem-solving (Doyle, 1983). We discuss this point in depth in the final section of this chapter.

A related set of instructional practices was found to be effective in a recent comprehensive review of studies on academic interventions with LD students. They include instruction that is (1) goal-directed (has a close correspondence with terminal objectives); (2) practice-loaded; (3) strategy-laden (teaches students the processes for performing academic tasks); (4) independence-oriented (provides a great deal of teacher direction in initial stages followed by increasing amounts of student self-direction); and (5) detailed and comprehensive (Lloyd, 1988). It should be noted that the above characterizations of effective instruction with special education students are not setting-bound. That is, no evidence supports the notion that a specific practice works only in a specific special education program setting.

DESCRIPTION OF CURRENT PRACTICE

As described in the previous section, the various preventive and remedial programs falling under the rubric of special and compensatory education were initiated independently of one another as well as from the mainstream of regular education. Their separate roots are still very evident in the mutually exclusive funding, entitlement, and administrative procedures that govern current practice. Services to compensatory education students and the mildly handicapped students are regulated by two very separate administrative bureaucracies and are typically delivered without significant interprogram coordination.

Mildly handicapped special education students generally receive their education in one of three settings: (1) self-contained classrooms from which they are mainstreamed to some extent, usually for nonacademic classes; (2) resource rooms in which they receive special help for reading and math (students are "pulled out" of their regular classroom to attend resource room instruction); or (3) regular room placement with a resource teacher who helps occasionally or daily to see that the targeted student is keeping pace. In self-contained classes there are between twelve and fifteen students with one specially certified teacher and, depending on the disability, one aide. Almost 70 percent of the school day is devoted to reading and little or no time is spent on social studies or science (Leinhardt, Zigmond, and Cooley, 1981; Norman and Zigmond, 1980). In resource rooms there are usually six to twelve students who go there for one or two periods a day (less than 30 percent). Both settings tend to emphasize behaviorist approaches to instruction and assessment. That is, specific objectives are set and students work (often using worksheets) to master limited and subsequently tested skills. Global, integrative work is uncommon.

Compensatory education students are either in regular classes with a teacher and an aide or with a teacher and a part-time specialist teacher, or they attend pullout classes, working with a specialist teacher (see Chapters 1 and 7). Significant percentages of both reading and math instruction are typically given in pullout rooms. Class size for pullout rooms is variable and, as with special education, the most successful and predominant style of instruction is behaviorally based.

Disadvantages of the Pullout Method

The pullout or resource room approach is currently the predominant method used to deliver educational services for low-achieving students (Carter, 1984). However, this method has not been shown to have positive effects on student learning. In fact, pullout programs too often result in a disjointed educational experience for the very children who are most in need of the best possible educational experience. In the following discussion, we consider five issues related to the delivery of instructional services using the pullout technique: (1) instructional fragmentation, (2) time erosion, (3) oversight responsibility for the individual student, (4) ownership of educational services, and (5) procedural requirements.

Foremost among problems associated with the pullout model is lack of attention to instructional coordination between what is taught in the regular classroom and what is taught in the pullout room. From the students' perspective, they may feel as if they are on a roller coaster of special assignments. Content may be duplicated or not covered at all, depending on the configuration and timing of services received. It is not unusual, for instance, for a child to receive two math classes and no science. Within a particular subject (e.g., math), it becomes the individual student's responsibility to make sense of the all-too-often disparate learning tasks that are assigned under the auspices of these two very different classroom situations. In order to gain a true understanding of a particular domain, the students must, on their own, integrate fragmentary instructional content into a meaningful and internally consistent conceptualization. Such fragmentation of instruction could be expected to pose problems for any student; for low-achieving students it is particuarly devastating. (See Chapter 11 for an excellent discussion of problems in instructional coordination between regular and pullout classes.)

From the teacher's perspective, multiple pullouts result in a managerial headache. It is not unusual for a regular classroom teacher's daily instruction to be almost continuously interrupted by students leaving for (or coming back from) Chapter 1 instruction, bilingual instruction, learning disability resource rooms, and so on. Such pullouts often happen in odd patterns throughout the school day. In cases where a single student has been declared eligible for multiple programs (e.g., Chapter 1, learning disabilities, speech therapy), there may be insufficient hours in the school day to remove the student for all of the extra assistance to which he or she is entitled (Carter, 1984). It is ironic that one of the instructional features consistently found to be related to increased student learning—time spent actively engaged with criterion (or tested) material—is exactly the feature that is undermined when low-achieving students spend unproductive time traveling to and from special assignments.

The lack of coordination of instructional content mirrors the more general problem of lack of responsiblity for the individual child. Typically, homeroom teachers accept an oversight responsibility for regular elementary school students. Homeroom teachers are likely to be in touch with the attendance patterns, emotional profiles, and typical achievement levels of the children who report to them first in the morning and last in the afternoon. Furthermore, elementary students often spend much of the school day receiving instruction from their homeroom teacher. Which professional oversees the child who spends significant chunks of the school day in two to three or more different places? It has been suggested that regular teachers often "tolerate" but show little sustained interest in the overall welfare of such students (e.g., Cohen, Intilli, and Robbins, 1978). In some ways, resource room assignment can be likened to departmentalization, which

Slavin (1987) suggests runs the risk of diffusing responsibility for individual children. An unforeseen consequence may be that the child fails to form a bond or identification with a single caring adult.

A closely related concern is the lack of local ownership over the educational services provided to children with special learning needs. Most personnel who run special programs in elementary school buildings are directly accountable to Chapter 1 supervisors, district special education directors, or other similarly "removed" supervisors. This represents a concomitant loss of control at the level of the building principal—another irony given findings from the school effectiveness literature on the importance of building-level leadership. Increasingly, empowerment has been stripped from building principals as special programs have become characterized by a narrowing of leadership (Heller, Holtzman, and Messick, 1982).

This program-specific, often geographically distant, leadership can be seen as related to the tremendous increase in the procedural requirements placed upon teachers and school administrators. The requirements include preparation of individual educational plans (IEPs), scheduling of meetings, and other accountability procedures necessary to ensure dollar flow. Such procedures are time consuming and often detract valuable resources from attention to more substantive aspects of the education of low-achieving children. It has also been suggested that a litigious atmosphere is created by an overemphasis on procedural requirements which, in turn, heightens distrust between teachers and parents (Reynolds and Wang, 1981).

This close procedural monitoring may also strain relationships between regular and remedial teachers. For example, federal guidelines clearly specify that Chapter 1 monies only be used to purchase material or hire personnel to assist Chapter 1 eligible students. Any spillover of benefits to regular students is prohibited. Strictly speaking, a Chapter 1 aide working in a regular classroom may not respond to a request for help by a non-Chapter 1 eligible student. Similarly, books bought with Chapter 1 monies must be clearly marked as such and not shared with other students. Clearly, the spirit of the law has been subverted by overly rigid procedures aimed at monitoring adherence to the letter of the law.

Questions about the Instructional Efficacy
of Separate Systems

Although there is widespread recognition of the problems associated with the pullout approach, many educators argue that improvements can be made without a complete overhaul of the overarching structure of educational programming for low-achieving students. Indeed, the stakes for maintaining the present separate systems are perceived to be quite high by many individuals who are involved in what Reynolds and Lakin (1987) have termed the "collateral enterprises of teaching, teacher supervision, child assessment, teacher training, advocacy, product development, research and scholarly writing, and professional organization." These collateral enterprises have developed hand in hand with, in particular, the various special education classifications (e.g., learning disabilities, mental retardation) and are often perceived to be dependent on the continuation of a system that is built around various categorical procedures.

Arguments against retaining the present system, on the other hand, hinge on evidence that children assigned to resource, pullout, or self-contained settings are *not* receiving qualitatively better instruction. This evidence comes from several fronts. In the following discussion we will briefly summarize selected findings from three lines of work that cast doubt on the instructional efficacy of continuation of the present structure of separate educational systems for low-achieving children. They are: (1) comparative studies of the opportunity to learn in remedial settings versus regular classrooms, (2) work in the area of special education classification, and (3) the growing knowledge base on effective instructional practices that are not classsification- or setting-bound.

Opportunity to Learn

Comparative studies have suggested that placement in Chapter 1 or special education settings does not guarantee increased opportunity to learn academic material. For example, data gathered through intensive observations of nearly 100 Chapter 1 and non-Chapter 1 fourth-grade students from four different schools suggest that the assumption that placement in a Chapter 1 setting will provide more structure and opportunity to engage in reading and math may be incorrect (Stanley and Greenwood, 1983). Although different structural contexts are often provided in Chapter 1 settings, the effect on students' opportunity to learn may not be straightforward. For example, Stanley and Greenwood's data show that Chapter 1 students were engaged an average of eleven minutes *less* per day than students in non-Chapter 1 settings. Similarly, results from a series of studies conducted at the Institute for Research on Learning Disabilities at the University of Minnesota suggest that placement in special education settings is not necessarily associated with increased amounts of student engaged time (Thurlow, Graden, Greener, and Ysseldyke, 1982; Thurlow, Ysseldyke, Graden, Greener, and Mecklenberg, 1982; Ysseldyke, Thurlow, Mecklenberg, Graden, and Algozzine, 1984). For example, Ysseldyke et al. (1984) examined change in level of service from pre- to postplacement. Although their findings must be treated cautiously due to the small sample size, the results of their observations indicated that the students did not receive more intensive services in special education than they received in the regular education environment. Instead, it was found that amounts of academic instruction and responding time actually decreased two months after assignment to special education.

Several characteristics of remedial instruction may be seen as related to the depressed levels of academically engaged time often found in pullout programs. At the most obvious level, less instructional time can be seen as partly a result of time spent moving from class to class and getting down to work once arriving at the various settings. In addition, students in special settings may be spending considerable time in academically unproductive process training (Arter and Jenkins, 1979). Time spent on perceptual, social, and motor skills training represents a corresponding loss of time spent on academic skills. Finally, it has been suggested that the pace of instruction for low-ability students is slower and that teachers focus more on low-level objectives and routine procedures than they do with high-ability students (Shavelson and Stern, 1981; Weinstein, 1987). The overall effect of the above characteristics of instruction is less opportunity to learn what is subsequently valued and tested throughout the students' schooling careers. Furthermore, the problem of instructional fragmentation mentioned previously only compounds the effects of lack of opportunity to learn. When students are engaged in academic work, the content may seem unintegrated and meaningless. This experience stems from the use of different materials and methods in the different settings and/or to the lack of communication betweeen the different teachers about coordinating the instructional programs.

Classification Issues

Historically, the classification of special needs children into specific categories (e.g., LD, EMR) has served several functions. One of the more positive functions of the classification system has been the utilization of the various categorical labels as unifying symbols around which public and legal support has coalesced. Parents and other concerned parties have formed powerful advocacy groups for each of the categorical disabilities and have been successful in lobbying Congress for fiscal support for a variety of social and educational programs.

In addition to their public support function, categorical labels have been viewed as possessing a diagnostic and prescriptive function. Until recently, it was assumed that the various categorical disabilities accurately reflected different handicapping deficits, stemming from different root causes, and capable of being accurately diagnosed through standardized psychometric assessment procedures. Furthermore, once diagnosed, it was believed that treatments could then be prescribed or tailored to the specific "illness" that had been uncovered. These treatments would then be administered by professionals who were specially trained in the technical knowledge about the causes and cures of the problem.

The above model of classification and treatment has come under attack in recent years. For example, Reynolds and Lakin (1987) have argued that a choice of a classification system should be based on the purpose(s) it is meant to serve. Within education, the purpose is to effectively instruct children. However, historically classification procedures and systems of categorization have evolved from such nonteaching disciplines as psychology and medicine. Increasingly these systems and procedures have been recognized to have poor applicability to the purposes of instruction. There is little evidence to suggest that current procedures (i.e., assessing the child with a standardized instrument and then identifying him or her as LD, EMR, etc.) provide data relevant to decisions regarding the type of instructional program needed to improve the academic performance of special needs students (Jenkins and Pany, 1978). Nevertheless, enormous amounts of energy are funnelled into diagnosis and placement procedures under the current system (Ysseldyke and Algozzine, 1983). Such a focus diverts attention from more substantive issues, such as identification of the areas of knowledge and skill that low-achieving students lack. For a more thorough discussion of problems associated with current classification procedures, the reader is referred to Hobbs' (1975) major work in this area. Based on his findings, Hobbs has concluded that current classification and placement procedures used to assign students to special classes are "a major barrier to the efficient and effective delivery of services to them and their families" (Hobbs, 1975, p. 1274).

Knowledge Base on Effective Instruction
for Low-Achieving Students

There is a growing consensus on the features of instruction which successfully move the lower quartile of students closer to the mean. We have briefly touched upon some of these in the first part of the chapter; a more in-depth discussion and analysis of effective instruction for at-risk students is presented in the final section. At this point, it is important to note that a significant attribute of these instructional features is that they tend not to vary across programs or settings, and features which are found to be effective are effective in both compensatory and special education contexts. The presence of these effective instructional practices that do not seem to be tied to specific types of low-achieving children or to specific settings is a powerful argument that challenges the instructional rationale for separate systems.

In summary, the arguments against separate programs include (1) the decreased opportunity to learn in special settings; (2) the lack of specific instructional matches for traditional diagnostic labels; and (3) the existence of effective instructional features across settings and types of handicap. It has been our position that the weight of these arguments places the burden of proof on those individuals who advocate continuation of separate instructional programs for students at risk. The evidence presented above, we feel, provides serious challenges to the instructional efficacy of separate educational systems for low-achieving students. Considered in tandem with the disadvantages associated with "pullout" programs, a strong case emerges for serious consideration of a more unified instructional system. Such a system would merge the instruction of all types of low-achieving students and also, to the greatest extent possible, integrate instruction for low-achieving students with the mainstream educational program. Moreover, the existence of a set of instructional features which are effective across types of students and educational settings provides a foundation upon which to begin to assemble the necessary components of such a merged instructional program. The guiding principle of the program would be the targeting of educational treatments based on the type of instructional support needed, thereby labeling instruction and not children.

INSTRUCTIONAL CONSIDERATIONS UNDERLYING A MERGED SYSTEM

In this final section, a brief rationale for an instruction-driven approach to the development of a merged system is presented followed by a discussion of the current state of knowledge on effective instruction for at-risk students. The section concludes with an overview of promising agendas for continued development of the knowledge base on effective instruction for low-achieving students.

An Instruction-Driven Approach: Putting the Horse Before the Cart

Previous attempts to improve programming for special education and compensatory education students have often focused on noninstructional variables. Many efforts have emphasized the physical or temporal integration of low-achieving children without concomitant or prior attention to instructional integration. In other words, improvement efforts have often been defined in terms of the setting in which at-risk students are instructed and the amount of time they spend in various settings. For example, Epps and Tindal (1987) found that one of the properties of mainstreaming programs that is most often examined in efficacy studies is temporal integration, referring to the amount of time students spend in regular classrooms with their nonhandicapped peers.

Throughout history, much attention has been devoted to the question of the most appropriate setting in which to educate low-achieving students. Much of the early work in this area (pre-1970) hypothesized that separate classes were more effective (Heller, Holtzman, and Messick, 1982). Since the late 1960s and early 1970s, however, the majority of investigations have hypothesized that the mainstream is the most efficacious placement (Madden and Slavin, 1983; Polloway, 1984). The focus throughout, however, has been more on administrative arrangements than on instructional variables. Building on past work (Leinhardt, Bickel, and Pallay, 1982; Leinhardt and Pallay, 1982) and relevant recent work (Epps and Tindal, 1987), we take the position that debates that focus on the best setting (e.g., resource room versus self-contained classroom, etc.) in which to educate low-achieving students miss the mark. It is our belief that setting, because it is an easily understood, highly visible, and manipulable variable, has been overplayed by policymakers, researchers, parents, and teachers.

Furthermore, findings from studies that employed setting or time spent with nonhandicapped peers as the major independent variable have been inconsistent. Neither self-contained classrooms, resource rooms, nor regular classroom placement has been unequivocally supported as the most effective treatment. Many investigators (Epps and Tindal, 1987; Leinhardt and Pallay, 1982) have interpreted these findings as evidence that setting, as a global construct, is an inappropriate variable for efficacy studies. In fact, setting may often mask more significant, fine-grained variables such as the features of instruction that lead to positive student learning. It is our belief that educational setting is not the salient variable that determines the success of instruction. Rather, certain features of educational treatments affect student outcomes.

For the remainder of this chapter, we ask the reader to put not only setting questions, but also other programmatic and policy questions on hold, not because they are unimportant, but rather because to address them *a priori* is putting the cart before the horse. Instead, we would like to discuss a vision of a merged system that is built on evidence of effective instruction for low-achieving children. Using effective instructional practices as the foundation, issues of setting, timing, and policy can subsequently be addressed.

The Instructional Knowledge Base

Knowledge regarding what constitutes effective instruction for low-achieving students comes from diverse sources. First, a summary of the findings from studies of special education and compensatory education described earlier in this chapter will be presented, followed by a brief overview of recent work in the area of effective insruction for low-achieving students. Subsequently, we discuss a second line of work, research in the area of cognitive strategies, and highlight its implications for the instruction of at-risk students. Analyses of these two lines of work reveals substantial progress as well as several nagging concerns. The concerns, we shall argue, seem to revolve around insufficient attention to the content of instruction. The chapter concludes with a discussion of the potential of a third line of work, which is informed by serious consideration of both what is taught (the content of instruction) and how it is taught (the instructional approach).

Instruction That Works with Low-Achieving Students

Much of the initial knowledge concerning effective instruction for low-achieving students was gained by the evaluations of compensatory and special education programs described earlier in this chapter. Briefly, most of these evaluations have found that interventions that are behaviorally focused and spend the majority of time on highly directed, teacher-led instruction in basic skills in reading and math are effective in improving the achievement of at-risk students (Becker and Gersten, 1982; Bereiter and Kurland, 1981–1982; Gersten, 1984; Gersten, Carnine, Zoref, and Cronin, 1986; Leinhardt, 1976, 1977). Other components of successful programs included frequent monitoring of student work, and the provision of performance-based feedback and appropriate reinforcement (Stebbins et al., 1977). Evaluations of Chapter 1 programs have also identified the quantity of time spent on instruction as a potent indicator of student achievement. More specifically, the opportunity to learn material that is subsequently tested has been shown to correlate with student mastery of basic skills (Cooley and Leinhardt, 1980). As noted earlier, these studies of special and compensatory educational practices have provided very similar pictures of effective instruction regardless of programmatic or student classification labels. When grouped under the label of direct instruction (Rosenshine, 1983), the components are often summarized as systematic academic instruction planned and presented at least in part by the teacher, along with active academic responding by the students and modeling, monitoring, and feedback by and from the teacher. The main characteristic is focus and a lack of meandering around in the content under study.

Other more recent approaches to the identification of effective instructional techniques have aimed to identify features of instruction that are particularly successful for low-achieving students who are either mainstreamed or taught within Chapter 1 classes. Three efforts in this regard are reported on in this book. Larrivee (Chapter 10) has extended the process-product methodology frequently used in the effective teaching literature in general education to the identification of features of instruction that can aid low-achieving mainstreamed students. Her findings closely parallel the process-product findings from the regular education literature. In particular, effective teachers asked factual questions that were most often answered correctly by students, and gave positive feedback to correct answers as well as supportive, clarifying feedback to incorrect answers. They rarely criticized, were very responsive to students, and held high expectations. Interventions were supportive, student contact was teacher-initiated, and on-task behavior was reinforced. Finally, students worked at their own instructional levels and were appropriately engaged in learning activities; disciplinary actions were seldom needed.

Crawford (Chapter 9) has pulled together information from diverse sources (Brophy, 1986; Cooley and Leinhardt, 1980; Crawford, 1983;

Griswold, Cotton, and Hansen, 1985) and has identified consistent themes regarding school, teacher, and student variables that impact the achievement of educationally disadvantaged students. His synthesis identifies the following instructional activities as conducive to achievement gains in Chapter 1 classes: active, teacher-led instruction; busy monitoring of student learning; high expectations communicated by relatively difficult seatwork assignments, challenging verbal questioning, and a focus on academic content; recognition of positive student performance; one-to-one interactions (primarily in primary grades reading); content coverage and maintenance of a brisk pace (in math); encouragement of student involvement; and efficient management of nonacademic classroom activities. As with Larrivee's work, the above effective teaching behaviors have been identified using process-product methods. Although many of Crawford's findings agree with the results of process-product work done in regular classrooms, some are not congruent. Crawford argues that more studies are needed that examine the effect of setting or context on effective instruction with low-achieving students.

Finally, the approach used by Slavin and Madden (Chapter 2) has involved systematic analysis of in-place classroom programs that integrate at-risk students into the regular educational program. They first identified comprehensive classroom programs that were effective in increasing the achievement levels of at-risk students. The two categories of programs that were most effective were "continuous-progress" models and cooperative learning models. Subsequently they extracted the features or principles that are shared by continuous-progress and cooperative learning programs. These features include instruction directed to individual students' needs and provided in small, homogeneous groups; instruction from the teacher, not from written materials or from peers; constant assessment of students' progress accompanied by specific procedures to remediate any small problems before they become large ones; and the existence of a structured hierarchy of skills that students are expected to master.

The above characterizations of effective instruction for low-achieving students have several features in common. First, the teacher emerges as a central figure. Currently, the best-developed materials or technological tools are no match for a competent teacher who carries the material directly to the student. Second, effective instruction is clearly tied to academic content. Training in perception, motor skills, social skills, and other indirect activities does not promote development of school-based cognitive skills. Third, students must spend sufficient amounts of time being taught and practicing academic skills. Mastery does not materialize from brief encounters, but rather develops with academically engaged time spent on material that is at an appropriate level of difficulty and that is subsequently tested. Finally, monitoring, feedback, and high expectations are significant elements in increasing student learning. It seems noteworthy that a common set of core features has emerged from such a diverse group of studies. Moreover, the shared features are uniform across setting (i.e., studies of what is effective in mainstreamed settings reveal similar features as the studies conducted in compensatory and special education settings).

Nagging Concerns

Although the preceding work provides an overall sense of optimism, several concerns remain. One is the growing acknowledgment that the effects of direct instruction have not been documented with respect to the acquisition of higher-order cognitive skills. A second concern relates to the difficulty of developing guidelines for improved practice using some of the current findings (e.g., increasing time-on-task, monitoring student practice, giving performance-based feedback, setting high expectations, etc.). Each of these concerns is discussed below.

Direct Instruction and Higher-Order Cognitive Skills.   The power of direct instruction to facilitate the learning of lower-level skills such as basic facts has been firmly established. Not only do direct instructional techniques assure that teachers are teaching what is supposed to be taught, but also the segmentation of the to-be-learned material into manageable pieces along with active responding by students seems to be especially effective with low achievers. Nevertheless, concerns are growing regarding the efficacy of direct instruction with regard to the learning of higher-level cognitive skills such as problem-solving and reading comprehension (Peterson, 1986). This concern has been fueled by recent reports regarding the inability of *students in general* to engage in these high-level comprehension and problem-solving activities. Recent results of the National Assessment of Education Progress (NAEP), for example, have indicated that, although students are mastering the "basic" computational and decoding skills of mathematics and reading, they are failing to attain more abstract levels of competencies such as math problem solving (Carpenter, Corbitt, Kepner, Lindquist, and Rays, 1981). Similarly, declines in scores on reading comprehension tests have been documented beginning in the 1960s (Chall, 1983). The lack of these skills *among low achievers* has been viewed as especially worrisome because teachers often provide little exposure to such higher-level skills to this population. Despite evidence regarding the importance of high expectations for low-achieving students, the objectives of many "low" reading and math groups remain at the "mastery-of-facts" level. For example, it has been documented that whereas students in high reading groups come away understanding that the purpose of reading is comprehension, students in low reading groups often come away thinking that the sole purpose of reading is to read individual words accurately (Allington, 1983).

It has been suggested that direct instructional techniques are not suited to the development of higher-order cognitive skills (Doyle, 1983). However, several factors may be clouding the issue. First, measurement of higher-order understanding and cognitive skills is more elusive than assessment of basic facts. Although the psychometrics underlying standardized achievement tests (mostly tests of basic skills and facts) have become more and more refined, the validity and reliability of measures of problem-solving and other higher-order cognitive skills are still debated. Therefore, it may be unfair to indict direct instruction (or any other instructional approach) as inadequate for the teaching of higher-order skills. Second, the majority of direct instruction has focused on lower-level skills. It seems unreasonable to expect that instruction in decoding or pronunciation will increase students' text comprehension, or that instruction in addition facts will increase students' ability to solve word problems. For example, increases in student engaged time during reading lessons with an emphasis on accuracy have been associated with increased scores on measures of lower-order skill attainment, but not on measures of higher-order skills (Anderson, Mason, and Shirley, 1984). These findings might be interpreted as supporting the notion that direct instruction is not appropriate for the development of higher-order skills. A competing interpretation, however, is that the students simply learned what they were taught. No doubt, quantity of time will not make a difference if what is being taught is not what is subsequently tested. We have referred to this phenomenon elsewhere (LeMahieu and Leinhardt, 1985; Leinhardt and Seewald, 1981) as *overlap*.

Rather than question the overall appropriateness of direct instruction, it seems we need to begin to address the question, "Direct instruction *of what?*" We need to recast our notion of direct instruction from that of a comprehensive instructional prescription to that of an instructional approach for teaching material the nature of which must be specified. Logically, one could talk about using a direct instructional approach for the teaching of problem-solving or other higher-order cognitive activities such as writing an interpretive essay. The practical problem is that we are not adequately knowledgeable regarding what comprises expertise in these more complex domains. Researchers are beginning to make some progress toward identifying the component knowledge and skills that comprise expert performance in higher-order knowledge and skill areas. These advances will have important implications for instruction in more complex domains. We will review promising developments and emerging research agendas in this area later in this chapter.

Limitations of "Generic" Instruction.   A second concern with respect to the current evidence regarding effective instruction for low-achieving students is what can be referred to as the "vacuous" nature of many of the teaching principles derived from process-product and other closely related kinds of research programs. Research carried out in the process-product tradition attempts to correlate gains in student achievement with certain teaching behaviors, such as the types of questions asked and the amount of feedback given. This research, by and large, has focused on the general or "generic" teaching behaviors shared by effective teachers. The attempt has been to span many teachers and teaching situations with a focus on global behaviors in order to allow for replication and generalizability of the findings. This strategy has had a measure of success in that the process-product paradigm has generated many findings that have been replicated across studies, whereas other earlier research paradigms had not.

Summaries of studies using the process-product methodology often conclude with a "composite" of an effective teacher. Both Larrivee's and Crawford's summaries of findings (Chapters 9 and 10) are examples of composite summaries of effective teachers (i.e., the effective teacher asks factual questions, rarely criticizes, holds high expectations, etc.). Such summaries are attractive to policymakers and teacher trainers because they (1) often intuitively "make sense" and (2) can be put into the form of propositions which can then be advocated as prescriptions for classroom practice (e.g., teachers should provide suffficient wait time during oral questioning of students; teachers should use ordered turns in reading groups). Recently, however, the efficacy of this approach as a guide for practice has been questioned (Shulman, 1987). The questions revolve around the way in which composite summaries are produced, including the nature of the variables that make up composite summaries of effective teachers. Composite summaries are drawn from data collected on general, yet isolated variables that have been aggregated across several kinds of teachers and teaching situations. Researchers interpret and integrate these findings when they produce composite summaries of effective teachers. It is important to realize that the composites are *not* descriptions of actual teachers who have been observed by the researchers. Rather, they are the product of researchers who "pull together" findings from a variety of teachers. When guidelines for actual classroom practice are inferred from composite summaries, they often seem incomplete. What is lacking is information on when and how to apply the various principles or propositions.

A major limitation, then, is the lack of attention to the specific contextual factors that give texture and real-world (face) validity to the findings. Without more fine-grained attention to how these findings can be applied in specific contexts, their effect on practice becomes diluted. It has been suggested that some of these findings can perhaps more reasonably be viewed as *indicators* of effective teaching as opposed to a descriptive portrait of what constitutes effective teaching. For example, Shulman (1987) has argued that the *reasons* behind these findings ought to be analyzed and used to guide practice. In fact, investigators have already begun to look "beyond" these initial findings, moving toward more fine-grained descriptions of the thoughts and actions of effective teachers and their students.

The intensive work on the variable of time provides an excellent example of the evolution of a variable from a process-product-generated *indicator* of effective teaching to a more descriptive and in-depth characterization of what good teaching entails. Time is an important schooling variable. Its value relates to the fact that it is a finite commodity and that it is directly related to the opportunity to learn. The opportunity to learn, in turn, has been found to influence the amount that is learned (Carter, 1984; Fisher et al., 1978). Initially, the "discovery" of the importance of time was heralded with much optimism because time is a highly visible and manipulable construct. More than the earlier variables that consumed researchers' attention (e.g., SES), time was a variable over which teachers and principals (and legislators) felt they could exert some control.

It was not unusual for very early work in this area to make extravagant claims about the effects of time. For example, after reanalyzing a subset of the Coleman, Campbell, Hobson, McPartland, Mood, Weinfeld, and York (1966) data, Wiley and Harnischfeger (1974) concluded that simply increasing exposure to instruction (defined in terms of student attendance × number of hours per day × number of school days per year) would lead to increased student achievement. This initial enthusiasm was soon tempered, however. In a replication of Wiley and Harnischfeger's analyses using additional data sets, Karweit (1976) found that the effects of time were not so straightforward. Karweit (1977) went on to argue that previous analyses of the relationship between quantity of time and student achievement were incomplete, neglecting, in particular, attention to *how* time is spent. Soon afterward, Gage (1978) criticized continued investigations into engaged time with the observation that time is an empty vessel.

A new wave of research followed that sought to fill the "empty vessel" of time with more descriptive accounts of what was happening in classrooms and in the minds of teachers and students. Studies of time-on-task began to ask, "Time on *what* task?" In other words, the research community began to acknowledge that the amount of time engaged was not as important as how that time was spent. This represented a major shift in how time was treated in investigations of school learning. From an early focus on time as a variable in its own right, attention shifted to the use of time as a method of scaling information about other potentially important classroom events (Leinhardt, 1985).

This brief history of research on the variable of time is presented in order to highlight the crucial role played by those early inquiries. It is important to note that, although initial work in the area of time is now criticized as vacuous, it did provide a marker or a signpost that pointed researchers to an important area of classroom life heretofore neglected. Subsequently, researchers began to "unpack" this variable with ever-increasing, fine-grained analyses into what constitutes the effective use of time and why time spent is so important.

Most importantly, the evolution of research on time has had important implications for guiding the instruction of at-risk students. For example, we have already learned that time should be spent on material that we want children to learn. That is, students learn more when they are spending their time on material to be learned rather than on activities designed to teach them in a more indirect way (Carter, 1984; Cooley and Leinhardt, 1980; Gersten, 1984; Leinhardt and Seewald, 1981; Leinhardt, Zigmond, and Cooley, 1981; Rosenshine, 1978). Moreover, continued attention to how time is spent and why time is important will most likely provide an even more precise understanding of how to guide instruction for low-achieving students. For instance, in the future, we may learn that time has different implications for lower-order versus higher-order learning. Perhaps rapid pacing is conducive to the learning and maintenance of lower-order knowledge such as addition or subtraction facts, but not as appropriate for instruction on more complex topics such as problem solving in mathematics or other higher-order concepts in science or history.

In addition to the variable of time, the work to-date on effective instruction for at-risk students has provided us with many other indicators of effective teaching. Reviewed earlier, they include close monitoring of student performance, consistent feedback, and high and clear expectations. With these findings (and others) serving as signposts, researchers are now primed for more in-depth analyses of the hows, whens, and whys underlying these indicators of effective teaching.

Recent work suggests that advances in this area will be tightly intertwined with inquiries into how teaching and learning occur in various subject matter domains (Shulman, 1986). In other words, how teachers organize and deliver the content of instruction is seen as an important, but neglected aspect of effective teaching. For example, in order to provide effective guides for practice, we will need studies that tell us not only how rapidly to pace a unit on fractions, but also what the scope and content of that unit should be. Considered together with our knowledge of effective structural features of instruction (e.g., the importance of pacing, overlap, group size, etc.), additional knowledge of effective content features should provide us with a well-rounded guide to practice. The expertise of asking and answering this next wave of question is just beginning to develop; it is intertwined with the work on expertise in complex knowledge domains discussed earlier. As promised earlier, emerging findings in this area will be highlighted later in the chapter.

Cognitive Strategy Instruction

Another line of research that has informed our knowledge regarding effective instruction for at-risk students is work in the area of cognitive strategies. Cognitive strategies refer to skills, such as rehearsing, elaborating, organizing, summarizing, and self-questioning, that facilitate the acquisition of knowledge. Cognitive strategy work holds significance for the instruction of low-achieving students because: (1) evidence suggests significant differences between good and poor learners in their use of cognitive strategies and (2) work in the area of cognitive strategy training indicates that strategies can be taught successfully to low-achieving students and that, once learned, use of the strategies leads to increases in student learning. Each of these is discussed below, followed by a discussion of nagging concerns in this area.

Lack of Spontaneous Strategy Use by Poor Learners. Low-achieving students are often observed to exhibit deficits in the use of learning strategies. For example, early work in this area (Torgesen, 1977) revealed that poor students do not use the strategy of categorization as an aid when asked to remember a series of pictures or words. Similar observations regarding the failure of LD children to spontaneously use effective strategies have been made by Tarver, Hallahan, and Kaufmann (1976) and by Dawson, Hallahan, Reeve, and Ball (1980) in their studies of selective attention. In addition, Campione and Brown (1977) have noted that mentally retarded children do not use strategic behavior spontaneously and have difficulty selecting, modifying, and sequencing strategies. Similarly, Borys (1979) has demonstrated that retarded children have problems with self-questioning.

Much of the recent work in this area has been in the domain of reading comprehension. A number of reviews have been published of studies investigating good-reader/poor-reader differences in text processing (e.g., Golinkoff, 1976; Ryan, 1981). These reviews show consistent differences between good and poor readers in how they approach the task of reading. In general, studies point to the failure of poor readers (1) to conceptualize reading as a search for meaning rather than as a decoding task; (2) to monitor when they are experiencing problems in comprehension; (3) to engage in strategic behavior that will bring meaning to the text or restore meaning if there has been a breakdown in comprehension; (4) to skim, scan, reread, take notes, or make inferences; and (5) to modify how they read passages based on the difficulty of the material and/or their reasons for reading it.

Evidence regarding different levels of strategy use between good and poor learners in another domain (mathematics) comes from a series of studies conducted by Peterson and her colleagues (Peterson, Swing, Braverman, and Buss, 1982; Peterson and Swing, 1982; Peterson, Swing, Stark, and Waas, 1984; Peterson, 1986). They explored students' reports of their thoughts during both simulated and classroom instruction in mathematics. In general, they found that low-achieving students do not spontaneously use the sophisticated kinds of strategies that have been identified by researchers as effective. High-achieving students, on the other hand, were more likely to report engaging in the following cognitive processes during classroom instruction in mathematics: (1) attending to the lesson, (2) understanding the lesson, (3) either employing a variety of specific cognitive strategies or engaging in these cognitive strategies more frequently, (4) engaging in strategies that involved problem-solving steps or showed insights into the mathematics, and (5) using the specific strategy of relating the new information to be learned to prior knowledge (Peterson, 1986, p. 22).

In general, results from a diverse group of studies have suggested inferior use of learning strategies by low-achieving students. Although these findings are important, they are also mostly descriptive; that is, the objective of these studies was to describe cognitive strategy use rather than to generate information on how to teach cognitive strategies. Another line of work, however, examines how children learn to use strategies and the role that instruction can play in facilitating such learning. We turn now to a discussion of these themes in cognitive strategies research.

Cognitive Strategy Instruction. Cognitive strategy instruction consists of deliberate, planned training that aims to teach students learning strategies that will enhance their knowledge and skills acquisition. Many training programs also work toward the development of metacognitive skills, that is, student awareness of when and how to use strategies. Currently, there is no consensus on the best way to train low-achieving students to acquire, use, and monitor cognitive strategies. Strides have been made, however, toward making cognitive strategies training research more informative to the actual classroom instruction of low-achieving students. Most early studies in this area were conducted in the laboratory (e.g., Schumaker, Deshler, Alley, Warner, and Denton, 1984; Wong and Jones, 1982). Although providing valuable information, their application to classroom practice was considered tenuous for several reasons. First, the majority of laboratory training studies were of short duration and consisted of training conducted by the investigator(s) rather than the classroom teacher. Second, learning outcomes measures were often narrowly defined and usually related directly to the experimental task (Peterson and Swing, 1983). Hence, even if successful student learning was demonstrated, the implications for ongoing academic work in the classroom remained unclear.

More recently, cognitive strategy training research has moved into the classroom (Brown and Palinscar, 1982; Palinscar and Brown, 1984; Paris, Cross, DeBritto, Jacobs, Oka, and Saarnio, 1984). These studies are characterized by the training of classroom teachers followed by the delivery of cognitive strategy instruction by the teachers to their own students over extended periods of time. One of the most frequently cited approaches to cognitive strategy training is reciprocal teaching (Palinscar and Brown, 1984). The objective of reciprocal teaching is student acquisition and effective use of comprehension-monitoring strategies. We will describe this approach briefly because it can be used to illustrate several important issues in this area of study.

Reciprocal teaching in reading can be characterized as a dialogue between teacher and students that takes place in a cooperative learning group and is structured by four specific comprehension-monitoring strategies. The four strategies are (1) summarizing (identifying main idea information); (2) questioning (self-questioning on information identified as important); (3) demanding clarity (noting when there has been a breakdown in comprehension and restoring meaning); and (4) predicting (hypothesizing what the author will discuss next). The procedure of reciprocal teaching features guided practice in applying these strategies to the task of text comprehension. The overall goal is the joint construction of the meaning of the text.

Participants in the dialogue take turns assuming the role of teacher. In the beginning of training, the teacher assumes primary responsibility for initiating and maintaining the dialogue. The teacher both provides instruction in and models the use of the four strategies. With each session, the teacher transfers more responsibility for the dialogue to the students while continuing to provide feedback and coaching. At the beginning of each session, the group reviews the strategies, the reasons they are learning the strategies, and the situations in which their utilization would be helpful.

Variants of this approach have been used in many classrooms, but Palinscar and Brown were the first to formally investigate the effectiveness of the reciprocal teaching approach. In a series of studies, Palinscar and Brown observed classrooms in which reciprocal teaching was conducted primarily by remedial reading teachers in their natural reading groups (Brown and Palinscar, 1982; Palinscar and Brown, 1984). The middle-school students participating in the studies were identified by their schools as reading at least one year below grade level with typical comprehension skills at least two years below grade level. The group sizes ranged from four to eighteen students and there were usually twenty days of instruction preceded by five-day baseline periods and both short- and long-term maintenance checks.

Findings from the studies indicated that students did learn the intended reading comprehension strategies and, over time, became increasingly able to implement them independently. Outside of the group, Palinscar and Brown documented large and reliable improvements in performance on daily comprehension tests that were independent of the training materials. Furthermore, improvements were noted on classroom measures of comprehension taken in nonreading classes (e.g., social studies and science) and on transfer tests, such as writing summaries, predicting test questions, and detecting text anomalies.

On the surface, reciprocal teaching appears deceptively simple. Closer examination of the procedure, however, reveals attention to several dimensions acknowledged to be important throughout the cognitive-strategies training literature. They are (1) generalization and transfer, (2) the degree to which cognitive-strategies instruction is embedded in academic content, and (3) the instructional approach used to teach cognitive strategies. Each of these dimensions is discussed below. As will become evident, quite a lot has been learned regarding how to teach cognitive strategies, but several questions remain. The following discussion attempts to overview both ongoing concerns and the current state of knowledge in this area.

1. *Generalization and transfer.* A problem that has continually plagued cognitive-strategy instruction has been the tendency for students not to apply the learning strategies outside of the experimental situation in which they were learned. For example, mildly retarded and learning-disabled students who were taught learning strategies for dealing with specific memory problems often failed to demonstrate ongoing use of those strategies unless "nudged" by persistent prompting by the trainer. In addition, evidence of transfer to other similar memory tasks was sparse (Borkowski and Cavanaugh, 1979; Brown, 1978; Campione and Brown, 1977; Torgeson, 1977). It should be noted that the earliest training studies were generally not as concerned about this lack of generalization or transfer as were later studies. The aim of these earlier studies was to demonstrate that the strategies could be taught and that their use would benefit the acquisition of knowledge and skills. After much evidence accumulated regarding the "teachability" of cognitive strategies, however, researchers turned their attention to how continued, appropriate use of the strategies outside of the immediate experimental condition could be facilitated.

The generalization and transfer of cognitive strategies seems to be facilitated by explicit training in the *role* of the strategy as well as training in the strategy itself (Brown, Bransford, Ferrara, and Campione, 1983). Rather than simply requiring students to execute the strategy, the instructor informs the students about the use of the strategy and tells them why and in what situations it will work for them. In addition, students are given practice in controlling and overseeing the use of the strategies being taught. In reciprocal teaching, for example, instruction continually works toward the students' understanding of the goal of the strategy they are using. At the beginning of each session, the group reviews not only the four strategies, but also the reasons they are learning the strategies and the types of learning situations in which they would be particularly useful. In addition, reciprocal teaching aims to help students monitor the use of their strategies (i.e., to check to see if the strategies are working and make appropriate corrections if they are not).

Within a taxonomy of training approaches described by Campione, Brown, and Ferrara (1982), reciprocal teaching is an example of *self-control training,* the most comprehensive level of instruction. Campione and his colleagues have categorized training studies according to the degree to which students receive training in the usefulness of strategies and the monitoring of their use. The first level is called *blind* training, and refers to an instructional situation in which the student remains naive regarding the role of the to-be-learned strategy. The investigator simply tells the learner what strategies to perform with no information regarding why these particular strategies have been selected or in what situations they might be appropriate. In the second level, *informed* training, the student receives information regarding the usefulness of the strategies (e.g., how the strategies help performance, with what success, and in what situations). This information is intended to increase the learner's awareness of the role and significance of the strategies. Finally, in the third level, *self-control* training, the student receives all of the information given in the first two levels plus instruction in how to monitor and evaluate strategy use. The student is taught both how to produce and *regulate* cognitive-strategy activity through explicit instruction in planning, checking, and monitoring.

Evidence suggests that students with learning problems profit most from interventions that can be described as self-control training (Miller, 1985; Kurtz and Borkowski, 1985). For example, Kurtz and Borkowski (1985) randomly assigned 130 fourth, fifth, and sixth graders to one of three treatment conditions. In the first condition, the students received straightforward strategy instruction on how to summarize, identify main ideas, and generate topic sentences. In the second condition, the students received this instruction *plus* instruction regarding the value of monitoring reading strategies, the importance of deliberate strategy selection, the flexible use of strategies, and the need to work slowly. The third group was a control group that simply read the experimental material and wrote summaries. Results indicated that the second group that received the metacognitive instruction performed the best. Thus, although students without diagnosed learning problems can often benefit from blind or informed training, remedial students instructed under these less explicit conditions frequently fail to acquire and/or generalize cognitive strategies. In order for instruction in cognitive strategies to have carryover effects for low-achieving students, one prerequisite seems to be that the students are made aware of not only the significance of the strategies, but also how their use of the strategies can be regulated and, if necessary, readjusted.

2. *Cognitive strategy instruction and academic work.* The issue of the degree to which cognitive strategy instruction should be embedded in regular academic work is related to the issue of generalization and transfer. Should the teaching of cognitive strategies be incorporated into students' regular academic work in the various subjects in order to ensure the most reliable use of the strategies in academic learning? Or can cognitive strategies be taught separately from academic content and still result in their transfer to academic work? These questions are often debated and although unequivocal answers are not available, current evidence suggests it is best to teach cognitive strategies in the context of regular academic work.

Reciprocal teaching is an example of cognitive-strategies training that is designed to be delivered within an academic work context. In this procedure, strategies are always modeled in appropriate academic contexts, not as isolated separate skill exercises. The four strategies are embedded in the actual task of reading, and the students understand that the overall goal of the activity is to construct the meaning of the passage being discussed.

Cognitive-strategies training programs based on the explicit teaching of learning strategies independent of specific academic content have also been advocated. Many of these training programs have been adopted by a number of school districts in recent years. These programs are often referred to as *thinking-skills* programs. Examples include the *Instrumental Enrichment Program* (Feuerstein, 1980), the *Philosophy for Children Program* (Lipman, Sharp, and Oscanyan, 1980), and Whimby and Lochhead's short course in *Problem Solving and Comprehension.* Feuerstein's program consists of thirteen types of exercises (e.g., identifying geometric figures embedded in dots, completing number sequences) repeated in cycles. After students work individually on each exercise, they participate in a classroom discussion that provides them with the opportunity to learn from other students' strategies. The teacher's task throughout is to encourage cognitive activities appropriate to the materials. In the *Philosophy for Children Program,* students are provided with stories about groups of children and adults who engage in dialogue concerning issues that arise in the course of everyday life. Different aspects of these stories illustrate various "thinking about thinking" skills such as assessing factual information objectively, formulating cause-effect relationships, and drawing generalizations. The situations in which the *Philosophy for Children* material is posed are concrete as opposed to abstract as in the Feuerstein program. Finally, the *Problem Solving and Comprehension* course involves practice on a variety of well-defined problems in the context of a thinking-aloud procedure that provides for feedback regarding the processes of thinking as well as the products of thinking. The problems are of four basic types: verbal reasoning, analogies, analysis of trends and patterns, and mathematical word problems.

Data to support the effectiveness of these approaches are sparse. Feuerstein has collected data (1979, 1980) that indicate that teachers enjoy and approve of this kind of instruction and that students exposed to this instruction have demonstrated improvement on standardized tests of intelligence. Very little data, however, are available regarding its effects on classroom learning, particularly in the area of generalization to academic skill areas. In a review, Nickerson (1984) proposed that the developers, convinced of the inherent worth of their programs, have not been inclined to evaluate them. In addition, an analysis of the these three programs by Bransford, Arbitman-Smith, Stein, and Vye (1985) suggests that, although all three programs provide some ingredients necessary for transfer, "there is no strong evidence that students in any of the three thinking-skills programs improved in tasks that were dissimilar to those already explicitly practiced" (p. 202).

The debate regarding whether or not cognitive-strategies training should be embedded in academic content ties into a related, unresolved issue in this area: the degree and type of interdependence between knowledge-base components and strategy components in intellectual functioning. Recent models of good strategy use have suggested that strategic knowledge is only one type of knowledge possessed by competent strategy users (Pressley, Borkowski, and Schneider, in press). These users also possess a great deal of knowledge about the world in general and about specific content areas. In other words, they also have an extensive declarative knowledge base. Similarly, recent conceptual frameworks of intellectual functioning view competent performance as multifaceted. Intelligent performance is suggested to be comprised of several components, including cognitive strategies, metacognitive knowledge and skills, and knowledge-based components (Brown, Bransford, Ferrara, and Campione, 1983; Flavell, 1985; Sternberg, 1985).

How strategy and knowledge-base components interact to provide for competent performance poses a challenging question. It has been suggested than an individual's knowledge base can have an enabling or an inhibiting effect on strategy execution (i.e., an individual may have learned a variety of strategies but the extent to which he or she is able to apply them will depend on the extensiveness of his or her knowledge base). For example, Levin and Pressley (1981) have suggested that an effective reading strategy is to access prior knowledge about a topic before reading a passage about the topic. If an individual has no prior knowledge about the topic, however, this strategy (no matter how well learned and/or appropriately accessed) will be ineffective. A similar example involves the use of categorization as an aid to remembering a set of words or pictures. When an individual groups a series of items into meaningful categories, the capacity of her or his short-term memory is "stretched." Instead of needing to remember, for example, sixteen separate items, the individual only needs to remember four categories. These four categories, in turn, stimulate the recall of the individual items. A scuba diver who takes on the task of memorizing the following set of terms will find the categorization strategy much more effective than will a land lover: *snorkel, regulator, narcosis, compass, bends, fins, depth gauge, mask, embolism.* Because the individual terms are meaningful to the diver, grouping them in a meaningful way is both possible and effective.

To date, most approaches to cognitive-strategy instruction do not deal extensively with the interaction of knowledge and strategy use. Although reciprocal teaching occurs within the context of a particular academic domain (i.e., reading), the knowledge component of reading is difficult to define. Reading as it is taught in elementary schools may be a *process-heavy* kind of intellectual skill; note that once students master vocabulary, syntax, and comprehension skills, their reading instruction *per se* ceases and they proceed to the *use* of reading in the learning of other subject areas (e.g., science and social studies). The knowledge components of these subjects consist of the substantive facts and concepts that make up the discipline; the knowledge components of "generalized" reading, on the other hand, cannot be so neatly (precisely) defined. Hence, even though reciprocal teaching is, in general, viewed as integrated with academic content, one can argue that the nature of the knowledge-base components of reading is qualitatively different from the nature of the knowledge-base components in other subject areas. Thus it may be necessary to develop more examples of instruction that attend to both knowledge and strategy components in other domains (e.g., math, science, history, etc.).* Insufficient attention to strategy-by-knowledge-base interaction may have potentially the most worrisome effect on low-achieving students. These students have been viewed as having an impoverished knowledge base in comparison to their normal-achieving peers. To the extent that a well-articulated knowledge base is a prerequisite to enhanced strategy use, the deficits that low-achieving students possess in this regard could be particularly devastating. Unless future work in this area demonstrates how the knowledge base and strategy use can be developed hand-in-hand, continued isolated inquiry into cognitive-strategies training with low-achieving children may be nonproductive.

In order for future work to be inclusive of both strategy and knowledge components, much more detailed information is needed regarding the nature of competent performance in complex domains. A revised instructional program could then be informed by this fine-grained analysis of both strategic and knowledge components of competent performance. Once again, the reader is reminded that work in this area has only recently begun. Our discussion highlights, however, that the pay-off of investigations into the nature of performance in complex tasks may extend to advances in cognitive-strategies training programs as well.

3. *Instructional approach.* Instruction in cognitive strategies can take a number of forms, ranging from discovery methods to direct instruction approaches. We will briefly review three instructional approaches— discovery, direct instruction, and proleptic instruction—with particular attention to the appropriateness of each approach for low-achieving students.

Discovery methods are often promulgated as the ideal approach for promoting students' development of thinking skills. Discovery approaches

---

* This discussion is not meant to give the impression, however, that knowledge is not important in reading. Bransford (1979) and others (Spilich, Vesonder, Chiesi, and Voss, 1979) have done extensive work that demonstrates the important role of background knowledge in reading comprehension. The issue is more related to ease of characterization of the knowledge base and (perhaps) the degree to which less knowledge can be offset by more strategy.

are characterized by an unstructured learning environment and student-directed learning. Children are encouraged to engage in a number of stimulating activities and given the opportunity to ask questions of both peers and teachers. Advocates note that learning by discovery is motivating and that it leads to retention and deep understanding, thereby increasing chances of transfer. A related approach, guided discovery, suggests a more structured environment which, its proponents argue, more often leads to student "discovery" of appropriate strategies. In a guided discovery lesson, for example, the teacher arranges for his or her students to experience a conflicting situation, the resolution of which requires development of sophisticated strategies. The challenge is how to engineer learning encounters so that the discovery of appropriate strategies takes place. An example of a guided discovery method is inquiry teaching (Collins and Stevens, 1982). It should be noted that critics of the discovery approach (e.g., Wittrock, 1966) question its efficiency as an instructional method, especially with slower learners.

Direct instruction approaches fall at the other end of the spectrum; they are characterized by highly structured, teacher-led training. Direct instruction approaches vary in their degree of comprehensiveness. On the one hand, direct instruction of cognitive strategies can include training in the strategies themselves along with verbal encouragement that students use the strategies. On the other hand, direct instruction can also include explicit explanations regarding when and how to use the strategies along with teacher demonstration and student practice with subsequent teacher feedback. Duffy, Roehler, Vavrus, Book, Meloth, Putnam, and Wesselman's (1984) work on explanations, referred to as direct explanations, is an excellent example of comprehensive direct instruction in cognitive strategies. (Evidence of the effectiveness of their direct explanation approach with low-group, third-grade students has been suggested by Roehler, Duffy, Putnam, Wesselman, Sivan, Rackliffe, Book, Meloth, and Vavrus [1986].)

The final method is termed dyadic, or proleptic, instruction and is rooted in the learning theories of Vygotsky (1978). According to Vygotsky, learning occurs through social mediation in heterogeneous, cooperative group settings. Less expert group members observe the more advanced learning strategies of more expert members; gradually they begin to internalize the strategies and take on more and more responsibility for their own learning. The explicit communication of effective strategies by the expert members is often viewed as a support or "scaffold" for the initially halting learning of the less sophisticated members. An important aspect of the scaffold concept is that provisions are made for its gradual removal as learners become less and less dependent on it for learning. The reciprocal teaching procedure described earlier is an excellent example of scaffolded, or proleptic, instruction. As noted earlier, after the four strategies are explicitly taught and modeled in a group situation, individual children are assisted in gradually internalizing the strategies and eventually leading the group in their use.

Pressley, Snyder, and Cariglia-Bull (in press) have recently reviewed these three approaches to cognitive-strategies instruction along with several other approaches. In summarizing their information, they were very careful to note that long-term experiments comparing different instructional approaches are lacking and hence definitive answers are far off. Given the current evidence, however, Pressley and associates concluded that comprehensive direct instruction (e.g., Duffy et al., 1984) and reciprocal teaching seem to be the most powerful approaches for student acquisition *and generalized use* of cognitive strategies. They go on to offer that proleptic instruction may be the best choice for use with low-achieving students: "It seems to us that of all the alternative teaching techniques, proleptic instruction is the one most likely to take any given nonstrategic child and turn her/him into a competent strategy user" (p. 49).

Similarly, Brown and Palinscar (1982) conducted a study aimed at analyzing the instructional components of reciprocal teaching. Training in the four comprehension-monitoring strategies was conducted under four different conditions. One was the traditional reciprocal teaching, a form of proleptic instruction. The second condition, reciprocal teaching/practice, included similar initial instruction, followed by much practice opportunity but minimal feedback. The third condition, demonstration, permitted little group interaction or practice. Finally, the fourth condition involved introduction of the skills (one at a time) via worksheets with lots of student practice with individual teacher assistance, thus providing the opportunity for a lot of teacher-student interaction. Results of the study suggest that traditional reciprocal teaching was most effective, followed by (but not closely) the fourth approach (worksheets and practice).

What is noteworthy about these findings is that a more economical means of cognitive-strategies training that is as reliable as proleptic instruction has not been identified. With low-achieving students, this mediated form of instruction, although most time-consuming, is also most effective. Essentially, proleptic instruction is individually tailored instruction. Although Palinscar reports teachers successfully using this technique in groups as large as eighteen, the feasibility of widespread adoption in regular classrooms as they exist today has been questioned. The problems would essentially be the same set of problems encountered in implementing an individualized program: limited time of the teacher to be a resource to each individual, keeping others students actively and meaningfully engaged while the teacher attends to an individual, and the difficulties involved in tracking separate student learning paths.

In addition to adjustments based on the labor-intensiveness of this form of instruction, adoption in classrooms of proleptic forms of instruction would also entail a reconceptualization of the role of the teacher. Many current teachers have adopted a role much more aligned with the direct instructional approach, that is, the teacher's responsibility is to (1) decide what is to be taught and (2) transmit that knowledge to students as effectively and efficiently as possible. Thus the teacher is in a very dominant, active role. By contrast, proleptic instruction places the teacher more in the role of a coach. In addition to modeling correct performance, the teacher must make decisions regarding the level of competence of each student. Then the teacher must provide supportive prompts and feedback to move the student to the next level of competence. The student, however, does most of the work; the teacher's job is to provide sensitive diagnosis, modeling, prompting, and feedback in order to move the student to higher and more independent levels of learning. The complexities involved in recasting teachers into the coaching role would require large-scale changes in teacher education programs.

In summary, the present data suggest several considerations that should underlie cognitive-strategies training with low-achieving students. First, poor learners need explicit instruction in how and when to apply cognitive strategies as well as how to monitor their use. When instruction stops at the level of simple instruction of what the strategies are, low-achieving students have difficulty applying them outside of the immediate training situation. Second, cognitive-strategy training has the best chance of being incorporated into the poor learner's repertoire if it is integrated with regular classroom instruction in the various subject matter domains. Although explicit teaching of cognitive strategies separate from academic content may have many positive benefits (teachers like it, it improves IQ scores), there is little evidence to suggest that it consistently helps students in their academic work. Additional investigations into the nature of expertise in various domains will be required in order to provide cognitive-strategies instruction that is meaningfully integrated with the knowledge-base components of various academic domains. Third, and last, current evidence suggests that the proleptic instructional approach as illustrated by reciprocal teaching seems to offer the surest bet that cognitive strategies will be acquired, used, and monitored with regularity by low-achieving students. More within-experiment comparisons of the different instructional methods need to be undertaken, however, before firm conclusions can be reached in this regard. In addition, parallel work in the area of teacher training would be required before proleptic instruction could be implemented on a widescale basis.

Promising Agendas for Continued Development of the Instructional Knowledge Base

The preceding information has summarized many firm findings upon which we can begin to build merged instructional programming for low-achieving students. In addition, nagging concerns regarding the present knowledge base have been discussed. In particular, the following three general concerns have been noted: (1) in direct instruction: a need to examine new forms that it might take in order to teach adequately higher-order cognitive skills; (2) in the process-product findings: the need to unpack generic variables in order to get at more fine-grained guides for practice; and (3) in cognitive strategies research: the need to address knowledge components of effective strategy use and the implementation requirements of various instructional approaches to strategy training.

A common feature shared by these three concerns is the need to address the content of instruction. In particular, the concerns highlight sparse attention to teaching and learning in semantically rich domains that correspond to the basic academic disciplines of reading, mathematics, writing, science, history, and so on. We know very little about how to teach and how students learn the kind of material that is (or should be) the mainstay of the academic curriculum.

Up to this point, the majority of instructional investigations have focused on the structural and delivery aspects of effection instruction. Much valuable information has been learned in these areas. For example, monitoring, feedback, and the effective use of time are important elements of effective teaching; similarly, small-group instruction arranged in hierarchical levels of difficulty and geared to the level of the child is conducive to increased student learning. Notably lacking, however, has been attention to the actual material being taught, that is, how teachers organize and deliver the content of academic lessons and how students come to understand that material. This latter information, it seems, would be an indispensable prerequisite (or at least a corequisite) to decisions regarding how to arrange the structural and delivery elements of teaching. This is not to belittle the importance of information on structural and delivery aspects of instruction. Rather, it is meant to point to the potential power of an instructional system that considers both *what* is taught and *how* it is taught.

These are not easy questions. At present, investigations into areas such as these are just beginning to take shape. This new genre of research on subject matter content is informed by several lines of work. For example, curriculum specialists are beginning to raise new concerns about the nature of subject matter competence, and cognitive psychologists have begun to focus on the identification of knowledge and skills associated with the acquisition of competence in specific content domains. The final section of our chapter highlights selected aspects of this research in three content areas: science, mathematics, and history.

Science. Research in the content area of science has been undertaken by cognitive psychologists, developmental psychologists, and researchers interested in the design of instruction. By and large, cognitive psychologists have focused their attention on the question of how students learn scientific information; instructional psychologists, on the other hand, have begun to wrestle with the practical problem of how the findings and insights derived from cognitive research on science learning can inform classroom practice.

Investigations into the acquisition of scientific knowledge have generally focused on two interrelated areas: the identification of the conceptions that uninstructed students possess regarding various scientific phenomena, and the characterization of "knowledge-building" skills of more versus less able students. Several studies have shown that uninstructed students have definite conceptions about various natural phenomena and that these conceptions are highly resistant to change. For example, "naive" subjects (ages eight to eleven) think that light from a candle goes further at night and that friction only occurs between moving surfaces (Stead and Osborne, 1980). It has been argued that the development of effective techniques to confront and modify such misconceptions must be a priority for future research (Erikson, 1983; Resnick, 1983).

More recently, the thrust of the work in this area has been aimed at the identification of how children learn the extensive information associated with the various science topics included in most school science curricula. A characteristic of this and all research in the content areas is the maintenance of a clear distinction between the memorization of scientific facts and the development of the kind of scientific understanding that allows students to answer questions about complex topics that require analysis, application, and integration. Emphasis is placed on the latter (i.e., the development of deep understanding of complex topics). For example, in a line of work being conducted by Chi and colleagues (e.g., Chi, Bassok, Lewis, Reimann, and Glaser, under review), careful attention is being devoted to the explication of the "knowledge-building" skills used by more versus less successful students when learning new science topics. Preliminary findings suggest that the knowledge-building skills used by successful students (1) assist them in going beyond the information that is presented to them, (2) help them to organize their knowledge in meaningful ways, and (3) give their knowledge conceptual power. Efforts are now underway to characterize the nature of the contents of the knowledge-building skills used by successful science students. The ultimate goal is to be able to instruct less able students in the use of these exemplary knowledge-building skills once they have been identified.

In the meantime, classroom application work is also being initiated. Instructional psychologists have begun training and implementation research programs, the goals of which include training science teachers to (1) analyze student understanding of science concepts, (2) analyze science instructional materials, and (3) modify existing instructional materials and procedures. For example, Gunstone, Champagne, and Klopfer (1981) have designed and tested innovative instructional strategies in physics that include qualitative analyses of problems and ideational confrontation. Research-based training programs such as these represent a link between the basic inquiries of cognitive psychologists and the real world of the classroom, thereby testing ideas in practice and providing continued suggestions from and for practicing teachers.

History.   Appreciation for the work undertaken in the area of history relies on the following awareness: Most history or social studies instruction delivered in our elementary and middle schools today is heavily influenced by commercial textbooks. Both the content that is covered and the instructional strategies used to present the content are deeply influenced (Shaver, Davis, and Helburn, 1979). Therefore, detailed analyses of existing textbooks is one method of increasing our understanding of the current state of history instruction. Such an investigation of intermediate-grade history textbooks by Beck, McKeown, and Gromoll (in preparation) has revealed a serious lack of explanatory elements including the significance, interrelatedness, and causal connectedness of historical events or facts. In other words, textbooks typically outline a series of events without stating the relationships between and among those events. For example, in a unit on the American Revolution, textbook authors might present a description of the Boston Tea Party, followed by a discussion of the passage of the Intolerable Acts, followed, in turn, by a discussion of the closing of the Port of Boston. Left unstated, however, are the highly explanatory causal connections between and among these three events—connections which, if understood, contribute to a deep understanding of the causes of the American Revolutionary War.

At a deeper level, the texts were also found lacking in their conveyance of "big concept" ideas (i.e., ideas not tied to concrete events or persons, but rather ideas that conceptually unite a movement or a historical period (e.g., the growing sense of U.S. identity of the thirteen colonies, the concept of self-government, etc.). These findings on the superficial level of treatment of historical topics by textbooks are just a first step, however. Needed are further inquiries into the nature of how students learn complex historical material and how teachers can assist them through the modification and supplementation of existing textbook materials and procedures. In addition, work is needed in the area of identifying key components of teacher explanations that lead to increased depth of student understanding.

Mathematics.   Mathematics has been one of the more intensively studied content areas. Math educators, developmental psychologists, and (more recently) cognitive scientists have provided new insights into the nature of mathematical knowledge and how it is acquired. By and large, there is considerable optimism surrounding the potential of this research to provide classroom teachers with a reasonable account of how various topics within the math curriculum are learned by students and how they can best be taught.

One branch of this research is focused on the nature of the intuitive mathematical knowledge and competencies of young, uninstructed children (Ginsburg, 1977; Resnick, 1987). A troubling question is why this informal knowledge does not seem to support formal math learning in school. A closely allied line of work looks at the actual and potential cognitive linkages between "various ways of knowing mathematics." Although various researchers use different labels for these different "ways of knowing math," most taxonomies include intuitive or naive knowledge, computational knowledge (knowledge of procedural rules), concrete knowledge (knowledge of how to manipulate objects to solve a problem), and principled knowledge (knowledge of the conceptual underpinnings of mathematics). Whereas some researchers have focused on how learners connect concrete experiences, procedural skill, and conceptual understanding (e.g., Resnick and Omanson, 1987), other investigators have chosen to focus on the potential role of classroom instruction in improving competency in each of these categories of knowledge or in strengthening the connections among them. For example, Lampert (1986) has described a set of instructional strategies for teaching multidigit multiplication to fourth graders which seems to promote the integration of students' knowledge of rote procedures, their intuitive understanding of how to operate on concrete quantities, and a deeper conceptual knowledge of the mathematical principles that legitimate the procedures. The lesson activities described (and taught) by Lampert were designed to give children practice in realms where various relevant math principles (e.g., place value, the distributive property of multiplication over addition) were transparent in the steps of the procedures used to arrive at an answer. For instance, Lampert used various grouping exercises with U.S. coins which capitalized on the parallels between the relative values of different kinds of coins and the way we use place value to compose numbers.

Similarly, Leinhardt has provided analyses of the teaching and learning of subtraction in the second grade (1987) and the teaching and learning of the equivalence of fractions in the fourth grade (1988a,b; Leinhardt and Smith, 1985). A primary focus of Leinhardt's work has been the detailed examination of what she considers to be a core feature of a math instructional episode: the explanation of new material and its logical connection to prior material. The aim of this work is the identification of key explanatory components that lead to increased student understanding. The research has been carried out by analyzing a series of math lessons by an expert teacher and by simultaneously monitoring the growth and structure of students' knowledge bases as the lessons progressed. What emerges from this detailed trace of instruction and student learning is a list of features to look for in an expert explanation of one particular topic within elementary mathematics.

SUMMARY AND CONCLUSIONS

In this chapter, we have attempted to place current instructional practice and research into the context of the changing educational responses to the needs of low-achieving students. Our review has traced these changing responses and has characterized them as passing from neglect, to segregated attention, to (attempted) integration. Seen through the lens of instruction, we have charted progression from an orientation marked exclusively by care and nurturance, to one of nonacademic skill training, to a present-day approach dominated by the teaching and learning of academic skills and facts through teacher-led, direct instruction. The advances have been great, yet much remains to be accomplished. Integration is still often nominal and much of the learning is still lower-order and often not easily transferred to new areas.

At the beginning of the chapter we stated that it is important to take stock of what we know about the education of low-achieving students and what we still need to know. From the perspective of instruction and learning, this chapter outlines several things that we do know about effective instruction for at-risk students: for example, teaching children directly the material we want them to learn pays off, and mixed-ability small-group learning promotes improved achievement. This chapter also points to gaps in our knowledge: for example, how is a specific piece of complex material taught and learned? How can we best foster mathematical problem solving? Although our coverage of the terrain has not been comprehensive, we hope that we have succeeded in highlighting what is known and what is not known or only beginning to be known.

We have also made suggestions for the direction of future work in this area. We hope that our overview of work being carried out under the broad umbrella of research in the content areas illustrates the potential of this line of work for informing the instruction of remedial students, as well as the complementary role that findings from such work can play to our existing knowledge regarding general effective teaching practices. Hopefully, the answers to questions asked by content researchers will provide a balance to the pedagogical answers that have been aggregating over the past twenty years.

In particular, we see research in the content areas as holding promise for low-achieving students in two realms: (1) the identification of the strategies used by more able students to learn subject matter and (2) the identification of the key components of effective teachers' lessons. The elucidation of methods by which successful students learn subject matter may provide detailed guidance on how best to instruct less able students. The identification of key components of exemplary lessons, on the other hand, may begin to provide a linkage between the organization and substance of teacher-presented material and the structure and content of student knowledge. In other words, we hope to learn about the nature of transmissions (i.e., how complex bodies of knowledge are transferred from teacher to student).

We see both of these advances as particularly timely for movement to the next stage of knowledge regarding effective instruction for low-achieving students. This is for two reasons. First, the teaching and learning of subject matter in remedial education has, by and large, been neglected. Although emphasis has recently been placed on the provision of instruction in the basics (i.e., reading and math), topics such as science and social studies have, for the most part, remained untouched. Second, in the past we have (at least implicitly) condoned the adoption of two different sets of goals for low-achieving and regular students. A goal of general education is to advance students to high levels of understanding of complex material. By contrast, the education of at-risk students has often aimed lower, that is, to the mastery of lower-level facts and routine procedures. This discrepancy in goals undoubtedly has multifaceted roots. A contributing factor, however, may be researchers' successful analyses of the learning requisites of facts and procedures, thereby facilitating the prescription of methods of teaching these skills effectively to low-achieving students. It is our hope that the new investigations into learning complex material will lead to a clearer understanding of the components of competent performance in higher-order domains and subsequently to prescribed methods of teaching those components to students who lack them.

This movement toward the study of the teaching and learning of higher-level topics within particular content domains, we believe, represents a potential breakthrough for the education of remedial students in particular. In the past, we have been too easily satisfied by (apparent) gains in learning which vanished once the props were removed or the unit had passed. As we learn more about how complex topics can be best taught and understood, we will expand our expectations to include the ability to analyze, apply, and integrate material in conceptually powerful ways. Similarly, we will demand instruction that helps students link new knowledge to what they already know and assists them in going beyond the material presented—to reason about the material in principled ways. This is a significant leap that places new and unfamiliar demands on both teachers and learners. Nevertheless, the decision to work toward these new levels of understanding represents the only choice if we truly subscribe to equal educational opportunity for all students. We have a new ally in our march toward equality: the beginnings of a new set of effective instructional features for low-achieving students. It is our belief that this new wave of content-relevant features holds the potential to promote increased depths of understanding of all levels of material by all students.

REFERENCES

Allington, R. L. (1980). Teaching reading in compensatory classes: A descriptive summary. *The Reading Teacher, 57,(8)*, 178–183.

Allington, R. L. (1983). *Designing effective compensatory reading instruction: A review.* New York: State University of New York at Albany.

Anderson, R. C.; Mason, J.; and Shirley, L. (1984). The reading group: An experimental investigation of a labyrinth. *Reading Research Quarterly, 20*, 6–38.

Arter, J. A., and Jenkins, J. R. (1979). Differential diagnosis-prescriptive teaching: A critical appraisal. *Review of Educational Research, 49*, 517–555.

Barnett, W. S. (1985). Benefit-cost analysis of the Perry Preschool Program and its policy implications. *Educational Evaluation and Policy Analysis, 7,(4)*, 333–342.

Beck, I. L.; McKeown, M. G.; and Gromoll, E. W. (in preparation). *Requirement for historical knowledge: Exposing the reasoning.*

Becker, W. C., and Gersten, R. (1982). A follow-up of Follow Through: The later effects of the direct instruction model on children in fifth and sixth grades. *American Educational Research Journal, 19,(1)*, 75–92.

Bereiter, C., and Kurland, M. (1981–82). A constructive look at Follow Through results. *Interchange, 12,(1)*, 1–21.

Berrueta-Clement, J. R.; Schweinhart, L. J.; Barnett, W. S.; Epstein, A. S.; and Weikart, D. P. (1984). *Changed lives: The effects of the Perry Preschool Program on youths through age 19.* Ypsilanti, MI: The High/Scope Press.

Borkowski, J. G., and Cavanaugh, J. (1979). Maintenance and generalization of skills and strategies by the retarded. In N. R. Ellis (Ed.), *Handbook of mental deficiency: Psychological theory and research.* Hillsdale, NJ: Erlbaum, pp. 190–220.

Borys, S. (1979).Factors influencing the interrogative strategies of mentally retarded and nonretarded students. *American Journal of Mental Deficiency, 84*, 280–288.

Bransford, J. D. (1979). *Human cognition: Learning, understanding, and remembering.* Belmont, CA: Wadsworth.

Bransford, J. D.; Arbitman-Smith, R.; Stein, B. S.; and Vye, N. J.(1985). Improving thinking and learning skills: An analysis of three approaches. In J. W. Segal, S. R. Chipman, and R. Glaser (Eds.), *Thinking and learning skills: Vol. 1. Relating instruction to research.* Hillsdale, NJ: Erlbaum, pp. 133–206.

Brophy, J. (1986). *Research linking teacher behavior to student achievement: Potential implications for Chapter 1 students.* East Lansing, MI: Institute for Research on Teaching, Michigan State University.

Brown, A. L. (1980). Knowing when, where, and how to remember: A problem of metacognition. In R. Glaser (Ed.), *Advances in instructional psychology,* vol. l. Hillsdale, NJ: Erlbaum, pp. 77–165.

Brown, A. L.; Bransford, J. D.; Ferrara, R. A.; and Campione, J. C. (1983). Learning, remembering, and understanding. In J. H. Flavell and E. M. Markman (Eds.), *Handbook of child psychology: Vol. 3. Cognitive development,* 4th ed. New York: Wiley, pp. 77–166.

Brown, A. L., and Palinscar, A. S. (1982). Inducing strategic learning from texts by means of informed, self-control training. *Topics in Learning and Learning Disabilities, 2,(1),* 1–17.

Campione, J., and Brown, A. (1977). Memory and metamemory development in educable retarded children. In R. Kail and J. Hagen (Eds.), *Perspectives in the development of memory and cognition.* Hillsdale, NJ: Erlbaum, pp. 367–406.

Campione, J. C.; Brown, A. L.; and Ferrara, R. A. (1982). Mental retardation and intelligence. In R. J. Sternberg (Ed.), *Handbook of human intelligence.* Cambridge, England: Cambridge University Press, pp. 392–490.

Carpenter, T. P.; Corbitt, M. K.; Kepner, H. S.; Lindquist, M. M.; and Rays, R. E. (1981). National assessment. In E. Fennema (Ed.), *Mathematics education research: Implications for the '80s.* Alexandria, VA: Association for Supervision and Curriculum Development, pp. 22–38.

Carter, L. F. (1984). The sustaining effects study of compensatory and elementary education. *Educational Researcher, 13,(7),* 4–13.

Chall, J. S. (1983). Literacy: Trends and explanations. *Educational Researcher, 13,(7),* 4–13.

Chi, M. T. H.; Bassok, M.; Lewis, M. W.; Reimann, P.; and Glaser, R. (under review). *Self-explanations: How students study and use examples in learning to solve problems.*

Cohen, E. G.; Intilli, J. K.; and Robbins, S. H. (1978). Teacher and reading specialists: Cooperation or isolation? *Reading Teacher, 32,* 281–287.

Coleman, J. S.; Campbell, E. A.; Hobson, C.; McPartland, J.; Mood, A.; Weinfeld, F.; and York, R. (1966). *Equality of educational opportunity.* Washington, DC: Government Printing Office.

Collins, A., and Stevens, A. L. (1982). Goals and strategies of inquiry teachers. In R. Glaser (Ed.), *Advances in instructional psychology,* vol. 2. Hillsdale, NJ: Erlbaum, pp. 65–119.

Cooley, W. W., and Leinhardt, G. (1980). The instructional dimensions study. *Educational Leadership, 2,(1),* 7–25.

Crawford, J. (1983). A study of instructional processes in Title I classes: 1981–82. *Journal of Research and Evaluation of the Oklahoma City Public Schools, 13.*

Cross, K. P. (1984). The rising tide of school reform reports. *Phi Delta Kappan, 65,* 167–172.

Dawson, M. M.; Hallahan, D. P.; Reeve, R. E.; and Ball, D. W. (1980). The effect of reinforcement and verbal rehearsal on selective attention in learning disabled children. *Journal of Abnormal Child Psychology, 8,* 133–144.

Dougherty, J. C., IV (1985). *Report on changes under Chapter 1 of the Education Consolidation and Improvement Act* (Serial No. 99-B). Washington, DC: U.S. Government Printing Office.

Doyle, W. (1983). Academic work. *Review of Educational Research, 53,* 159–200.

Duffy, G. G.; Roehler, L. R.; Vavrus, L. G.; Book, C. L.; Meloth, M. S.; Putnam, J.; and Wesselman, R. (1984, April). *A study of the relationship between direct teacher explanation of reading strategies and student awareness and achieve-*

ment outcomes. Presented at the annual meeting of the American Educational Research Association, New Orleans.

Education Consolidation and Improvement Act of 1981, P.L. 97–35, 95 Stat. 367 (August 31, 1981).

Epps, S., and Tindal, G. (1987). The effectiveness of differential programming in serving mildly handicapped students: Placement options and instructional programming. In M. C. Wang, M. C. Reynolds, and H. J. Walbert (Eds.), *Handbook of special education: Research and practice.* Oxford, England: Pergamon Press.

Erickson, G. (1983). Student frameworks and classroom instruction. In H. Helm and J. D. Novak (Eds.) *Proceedings on the international seminar on misconceptions in science & mathematics.* Ithaca, NY: Cornell University.

Feuerstein, R. (1979). *The dynamic assessment of retarded performers: The learning potential assessment device, theory, instruments, and techniques.* Baltimore, MD: University Park Press.

Feuerstein, R. (1980). *Instrumental enrichment: An intervention program for cognitive modifiability.* Baltimore, MD: University Park Press.

Fisher, C. W.; Filby, N.; Marliave, R.; Cahen, L. S.; Dishaw, M.; Moore, J.; and Berliner, D. (1978). *Teaching behaviors, academic learning time, and student achievement: Final report of Phase III-B, Beginning teacher evaluation study* (Tech. Rep. No. U-1). San Francisco: Far West Laboratory for Educational Research and Development.

Flavell, J. H. (1985). *Cognitive development.* Englewood Cliffs, NJ: Prentice-Hall.

Fullan, M., and Pomfret, A. (1977). Research on curriculum and instruction implementation. *Review of Educational Research, 47,(1),* 335–397.

Gage, N. L. (1978). *The scientific basis of the art of teaching.* New York: Teachers College Press, Columbia University.

Gersten, R. (1984). Follow Through revisited: Reflections on the site variability issue. *Educational Evaluation and Policy Analysis, 6,(4),* 411–423.

Gersten, R.; Carnine, D.; and White, W. A. T. (1984). The pursuit of clarity: Direct instruction and applied behavior analysis. In W. L. Heward, T. E. Heron, D. S. Hill, and J. Trap-Porter (Eds.), *Behavior analysis in education.* Columbus, OH: Charles E. Merrill Publishing Co., pp. 38–57.

Gersten, R.; Carnine, D.; Zoref, L.; and Cronin, D. (1986). A multifaceted study of change in seven inner-city schools. *The Elementary School Journal, 86,(3),* 1–20.

Ginsberg, H. P. (1977). *Children's arithmetic: The learning process.* New York: Van Nostrand Reinhold.

Golinkoff, R. (1976). A comparison of reading comprehension in good and poor comprehenders. *Reading Research Quarterly, 11,* 623–659.

Griswold, P.; Cotton, K.; and Hansen, J. (1985). *Effective compensatory education sourcebook, Volumes I and II.* Washington, DC: U.S. Department of Education.

Gunstone, R. F.; Champagne, A. B.; and Klopfer, L. E. (1981). Instruction for understanding: A case study. *Australian Science Teachers Journal, 27,(3),* 27–32.

Haney, W. (1977). *The follow-through planned variation experiments,* vol. 5. Cambridge, MA: The Huron Institute.

Heller, K. A.; Holtzman, W. H.; and Messick, S. (Eds.). (1982). *Placing children in special education: A strategy for equity.* Washington, DC: National Academy of Sciences Press.

Hobbs, N. (Ed.). (1975). *The future of children.* San Francisco: Jossey-Bass.

Human Services Authorization Act of 1984, P.L. 98–558, 98 Stat. 28–78 (October 30, 1984).

Jenkins, J. R., and Pany, D. (1978). Standardized achievement tests: How useful for special education? *Exceptional Children, 44,* 448–453.

Karweit, N. (1976). A reanalysis of the effect of quantity of schooling on achievement. *Sociology of Education, 49,* 236–246.

Karweit, N. (1977). The organization of time in schools: Time scales and learning. Unpublished manuscript, Johns Hopkins University, Center for Social Organization of Schools, Baltimore.

Kurtz, B. E., and Borkowski, J. C. (1985, March). *Metacognition and the development of strategic skills in impulsive and reflective children.* Paper presented at the meeting of the Society for Research on Child Development, Toronto, Canada.

Lampert, M. (1986). Knowing, doing, and teaching multiplication. *Cognition and Instruction, 3,(4),* 305–342.

Lazar, I., and Darlington, R. (1982). Lasting effects of early education: A report from the Consortium for Longitudinal Studies. *Monographs of the Society for Research in Child Development,* 47 (Serial No. 195).

Lazerson, M. (1983). The origins of special education. In J. G. Chambers and W. J. Hartman (Eds.), *Special education policies.* Philadelphia: Temple University Press, pp. 15–47.

Leinhardt, G. (1976). Observation as a tool for evaluation of implementation. *Instructional Science, 5,* 343–364.

Leinhardt, G. (1977). Program evaluation: An empirical study of individualized instruction. *American Educational Research Journal, 14,(3),* 277–293.

Leinhardt, G. (1980). Modeling and measuring educational treatment in evaluation. *Review of Educational Research, 50,(3),* 393–420.

Leinhardt, G. (1985). Instructional time: A winged chariot? In C. S. Fisher and D. C. Berliner (Eds.), *Perspectives on instructional time.* New York: Longman, pp. 263–282.

Leinhardt, G. (1987). The development of an expert explanation: An analysis of a sequence of subtraction lessons. *Cognition and Instruction, 4,(4),* 225–282.

Leinhardt, G. (1988a). Expertise in instructional lessons: An example from fractions. In D. A. Grouws and R. J. Cooney (Eds.), *Perspectives on research on effective mathematics teaching.* Hillsdale, NJ: Erlbaum, pp. 47–66.

Leinhardt, G. (1988b). Getting to know: Tracing students' mathematical knowledge from intuition to competence. *Educational Psychologist, 23,(2),* 119–144.

Leinhardt, G.; Bickel, W.; and Pallay, A. (1982). Unlabeled but still entitled: Toward more effective remediation. *Teachers College Record, 84,(2),* 391–422.

Leinhardt, G., and Pallay, A. (1982). Restrictive educational settings: Exile or haven? *Review of Educational Research, 52,(4),* 557–578.

Leinhardt, G., and Seewald, A. M. (1981). Overlap: What's tested, what's taught? *Journal of Education Measurement, 18,(3),* 171–177.

Leinhardt, G., and Smith, D. (1985). Expertise in mathematics instruction: Subject matter knowledge. *Journal of Educational Psychology, 77,(3),* 247–271.

Leinhardt, G.; Zigmond, N.; and Cooley, W. (1981). Reading instruction and its effects. *American Educational Research Journal, 18,(3),* 343–361.

LeMahieu, P., and Leinhardt, G. (1985). Overlap: Influencing what's taught. A process model of teachers' content selection. *Journal of Classroom Interaction, 21, (1),* 2–11.

Levin, J. R., and Pressley, M. (1981). Improving children's prose comprehension: Selected strategies that seem to succeed. In C. M. Santa and B. L. Hayes (Eds.), *Children's prose comprehension: Research and practice.* Newark, DE: International Reading Association, pp. 44–71.

Lipman, M.; Sharp, A. M.; and Oscanyan, F. S. (1980). *Philosophy in the classroom.* Philadelphia, PA: Temple University Press.

Lloyd, J. W. (1988). Direct academic interventions in learning disabilities. In M. C. Wang, M. C. Reynolds, and H. J. Walberg (Eds.), *Handbook of special education: Research and practices.* Oxford, England: Pergamon Press.

MacMillan, D. L.; Keogh, B. K.; and Jones, R. L. (1986). Special education research on mildly handicapped learners. In M. C. Wittrock (Ed.), *Handbook of research on teaching.* New York: Macmillan, pp. 686–724.

Madden, N. A., and Slavin, R. E. (1983). Mainstreaming students with mild handicaps: Academic and social outcomes. *Review of Educational Research, 53,(4),* 519–569.

McKey, R. H.; Condelli, L.; Ganson, H.; Barrett, B.; McConkey, C.; and Plantz, M. (1985). *The impact of Head Start on children, families and communities* (A final report of the Head Start Evaluation, Synthesis and Utilization Project). Washington, DC: CSR.

Miller, G. E. (1985). The effects of general and specific self-instruction training on children's comprehension monitoring preformances during reading. *Reading Research Quarterly, 20,* 616–628.

Nickerson, R. S. (1984). *Teaching thinking: What is being done and with what results?* Cambridge, MA: Bolt, Beranck and Newman.

Norman, C. A., Jr., and Zigmond, N. (1980). Characteristics of children labeled and served as learning disabled in school systems affiliated with child service demonstration centers. *Journal of Learning Disabilities, 13,(10),* 542–547.

Palinscar, A. S. (1985, April). *The unpacking of a multi-component, metacognitive training package.* Paper presented at the annual meeting of the American Educational Research Association, Chicago.

Palinscar, A. S., and Brown, A. L. (1984). Reciprocal teaching of comprehension fostering and comprehension monitoring activities. *Cognition and Instruction, 1,(2),* 117–175.

Paris, S.; Cross, D.; DeBritto, A.; Jacobs, J.; Oka, E.; Saarnio, D. (1984, April). *Improving children's metacognition and reading comprehension with classroom instruction.* Paper presented at the annual meeting of the American Educational Research Association, New Orleans, LA.

Peterson, P. L. (1986, June). *Selecting students and services for compensatory education: Lessons from aptitude-treatment interaction research.* Paper prepared for the Conference on Effects of Alternative Designs in Compensatory Education, Washington, DC.

Peterson, P. L., and Swing, S. R. (1982). Beyond time on task: Students' reports of their thought processes during classroom instruction. *Elementary School Journal, 82,* 481–491.

Peterson, P. L., and Swing, S. R. (1983). Problems in classroom implementation of cognitive strategy instruction. In M. Pressely and J. R. Levin (Eds.), *Cognitive strategies research: Educational applications.* New York: Springer-Verlag, pp. 267–286.

Peterson, P. L.; Swing, S. R.; Braverman, M. T.; and Buss, R. (1982). Students' aptitudes and their reports of cognitive processes during direct instruction. *Journal of Educational Psychology, 74,* 535–547.

Peterson, P. L.; Swing, S. R.; Stark, K. D.; and Waas, G. A. (1984). Students' cognitions and time on task during mathematics instruction. *American Educational Research Journal, 21,* 487–515.

Polloway, E. A. (1984). The integration of mildly retarded students in the schools: A historical review. *Remedial and Special Education, 5,(4),* 18–28.

Pressley, M.; Borkowski, J. G.; and Schneider, W. (in press). Cognitive strategies: Good strategy users coordinate metacognition and knowledge. In R. Vasta and G. Whitehurst (Eds.), *Annals of child development,* vol. 4. Greenwich, CT: JAI Press.

Pressley, M.; Snyder, B. L.; and Cariglia-Bull, T. (in press). How can good strategy use be taught to children?: Evaluation of six alternative approaches. In S. Cormier and J. Hagman (Eds.), *Transfer of learning: Contemporary research and applications.* Orlando, FL: Academic Press.

Resnick, L. B. (1983). Mathematics and science learning: A new conception. *Science, 220,* 477–478.

Resnick, L. B. (1987). The development of mathematical intuition. In M. Perlmutter (Ed.), *Perspectives on intellectual development: The Minnesota Symposia on Child Psychology,* vol. 19. Hillsdale, NJ: Erlbaum, pp. 159–194.

Resnick, L. B., and Omanson, S. F. (1987). Learning to understand arithmetic. In R. Glaser (Ed.), *Advances in instructional psychology,* vol. 3. Hillsdale, NJ: Erlbaum, pp. 41–95.

Reynolds, M. C., and Lakin, K. C. (1987). Noncategorical special education: Models for research and practice. In M. C. Wang, M. C. Reynolds, and H. J. Walberg (Eds.), *Handbook of special education: Research and practice.* Oxford, England: Pergamon Press.

Reynolds, M. C., and Wang, M. C. (1981, September). *Restructuring "special" school programs: A position paper.* Paper presented at the national invitational Conference on Public Policy and the Special Education Task of the 1980s. Wingspread Conference Center, Racine, WI.

Richmond, J. B.; Stipek, D. J.; and Zigler, E. (1979). A decade of Head Start. In E. Zigler and J. Valentine (Eds.), *Project Head Start: A legacy of the war on poverty.* New York: The Free Press, pp. 135–152.

Roehler, L. R.; Duffy, G. G.; Putnam, J.; Wesselman, R.; Sivan, E.; Rackliffe, G.; Book, C.; Meloth, M.; and Vavrus, L. (1986, March). *The effect of direct explanation of reading strategies on low group third graders' awareness and achievement: A technical report of the 1984-85 study.* Tech Rep. East Lansing, MI: Institute for Research on Teaching, Michigan State University.

Rosenshine, B. V. (1978, March). *Academic engaged minutes, content covered and direct instruction.* Paper presented at the annual meeting of the American Educational Research Association, Toronto, Canada.

Rosenshine, B. V. (1983). Teaching functions in instructional programs. *Elementary School Journal, 83,* 335–351.

Ryan, E. B. (1981). Identifying and remediating failures in reading comprehension: Toward an instructional approach for poor comprehenders. In T. G. Waller and G. E. MacKinnon (Eds.), *Advances in reading research*, vol. 2. New York: Academic Press, pp. 223–261.

Schumaker, J.; Deshler, D.; Alley, G.; Warner, M.; and Denton, P. (1984). Multipass: A learning strategy for improving reading comprehension. *Learning Disability Quarterly, 5*, 295–304.

Schweinhart, L. J., and Weikart, D. P. (1980). *Young children grow up: The effects of the Perry Preschool Program on youths through age 15*. Ypsilanti, MI: The High/Scope Press.

Schweinhart, L. J., and Weikart, D. P. (1985). Evidence that good early childhood programs work. *Phi Delta Kappan, 66,(8)*, 545–548.

Shavelson, R. J., and Stern, P. (1981). Research on teachers' pedagogical thoughts, judgements, decisions, and behavior. *Review of Educational Research, 51*, 455–498.

Shaver, J. P.; Davis, O. L.; and Helburn, S. M. (1979). An interpretive report on the status of precollege social studies education based on three NSF-funded studies. What are the needs in Precollege Science Mathematics and Social Science Education? Views from the Field (Document No. SE 80-9). Program integration, Directorate for Science Education.

Sheehan, R., and Keogh, B. K. (1984). Approaches to evaluation in special education. In B. K. Keogh (Ed.), *Advances in special education*, vol. 4. Greenwich, CT: JAI Press, pp. 1–20.

Shulman, L. S. (1986). Paradigms and research programs in the study of teaching: A contemporary perspective. In M. C. Wittrock (Ed.), *Handbook of research on teaching*. New York: Macmillan, pp. 3–36.

Shulman, L. S. (1987). The wisdom of practice: Managing complexity in medicine and teaching. In D. C. Berliner and B. V. Rosenshine (Eds.), *Talks to teachers: A Festschrift for N. L. Gage*. New York: Random House.

Slavin, R. E. (1987). Grouping for instruction in elementary school. *Educational Psychologist, 22*, 109–127.

Spilich, G. J.; Vesonder, G. T.; Chiesi, H. L.; and Voss, J. F. (1979). Text processing of domain-related information for individuals with high and low domain knowledge. *Journal of Verbal Learning and Verbal Behavior, 18*, 275–290.

Stanley, S. O., and Greenwood, C. R. (1983). How much "opportunity to respond" does the minority disadvantaged student receive in school? *Exceptional Children, 49,(4)*, 370–373.

Stead, B. F., and Osborne, R. J. (1980). Exploring science students' concepts of light. *Australian Science Teachers Journal, 26*, 84–90.

Stebbins, L. B.; St. Pierre, R. G.; Proper, E. G.; Anderson, R. B.; and Cerva, T. R. (1977). *Education as experimentation: A planned variation model. An evaluation of follow through* (Vol. IV-A, Rep. No. 76-196 A). Cambridge, MA: Abt Associates.

Sternberg, R. J. (1985). *Beyond IQ: A triarchic theory of human intelligence*. Cambridge, England: Cambridge University Press.

Tarver, S. G.; Hallahan, D. P.; and Kaufmann, J. M. (1976). Verbal rehearsal and selection attention in children with learning disabilities: A developmental lag. *Journal of Experimental Child Psychology, 22*, 375–385.

Thurlow, M. L.; Graden, J.; Greener, J. W.; and Ysseldyke, J. E. (1982). *Academic responding time for LD and non-LD students* (Research Report No. 72). Minneapolis, MN: University of Minnesota, Institute for Research on Learning Disabilities.

Thurlow, M. L.; Ysseldyke, J. E.; Graden, J.; Greener, J. W.; and Mecklenberg, C. (1982). *Academic responding time for LD students receiving different levels of special education services* (Research Rep. No. 78). Minneapolis, MN: University of Minnesota, Institute for Research on Learning Disabilities.

Torgeson, J. K. (1977). Memorization processes in reading-disabled children. *Journal of Educational Psychology, 69*, 571–578.

Vygotsky, L. S. (1978). *Mind in society: The development of higher psychological processes.* Cambridge, MA: Harvard University Press.

Weinstein, R. S. (1976). Reading group membership in first grade: Teacher behaviors and pupil experience over time. *Journal of Educational Psychology, 68*, 103–116.

White, K., and Castro, G. (1985). An integrative review of early intervention efficacy studies with at-risk children: Implications for the handicapped. *Analysis and Intervention in Developmental Disabilities, 5*, 7–31.

Wiley, D. E., and Harnischfeger, A. (1974). Explosion of a myth: Quantity of schooling and exposure to instruction, major educational vehicles. *Educational Researcher, 3,(4)*, 7–12.

Wittrock, M. C. (1966). The learning by discovery hypothesis. In L. S. Shulman and E. R. Keislar (Eds.), *Learning by discovery: A critical appraisal.* Chicago: Rand McNally, pp. 33–75.

Wolff, M., and Stein, A. (1966). *Study I: Six months later, a comparison of children who had Head Start, summer 1965 with their classmates in kindergarten.* Washington, DC: Research & Evaluation Office, OEO (EDO 15026).

Wong, B., and Jones, W. (1982). Increasing metacomprehension in L.D. and normally achieving students through self-questional training. *Learning Disability Quarterly, 5*, 228–238.

Ysseldyke, J. E., and Algozzine, B. (1983). LD or not LD: That's not the question. *Journal of Learning Disabilities, 16*, 29–31.

Ysseldyke, J. E.; Thurlow, M. L.; Mecklenberg, C.; Graden, J.; and Algozzine, B. (1984). Changes in academic engaged time as a function of assessment and special education intervention. *Special Services in the Schools, 1*, 31–44.

Zigler, E., and Anderson, K. (1979). An idea whose time had come: The intellectual and political climate. In E. Zigler and J. Valentine (Eds.), *Project Head Start: A legacy of the war on poverty.* New York: The Free Press, pp. 3–19.

7

THE QUALITY OF CHAPTER 1 INSTRUCTION: RESULTS FROM A STUDY OF TWENTY-FOUR SCHOOLS*

Brian Rowan

Michigan State University

Larry F. Guthrie

Far West Laboratory for Educational
Research and Development

Chapter 1 of the Education Consolidation and Improvement Act (ECIA) is the nation's largest federal education program, providing over $3 billion of aid to local school districts for support of compensatory education programs. Designed to increase educational opportunities and outcomes in school districts serving high proportions of low-income students, the Chapter 1 program signals the nation's commitment to improving education for disadvantaged students. Unfortunately, after two decades of continuous operation, evaluation research demonstrates that the program results in discouragingly small achievement gains for participating students.

In 1983, Congress mandated that a National Assessment of Chapter 1 be conducted in order to consider the current operations of the program and its prospects for its improvement. The Office of Educational Research and Improvement (OERI) of the United States Department of Education con-

* Work on this paper was supported by the Office of Educational Research and Improvement, Department of Education, under Contract No. 400-85-1015 to the Far West Laboratory for Educational Research and Development, San Francisco, California. The contents of this paper do not necessarily reflect the position or policies of the Department of Education. The authors thank Richard Allington, Lorin Anderson, Steve Bossert, Annegret Harnischfeger, Ginny Lee, and Jane Stallings for directing research at the various sites in this study.

ducted this National Assessment and is releasing three reports to Congress (Kennedy, Jung, and Orland, 1986; Kennedy, Birman, and Demaline, 1987; OERI, in press). These reports, based on secondary analyses of existing data as well as the results of original research, give a comprehensive overview of program operations at multiple levels of the educational system. They also provide educators and policymakers with an unprecedented opportunity to reassess and improve upon current methods of delivering compensatory education to disadvantaged students.

This chapter reports the results of a field study undertaken as part of the National Assessment. Among the original research studies sponsored by this initiative, the study discussed here was the only one that investigated the operations of the Chapter 1 program at the point of service delivery, in the schools and classrooms where participating students received the instructional services purchased by Chapter 1 funds. A major purpose of the research was to assess the "size, scope, and quality" of local Chapter 1 instruction and to consider strategies for improving the program's capacity to "meet the special educational needs of the children being served" (see Section 556 (b) (3) of Chapter 1, ECIA).

The study focused on three issues. First, it gathered descriptive data on the characteristics of Chapter 1 instruction and compared these to the features of an effective instructional program as found in previous research. The purpose was to provide information on the quality of Chapter 1 instruction in local schools. Second, the study investigated whether variations in instructional quality could be accounted for by local design decisions, particularly decisions about the implementation of different models of service delivery (e.g., pullout, in-class, replacement, or add-on models). Finally, the study analyzed the extent and nature of coordination between Chapter 1 and regular instructional programs. The overall purpose of the study was to gather descriptive data on the design and operations of the program at the point of service delivery and to formulate strategies for improving Chapter 1 instruction.

DATA AND SAMPLE

The study was conducted in six states in diverse geographic regions of the country. Twenty-four schools were selected using a purposive sampling plan that took into account the following facts: (1) since approximately 90 percent of the school districts in the United States receive Chapter 1 funds (Kennedy, Jung, and Orland, 1986), the sample was chosen to include schools in large and small districts in urban, suburban, and rural communities; (2) since districts are more likely to provide Chapter 1 services in elementary than in secondary schools (Advanced Technology, 1983), the sample included more elementary than secondary schools; and (3) since

Chapter 1 regulations permit schools to use a variety of service delivery models (e.g., pullout, in-class, replacement, add-on), the sample was chosen to include schools implementing the full range of service delivery models.

The final sample included seventeen elementary schools, three intermediate schools, and four high schools. Fifteen schools were located in urban areas, four in suburban areas, and five in rural areas. District enrollments varied from a high of over 430,000 students to a low of approximately 900 students. Most of the schools offered Chapter 1 instruction in both reading and math, although this was more true of the elementary than the secondary schools in the sample. Moreover, most of the schools used more than one service delivery model to deliver Chapter 1 instruction (e.g., pullout was used in math, in-class for reading).

At each school in the sample, teams of three to four researchers spent a month conducting interviews with school staff and observing the instruction received by students. During the course of the study over 2,000 hours of academic instruction were observed, and interviews were conducted with over 400 teachers, administrators, and students. These procedures yielded descriptive data on patterns of Chapter 1 service delivery in schools (e.g., the delivery models in use, service schedules, and staffing patterns) and data on the characteristics of the instruction received by Chapter 1 students.

The major task of the study was the observation of students' instruction over the course of an entire school day. Only students who participated in the Chapter 1 program were observed. At each school, eight students were observed for an entire school day, and two students were observed for an entire school week. During these observations, researchers used a coding scheme that recorded the amount of time students spent receiving instruction in various subjects, the instructional formats that students engaged in during lessons, the sizes of the instructional groups in which students participated, and the instructors from whom students received instruction. Observers also kept a running narrative record that focused on the materials being used for instruction, the nature and skill levels of instructional tasks on which students worked, the nature of verbal interactions between teachers and students, and the engagement and success rates of students during instruction. Thus both quantitative and qualitative data on students' instructional experiences were collected over the course of a school day (or week).

In addition to observations of Chapter 1 students, interviews were conducted at each school with classroom teachers, school administrators, and Chapter 1 staff (resource teachers, aides, and coordinators). The data from these interviews were used to assemble descriptions of the service delivery model(s) in use at a school, the scheduled frequency of Chapter 1 and other special instructional services, and a number of other topics not germane to this chapter but discussed in the final report of the research project (Rowan, Guthrie, Lee, and Guthrie, 1986).

The resulting data set reflected the multilevel concerns of the research project. Interview data provided information on the design characteristics of Chapter 1 projects in the seventeen elementary and seven secondary schools included in the study. And within these schools, student observations provided information on the characteristics of instruction received by Chapter 1 students. In the final analysis, the study obtained data on 241 Chapter 1 students (166 in grades 2 and 4; 75 in grades 8 and 10) and observed a total of 2,062 hours of academic instruction (1,357 hours in grades 2 and 4; 705 hours in grades 8 and 10).

RESEARCH AND POLICY ISSUES ADDRESSED BY THE DATA

The data were used to provide information on a number of questions about the design and implementation of Chapter 1 instructional programs in local settings. This section reviews these questions and shows how they are related to a number of research and policy issues in the area of compensatory education.

Quality of Instruction in Chapter 1 Projects

The National Assessment of Chapter 1 was designed to gather information on the quality of instruction received by compensatory education students. In order to meet this goal, this study needed to develop an approach to gathering data that differed from much past evaluation research, particularly the large-scale outcomes studies that often have been used to evaluate the effectiveness of the Title I and Chapter 1 programs. These studies often take a macro approach to the evaluation of federal education programs. Researchers assume that all students who participate in a federal program receive comparable instructional treatments and thus that evaluations of program effectiveness can be accomplished by inspecting highly aggregated data on instructional outcomes. A number of observers have noted the shortcomings of this approach. A problem is that the instructional "treatments" received by compensatory education students vary markedly from school to school, contrary to the assumptions of the macro approach to evaluation (Averch, Carroll, Donaldson, Kiesling, and Pincus, 1972; Wiley, 1979; Carter, 1984).

Mindful of this criticism, researchers have begun to advocate a micro approach to the evaluation of federal education programs. In this approach, the school-to-school variation in instructional programs is recognized and described in detail. This study follows this tradition of evaluation research. Data were collected on the characteristics of instruction provided to Chapter 1 students at schools in the sample, and these data were compared to the features of an effective instructional program identified by past educational research. The major purpose of the analysis was to examine the processes within schools that lead to instructional outcomes and to describe the extent of variation in quality of instruction in a variety of local settings.

The definition of *quality* instruction used in this study was derived from past research on teaching and instruction. On the basis of this literature, the following variables were identified as components of an effective instructional program:

Time. Educational research has shown a consistent relationship between the amount of time students spend on academic tasks and their subsequent performance on achievement tests (Walberg and Frederick, 1983). The relationship of time to student achievement is greater in studies that measured engaged time rather than allocated time. Engaged time is that fraction of allocated time that students spend actively working on academic tasks (Fisher, Berliner, Filby, Marliave, Cahen, and Dishaw, 1980). The present study recorded the amount of time students in the sample spent in instruction in various subjects in both the regular and Chapter 1 programs. In addition, qualitative data on student engagement and success were gathered. These data were used to assess the extent to which Chapter 1 instruction contributed to students' academic learning time.

Class Size. Past research also indicates that student achievement is increased when learning activities take place in smaller groups (Cahen, Filby, McCutcheon, and Kyle, 1983). For example, a meta-analysis of studies of class size by Glass, Cahen, Smith, and Filby (1982) presented a curve that traced the effects on learning of reductions in group size. This curve suggested that reductions in class size had minimal effects until instructional groups reached a size of about ten students. Below this number, reductions in class size tended to have larger effects. This same meta-analysis also suggested that reductions in class size had larger effects when the reduction occurred for longer periods of time. For example, Glass and associates (1982) arbitrarily divided studies into those that reduced group size for more or less than 100 hours and found that reductions lasting longer than 100 hours had larger effects than those lasting less than 100 hours. The present study recorded the sizes of the instructional groups in which students in the sample participated, both in the Chapter 1 program and in the regular program. These data were then used to examine whether changes in student grouping arrangements could be expected to contribute to increased achievement of Chapter 1 students.

Instructional Formats. A third component of instructional quality consists of the formats used by teachers during lessons. A great deal of research has searched for instructional formats that result in effective instruction for low-income, low-achieving students (for a review, see Brophy and Good, 1986). In the 1970s, researchers held out high hopes for individualized instructional formats, but the Instructional Dimensions Study (Cooley and Leinhardt, 1980), sponsored by the National Institute of Education (NIE) during its last evaluation of compensatory education (NIE, 1976), provided little support for the effectiveness of this approach, at least as measured in the study. Alternatively, much more empirical support has been found for an approach that has come to be known as "direct instruction" (Brophy and Evertson, 1974; Good, 1978; Stallings and Kaskowitz, 1974; for a review, see Rosenshine, 1983). In this approach, teachers actively present lessons and provide students with guided practice in new academic skills. This approach contrasts sharply with the frequent use of independent seatwork as an instructional format, a feature common to many individualized programs. Although good instruction always includes some independent practice, and this kind of practice usually occurs during seatwork, recent research suggests that an overreliance on seatwork, especially its use to present new skills, is less effective than more "direct" instructional formats (Anderson, Brubaker, Alleman-Brooks, and Duffy, 1985; Brophy and Good, 1986). On the basis of these findings, the present study recorded the amount of time students spent in independent seatwork as opposed to more "direct" instructional formats such as lecture/recitation activities.

Curriculum Content.   Discussions of instructional quality must consider not only how students are taught, but also what they are taught (Carter, 1984; Cooley and Leinhardt, 1980). Increasingly, thoughtful observers are beginning to question the curriculum content of compensatory education programs (Botel, 1978; Allington, Steutzel, Shake, and Lamarche, 1986). Past research suggests that compensatory students spend much time working on "lower-order" academic skills. For example, students practice phonics skills but do little reading of connected text, or students practice basic arithmetic skills but do not apply these skills in problem-solving situations. Recent research also suggests that the "direct" instruction formats that many educational researchers advocate for use with low-income, low-achieving students may be of limited utility for instruction in higher-order thinking skills (Peterson, 1986). As a result of this debate, this study recorded the skills to which students in the sample were exposed, both in the Chapter 1 program and the regular program, and the study assessed the extent to which Chapter 1 instruction was focused on low-level basic skills, such as phonics drills and arithmetic facts, or whether Chapter 1 students had an opportunity to engage in higher-order skills, such as the reading of connected text and the completion of problem-solving exercises.

The Design and Implementation of Instructional Services

The study was not simply interested in charting the characteristics of Chapter 1 and regular instruction in a diverse sample of schools. An additional purpose was to assess the extent to which instructional quality varied as a result of the Chapter 1 service delivery model used by schools. In particular, the study sought to describe the types of project designs used in schools and to assess the effects of these designs on the scope and quality of instruction received by Chapter 1 students.

Questions about local design practices often focus on a specific issue: the relative merits of implementing pullout versus alternative models of service delivery. Early research on this question found that almost all Title I projects used pullout models (Glass and Smith, 1977), but later research discovered a slight trend away from this tendency, with school districts increasingly replacing pullouts with alternative designs involving in-class and replacement designs (Advanced Technology, 1983). This study was particularly interested in whether the implementation of these different service delivery models had consequences for the scope and quality of instruction received by Chapter 1 students, since it was felt that evidence on this point could help policymakers and practitioners better understand the instructional consequences of local choices about service delivery models.

Much early research suggested that the use of pullout models was detrimental to instruction. Glass and Smith (1977, p. 5), for example, argued that "research does not support the wisdom of instruction under conditions like those that prevail in pullout programs." Kimbrough and Hill (1981) expanded on this critique when they argued that pullouts disrupted ongoing lessons in regular classrooms and caused students to miss some portion of their regular instruction. Other research suggested that the implementation of pullout designs can result in a lack of coordination between compensatory and regular instructional programs and that this can adversely affect student success in regular classroom lessons (Johnston, Allington, and Afflerbach, 1985).

Other researchers have developed a more balanced analysis of service delivery models. Archambault (1986), for example, reviewed a number of studies of the effects of pullout models on instruction and found that study results were inconsistent. He concluded that choice of a particular delivery model was less important to the quality and effectiveness of Chapter 1 instruction than a number of other factors, including curricular, staffing, grouping, and teaching practices. Archambault's work suggests a broader view of project design that includes a number of factors in addition to the particular service delivery model being implemented locally.

Past evaluations of compensatory education suggest further considerations about local design practices. Carter (1984) noted that project designs in compensatory education are characterized by few uniformities. In part, this variability in design is due to the weak constraints placed on schools in federal education laws and policies. As Gaffney (1986) discussed, Chapter 1 legislation and federal education statutes give local school systems wide latitude in the design of local Chapter 1 projects. In addition to allowing schools to implement a number of different service delivery models (e.g., pullout, in-class, replacement, add-on), federal statutes prohibit the federal government from exercising any direct supervision or control over the curriculum, program of instruction, administration, or personnel of any school system (Gaffney, 1986). Given these circumstances, it would not be surprising to find that schools operating the same nominal service delivery model have few other instructional design features in common.

Given the lack of restrictive guidelines about local project design, there is a need to investigate the extent to which schools uniformly implement various service delivery models and to examine service delivery models in the context of other instructional design features. Accordingly, the sample for this study included schools that used a variety of service delivery models, but these models were nested within sites that also contained a variety of other design features, including a variety of curriculum, staffing, scheduling, and management practices. This sampling strategy allowed an investigation of the extent to which projects using the same nominal service delivery model (e.g., pullout) were similar in other design features. It also allowed an analysis of the extent to which overall project design features affected the scope and quality of instruction received by Chapter 1 students. The purpose was to provide practitioners and policymakers with a better understanding of the instructional implications of design choices.

Chapter 1 and the Regular Instructional Program

A final set of questions concerned the relationship between Chapter 1 and regular instruction. Obviously, student achievement ultimately results from the combination of instruction in both of these programs, and most educators view compensatory education as a supplement to a student's regular program of instruction. Thus an important topic of concern in this study was how Chapter 1 instruction fit within a student's overall instructional program.

The last major evaluation of compensatory education (NIE, 1976) contained a number of findings relevant to this issue. A basic picture that emerged from this evaluation was that Title I instruction often substituted for, rather than added to, students' regular instructional programs. For example, the NIE (1976) study found that the average compensatory education student spent between 4 and 5½ hours a week in compensatory instruction, almost always after having been "pulled out" of the regular classroom during which time about 40 percent of participating students missed instruction in a variety of regular classroom subjects.

Policy analysts have discussed these findings in conjunction with criticisms of current program practices. For example, Brown (1982) and Walberg (1984) argued that compensatory education programs are not truly compensatory because they rarely add more instructional time to a student's instructional day. Almost all projects offer instruction during the regular school calendar and participating students often miss some portion of regular classroom instruction. A closely related criticism was offered by Kimbrough and Hill (1981), who argued that the widespread use of pullout models disrupted the instruction not only of pulled-out students, but also of students who remained in the classroom.

It is interesting to contrast these criticisms, offered by policy researchers and academics, with the views of teachers. In 1978, the NIE sponsored a conference in which teachers were invited to discuss research on compensatory education. By and large, teachers were not much concerned with the fact that compensatory instruction caused some students to miss a portion of the regular curriculum. Some argued that mastery of basic reading and mathematics skills was paramount. Nevertheless, teachers at the conference did recognize that coordination problems existed, especially when pullout models were in use, and many teachers reported that they "saved" time for instruction in important subjects until it could be offered when all students were present (see Advanced Technology, 1983, pp. 5–30 for survey findings that confirm teachers' views).

It is important to consider not only what students miss when they receive Chapter 1 lessons, but also the extent to which lesson content in Chapter 1 and regular classrooms is congruent. For example, Johnston, Allington, and Afflerbach (1985) concluded that most compensatory education students received compensatory reading lessons that bore little relationship to the reading lessons in their regular classrooms. They also reported that school personnel made little effort to systematically coordinate lesson content across instructional programs. On the basis of this and other evidence, they concluded that students would be more successful in the regular instructional program if they received compensatory instruction that was more congruent with what was offered in the regular program.

To investigate these issues, this study observed students over the course of an entire school day, a procedure that allowed us to chart the congruence of lessons across different programs. In addition, we used observations and interview data to address other relevant questions. For example, we were interested in understanding more about the problem of missed instruction. As the NIE (1976) study showed, only 40 percent of the teachers surveyed reported that Chapter 1 students missed some portion of their regular instruction. In this study, it was possible to analyze the extent to which school-level design decisions affected the problem of missed lessons. Moreover, the interview data allowed an investigation of how teachers managed instruction so that the disruption of Chapter 1 instruction was minimized. And finally, the data were used to investigate how regular classroom teachers, Chapter 1 staff, and school administrators coordinated instructional programs and whether various coordinative procedures resulted in lessons that were more or less congruent across programs.

FINDINGS

A massive amount of descriptive data was collected over the course of the study, including qualitative and quantitative data on schools, classrooms, and students. The approach to the analysis of data followed procedures developed in other multisite case studies (Miles and Huberman, 1984). Analysis began on a case-by-case basis using a variety of data reduction forms, resulting in the writing of extensive case studies of twelve schools (Lee, Rowan, Allington, Anderson, Bossert, Harnischfeger, and Stallings, 1986). Analysis then proceeded to cross-site comparisons and the development of important generalizations. The findings from this analysis were reported in the final report of the project (Rowan, Guthrie, Lee, and Guthrie, 1986).

This chapter summarizes the major findings from the cross-site analysis in three general areas: (1) the quality of instruction received by Chapter 1 students in the sample; (2) the degree to which quality of instruction varied as a function of the design characteristics of schools, particularly the service delivery models in use; and (3) the relationship between Chapter 1 instruction and regular instructional programs.

Quality of Instruction

Basic descriptive data on the quality of Chapter 1 instruction at the twenty-four schools in the study are presented in Tables 7–1 through 7–3. The data have been aggregated to the school level, and schools have been grouped by service delivery model (for elementary school reading projects, elementary school math projects, and secondary school reading and math projects). The first column in each table lists the number of days Chapter 1 instruction in a particular subject was observed at a school. The second column lists the number of times per week students were scheduled to receive Chapter 1 instruction. In most schools this schedule was fixed, but in some schools with in-class designs, scheduling was variable and it was necessary to infer a schedule from the observed data. The next two columns combine the data on schedules with the data on service minutes to yield estimates of the weekly and yearly time the average Chapter 1 student at a school spent in Chapter 1 services.

In addition to data on time allocations, the tables include data on three other variables. One is the percentage of observed Chapter 1 instruction

TABLE 7-1. Characteristics of Chapter 1 Instruction: Elementary School Reading Projects

Service Delivery Model	School	# Service Days Observed	Schedule	Aver. mins/ Service day	Estimated Weekly Time Mins.	Estimated Yearly* Time Hrs.	% Instructor[†] Type in CI			Aver. Group Size in CI	% in Formats[‡]			
							CT	RT	A		Lec/Rec	Stwk	Mgmt	Surr
Mixed														
	Parker	9	2x-5x/wk‖	30.7	26wk/62 10wk/155	52	0	1	99	5.9	42	38	7	13
	Westwood	14	5x/wk§	31.4	157	94	13	10	70	4.5	52	19	7	17
	Hayes	17	5x/wk§	42.1	210	126	3	71	27	3.9	67	24	4	1
Pullout														
	Kensington	18	5x/wk (9wks)	133.1	665	100	1	58	34	5.7	40	53	7	0
	St. Mary's	11	3x/wk	29.3	87	52	0	85	15	5.5	82	0	6	12
	Danville	14	4x/wk	50.1	200	120	7	73	20	6.6	65	18	6	10
	Central	15	5x/wk	32.2	160	96	1	39	60	5.2	79	10	6	5
	Hillside	15	4x/wk	46.5	188	113	10	64	26	4.1	35	8	15	41
	Johnson	15	4x/wk	30.9	124	74	1	75	24	6.5	78	14	6	0
	Winkler	14	5x/wk	28.4	140	84	0	67	33	3.1	59	39	2	0
	Tudor	4	5x/wk	25.6	130	78	3	97	0	3.8	12	44	10	34
In-class														
	Huxley	4	2.5/wk§	25.5	65	39	13	0	87	3.6	65	10	24	0
	Nelson	17	5x/wk	28.7	145	87	0	6	94	3.0	44	41	6	0
	Sumner	9	4x/wk§	21.3	84	50	0	0	100	3.7	94	0	0	0
	Evergreen	10	5x/wk	21.5	110	66	30	0	70	6.8	54	35	0	0
	Lowell	11	5x/wk	41.2	205	123	0	3	97	4.3	56	34	7	3
Replacement														
	Washington	18	5x/wk	111.4	555	333	90	0	10	9.1	50	35	12	2

Legend: CT=Classroom Teacher; RT=Resource Teacher; A=Aide; Lec/Rec=Lecture/Recitation; Stwk=Seatwork; Mgmt=Management; Surr=Surrogate

* Yearly time =(Weekly time × 36 weeks) ÷ 60 minutes

[†] Percentage may not equal 100 because Testing and Other formats are not included

[‡] Percentage may not equal 100 because Classroom Teacher & Aide and Other Instructor categories are not included

§ Time variable—Schedule estimated from observational data

‖ Time variable—Estimate=26 weeks at 2x/wk and 10 weeks at 5x/wk

TABLE 7-2. Characteristics of Chapter 1 Instruction: Elementary School Math Projects

Service Delivery Model	School	# Service Days Observed	Schedule	Aver. mins/ Service day	Estimated Weekly Time Mins.	Estimated Yearly* Time Hrs.	% Instructor† Type in C1			Aver. Group Size in C1	% in Formats‡			
							CT	RT	A		Lec/Rec	Stwk	Mgmt	Surr
Mixed														
	Huxley	7	2x/wk§	27.6	56	34	26	28	46	6.5	53	4	2	22
	Parker	5	2x/wk§	16.0	36	22	0	45	55	13.5	16	25	11	30
	Westwood	8	3x/wk§	14.1	42	25	0	0	100	7.9	31	19	9	42
	Nelson	2	5x/wk	28.0	140	84	0	100	0	3.0	16	64	11	0
Pullout														
	Danville	2	4x/wk	60.5	244	146	22	78	0	4.2	36	37	1	7
	Central	6	2.5x/wk	22.8	58	35	3	5	92	5.1	76	0	24	0
	Hillside	7	4x/wk	43.3	172	103	0	100	0	3.8	25	13	16	41
	Johnson	9	4x/wk	40.2	160	96	22	30	48	5.0	54	31	7	0
	Winkler	13	5x/wk	24.8	125	75	3	36	58	1.6	62	12	5	17
	Tudor	13	5x/wk	38.4	192	115	0	100	0	3.9	7	92	1	0
In-class														
	Sumner	11	4x/wk	30.3	129	72	27	0	73	7.2	41	53	3	0
	Lowell	6	5x/wk	23.2	115	69	5	0	95	1.7	44	38	1	17
Replacement														
	Washington	17	5x/wk	25.1	125	75	96	0	4	9.4	26	59	11	0
	Evergreen	14	5x/wk	55.5	280	168	77	0	23	5.5	41	28	13	18

Legend: CT=Classroom Teacher; RT=Resource Teacher; A=Aide; Lec/Rec=Lecture/Recitation; Stwk=Seatwork; Mgmt=Management; Surr=Surrogate

* Yearly time=(Weekly time × 36 weeks) ÷ 60 minutes

† Percentage may not equal 100 because Testing and Other formats are not included

‡ Percentage may not equal 100 because Classroom Teacher & Aide and Other Instructor categories are not included

§ Time variable—Schedule estimated from observational data

TABLE 7-3. Characteristics of Chapter 1 Instruction: Secondary School Reading and Math

Service Delivery Model	School	# Service Days Observed	Schedule	Aver. mins/ Service day	Estimated Weekly Time Mins.	Estimated Yearly* Time Hrs.	% Instructor† Type in C1			Aver. Group Size in C1	% in Formats‡			
							CT	RT	A		Lec/Rec	Stwk	Mgmt	Surr
Grade 8														
Reading														
Pullout	Einstein	4	2x/wk	35.8	72	43	6	94	0	3.0	8	20	6	61
Pullout	Kehoe	12	2.5x/wk	40.8	103	62	0	82	8	2.9	17	65	8	7
Replacement	Lakeview	13	5x/wk	64.7	325	195	95	0	5	15.7	1	50	42	0
Replacement	Taylor	6	5x/wk	56.2	280	168	2	81	0	5.1	17	55	4	21
Grade 10														
Reading														
Mixed	Salvador	5	1.5x/wk§	12.0	18	11	0	0	100	6.3	35	9	0	57
Replacement	Coolidge	16	5x/wk	29.3	145	87	2	96	0	4.3	9	47	10	30
Replacement	Stevenson	16	5x/wk	39.8	200	120	7	64	22	8.0	65	5	23	6
Grade 8														
Math														
Pullout	Einstein	3	2x/wk	29.7	59	35	37	63	0	4.3	50	11	2	37
Replacement	Lakeview	14	5x/wk	36.6	185	111	93	0	7	11.8	3	55	41	0
Replacement	Taylor	15	5x/wk	57.3	285	171	0	91	7	12.6	51	42	7	0
Grade 10														
Math														
Mixed	Salvador	5	2x/wk§	14.0	28	17	0	0	100	6.9	3	0	0	19

Legend: CT=Classroom Teacher; RT=Resource Teacher; A=Aide; Lec/Rec=Lecture/Recitation; Stwk=Seatwork; Mgmt=Management; Surr=Surrogate

* Yearly time=(Weekly time × 36 weeks) ÷ 60 minutes

† Percentage may not equal 100 because Testing and Other formats are not included

‡ Percentage may not equal 100 because Classroom Teacher & Aide and Other Instructor categories are not included

§ Time variable—Schedule estimated from observational data

conducted by classroom teachers, resource teachers, or instructional aides. The next two variables are measures of instructional formats. The first is the average size of the instructional groups in which Chapter 1 students participated during Chapter 1 instruction; the second is the percentage of Chapter 1 instructional time that students spent in different instructional formats (these percentages may not total 100 since testing and other formats are not included in the table).

The data confirm that the characteristics of Chapter 1 instruction varied greatly across schools, even those using the same nominal service delivery model. Nevertheless, we begin by describing the modal patterns in the data. At the elementary level, in both reading and math, the modal pattern was to offer Chapter 1 instruction four to five times a week for thirty to forty minutes per session. Across all schools, Chapter 1 lessons in reading in grades 2 and 4 averaged between 50 percent to 60 percent lecture/recitation, this study's measure of "direct" instruction. Chapter 1 math lessons at this level provide somewhat less "direct" instruction, averaging between 35 to 45 percent lecture/recitation across all schools. Finally, the one uniform characteritistic of both Chapter 1 reading and math lessons at the elementary level was the small size of instructional groups. In both reading and math, Chapter 1 group sizes averaged from five to seven students.

Fewer students and schools were observed at the secondary level, and variations across Chapters 1 projects was great, thus making generalizations more tenuous. The modal pattern was to offer Chapter 1 instruction in both reading and math five times per week, usually during a scheduled period of the school day. The length of this period varied across schools, depending on school schedules, but a period usually was between forty and fifty minutes in length. With respect to the amount of "direct" instruction observed, a bimodal tendency emerged. In schools that used self-paced, individualized curricula, secondary school students often spent a vast majority of their Chapter 1 time in independent seatwork. In these schools, "direct" instructional formats, such as lecture/recitation, were observed only about 10 percent of the time. On the other hand, some secondary school projects used a more conventional teaching technique which consisted of 30 to 40 percent lecture/recitation, this study's measure of "direct" instruction. Finally, in some secondary schools, Chapter 1 group sizes in reading or math were above ten students, but across all secondary schools in the sample, Chapter 1 group sizes averaged between six to seven students.

An interesting question is whether the instruction received by students in Chapter 1 settings differed substantially from that received in regular classrooms. Table 7–4 presents data comparing lesson formats and group sizes across the two programs for students in the sample. At the elementary level, the mix of instructional formats across the two program settings is roughly comparable, although Chapter 1 lessons appear to consist of roughly

TABLE 7–4. Percentage of Time Spent in Different Instructional Formats by Subject and Grade Level

Program	Total Hrs. Observed	% Lec/Rec	% Seat-work	% Surro-gate	% Other	% Manage-ment	Aver. Group Size
			Reading Format				
Grade 2							
Regular	140.4	50.6	34.6	1.5	4.2	9.1	16.6
Chapter 1	53.8	60.2	17.1	12.6	2.6	7.5	5.0
Grade 4							
Regular	122.2	41.9	42.5	1.1	4.2	10.2	19.5
Chapter 1	101.1	48.1	39.1	3.5	1.0	8.4	6.6
Grade 8							
Regular	18.9	35.7	38.3	8.7	6.9	10.4	13.4
Chapter 1	30.2	8.9	52.7	10.7	5.0	22.7	9.3
Grade 10							
Regular	30.4	42.8	24.7	13.3	1.4	17.7	17.5
Chapter 1	19.4	41.0	22.1	18.6	1.6	16.8	6.4
			Mathematics Format				
Grade 2							
Regular	27.2	55.4	25.8	3.4	3.5	11.9	19.4
Chapter 1	23.8	42.4	26.6	15.1	7.9	8.0	6.5
Grade 4							
Regular	22.2	53.5	31.7	0.8	0.8	13.3	22.0
Chapter 1	28.6	34.4	42.3	11.1	2.3	9.9	5.6
Grade 8							
Regular	4.0	52.7	16.5	2.0	16.0	14.8	19.3
Chapter 1	27.2	31.7	48.9	—	0.2	17.2	5.6
Grade 10							
Regular	2.5	28.7	38.0	—	5.3	28.0	14.5
Chapter 1	1.1	2.9	—	18.8	78.3	—	6.9

10 percent more "direct" instruction and somewhat more surrogate (e.g., computer-assisted) instruction than regular classrooms. As discussed above, at the secondary level, the Chapter 1 projects at schools in the sample provided a bimodal distribution of instructional formats. In the schools with self-paced, individualized curricula in reading (Lakeview and Taylor), students were provided with much less "direct" instruction in Chapter 1

lessons than in regular lessons. At the tenth grade, only one school in the sample offered Chapter 1 instruction in math, and in this school, 78 percent of Chapter 1 instructional time was given over to testing. Apart from these schools, however, group-paced instructional formats were used to provide Chapter 1 instruction, and in these schools there was little difference in the amount of "direct" instruction across programs.

Table 7–4 does show a major difference between Chapter 1 and regular lessons, however. At both the elementary and secondary levels, and in both reading and math, Chapter 1 group sizes were much smaller than those in the regular program. Indeed, based on prior studies of class size, it seems safe to conclude that the average size of instructional groups in Chapter 1 settings represented an important advantage of Chapter 1 over regular classroom instruction. For example, across all schools in the sample (i.e., both elementary and secondary schools) instructional groups in regular reading/ language arts had an average size of 17.6 students and Chapter 1 groups had an average size of 6.6 students. In math, regular classroom groups averaged 20.2 students and Chapter 1 groups averaged 7.7 students. In fact, an examination of Tables 7–1 through 7–3 demonstrates that small group size was the most uniform characteristic of Chapter 1 instruction.

This finding is especially important and requires further interpretation. As meta-analyses have shown, the magnitude of reductions in group sizes between Chapter 1 and regular classrooms at schools in the sample were substantial enough to expect the reductions to affect student achievement positively. However, as these same meta-analyses demonstrate, group size reductions have larger effects the longer the period of time in which students experience such reductions. As Tables 7–1 through 7–3 show, most of the Chapter 1 students in this study could be expected to receive less than 100 hours of Chapter 1 instruction over the course of a thirty-six-week academic year. But if students experienced longer periods of Chapter 1 instruction, it seems reasonable to expect that any positive effects of the reduced group sizes purchased by Chapter 1 funds would be enhanced.

A final question investigated by this study was the extent to which Chapter 1 instruction offered students opportunities to practice "higher-order" skills. In general, the narrative records from classroom observations showed that Chapter 1 reading and math projects did not focus on these kinds of tasks. In math, Chapter 1 students in both elementary and secondary schools worked primarily on computational tasks involving basic arithmetic facts. Word problems were common, but they did not constitute the core of instruction, and little attempt was made to engage students in tasks that required the use of mathematical models to synthesize or evaluate ideas. In reading, the general pattern also was for Chapter 1 lessons to focus on lower-order tasks. With a few notable exceptions, students at all grade levels spent a good deal of time on worksheets that involved little reading of connected text. The low level of the Chapter 1 curriculum undoubtedly served a useful purpose by providing students with useful review and practice of basic skills, especially at the lower grades, but as students entered upper elementary school and passed into secondary schools, the continuing focus on basic reading skills appeared particularly incongruent with the reading tasks demanded in regular classrooms. This is unfortunate, for in schools where Chapter 1 classes did provide direct instruction in reading comprehension, the narrative records indicated that many Chapter 1 students were capable of performing higher-order tasks. Thus the low level of Chapter 1 reading instruction often prevented local projects from presenting Chapter 1 students with challenging materials that extended and enriched learning.

Design Characteristics and Quality of Chapter 1 Instruction

As Tables 7–1 through 7–3 demonstrate, there was much variation around the modal patterns of instruction discussed above. An important purpose of this study was to investigate the extent to which this variation could be accounted for by differences in instructional design features at the various schools in the sample. A basic finding emerged from this analysis. Contrary to the assumption of much of the policy literature in compensatory education, there was little evidence in this study that instructional quality varied as a result of the particular service delivery model used by a local Chapter 1 project. Instead, other design features appeared more important.

Consider the data on the effects of different service delivery models (e.g., pullout, in-class, replacement, add-on). Past research led us to be particularly interested in the question of whether pullout programs offered ''inferior'' instructional services. At the elementary level, there was no indication of this. On the whole, pullout projects allocated about the same amount of time to Chapter 1 instruction, provided the same small group size, and were characterized by the same amount of ''direct'' instruction as projects with in-class and replacement designs. A similar pattern was evident at the secondary level.

Only the add-on designs observed at the elementary levels appeared to provide an advantage over alternative designs, and then only on one dimension of instructional quality: instructional time. In schools with pullout and in-class designs, it was common for Chapter 1 instruction to constitute roughly 30 to 40 percent of the total reading instruction received by Chapter 1 students. However, these delivery models rarely added more than ten to fifteen minutes to the daily time spent by students in reading and math, and this added time often came at the expense of time taken away from other academic subjects. In schools with replacement projects, Chapter 1 instruction generally constituted 100 percent of the instruction received by students in reading or math, and thus these projects added little or no time to students' instructional days and resulted in little or no redistribution of time across academic subjects. Thus, overall it appeared that most Chapter 1 projects added no time to a student's instructional day and resulted only in a very modest redistribution of time across subjects. Only the add-on projects, which offered Chapter 1 instruction outside of the regular school schedule (before or after school), appeared to actually add instructional time in basic skills without taking time away from other subjects (see Rowan et al., 1986, chapter 6 for a more detailed analysis of these findings).

Service delivery models also differed on another dimension: staffing patterns. However, this did not appear to markedly affect the quality of instruction received by Chapter 1 students, at least as measured by quantitative variables. For example, in-class projects in the sample were staffed almost exclusively by instructional aides, whereas pullout and replacement models were often staffed by a combination of resource teachers and aides. To examine whether there were differences in the type of instruction offered by various types of instructors, we compared the instructional formats of lessons taught by resource teachers and aides. The analysis revealed no consistent differences. In reading, aides provided 15 percent more "direct" instruction (lecture/recitation); in math, aides provided about 5 percent less "direct" instruction. The narrative field records suggested that resource teachers generally provided well-organized lessons, used effective teaching practices, and kept students motivated and engaged in lessons. There were also many excellent instructors among the aides observed in this study, but there was also more variation in quality across aides; a few aides presented confusing and wrong information to students or were unable to keep students motivated and engaged in lessons. On the whole, however, it did not appear that staffing patterns made a significant difference to the instruction received by Chapter 1 students.

The field records were also used to evaluate the criticism that pullout instruction wastes time for pulled-out students and disrupts ongoing instruction in the regular classroom. To examine this criticism, a comparison was made between five elementary schools where all observed Chapter 1 instruction was offered in a pullout setting with two elementary schools that used an in-class setting exclusively. In the two in-class projects, transition times to and from Chapter 1 lessons averaged 2.28 minutes and 1.47 minutes. Of the five pullout projects, three had average transition times of about 3.5 minutes, one had an average time of 5.7 minutes, and the last had a transition time of 9.0 minutes. Clearly, the amount of time spent traveling to and from Chapter 1 services was less in the in-class projects, but only by one or two minutes in most cases. Transition times were lengthy only in schools where the Chapter 1 pullout rooms were at considerable distance from the regular classroom. Finally, the field records indicated that the movement of students into and out of classrooms was no more disruptive than movement within classrooms, and in elementary schools especially, students seemed quite accustomed to the movement and regrouping of students.

Design decisions other than the choice of a particular service delivery model appeared to have larger effects on quality of instruction in Chapter 1 programs. For example, schools used different curricula, and this appeared to have marked effects on the content covered by students, especially opportunity to practice higher-order skills in reading and math. In fact, variables measuring content covered have been found to affect achievement in at least two previous studies of compensatory education, the Instructional Dimensions Study (Cooley and Leinhardt, 1980) and the Sustaining Effects Study (Carter, 1984). Thus curricular decisions, which were unrelated to the use of a particular service delivery model, appeared to have important effects on instructional quality.

In addition, the adoption of curricula designed for self-paced instruction through sequenced curriculum hierarchies appeared to have marked effects on the instructional treatments received by Chapter 1 students. This is because these kinds of curricula often resulted in a heavy reliance on student seatwork. As the Instructional Dimensions Study (Cooley and Leinhardt, 1980) demonstrated, the use of individualized, sequenced curricula, in and of itself, does not appear to be related to student achievement. What is needed, apparently, is active instruction by teachers. In fact, this kind of "direct" instruction was found by the Sustaining Effects Study (Carter, 1984) to be related to improved instructional outcomes.

Examples of Chapter 1 classrooms relying on individualized curriculum hierarchies and seatwork were particularly evident in the secondary schools in the sample. A particularly interesting case is Lakeview school (see the data in Table 7-3). At this school, in both reading and math classes, students entered a classroom with twelve to fifteen other students and immediately began working independently on the individualized curriculum packets. Although aides circulated and monitored student seatwork, the majority of actual instruction was offered to students by the resource teacher, who sat at a desk near the front of the room and conducted "staccato" recitations with students. As Table 7-3 shows, students at this school received only 1 to 3 percent "direct" instruction. In addition, about 40 percent of student time was spent in management, as students waited for aides to check their assignments or for the resource teacher to meet with them. Although this case is extreme, Table 7-3 shows that most of the secondary schools in the sample operated this kind of individualized program and offered very little "direct" instruction to students. In all likelihood, such individualization was a convenient grouping strategy in the face of the wide variation in student achievement levels in secondary school Chapter 1 classrooms, but there is little evidence to support the efficacy of this kind of approach.

The Relationship Between Chapter 1 and Regular Instruction

A final issue addressed by this study was the relationship between Chapter 1 and regular instruction. Previous research and policy analyses have been critical of the Chapter 1 program on several counts related to this issue. The program has been criticized for adding little instructional time to participating students' instruction and for taking time away from instruction in other subjects; the program also has been criticized for providing instruction that is incongruent with instruction received in the regular classroom (Walberg, 1984; Johnston, Allington, and Afflerbach, 1985).

The data on students' instructional days only partially confirmed the first criticism. As discussed above, Chapter 1 instruction in most schools occurred within the school day and thus added little time to a student's total daily instruction. At the same time, however, this pattern did not appear to cause students to miss large amounts of instruction in other academic subjects. An analysis of quantitative data suggested that, on average, students gained only about ten minutes of instruction in reading or math on a day when they received Chapter 1 services, and while this slight gain came at the expense of instruction in other academic subjects, it did not appear to result in radical redistribution of learning time across academic subjects. The qualitative data suggested an explanation for this finding. Most of the schools in the study scheduled Chapter 1 classes so that they would be minimally disruptive to students, and this usually involved offering Chapter 1 services while same-subject instruction was being offered in the regular classroom. The only exceptions to this general tendency were an extended pullout program in one elementary school, which pulled students out of their regular classrooms for two hours in the afternoon during a nine-week period of the school year, and several secondary school replacement projects in which Chapter 1 instruction replaced various electives in students' academic programs. Thus the data suggested that in most schools participation in the Chapter 1 program had little effect on the amount of time students spent in different academic subjects (see Rowan et al., 1986, chapter 6).

Despite this consistent scheduling pattern, there were important differences in the extent to which regular and Chapter 1 instructional programs were coordinated at sites in the study. In particular, the study found that the relationship between the content of lessons in the Chapter 1 and regular programs varied greatly across sites. In the final report of the study, a typology was developed to describe the relationship between the content of lesson assignments across programs in a school. In some schools, a "supportive" assignment pattern existed. In this pattern, Chapter 1 lesson assignments were explicitly designed to reinforce lesson content previously covered in the regular classroom. Other schools developed "alternative" assignment patterns in which Chapter 1 lessons bore little or no relationship to lessons in the regular program. Thus the data in this study did not confirm a simple generalization about the lack of congruence between Chapter 1 and regular instruction. In fact, over half of the elementary schols in the sample, and two of the seven secondary schools in the study, maintained a "supportive" assignment pattern that established congruent lesson content in the Chapter 1 and regular instructional programs (see Rowan et al., 1986, chapter 8 for a discussion of these findings).

An important question is whether one type of assignment pattern is more effective than another in promoting student achievement. In this study, data on student success rates were used to provide insight into this question. An analysis of the narrative field records suggested that there was no simple relationship between assignment patterns and student success in lessons. For students who were performing near grade level, "supportive" Chapter 1 assignments which reinforced regular classroom instruction appeared effective in maintaining and promoting student success in the regular academic program. However, "alternative" assignment patterns appeared more appropriate for students who were performing well below grade level or who had instructional needs that were not addressed by regular curricula. Because these students usually required instruction that was far off the pace of that which occurred in the regular classroom, they usually did not experience much success during regular lessons and benefitted much more from the more appropriate instruction provided by the "alternative" assignments in the Chapter 1 program. Thus the data suggest that for the slowest students in a school, a Chapter 1 program that replaces grade level instruction may be the most appropriate, whereas for students near grade level, "supportive" assignments in Chapter 1 can sustain grade level performance. Despite the fact that no single assignment pattern appeared appropriate for all students, not a single Chapter 1 program in this study provided different assignment patterns to students with different instructional needs.

Finally, it was found that formal procedures for coordinating Chapter 1 and regular instruction were necessary but not sufficient to the integration of the two instructional programs within a school. Formal policies about curriculum and evaluation, formal organization of school staff into teams or planning units that included Chapter 1 staff, and the formal scheduling of joint planning times for Chapter 1 and regular staff all facilitated coordination of Chapter 1 and regular instruction. However, schools that showed the tightest coupling between Chapter 1 and regular instruction were those in which staff endorsed a norm of collegiality and had developed shared beliefs about instruction.

CONCLUSIONS

A major purpose of this study was to review the evidence on the quality of instruction in a variety of Chapter 1 schools and to formulate some suggestions for improvement. The great variety in Chapter 1 "treatments" across schools makes generalizations about program improvement very difficult. However, there was one uniform characteristic of Chapter 1 instruction in the schools in this study. All of the Chapter 1 projects offered instruction in small groups. It makes sense to assume that the results of past large-scale evaluations of the Chapter 1 program have been influenced by this trend, and that participation in smaller-sized Chapter 1 instructional groups has given students in the Chapter 1 "treatment" a small advantage over students not participating in Chapter 1. At the same time, however, the small effects of the Chapter 1 program in macro evaluations makes sense in light of this finding. Since Chapter 1 instruction usually accounts for less than 100 hours of learning time over the course of an academic year, the effects of reduced group size on student achievement should not be large.

The data also suggest another reason why past evaluations have found weak effects of program participation on student achievement. In general, participation in Chapter 1 services had very little effect on the total amount of time students in this study spent in reading and math lessons. This was especially true of many replacement projects, and it was also true of most pullout and in-class projects. Instead of adding to the amount of time students spent in reading and math lessons, schools simply redistributed a fixed amount of instructional time across programs. This process would not give Chapter 1 students who were "slow learners" any additional time to learn basic skills.

Apart from these general observations, however, it appears that Chapter 1 projects implemented instructional programs with very site-specific characteristics. This finding has a number of implications for how policymakers, researchers, and practitioners think about improving the program. The analyses reported here suggest:

1. Policymakers and practitioners should recognize that improvement in the Chapter 1 program will occur on a site-by-site basis. Given the weak constraints of federal statutes and regulations and the variable implementation of project design features at local sites, it appears unlikely that sweeping reforms can effect uniform changes in local instructional programs.

2. Policymakers and practitioners should recognize that the adoption of a particular service delivery model (e.g., pullout or in-class) is not the major consideration in thinking about how to improve Chapter 1 instruction. Other variables, such as the amount of "direct" instruction or the nature of the curriculum are more likely to affect the quality of instruction received by students.

3. Policymakers and practitioners should consider how time can be better used in Chapter 1 projects. Instead of redistributing the fixed amount of time in students' daily schedules across different programs, Chapter 1

funds might be better used to purchase add-on services that increase the amount of time students spend in basic skills instruction. By placing Chapter 1 instruction outside the regular school day, these designs not only add to instructional time, but also prevent students from missing instruction in other academic subjects.

4. Policymakers and practitioners need to give more careful attention to the curriculum linkage between Chapter 1 and regular instruction. The implementation of "supportive" or "alternative" lesson assignments should be done only after a careful assessment of whether or not students' needs can be met by the regular curriculum. When students' needs are unmet by the regular program, alternative instructional assignments may be required; when students can be maintained at grade level with minimal support, supportive assignments are appropriate.

5. Chapter 1 projects at all levels should expose students to higher-order thinking skills, especially opportunities to read connected text and to apply mathematics to real world problems. Although the focus of Chapter 1 instruction on basic skills provides students with useful review and practice, as students become older this review does little to support student learning in the regular classroom curriculums.

6. Chapter 1 projects in secondary schools should move away from self-paced instructional formats that rely on independent seatwork. Too often, secondary school Chapter 1 projects allowed the materials, rather than the instructor, to provide the instruction for Chapter 1 students.

The implementation of these suggestions has the potential to increase the scope and quality of Chapter 1 instruction and could allow local projects to better meet the special educational needs of the students served.

REFERENCES

Advanced Technology, Inc. (1983). *Local operation of Title I, ESEA 1976–1982: A resource book*. Reston, VA: Author.

Allington, R.; Steutzel, H.; Shake, M.; and Lamarche, S. (1986). What is remedial reading? A descriptive study. *Reading Research and Instruction*.

Anderson, L. M.; Brubaker, N. L.; Alleman-Brooks, J.; and Duffy, G. G. (1985). A qualitative study of seatwork in first grade classrooms. *Elementary School Journal, 86*, 123–140.

Archambault, F. X. (1986). *Instructional setting: Key issue or bogus concern?* Paper prepared for the National Institute of Education Conference on the Effects of Alternative Designs in Compensatory Education, Washington, DC.

Averch, H. A.; Carroll, S. J.; Donaldson, T. S.; Kiesling, H. J.; and Pincus, J. (1972). *How effective is schooling? A critical review and synthesis of research findings*. Santa Monica, CA: Rand Corporation.

Botel, M. (1978). Aspects of planning, organization, and management of selected reading programs. In National Institute of Education, *Perspectives on the Instructional Dimensions Study*. Washington, DC: Author.

Brophy, J., and Evertson, C. (1974). *Process-product correlations in the Texas Teacher Effectiveness Study: Final Report*. Austin, TX: Research and Development Center for Teacher Education.

Brophy, J., and Good, T. (1986). Teacher behavior and student achievement. In M. C. Wittrock (Ed.), *Handbook of research on teaching*, 3rd ed. New York: Macmillan.

Brown, F. (1982). Improving schooling through Title I: A model for change. *Education and Urban Society, 15*, 125–142.

Cahen, L. S.; Filby, N. N.; McCutcheon, G.; and Kyle, D. W. (1983). *Class size and instruction*. New York: Longman.

Carter, L. F. (1984). The sustaining effects study of compensatory education. *Educational Researcher, 13*, 4–13.

Cooley, W. W., and Leinhardt, G. (1980). The instructional dimensions study. *Educational Evaluation and Policy Analysis, 2*, 7–26.

Fisher, C. W.; Berliner, D. C.; Filby, N. N.; Marliave, R.; Cahen, L. S.; and Dishaw, M. M. (1980). Teaching behaviors, academic learning time, and student achievement: An overview. In C. Denham and A. Lieberman (Eds.), *Time to learn*. Washington, DC: National Institute of Education.

Gaffney, M. J. (1986). *Chapter 1: The choices for educators*. Paper prepared for the National Institute of Education Conference on Effects of Alternative Designs in Compensatory Education, Washington, DC.

Glass, G. V.; Cahen, L. S.; Smith, M. L.; and Filby, N. N. (1982). *School class size*. Beverly Hills, CA: Sage.

Glass, G. V., and Smith, M. L. (1977). *"Pullout" in compensatory education*. Boulder, CO: University of Colorado Laboratory of Educational Research.

Good, T. (1978). *The Missouri Mathematics Effectiveness Project*. Columbia, MO: University of Missouri, School of Education.

Johnston, P.; Allington, R.; and Afflerbach, P. (1985). The congruence of classroom and remedial instruction. *Elementary School Journal, 85*, 465–477.

Kennedy, M. M.; Birman, B. F.; and Demaline, R. E. (1987). *The effectiveness of Chapter 1 Services*. Washington, DC: Office of Educational Research and Improvement, U.S. Department of Education.

Kennedy, M. M.; Jung, R.; and Orland, M. (1986). *Poverty, achievement, and the distribution of compensatory education services*. Washington, D.C.: Office of Educational Research and Improvement, U.S. Department of Education.

Kimbrough, J., and Hill, P. T. (1981). *The aggregate effects of federal education programs*. Santa Monica, CA: Rand Corporation.

Lee, G. V.; Rowan, B.; Allington, R. A.; Anderson, L. W.; Bossert, S. T.; Harnischfeger, A.; and Stallings, J. A. (1986). *The management and delivery of instructional services to Chapter 1 students: Case studies of twelve schools*. San Francisco, CA: Far West Laboratory for Educational Research and Development.

Miles, M. B., and Huberman, A. M. (1984). *Qualitative data analysis: A sourcebook of new methods*. Beverly Hills, CA: Sage.

National Institute of Education (1976). *Evaluating compensatory education: An interim report on the NIE Compensatory Education Study*. Washington, DC: Author.

Office of Educational Research and Improvement (in press). *Final Report of the National Assessment of Chapter 1*. Washington, DC: Author.

Peterson, P. L. (1986). *Selecting students and services for compensatory education: Lessons from aptitude-treatment interaction research*. Paper prepared for the National Institute of Education Conference on the Effects of Alternative Designs in Compensatory Education, Washington, DC.

Rosenshine, B. (1983). Teaching functions in instructional programs. *The Elementary School Journal, 83*, 335–352.

Rowan, B.; Guthrie, L. F.; Lee, G. V.; and Guthrie, G. P. (1986). *The design and implementation of Chapter 1 instructional services: A study of 24 schools*. San Francisco, CA: Far West Laboratory for Educational Research and Development.

Stallings, J. A., and Kaskowitz, D. (1974). *Follow Through classroom observation evaluation 1972–1973*. Menlo Park, CA: Stanford Research Institute.

Walberg, H. J. (1984). *Federal (Chapter 1) educational spending and effects on poor children*. Washington, DC: Learn, Inc.

Walberg, H. J., and Frederick, W. C. (1983). Instructional time and learning. In H. Mitzel (Ed.), *Encyclopedia of educational research,* vol. 2. New York: Free Press.

Wiley, D. E. (1979). Evaluation by aggregation: Social and methodological biases. *Educational Evaluation and Policy Analysis, 1,* 41–45.

8

INSTRUCTIONAL SETTING AND OTHER DESIGN FEATURES OF COMPENSATORY EDUCATION PROGRAMS

Francis X. Archambault, Jr.

University of Connecticut

The past decade has been a particularly fruitful one for research on effective educational programs. We have learned a great deal about factors that distinguish effective from not-so-effective schools. We have also uncovered a wealth of information about teaching practices that contribute to improved student performance. Much of what we have learned from the effective schools literature can be used in schools serving the academically disadvantaged. In fact, such research has usually been conducted in this type of environment. Fortunately, some of the effective teaching research is also transportable to these schools and the classrooms within them. Nonetheless, much remains to be learned about the types of classroom practices and strategies that will lead to improved performance for compensatory education students.

This chapter is concerned with what the literature says about the effects of certain design features of compensatory education programs. Specifically, it focuses on the effect of instructional setting (i.e., whether instruction is delivered in class or outside the regular classroom in a pullout setting), the size of the class and the types of groups in which instruction is offered, and the effectiveness of various types of instructors. Because the large majority of the dollars allocated to compensatory education provides remedial instruction in reading, language arts, and mathematics for elementary school students, these content areas and grade levels are emphasized. Further, because most compensatory instruction is provided in a pullout setting, and since the choice of setting may influence other design features, this design feature is emphasized.

THE OVERALL EFFECT OF COMPENSATORY EDUCATION

In 1965, Congress passed the Elementary and Secondary Education Act (ESEA). Title I of this Act was designed to improve the educational opportunities of the poor and educationally disadvantaged by providing federal dollars to all states and, through them, to local school districts most in need. Given the proposed large investment in Title I and the concern of many congressional leaders that federal funds would not be used as intended, ESEA required that the Title I program be evaluated. These evaluations were the first systematic studies of the overall effect of compensatory education programs. However, even before these studies had begun, the Coleman Report conclusion that "schools bring little influence to bear on a child's achievement that is independent of his background and general social control" (Coleman, Campbell, Hobson, McPartland, Mood, Weinfeld, and York, 1966, p. 274) was being interpreted by many as an indictment of Title I (Stickney and Plunkett, 1982).

Wargo, Tallmadge, Michaels, Lipe, and Morris (1972) provide the best review of the early evaluations of Title I. They concluded that there was little evidence to support the contention that Title I had a positive impact on participating students. Stickney and Plunkett (1982) have argued that the disappointing findings of these early evaluations may have been different had the scores for all participants not been lumped together. That is, some children did appear to benefit from Title I, but, when their scores were combined with those of students who did not, the positive effect was neutralized. McLaughlin (1975) reached a different conclusion. She argued that the initial attempts to evaluate Title I were unsuccessful because of the newness of the program, the diverse nature of the instructional components, and problems in obtaining cooperation between the federally sponsored evaluators and local school personnel.

Carter (1984) has reported on a more recent study of Title I, one that he claims is the largest study of elementary education ever conducted. This research, known as the Sustaining Effects Study, focused on about 1,100 to 3,000 Title I students, about 1,300 to 2,000 needy students, and about 1,700 to 2,500 regular students in each of the grades 1 through 6. Title I students were reported by their school to be receiving some Title I services, needy students were reported by their teachers as being in need of Title I but not receiving them, and regular students were reported as not needing Title I services and not receiving them. The major results of this investigation were the following:

1. Compared to needy students, Title I students showed significant gains in mathematics for each of the six grade levels.

2. Compared to needy students, Title I students showed significant gains in reading for grades 1 through 3 but not for grades 4 through 6.

3. The largest gains in reading and mathematics occurred in the first grade.

4. The rate of gain for Title I students was at least equal to that for regular students, whereas the rate of gain for needy students who did not receive Title I was not as great as that of either Title I students or regular students.

5. Title I services were found to be effective for students who were only moderately disadvantaged (near average in achievement) but they did not improve the relative achievement of the most disadvantaged part of the school population.

6. By the time students reached junior high school, there was no evidence of sustained or delayed effects of Title I.

How should these results be interpreted? Does compensatory education have a sufficiently positive impact on students to justify the enormous amount of money (over $40 billion) that has been allocated to it?

Wang (1980) reported that although compensatory education has had a positive impact on achievement growth, the effects of compensatory education efforts are not large. In fact, she concluded that the "evidence for positive effects of special instruction on achievement growth is sparse" (p. 8). Hallinan (1986) concludes that the results of the Sustaining Effects Study are disappointing. She argues that "the desired outcome of a program of this magnitude would be steady, significant achievement gains that are sustained throughout a student's school career" (p. 4). Cooley (1981) concludes that "on balance, Title I is not producing the kind of achievement impact that people had hoped it would" (p. 300).

Stickney and Plunkett (1982) offer a different conclusion for the Sustaining Effects findings, which they contend is influenced by data from the National Assessment of Educational Progress (NAEP). This latter research (NAEP, 1981) found that between 1970 and 1980 black nine-year-olds gained 9.9 percentage points on their reading assessment measure, whereas whites improved their achievement by only 2.8 percentage points. NAEP also reported significantly greater gains between 1970 and 1980 for students in Title I eligible schools for all three grade levels tested. According to NAEP "these significant changes and the overall pattern of a narrowing gap for most population groups at all ages strongly suggest that students in Title I schools are improving at a faster rate than students in non-Title I schools" (cited in Stickney and Plunkett, 1982, p. 381). Stickney and Plunkett caution that since the NAEP conclusions are based on correlations, one cannot argue that Title I has caused greater pupil achievement. However, they do conclude that the Sustaining Effects and NAEP studies "have finally reported what a host of smaller scale evaluations have suggested for years: Title I is associated with greater than expected pupil gains'' (p. 380). Forbes (1985) is even more sanguine about the positive impact of compensatory education programs. In a relatively recent Phi Delta Kappa article Forbes concluded the following:

> Many things that happened in the Seventies could have dramatically affected student achievement in reading, among them: Title I, desegregation, sensitivity to serving students who had been underserved in the past, movements to improve public education in the southeastern states, and a focus on social concerns. Of these, any could have had a major impact on student performance. But the movement that stands out above all others during the Seventies is the effort to better educate the economically disadvantaged. Title I and all the associated national and state efforts probably played a central role in the improvement of reading skills among those students who historically performed less well (p. 544).

In 1981, the Education and Improvement Act (ECIA) was enacted, thereby replacing Title I with Chapter 1. Although we have little systematic data on the effect of this relatively new Act, Carter (1984) claims that the results "for Title I will apply equally well to the new Chapter 1 compensatory education program" (p. 4). Cooley (1981), however, contends that the search for overall effects of Title I (now Chapter 1) is an inappropriate goal. Rather, he suggests that researchers and evaluators should stop trying to justify this federal funding program and focus instead on ways in which compensatory education practices can be improved. Thus, Cooley and others are arguing that we should not be asking whether programs like Chapter 1 make a difference, but rather how we can adjust or align the programs so that they do make a difference. As noted above, we have learned a great deal in the recent past about the characteristics and features of educational programs that work. It is now time to adopt certain features that have been shown to be effective in compensatory education environments and to test others that have shown promise in noncompensatory settings. Thus we now turn to a discussion of design features that must be considered in the delivery of compensatory educational programs.

SETTING FOR INSTRUCTION

The first design feature we consider is the setting or location for instruction. Compensatory education can be delivered within the regular classroom, outside the regular classroom, or partially inside and partially outside the regular classroom. Instruction delivered outside the regular classroom has been given the name *pullout instruction,* since recipients are removed or pulled out of their regular classroom and sent to another location. Usually, the location is within the same school building, and the instruction delivered there is usually provided by an instructional specialist working with smaller groups of children than there were in the classroom from which the Chapter 1 student was removed. Instruction delivered within the regular classroom is called *in-class* or *mainstreamed instruction.* One approach to mainstreaming is for the regular teacher to instruct Chapter 1 students while Chapter 1 personnel, either a specialist teacher or an aide, provide supplementary assistance. Another form of mainstreaming occurs when a Chapter 1 staff person instructs Chapter 1 students while the regular teacher works with the other students in the class. A third, albeit less popular strategy, is known as the *replacement model,* which provides in one classroom all the services a Title I student receives in a given subject. Finally, there are *add-on programs,* which result from an extension of the school year (i.e., summer programs), the school week, or the school day.

What do we know about the popularity of these approaches? Carter (1984) reported that compensatory instruction was typically provided in a pullout setting, as did Vanecko, Ames, and Archambault (1980), Archambault and St. Pierre (1980), Kennedy (1978), and Stonehill and Anderson (1982). NIE (1977) reported that almost 75 percent of the students in Title I reading programs received their instruction in a pullout setting. About 41 percent of the compensatory language arts instruction was also delivered in a pullout setting, as was about 45 percent of the mathematics instruction. NIE also reported that about 24 percent of compensatory education students receive their regular instruction in groups comprised of only CE students. Glass and Smith (1977) claim that when the NIE pullout figures are corrected to eliminate pupils in 100 percent Title I-eligible classrooms who do not need to be pulled out, the pullout rates in all other classrooms rise to 84 percent for reading, 54 percent for mathematics, and 50 percent for language arts. Glass and Smith go on to argue that when one considers further that pupils might be "pulled out" for one of these subjects and not the other, it is plausible to say that in classes not 100% Title I eligible *"the practice of 'pull out' for compensatory teaching is nearly universal"* (p. 2).

More recently, Advanced Technology, Inc. (1983) reported that over 90 percent of the districts in their sample employed a pullout design exclusively or in combination with an in-class model; only 30 percent of the districts used an in-class design. Advanced Technology also reported, however, that pullout programs were being used less frequently than they had been in the past and that the use of in-class designs was on the rise, particularly in larger school districts (i.e., over 10,000 students). They found much less frequent use of the replacement model. Although this chapter will not address the use of add-on programs, partly because the data on them are particularly skimpy, it is interesting to note that summer programs were available in over half (51 percent) of the 5,010 schools surveyed in the Sustaining Effects Study. As reported by Heyns (1986), larger schools are more likely to conduct summer programs than smaller schools. Interested readers are referred to the Heyns paper for more details on summer programs. It should be noted, however, that she concludes that such programs are not unequivocally successful.

Impact of Setting on Achievement

Given the predominant use of the pullout and in-class modes of instruction, this discussion of the impact of setting on achievement will focus on these two models. In general, the literature leads to the following conclusions: (1) in some cases, compensatory education in a pullout setting results in higher student achievement than in-class instruction; in other instances, in-class instruction has a more positive effect; and in still others, and these appear to be the majority of cases, the setting for instruction has no significant effect on student achievement; (2) the findings on the cost effectiveness of the approaches are also mixed; and (3) the type of instruction delivered within a particular setting is more important than the setting itself.

One of the first large-scale investigations of the effect of instructional setting for compensatory education students was the third-year evaluation of the Emergency School Aid Act (Coulson, Ozenne, Hanes, Bradford, Doherty, Duck, and Hemenway, 1977). In one part of this evaluation residual gain scores on individual student reading and math tests were regressed on nineteen variables that were thought to be related to achievement. One of the nineteen variables was the proportion of reading or math instruction received in a pullout environment. The 8,319 students participating in this research were drawn from two types of compensatory education programs and from grades 3, 4, and 5. Since both reading and mathematics scores were analyzed, a total of twelve regression equations were derived, one for each program, grade level, and content area. For eight of these analyses, no significant differences were found for the pullout variable. In the other four instances, three of which were concerned with reading, pullout was found to have a significant negative effect on achievement. Leinhardt and Palley (1982) interpret these findings to mean that "a change from receiving no pullout instruction in reading to receiving one half reading instruction in pullout would be associated with a small reduction in the dependent measure" (p. 569). They also argue that no matter what the dependent measure was, the effect was very small.

Perhaps even more important than the small effect size is the strong possibility that pullout was associated with less gain because (1) less able students tended to get pullout instruction and (2) the pretest did not control adequately for such differences. Further, and as suggested by Coulson and colleagues (1977), schools were more likely to use pullout instruction when they had students with more severe problems.

The Instructional Dimensions Study (IDS) conducted for NIE by the

Learning Research and Development Center (LRDC) at the University of Pittsburgh also was concerned with the effect of pullout. This research focused on reading and mathematics instruction in first and third grade and used classrooms as the basic unit of analysis. Here the variable "setting" was scaled as a composite of the time students were in supplemental instruction outside the regular classroom and the number of children in a classroom that were pulled out for instruction. NIE (1977) reported that the results uncovered in this research differed by content area and grade level. First-grade students receiving instruction in the regular classroom (i.e., the in-class setting) made significantly larger gains in reading and mathematics than those in pullout settings. However, at the third-grade level, setting had no significant effect on reading achievement and pullout was associated with larger achievement gains in mathematics. NIE interpreted these results to mean that neither setting is consistently associated with greater instructional effectiveness.

Frechtling and Hammond (1978) reported on a reanalysis of the NIE findings. These researchers, who were part of the team monitoring the IDS study for NIE, noted that rechecking and cleaning the data changed the previously described picture slightly. As before, in-class instruction was found to have a positive effect on achievement at grade 1 for both reading and mathematics. At grade 3, however, in-class instruction was found to be more effective for reading (there was no difference previously) whereas no significant difference was found for instructional setting when mathematics was considered (pullout was more effective previously) (see Figure 8-1). Frechtling and Hammond (1978) argued that despite these changes in the previously reported findings they would "be uncomfortable concluding from the IDS data that districts should use only the inclass approach" (p. 9). They offered several reasons for their position: (1) the IDS findings were based on data from districts that were "special" and not nationally representative; (2) they had a gut feeling that mainstreaming (i.e., in-class instruction) may pose problems for many teachers and simply not be possible in some instances; and (3) they were unwilling to generalize from a single study. On this last point, they argued that "the IDS, despite all its virtues, is only one study, and convergent evidence from other work is not yet strong enough" (p. 9).

Cooley and Leinhardt (1980) and Leinhardt and Palley (1982) also report on the IDS study and, to make matters somewhat more confusing, their findings are different from those reported by NIE. Cooley and Leinhardt (1980) reported that setting was related to student achievement gain only in third-grade reading and that more time in pullout was associated with less gain. As can be seen in Figure 8-1, this is quite different from NIE's interpretation of the findings.

Leinhardt and Palley (1982) discuss a reanalysis of the IDS data in which they at least partially addressed a criticism by Glass and Smith (1977) that the pretest measure used was too difficult and thus did very little to

FIGURE 8–1.   Various Perspectives on the Pullout Findings of the Instructional Dimensions Study*

NIE's Perspective

A

Grade	Reading	Math
1	I+	I+
3	ND	P+

Based on NIE, 1977

B

Grade	Reading	Math
1	I+	I+
3	I+	ND

Based on Frechtling and Hammond, 1978

LRDC's Perspective

C

Grade	Reading	Math
1	ND	ND
3	I+	ND

Based on Cooley and Leinhardt, 1980

D

Grade	Reading	Math
1	P+	P+
3	ND	P+

Based on Leinhardt and Palley, 1982

Key: I^+ = in-class students outperform pullout students; P^+ = pullout students outperform in-class students; ND = no difference.
*The Instructional Dimensions Study was commissioned and monitored by NIE and conducted by the Learning Research and Development Center at the University of Pittsburgh.

adjust for initial group differences. In these analyses they included only children who had received pullout instruction and they treated setting as a student level variable rather than the classroom level variable employed in their previous analysis. They also changed the nature of the setting variable, redefining it as the number of minutes a child was in pullout. This reanalysis led them to conclude the following:

> Reanalyzing the data with only those children that received pullout changed the picture dramatically. In the analysis with the non-pullout students, there was a negative relationship between the time spent in pullout and posttest in all cells. When the non-pullout students were excluded from the analysis, the results completely changed. There was a positive significant relationship between pullout and posttest in all cases except third grade reading (p. 568).

By way of explaining differences across the two analyses, Leinhardt and Palley (1982) offer the following:

> The most plausible interpretation of these results is that the nonpullout students had more academic knowledge than the pullout students, that is, the

poorer students were chosen for pullout. Hence, pullout was associated with less achievement because it had less able students and not because it was an inferior practice. Pretest did not adequately adjust for all the initial differences. In this case, the underadjustment would be particularly faulty for the first grade since (as Glass and Smith, 1977, pointed out) the pretest was not a good measure of initial abilities. Examining the results with the nonpullout students removed, we see the following: Pullout is still associated with less gain in third grade reading but not in the other three cases. Overall, the more time a student spent in the segregated pullout class, the greater the gain. It seems likely that effective practices were being implemented in these settings. It cannot be determined whether students who were pulled out suffered some initial losses due to having been removed from the regular class. We can say that once pulled out, they increasingly gained from more pullout instruction (p. 568).

Prior to these reanalyses, Glass and Smith (1977) looked at the results of both the IDS study, as reported by NIE, and the ESAA evaluation and found that the ESAA study provided a better data base and more believable evidence for assessing the effects of pullout. Their review of the ESAA findings led them to conclude that there was a consistent negative relationship between the percentage of time pupils spend in the pullout setting and their mathematics and reading achievement. They also concluded that "pupils pulled out of their regular classrooms would have to receive remarkably effective compensatory programs to offset the potential risks incurred. In our opinion, the 'pulled out' pupil is placed in moderate jeopardy of being dysfunctionally labelled, of missing opportunities for peer tutoring and role modeling, and of being segregated from pupils of different ethnic groups" (p. 41). Finally, they concluded that the "pulled out" procedure *per se* had no clear academic or social benefits and may, in fact, be detrimental to pupils' progress and adjustment to school.

From their paper, it appears that Glass and Smith were willing to base their conclusions about pullout on the results of a single study. Obviously, other studies influenced their decision, as suggested by their review of the impact of variables such as ability grouping, labeling, peer tutoring, racial desegregation, and mainstreaming the handicapped. But, it appears that the ESAA findings were the *sine qua non* of their argument. With these findings in hand they could argue that pullout is not only ineffective in improving achievement but that it also produces harmful labeling of students, it serves as a means for resegregating students, and so forth. But is pullout truly ineffective in improving achievement? The reanalysis of the IDS data argue that it is not, and, based on these findings, it appears that Glass and Smith (1977) may have been too negatively disposed to the impact of pullout, at least on achievement. But, at the same time, the reanalyzed IDS data do not suggest that pullout is the best method for improving the achievement of compensatory education students. Rather, they seem to suggest that pullout is one method that should be considered. Cooley (1981) captures the essence of these mixed reactions: "No doubt there are schools in which the pullout practice is being done well, but there are certainly schools in which they may be doing more harm than good" (p. 300).

More recently, a few studies have looked at the impact of pullout on achievement, but, with one exception, these studies are much narrower in scope and in significance than those reported above. Consequently, they do little more than add fuel to the setting debate fire. Nonetheless, they are worthy of consideration, and we turn now to a brief discussion of them.

The Sustaining Effects Study did not directly address the question of the impact of pullout on achievement. However, Carter (1984) did conclude that pullout was the most typical mode of instruction in Title I programs and that Title I did make a difference in achievement, if only for moderately academically disadvantaged students. It could be argued that Carter thus indirectly concluded that pullout has some effect on achievement. However, and as is increasingly the case in the literature, Carter was more interested in describing the effect that particular classroom practices had on achievement than in discussing the effect of setting. Those variables that his research found to be important were opportunity to learn, lower student/staff ratio, allocation of teachers' time, classroom management practices, source of student off-task behavior, supervision of students, and coordination of instruction. He also found years of teaching experience and the instructional leadership of the principal to be important variables.

Yap (1983) also addressed the question of pullout in his secondary analysis of data acquired over a three-year period (1978 to 1981) throughout the state of Hawaii. In this research, Yap compared pullout programs with both in-class and combined in-class/pullout programs. These comparisons were performed separately for reading and mathematics, and for reading only by year, using analysis of covariance procedures in which an NCE gain score was the dependent variable, type of program was the independent variable, and pretest NCE and per pupil cost were covariates. Yap offers no explanation for his selection of per pupil cost as a covariate. Moreover, although he reports sizeable differences in per pupil cost (e.g., almost $350 more per pupil in 1978–79 for pullout versus in-class instruction), he does not describe how this covariate effects the dependent measure, if at all, and it is not possible to determine from the results whether it did. Yap also does not explain why he chose to use the more unreliable gain score as the dependent variable, particularly given the use of the NCE pretest score as a covariate.

Yap reported that there were some 300 "projects" involved in his research. That is, 287 schools were involved in the reading analysis and 26 were involved in the mathematics analysis. For reading, 75 schools were involved in 1978–79, 109 schools in 1979–80, and 103 schools in 1980–81, and in all years over 60 percent of them were pullout schools. Yap bases his major conclusions on school level comparisons. This means that NCEs had to be aggregated across grades. It also means that only one type of setting must have been employed at a given school. Yap offers no guidance as to whether this did occur.

Clearly, Yap's study had some weaknesses, and, consequently, his results are somewhat suspect. Nonetheless, it is interesting to note that Yap found no negative achievement effects resulting from pullout. In fact, his school-level analyses reveal a trend indicating the superiority of pullout programs over both in-class and combined pullout/in-class programs. Given small sample sizes and missing data problems, Yap reported that he was unable to ascertain through a formal analysis of variance or covariance whether grade level interacted with setting. However, an inspection of unadjusted and adjusted means indicated to Yap (no means were presented) that, although such effects were not substantial, there may be grade level differences. Taken together, these results led Yap to conclude that in terms of achievement gain, students who received Chapter 1 instruction in the pullout setting are likely to perform as well as, if not better than, their counterparts in other settings. He also concluded that, despite some drawbacks, the pullout setting was a viable option for providing services to Chapter 1 youngsters.

In a 1985 paper, Yap also argued for the cost effectiveness of the pullout approach. Using the data described above, with all of the inherent weaknesses ascribed to them, he found that pullout produced a unit of NCE gain for every $81 spent. Corresponding figures for in-class and combination programs were $84 and $86, respectively. These findings disagree with Fitzgerald and Hunt (1985). In this study of about one-third of the school districts in Minnesota, pullout and in-class settings were found to be equally effective in producing student achievement gains. However, the pullout setting was found to be more costly and to show a trend toward lower cost effectiveness than in-class instruction. Fitzgerald and Hunt argue that these increased costs might be due to the use of licensed teachers in pullout settings and teacher aides for supplemental in-class instruction. Given the scope of this study (141 randomly selected districts) and the quality of the methods used throughout, it is possible that the Fitzgerald and Hunt findings on cost effectiveness are closer to reality than those reported by Yap.

Nearine and Pecheone's (1984) study of the Intensive Reading Instruction Team (IRIT) Program, which was implemented in Hartford, Connecticut, and validated by the state of Connecticut and the JDRP, also reported positive effects for pullout. This study included 698 students in grades 3 through 6 whose pre-entry reading performance on the Metropolitan Achievement Test fell below the 23rd percentile. The comparison group contained 124 third-grade through sixth-grade students who also scored below the 23rd percentile but who were not selected for the program (i.e., a matched sample). Since students entered this ten-week intensive program at different times during the school year, comparisons could also be made across three "cycles." Thus posttest performance of students completing earlier cycles could be compared with pretest performance of students entering a later cycle. Nearine and Pecheone reported gains of at least six NCEs across the various reading and language arts analyses. They also reported that students who competed an IRIT cycle performed higher than students entering the next cycle. Finally, they found that the gains in reading were sustained throughout the school year (i.e., beyond the time of IRIT instruction). However, they did not find significant posttest differences between IRIT students and those in the comparison group, who outperformed the IRIT students on the pretest, although not significantly.

Knight (1979a, 1979b, and 1979c) also reported positive effects of pullout in studies of several schools in New York City. In each of these studies the actual posttest scores of pullout participants were compared against the scores students would be expected or predicted to receive without intervention. In all of the comparisons performed across the three studies, actual posttest performance exceeded predicted levels. Further, all but six of the more than twenty-five comparisons across various grade levels and content areas were statistically significant. However, the weaknesses of the research design and alpha problems associated with multiple comparisons render these findings somewhat suspect.

Finally, Madhere (1981) reported that pullout was more effective than in-class instruction in improving student achievement. Madhere also argued that pullout appeared to be most effective in an environment where the Title I pupils constitute a majority of the students in the school. He contended that in such a context, the impact of labeling a student in need of assistance, a negative consequence according to the critics of pullout, may be meaningless.

Doss and Holley (1982), on the other hand, reported that pullout programs were not effective. They argued that compensatory programs conducted during the regular day inevitably supplanted regular instruction. They also argued that one of the reasons for the ineffectiveness of pullout programs was the regular classroom teacher's decreased sense of responsibility for the special program student. Based on Glass and Smith's (1979) meta analysis of class size and achievement, they argued that reducing class size to fifteen and delivering instruction within the regular classroom would not only redress some of the problems occurring within pullout programs, but would also improve student performance. Since this approach was permissible under the "schoolwide projects" provision of Title I in force at that time, such a program was implemented on a pilot basis in 1980–81 in two Austin, Texas, elementary schools. Analyses were conducted on reading and mathematics achievement for students in grades 2 through 6 in those schools and in certain Title I schools using pullout programs. From these analysis, Doss and Holley concluded that in most schoolwide projects students outscored Title I regular students of the same pretest level and that the impact of the schoolwide projects were generally uniform across all levels of the pretest. On average, the advantage of the schoolwide projects across grades were 2.1 months in reading, 2.5 months in language arts, and 2.2 months in mathematics. However, these gains were purchased at such great expense ("lowering the PTR [pupil/teacher ratio] from 25–1 to 15–to–1 would increase personnel costs by 67% in the schools and grades where applied" [Doss and Holley, 1982, p. 10]) that the schoolwide project model was not adopted in other Austin schools. Levine and Stark (1982) also report the schoolwide projects implemented in the Los Angeles Unified School District were so poorly received that they were discontinued, partly because they were very expensive and partly because there were questions about how well they worked.

What, then, can we say about the effect of pullout on achievement? Based on the research that has been conducted to date, we cannot conclude with confidence either that pullout is more effective than in-class instruction or that the opposite is true. We can conclude, however, that the achievement findings provide little support for the overwhelming, and in some locations almost exclusive, use of the pullout model. Rather, the findings suggest that both pullout and in-class instruction can be effective, given appropriate circumstances, and, as reported by Carter (1984), Leinhardt and Palley (1982), Tobias (1982), and others, it is likely that these circumstances, particularly the type and quality of the instruction delivered within an instructional setting, are more important than the setting itself. Despite this general sense, however, it must be reported that pullout programs have been opposed for reasons other than their impact on achievement.

Other Effects of Instructional Setting

In addition to achievement findings, the literature also includes an increasing amount of other information on the effects of in-class versus pullout programs. Included among the long list of issues that have been addressed are the following:

1. The stigma associated with receiving Chapter 1 instruction, particularly in a pullout setting
2. The levels of communication, cooperation, and coordination possible in the two settings
3. The levels of teacher autonomy and control afforded by the settings
4. The amount and type of content lost when compensatory instruction is received, particularly in pullout programs
5. Class size shifts and resultant gains
6. Grouping patterns, individualization, and segregation in in-class and pullout settings

7. The relationship among peers and the opportunity for peer tutoring
8. The types of instructors and their roles in different settings.

The first four of these issues will be addressed in this section. The remaining four issues will be addressed in sections that follow. In either case, much of what we know about these issues is derived from relatively small-scale observational studies, studies of relatively modest scope reporting on the results of interviews with program students, teachers, and administrators, and somewhat narrow surveys of the perception of these and other groups. Moreover, as was the case with the review of the impact of setting on achievement, the data that are available are generally equivocal.

Stigma.   Leinhardt and Palley (1982) reported that despite contrary research findings, special educators strongly believe that special placement makes the target child feel rejected rather than rescued. Likewise, many educators believe that compensatory education students feel different if they are labeled as Chapter 1-eligible and are pulled out of their regular classrooms for special instruction (e.g., Leinhardt and Palley, 1982; Shuy, 1978; Glass and Smith, 1977). Some argue, on the other hand, that stigmatization occurs in mainstream programs as well (Noddings, 1978). On this score, at least one author has suggested that stigmatization may be greater in the mainstream setting since in this environment compensatory education students are both singled out and remediated in front of their classmates (Hayes, 1983). From a slightly different perspective, it has also been argued that pullout is an effective instructional strategy in an environment where Chapter 1 students constitute a majority, and that in such settings labeling may be meaningless (Madhere, 1981).

Even though the research evidence is inconclusive, it appears reasonable to argue that stigmatization occurs in both in-class and pullout settings: in the in-class setting because students receive extra instruction in front of their peers, and in the pullout setting because students are easily identifiable. It also appears that it is not the setting itself that aggravates the feeling of being different, but the sensitivity or insensitivity of teachers operating within the setting (Noddings, 1978). Kennedy's (1978) advice on this issue seems particularly compelling:

> Compensatory education students are less likely to be subjected to labeling and its negative effects in environments where teachers actively encourage children's respect for and appreciation of a variety of human differences; in environments where similarities between learning tasks and materials are emphasized; and in environments where Title I and non-Title I children frequently move, in an organized way, to other parts of the building or classroom to receive special instruction (p. 35).

Communication, Cooperation, and Coordination. One of the most frequently cited advantages of the in-class setting is the increased communication, cooperation, and coordination among regular classroom and compensatory education instructors that it affords. Advocates of in-class instruction argue that because specialist teachers or aides hired with compensatory education funds provide their instruction in the same classroom as the regular teacher, there will be increased interaction and cooperation in planning for instruction (Bean and Eichelberger, 1985; Kennedy, 1978; Hayes, 1983; Neumann, 1985), better integration of remedial and regular instructional strategies (Allington, 1986; Bean and Eichelberger, 1985; Kaestle and Smith, 1982), better opportunities for individualization and small-group instruction (Bean and Eichelberger, 1985), and a better flow of information on student progress (Harnischfeger, 1980). There will also be fewer disruptions caused by students moving in and out of the regular classroom (Hayes, 1983), and thus more continuity in instruction, as well as an increased opportunity for regular classroom teachers to observe other, perhaps more effective, approaches for working with compensatory education students (Kennedy, 1978).

Allington (1986) has offered some particularly powerful comments on one of the consequences of pullout, namely the fragmentation of instruction. He suggests that pullout remedial reading instruction is typically independent from the reading instruction offered in the regular classroom and that it generally employs different materials and teaching methods. He argues further that neither the classroom teacher nor the compensatory education specialist is likely to know what type of instruction the other is offering. Consequently, he claims that few remedial students actually receive instruction that supplements their core curriculum; rather, they are taught by classroom and remedial teachers who express different beliefs about student needs, offer different objectives as targets for instruction, and use reading material that represent different models of the reading process. As a result, he argues, students who are in need of remediation are offered instruction that seems likely to increase their confusion rather than reduce it. Allington also acknowledges, however, that pullout programs can offer instruction that is congruent with that provided in the regular classroom (i.e., same or similar material, same reading strategy used, and same reading skill taught), and, therefore, that the lack of congruence may be related to factors other than the instructional setting itself.

Despite this indictment of pullout programs, it appears that in-class programs also present problems, some of which are the same as those prevalent in pullout settings. Bean and Eichelberger (1985), for example, noted differences in classroom teachers' and specialists' teaching styles and instructional strategies when a large city school district changed from a pullout program to one in which specialists worked in the regular classroom. Moreover, although teachers in this new program reported increased

interaction and cooperation, they also reported problems with scheduling and inadequate joint planning time; reading specialists, on the other hand, reported that there was a lack of teacher interaction, that they weren't sure what their role was in the classroom, that they had insufficient materials, and that there was inadequate management. Bean and Eichelberger (1985) concluded that these problems were due to two teachers sharing the same room and that, despite the in-class arrangement, team teaching was difficult.

Vasquez and Nuttall (1983) reached similar conclusions. These researchers also argued that it is the classroom teacher, not the specialist, who is forced to schedule activities that will accommodate another class in the same room and that the coordination between the regular and compensatory program is still accomplished outside of the regular classroom, before school, during recess, during lunch, or after school. They argued further that even though the materials used in the regular and remedial programs are more likely to be similar in in-class programs, pullout programs use a greater variety of instructional materials. Specialist teachers working in the regular classrooms apparently find it difficult to transport books and other paraphernalia from classroom to classroom (Bean and Eichelberger agree), find it harder to use audiovisual materials because they would be distracting to the regular classroom teacher, and, for that same reason, avoid materials that require recitations or other "out-loud" work. Despite his enthusiasm for the in-class approach, Neumann (1985) concluded that where this type of setting is used specialists must be highly organized, must be flexible enough to work in several environments, and must have the diplomacy and personality needed to work jointly with colleagues.

Taken together, these results suggest that even though in-class programs offer the opportunity for increased communication, cooperation, and instructional continuity, they do not ensure that they will occur. Perhaps, as suggested by Kennedy (1978), the key to good coordination between compensatory and regular instruction is not the setting for instruction but rather the quality of the joint planning that occurs, the amount of decision-making power given to teachers and specialists by their respective administrators, and the flexibility in scheduling. Whether these characteristics occur more frequently in in-class settings remains to be seen.

Teacher Autonomy and Control.   Critics of the pullout model have argued that when students receive remedial instruction outside the regular classroom neither the regular teacher nor the compensatory education specialist is willing to accept full responsibility for the students' progress (Allington, 1986; Doss and Holley, 1982). If they so desire, classroom teachers can claim that less than acceptable progress is attributable to shortcomings of either the student or the compensatory instruction; compensatory education specialists, on the other hand, can attribute such a result to either the student or inadequate regular classroom instruction. To

avoid such academic fingerpointing, some have argued that the adoption of the in-class model would allow the teachers who share the same space to share this responsibility or the administrators coordinating the program to decide on whose shoulders the responsibility should rest. Despite the wisdom of this argument, it appears that the adoption of an in-class arrangement will again not ensure the expected outcome. Bean and Eichelberger (1985), for example, reported that both teachers and specialists had problems with two instructors in one room and that the problem of leadership or control was a real issue. Vasquez and Nuttall (1983) reached a similar conclusion, as did Shuy (1978), who found that some of the teachers in the Instructional Dimensions Study favored pullout because it gave them greater autonomy. On the other hand, Shuy also reported that some teachers favored the in-class approach because it gave them more control. Unfortunately, the literature does not allow one to resolve this apparent conflict.

Content Lost.   It was argued earlier in this chapter that students receiving compensatory instruction in a particular content area (e.g., reading) do so at the expense of regular instruction in that same content. Harnischfeger (1980) concluded that pullout pupils "often receive less reading time than the rest of the class because the pulling out—going some place and coming back—also entails loss of instructional time for students who need more" (p. 4). Regardless of whether this is true, and there is some evidence to suggest that the total time allocated to basic skills instruction is greater for compensatory education students than for their noncompensatory education peers (Archambault and St. Pierre, 1980), the implication is that some approach other than or in addition to pullout would be more effective.

Harnischfeger's solution would be to lengthen the school day for compensatory education students (i.e., an add-on approach). Others argue that providing in-class instruction would solve the problem because then the time lost by traveling from place to place would be retained. Allington (1986), for example, suggests that as much as fifteen minutes per day, or forty hours per academic year, might be saved in this manner. However, neither Allington nor anyone else that this reviewer has been able to uncover provides direct evidence on what would actually be done with the newly found time were compensatory instruction to be provided in the classroom. Would the interruptions prevalent in in-class programs (Hayes, 1983) prove to be less troublesome than the disruption associated with pullout programs? Would the presence of more than one teacher in a single classroom result in greater confusion than occurs in pullout programs, particularly when such programs are adopted on a wholesale basis? Additional research is needed before we can determine with any confidence whether in-class compensatory education programs result in more or less time allocated to instruction. Additional research is also needed to determine whether such differ-

ences in allocated time are accompanied by differences in the amount of time that students in various settings actually engage or actively participate in instruction.

CLASS SIZE, INDIVIDUALIZATION, AND GROUPING

Compensatory instruction is delivered in smaller classes and groups than regular classroom instruction. It is also more likely than regular instruction to incorporate components of individualized instructional programs. Pullout instruction, which comprises the large portion of compensatory instruction, is delivered in groups that are more homogeneous in ability than those in the classrooms from which compensatory students are removed. Do the reductions in class and group size and the increase in individualization of instruction have a positive affect on students? Is homogeneous ability grouping preferred to heterogeneous ability grouping? We turn now to a discussion of these issues.

Glass and Smith (1979) reported on the results of a meta-analysis of seventy-seven studies involving 725 comparisons of larger and smaller classes. They found that 60 percent of the achievement comparisons favored smaller classes and that the effect was particularly strong when the classes contained fifteen or fewer pupils. They also found that this relationship did not change significantly for students of different ability levels. On the other hand, a review of twenty-four studies conducted by the Educational Research Service (1978) concluded that research provided no clearcut guidelines for an optimum class size. The ERS review also concluded, however, that pupils with lower ability tend to benefit from smaller classes more than pupils of average ability and that smaller classes can positively affect the scholastic achievement of economically or socially disadvantaged pupils. Cooper (1986), in his comprehensive review of the literature, summarizes the effect of class size on achievement as follows:

> Both the (Glass and Smith) meta-analysis and the ERS review concluded that smaller class sizes benefit the population of students served by Chapter 1 programs. Glass and Smith did so by finding the benefit of small classes held for students regardless of their intelligence level. ERS found the benefit for low ability or economically disadvantaged children only. Further, the typical size of compensatory education instructional groups falls within the range about which there appears to be some agreement. It will be recalled that from one-third to all of Title I students in the districts sampled by the (Title I) Demonstration Study (Archambault and St. Pierre, 1979) received compensatory instruction in groups of one to five students. All the reviewers agreed that this is the end of the class size curve where effects are most dramatic and dependable (p. 9).

Hedges and Stock (1983) cite two problems with Glass and Smith's estimation procedures. First, they argued that they overestimated effect sizes when study Ns were small. Second, they argued that the variance of a student's effect size estimate was not based on its sample size, as it should have been. Hedges and Stock (1983) thus reanalyzed the same class size data taking these problems into account. As might be expected, they found a smaller effect size than Glass and Smith. However, they also found that smaller classes still led to higher expected achievement and that the shape of the curve expressing the relationship between class size and achievement found by Glass and Smith remained unchanged.

Slavin (1984) has criticized both the Glass and Smith study and the Hedges and Stock reanalysis. He argues that the Glass and Smith results were heavily influenced by studies of tutoring (i.e., one-to-one instruction, or a class size of one). This claim is based on his review of fourteen studies listed by Glass and Smith in which students were randomly assigned to large or small groups. Fourteen of the thirty contrasts in this studies involved comparisons of classes with a median size of twenty-three to those with class sizes of one to five, and ten of these involved classes with one student. The median effect size for these comparisons was 0.545. Nine involved comparisons of classes with a median size of 35 to classes ranging in size from fourteen to seventeen pupils. The median effect size for these studies was 0.08. Finally, for comparisons involving classes with more than twenty students (i.e., median larger classes of thirty-seven and median smaller classes of twenty-six), the median effect size was 0.04. Thus, Slavin concludes that the effects of tutoring are positive but that "there is nothing in the Glass et al. meta-analysis to contradict an assertion that class size makes no meaningful difference in achievement unless the smaller class has no more than three students" (p. 11).

Slavin's criticism of Hedges and Stock (1983) focuses on their study selection procedures. That is, although he agrees with Hedges and Stock's conclusion about overestimated effect sizes, he believes that Hedges and Stock's reanalysis produced the same general conclusion as Glass and Smith because they chose to include the same studies as the earlier researchers.

It appears, then, that for the total population the relationship between class size and achievement is not yet fully understood. For compensatory education students, however, there is some evidence to suggest that smaller class sizes may be beneficial. This conclusion is based on the ERS finding that pupils with lower ability tend to benefit from smaller classes. It is also based on Cooper's conclusion that the most dramatic effects of class size are at the end of the class size curve, namely classes of five students or less, the size of the group in which Chapter 1 students are mostly likely to receive compensatory instruction.

The Glass and Smith study also looked at the effect of class size on variables other than achievement. They concluded that teacher morale is higher, that their attitude toward pupils is more positive, and that their satisfaction with their own performance is greater in smaller classes. They also found positive effects of smaller classes on "student attitude," which included attitudes toward the teacher, school, and themselves (i.e., self-concept), as well as positive effects on student motivation. Cooper (1986) summarizes these other results of the Glass and Smith study:

> This category of effects [student attitudes] demonstrated a difference of 29 percentile ranks between students in classes of size 40 and size 10. Another group of effects involving measures of student participation showed a difference between classes of 10 and 40 students equal to 23 percentile ranks. Finally, a group of variables measuring different types of student misbehaviors also favored smaller classes, but the number of comparisons was too small to estimate a percentile rank difference (p. 11).

Individualization

Since the average class size for compensatory instruction in reading, language arts, and mathematics are all below fourteen and the average size of the regular classroom is twenty-seven (Archambault and St. Pierre, 1979; Carter, 1984; NIE, 1977), it would appear from the above that smaller class sizes would be preferred. Moreover, if students in these smaller classes are also receiving more individualized instruction, as Glass and Smith (1980) say they do, then it would be logical to conclude that class sizes for compensatory education students, whether the instruction is compensatory or not, should be small (i.e., at least less than fifteen), and that individualized instruction should be emphasized. Before we leap to this conclusion, however, we should review what other researchers have to say.

The Class Size and Instruction Program (CSIP) research of Cahen, Filby, McCutcheon, and Kyle (1983), which included four second-grade classes selected from an innercity school in California and a rural school in Virginia, investigated what happens in classrooms when class size is reduced. These researchers concluded that smaller classes made discipline easier and that teachers in them spend more time teaching and less time policing. They also found that students paid closer attention in smaller classes and that group discussions involved more of the students in the group. Finally, the researchers concluded that the effect of participation may be most pronounced for low achievers because "in a small group, where control is perceived to be easier, the teacher may feel she or he can take time to draw all students into the lesson" rather than "rely on volunteers or high ability students in order to keep things moving along" (cited in Cooper, 1986, p. 13).

The Class Size and Instruction Program as well as the Sustaining Effects Study (Carter, 1984) reported on behavior management issues associated with the sizes of classes and groups within them. The Sustaining Effects Study found that the smaller instructional groups and lower student-to-instructor ratios associated with Title I programs were associated with more student on-task behavior, less teacher time in behavioral management, a more harmonious class environment, and a higher quality of cognitive monitoring, task monitoring, and organization of activities. The CSIP researchers reached the same general conclusions.

CSIP also looked at the relationship between class size and individualization. Although the CSIP researchers recognized that smaller classes provided the opportunity for greater individualization of instruction, they found that smaller classes did not lead to dramatic increases in the amount of individualization. Instead, they found that group instruction continued and the curriculum remained the same. Harnischfeger (1980) concluded that, even when class sizes are reduced drastically, many teachers do not significantly change their teaching strategies. She suggests that the only consequence of smaller class sizes is smaller subgroups but not fewer groups, and, on the average, no increased teacher/pupil interaction. Harnischfeger goes on to argue that instead of a teacher working with small groups one at a time while the rest of the class is on their own, he or she should consider whole-class instruction. If they do, Harnischfeger argues, their students will benefit by receiving more direct instruction.

Despite the evidence provided by the CSIP researchers, one might argue that the findings are suspect because of the small sample of schools and classrooms (i.e., two schools and four classrooms involved in the research) and that individualization does occur more frequently in smaller classes. Suppose this were true? What do we know about the impact of individualization on student outcome measures?

Cooley and Leinhardt (1980) reported they did not find any clear evidence for the superiority of individualized instruction over other methods of compensatory education. Their review of the literature also suggested that this finding is consistent with other attempts to establish the effectiveness of individualization. Brophy (1986) has argued that the problem is not with the conceptual model of individualization, which calls for beginning where students are and moving them along at their own pace. Rather, the problem is that:

> Individualized instruction in the typical classroom shifts a great deal of responsibility for planning and managing learning from the teacher to the students themselves and shifts responsibility for carrying the content to the students from the teacher to the materials. This is workable and may even have certain advantages when the teacher is continually available to provide close supervision and immediate help when needed, but it does not work well when students must function on their own for extended periods of time, trying to learn through interacting with the curriculum materials without much guidance or help from the teacher (pp. 13–14).

Brophy does state, however, that the individualized training package approach can be used effectively in special classrooms with small student/ teacher ratios. Basing his conclusion on the results of a study by Crawford (1983), Brophy indicates that under such conditions "teachers can move the students through curriculum at a faster pace, can provide more tutorial and individualized instruction, and can assign more difficult work because they are able to monitor everyone's progress and provide immediate help when needed" (p. 14). Nonetheless, Brophy's review underscores the role of active instruction from the teacher in producing achievement gains:

> Such instruction can be provided in tutorial form in special classes with small student/teacher ratios, and it can be provided to small groups in classrooms where the teacher has developed appropriate assignments and installed effective seatwork management procedures so that students are engaged in worthwhile academic activities in between their small group lessons from the teacher. The individualized approach is not feasible in the typical classroom, however, and even the small group approach is likely to strike most teachers as more trouble than it is worth unless they have an aide available to supervise seatwork while they teach small group lessons (or unless they believe that the class is so heterogeneous that they are forced to provide differentiated instruction to small homogeneous groups). Consequently, most teachers will opt for the traditional whole-class instruction/recitation/seatwork method as their primary approach to instruction (p. 15).

What does Brophy mean by active teaching? Active teaching connotes frequent lessons (whole class or small group, depending on grade level and subject matter) in which the teacher presents information and develops concepts through lecture and demonstration, elaborates this information in the feedback given following responses to recitation or discussion questions, prepares the students for followup assignments by giving instructions and going through practice examples, monitors progress on assignments, and follows up with appropriate feedback and reteaching when necessary. There is a great deal of teacher talk, but most of it is academic rather than procedural or managerial, and much of it involves asking questions and giving feedback rather than extended lecturing.

Grouping

The issue of grouping for instruction has been alluded to several times in the preceding discussion, but to this point we have said little or nothing about how and why groups are formed and the effects of different grouping patterns. In general, ability grouping refers to the practice by which students in more heterogeneous classes or groups are arranged into more homogeneous classes or groups for all or a portion of their instruction. Most U.S. schools follow this practice and most teachers overwhelmingly support it, probably because they believe that homogeneous groups are easier to teach than heterogeneous groups. Dividing students according to ability allows teachers to increase the pace and level of instruction for high achievers and provide more repetition, review, and remediation for low achievers. Ability grouping is also supposed to provide a spur to high achievers by making them work harder to achieve, and to place success within the grasp of low achievers, who are protected from having to compete with their more able agemates (Atkinson and O'Connor, 1963). Critics argue that ability grouping confers unnecessary distinction on those in the fast track while placing a stigma on those in slow groups (Kulik and Kulik, 1982). They also contend that being placed in a low-achieving class or track has damaging psychological effects on students (Oakes, 1985; Rosenbaum, 1980; Schafer and Olexa, 1971).

Slavin (1986), in his "best evidence synthesis" of the literature on ability grouping in the elementary school, carefully distinguishes within-class from between-class ability grouping. Within-class ability grouping refers to the assignment of students to more homogeneous groups within a heterogeneous class arrangement. The most common form of within-class grouping is the use of reading groups, where teachers assign students to one of a small number of groups on the basis of reading level. These groups work on different materials at rates unique to their needs and abilities. Other forms of within-class ability grouping may be found in mathematics, where the teacher presents a lesson to the class as a whole, and afterwards, while the students are working problems, the teacher provides enrichment or extension to a high-achieving group, remediation or reexploration to lower achievers, and something in between to average achievers. According to Slavin, group-paced mastery learning (Bloom, 1976) may be seen as one form of flexible within-class grouping. Individualized or continuous-progress instruction may be seen as extreme forms of ability grouping.

Slavin (1986) also contends that between-class groups take many forms. In fact, he describes the following seven types:

1. Ability Grouped Class Assignment: Students are assigned on the basis of ability or achievement to one self-contained class (usually at the elementary level) or to one class that moves together from teacher to teacher, as in block scheduling in junior high schools.
2. Curriculum Tracking: A special form of ability-grouped class assignment unique to the secondary level in which students are assigned by ability or achievement to tracks, such as college preparatory, general, or vocational. Students may take all or only some of their courses within these tracks.
3. Regrouping for Reading or Mathematics (Ability Grouping for Selected Subjects): Students are assigned to heterogeneous homeroom classes for

part or most of the day, but are "regrouped" according to achievement level for one or more subjects.

4. Joplin Plan: A special form of regrouping for reading in which students are assigned to heterogeneous groups for most of the day but are regrouped for reading across grade levels (Floyd, 1954). For example, a reading class at the fifth-grade, first-semester reading level might include high-achieving fourth graders, average-achieving fifth graders, and low-achieving sixth graders. Reading group assignments are frequently reviewed, so that students may be reassigned to a different reading class if performance warrants if.

5. Nongraded Plans: In its broadest application, grade-level designations are entirely removed, and students are placed in flexible groups according to their performance level, not their age (Goodlad and Anderson, 1963). Students move from group to group and complete the curriculum at their own pace so that some students might complete the primary grades, for example, in two years while others would require four years.

6. Special Classes for High Achievers: Plans in which gifted, talented, or otherwise superior students are assigned to a special class for all or part of their school day, while other students remain in relatively heterogeneous classes.

7. Special Classes for Low Achievers: The assignment of students with learning problems to special or remedial classes for part or all of their school day.

Dreeban (1984) suggests that factors other than students' ability or past achievement also affect their assignment to groups. Included among these additional factors are the distribution of students' aptitudes or achievement in the school or classroom, organization constraints within the school or classroom, and student management and discipline. With regard to assignment within classes, teachers also consider the number, size, and diversity of students within groups when assigning other students to the group. Generally, teachers form at least three groups, and groups formed on the basis of ability may vary widely on other dimensions. Nonetheless, instruction is geared to the level of ability attributed to the group.

With regard to within-class grouping, a recent review of the literature by Wilkinson (1986) has concluded that students in low-ability reading groups fare poorly:

> Students in low groups receive less time to read in comparison with students in high groups; oral reading errors made by lows are more frequently corrected than those made by highs (i.e., they are interrupted more frequently); lows are given more instruction in decoding and teacher prompts are more focused on

phonics for lows than for high; lows are frequently less attentive than highs (Allington, 1980; Eder, 1981, 1982, 1983, 1984; Rist, 1970; Stern & Shavelson, 1981). Eder (1981) argues that these practices result in lower reading-test performance and lower oral-reading grades for the low ability groups. The poor achievement of the lows is thus the result of low expectations by the teachers and/or the poor quality of teaching that they receive. At first glance, these studies suggest that the differential treatment received by the low ability students is the culprit, the cause of their poor reading achievement (pp. 12–13).

Wilkinson continues:

> The implications for low achieving students seems clear: Homogeneous ability grouping is detrimental to learning for students assigned to low groups (Eash, 1961; Persell, 1977). These studies reveal mechanisms through which the negative effect of assignment to a low ability group occurs. There are differences in the instructional processes and learning environments of different ability groups. Teachers and students interact in different ways across ability groups. We are compelled to agree with Hallinan's (1984, p. 233) conclusion that: 'At present, the great majority of studies demonstrate that assignment to a low track or ability group places students at a disadvantage in terms of learning opportunities' (p. 13).

Wilkinson also concluded that low-ability students seem to benefit in achievement by being placed in small, heterogeneous ability groups (Swing and Peterson, 1982) and that these groups can provide environments that are positive for learning (Cohen, 1984; Webb, 1982, 1985; Webb and Kenderski, 1984; Peterson, Wilkinson, Spinelli, and Swing, 1984).

Slavin's (1986) review of the literature on within-class ability grouping reached a different conclusion. Basing this portion of his review exclusively on research in mathematics (because no reading studies met stated criteria for inclusion—see Slavin, 1986, pp. 15–16 for a discussion of these criteria), Slavin found that every one of the eight studies he located favored homogeneous within-class grouping, though not always significantly. Five of the studies also broke down achievement effects by student ability levels, but there was no clear pattern of results favoring ability grouping for one or another subgroup. On this score, Slavin concluded the following:

> Every subgroup gained more in classes using within-class ability grouping than in control (ungrouped) treatments. However, it is interesting to note that the median effect size for low achievers (ES = +.65) was higher than that for average (ES = +.27) or high achievers (ES = .41) (p. 84).

Slavin acknowledges that this evidence is surprising in light of several studies of ability grouping in reading suggesting that students in low reading groups experience a lower quality of instruction than do those in higher groups.

How can we explain the discrepant findings from the Wilkinson and Slavin reviews? One possible explanation is that Wilkinson draws heavily on studies in reading, whereas Slavin focuses only on mathematics. More important than this, however, is the fact that much of the research cited by Wilkinson deals with observations that students in low reading or math groups learn less than students in higher groups, not less than other low-achieving students in contrasting arrangements. Thus, according to Slavin, it is hardly surprising that high and low achievers differ and that their teachers' behavior differs accordingly. Slavin (1986) argues further that:

> Comparisons of achievement gains in high and low reading groups are found to show an advantage of being in the high group because high achievers learn more rapidly than low achievers, and unless measures used to control for initial ability are perfectly reliable and perfectly predictive of later reading achievement, assignment to the high reading group will appear to lead to higher achievement (see Reichardt, 1979) (p. 58).

What, then, can we conclude about the effect of within-class ability grouping? At present, the best evidence in this area comes from Slavin's review, and, based on this, it seems safe to conclude that at least in mathematics and on achievement grounds, within-class ability grouping should be supported for all students, including low achievers. However, and despite the results presented by Wilkinson, it does not appear reasonable to conclude at this time that either homogeneous or heterogeneous within-class ability grouping is preferred for delivering reading instruction to low-ability students. As suggested by Slavin, such a conclusion can be reached only when experimental comparisons of grouped and ungrouped reading classes have been performed.

Turning now to between-class ability grouping, Glass and Smith (1977) called the research literature on ability grouping "a confusing welter of contradictory, tendentious, antiquated and dubious studies" (p. 32). Nonetheless, drawing from the reviews of Miller and Otto (1930), Billet (1932), Cornell (1936), Ekstrom (1959), Eash (1961), and Goldberg, Passow, and Justman (1966), Glass and Smith (1977) concluded that ability grouping is not an important variable in itself, and that it is worth considering only as it relates to or potentiates other changes in instructional activities. They also concluded that "the accumulated research literature of several decades shows such as unstable pattern of what takes place between teachers and pupils in homogeneous as opposed to heterogeneous classrooms that no generalizations are possible (or useful) about the effects of ability grouping" (pp. 34–35).

Kulik and Kulik (1982) conducted a more recent meta-analysis of the effects of ability grouping on secondary school students. They found that in thirty-six of the fifty-one studies looking at achievement, the performance of students in grouped classes was better than the performance of students in ungrouped classes; in fourteen other studies, the performance was better in ungrouped classes; and in one study, there was no difference. A total of ten of the comparisons were statistically significant, eight of which favored grouping and two of which favored what Kulik and Kulik called "conventional instruction." The effect size was small, however, averaging about one-tenth of a standard deviation across studies. In the four programs designed especially for academically deficient students the effects were even smaller. In fact, they were near zero, indicating that students learned as much in mixed ability classrooms as they did in homogeneous classrooms. Kulik and Kulik did find, however, that homogeneous grouping was effective for high achievers.

Slavin (1984) criticized the Kulik and Kulik (1982) review on the grounds that many of the studies they included used matching or other nonrandom procedures to attempt to equate groups on initial ability, and that this procedure would result in selection bias. Moreover, Slavin argued that in studies of high achievers, this bias should favor homogeneous assignment for gifted students, as was found by Kulik and Kulik. Slavin also argued that since the mean effect size for studies using random assignment is zero, Kulik and Kulik's claim of positive effects of ability grouping rests entirely on nonrandomized studies.

In his own review of the ability grouping literature, Slavin (1986) argues that research clearly does not support the assignment of students to self-contained classes according to ability, nor does it support the conclusion that ability grouping is beneficial for high-ability students and detrimental for low-ability students, as suggested by Eash (1961), Esposito (1973), and Begle (1975). The literature does suggest, however, that cross-grade tutoring and comprehensive nongraded plans can be effective. Particularly noteworthy in this regard are the fourteen studies reviewed by Slavin using Joplin or Joplin-like plans. For eleven of these studies the Joplin plan classes achieved more than the control classes; for the remaining three studies no differences were found. In addition, the median effect size for these studies was found to be about 0.45. The results for the comprehensive nongraded plans are less consistent than for the Joplin-like plans, but the median effect size is still moderately positive (ES = .29). Based on this, Slavin concludes that the evidence supports the use of these plans. He also suggests that while the results of studies of regrouping for reading and mathematics are inconclusive, it is still quite possible that grouping for one or two subjects is instructionally effective.

Related to the literature on ability grouping is an increasingly large body of research on the relative effects of mainstreaming versus special class placement. Due in large part to the impact of the 1975 Education of All Handicapped Children Act (PL 94–142), which mandated that handicapped children had to be educated in the least restrictive environment, most of the recent research has focused on this special population, particularly the mildly handicapped, who prior to 1975 had most often been served in self-contained settings completely separate from the public schools. Because the results of these studies are not directly generalizable to the types of students served by compensatory education programs, these mainstreaming findings must be interpreted cautiously. However, it should also be recognized that the findings are not without merit and may be applicable to those now served by Chapter 1 and other state and local programs for the academically disadvantaged. In fact, as suggested by Leinhardt, Bickel, and Palley (1982), it may well be that some treatments are effective for both the mildly handicapped and the academically disadvantaged.

Leinhardt and Palley's (1982) informative review of the literature on mainstreaming and restrictive educational settings concluded that while there is a trend toward negative effects of isolated settings for low-ability children, it is neither strong nor highly consistent. They also concluded that children on the borderline of the cutoff for special placement suffer more when they are isolated than do children who are closer to the median of the group of children that receive special services. Finally, they concluded that the setting itself (i.e., mainstreaming versus isolated setting) is not a powerful direct inference on student achievement, but that it indirectly influences other relevant variables, most of which can occur in most settings.

Like Leinhardt and Palley (1982), Madden and Slavin (1983) also concluded from their review of the literature that full-time special education placements resulted in few consistent benefits for the mildly academically handicapped (i.e., learning disabled or educable mentally retarded). However, Madden and Slavin went further by concluding that regular class placement (i.e., mainstreaming) was preferred to special class placement on achievement grounds. The best evidence for this conclusion, Madden and Slavin argue, is the research of Calhoun and Elliott (1977) in which fifty black educable mentally retarded (EMR) students and fifty black emotionally disturbed students were randomly assigned to regular and special classes and followed over a three-year period. These researchers found that placement in regular classes had a more positive effect on the achievement of both groups that did special class placement. Interestingly, Madden and Slavin (1983) also cite a study by Leinhardt (1980) as support for regular class placement. In this study:

> Low achieving students in the regular class made significantly greater gains in reading achievement than did students in the special transition rooms, despite the fact that the transition rooms, which used the same curriculum, had much lower student teacher ratios and were staffed by some of the schools "best" teachers (Madden and Slavin, 1983, p. 524).

Madden and Slavin admit that their conclusions are based heavily on these two studies, However, they argue that their conclusion is warranted since the two studies are particularly well designed and their effects are quite large.

Despite his general conclusion that regular class placement is preferred for the mildly academically handicapped, Slavin suggests that the "effects of regular class placement depend substantially on the program in the regular class" (1986, p. 530). Specifically, he argues that individualized instruction is required for the positive effects to occur, and that this applies to social-emotional outcomes as well as achievement. He also suggests, however, that part-time resource programs can have a positive impact on the achievement of the mildly academically handicapped if they are of good quality, again hinting that this implies that individualized instruction occurs. In this regard, Slavin seems to be at odds with Brophy (1986) and others who are calling for less individualized instruction and more direct or active instruction.

Although Slavin is enthusiastic about regular class placement, he recognizes that the placement of mildly academically handicapped students in regular classes is fraught with problems. Included among these is the fact that regular class teachers feel poorly prepared to accommodate the needs of the mildly academically handicapped and that LD and EMR students in regular classes are less accepted and more rejected than their nonhandicapped peers. Slavin describes a variety of programs for overcoming these problems, and proposes that these programs and strategies be used either to restructure the regular classroom or to construct resource programs to supplement instruction in the regular class. Thus, in the language of ability grouping, Slavin appears to be calling for heterogeneous groupings of students, including the mildly academically handicapped, within-class. He also suggests, however, that some form of regrouping for certain types of instruction, probably employing pullout since he uses the resource room terminology, may be required.

But even if pullout programs can be justified on academic grounds, removing children from regular classrooms for compensatory instruction creates the possibility of resegregation. On this score, Glass and Smith (1977) have argued that pullout programs do not alter the racial mixture of schools but they may and probably do change the racial composition of the classes within them. Eyler (1982) is less equivocal. Citing the work of Hinkley, Beal, and Breglio (1978) and Brookover, Brady, and Warfield (1981), she argues that minority students receive larger amounts of compensatory instruction than nonminorities and that they are typically pulled out of less segregated classrooms and sent to more segregated special rooms to receive their instruction. Citing the work of Kimbrough and Hill (1981), Eyler argues that the potential for resegregation through compensatory services is exacerbated in schools that operate more than one categorical program and have substantial numbers of students who are eligible for more than one type of service. She also argues that the negative effects of resegregation are not offset by pullout's effects on achievement. To avoid problems created by pullout, Eyler recommends that compensatory services be delivered in class by specialists who act as consultants rather than simply as subject matter specialists. In this redefined role they would serve as resources to the regular classroom teacher rather than instructors of specific groups of students. They would assist teachers in assessing specific learning problems and preparing individual learning plans, train classroom aides and parent volunteers, and help the principal plan the schoolwide instruction program.

On the question of race relations, Slavin (1979, 1980) and Slavin and Madden (1979) reported that working together on school projects with a student of another race and competing together on interracial sports teams both had strong positive effects on racial attitudes and behaviors. However, teacher workshops, minority history, multiethnic texts, bisocial student advisory committees, and similar school programs made no difference in racial attitudes or interracial friendships. Given these results, it would appear that if pullout programs do lead to resegregation, as Eyler (1982) and others have argued that they do, the resultant reduction in contact between minority and nonminority students will reduce the possibility of improved relations among the races. To the extent that this occurs, it must be viewed as a serious negative consequence of homogeneous grouping that uses the pullout model.

TYPE OF INSTRUCTOR

As noted earlier, instructional specialists provide the large majority of compensatory instruction. Generally, these specialists have a higher level of educational attainment than regular classroom teachers. In general, they also have less experience, and, because of this, specialists are likely to receive less pay. Despite the widespread use of these better trained but less experienced teachers in compensatory education programs, the literature tells us surprisingly little about the effect they have on students. Glass and Smith (1977) report on two studies that claim to show that remedial reading specialists have a positive effect on reading performance (Flynn, Hass, and Al-Salam, 1976; Kiesling, 1971). However, neither this review nor the one reported here was able to uncover any additional information on this issue. Perhaps because of this lack of information, Ligon and Doss (1982) have suggested that compensatory funds be used to purchase additional classroom teachers rather than reading specialists, thereby reducing the size of the regular classes. Allington (1986), on the other hand, believes there is ample support for the continued use of reading specialists. He does feel, however, that reading specialists will be under increasing pressure to justify their positions, particularly to their classroom teacher peers.

Concerning the nature of their services, Eyler (1982) has suggested that the role of compensatory instructional specialists should be redefined to require them to work in in-class settings and serve as resources to the classroom teacher rather than as instructors of specific groups of students. Interestingly, Bean and Eichelberger (1985) have reported that reading specialists perceived that they placed less emphasis on both diagnosis of student weaknesses and teaching specific skills and more emphasis on working with content teachers when their school district changed from a pullout to an in-class approach. Classroom teachers concurred with specialists and also reported that specialists spend more time working with them. Despite the similarity between what Eyler (1982) proposed and what actually occurred in the Bean and Eichelberger (1985) study, the latter authors reported that teachers and specialists both agreed that reading specialists should focus on working with students with reading problems. Neither group saw the reading specialist as a resource to the classroom teacher, although both groups valued having interaction about specific children.

Shifting our attention to instructional aides, Schuetz (1980) reports that the evidence about their effectiveness is mixed. Qualitative studies have found that teachers using instructional aides spend more time on instructional activities, deliver more of their instruction in individual and small groups, feel they accomplish more, and feel that instructional aides are helpful. Quantitative studies of their impact on student achievement, however, are less conclusive. In fact, Schuetz reports positive, negative, and no effects attributable to instructional aides in her comprehensive review of the literature. Despite the lack of convincing evidence for their effectiveness, Schuetz provides useful information on the conditions that must be satisfied if aides are to be helpful: (1) teachers who use instructional aides must be genuinely receptive to them; (2) instructional aides must have the necessary literacy and computational skills to perform some useful instructional tasks in the classroom; (3) classroom management plans must be developed to take advantage of the presence of instructional aides; and (4) instructional aides must receive intensive training in the tasks they will be asked to perform.

Viewed as a whole, it is clear that the literature concerning the impact on student performance of specialist teachers and instructional aides is inconclusive. This may not be surprising, since by this time in the chapter most readers may have grown accustomed to equivocal results. What may be surprising, however, is the lack of evidence about the effectiveness of instructional specialists and instructional aides regardless of the type of instructional program or activity in which they are involved. Perhaps Allington (1986) is right in arguing that reading specialists will be called on increasingly to justify their positions. Whether he is or not, research clearly needs to be performed to determine exactly what impact reading specialists have on student performance and whether the continued use of compensatory education funds to purchase their services is warranted.

SUMMARY AND CONCLUSIONS

Since the passage of the Elementary and Secondary Education Act of 1965, billions of dollars have been spent each year to attempt to provide improved instruction for the poor and educationally disadvantaged. Despite the magnitude of this investment and the commitment of the many thousand people who have labored to ensure that these monies are well spent, the impact of compensatory education, although measurable and significant (Carter, 1984; Forbes, 1985; Stickney and Plunkett, 1982; Wang, 1980), has nonetheless been viewed as disappointing by some (e.g., Hallinan, 1986) and less than hoped for by others (e.g., Cooley, 1981). Cooley (1981), however, has also argued that the search for overall effects of compensatory education is an inappropriate goal. He suggests that researchers and evaluators should stop trying to justify this federal funding program and focus instead on ways in which compensatory education can be improved. With this goal in mind, a review of the literature was undertaken to determine what is known about the effectiveness of certain design features of programs for the educationally disadvantaged. Specifically, the review was concerned with the effects of particular instructional settings (i.e., whether the instruction was delivered in class or outside the regular classroom in a pullout setting), class size, instructional grouping practices, individualized instruction, and instructional specialists and aides.

Although recent research indicates that the in-class approach is being used more frequently (Advanced Technology, 1983), the literature clearly shows that most compensatory instruction is delivered in a pullout setting. It also shows that compensatory instruction is predominantly reading and mathematics instruction, and that it is provided primarily by instructional specialists and, to a lesser extent, instructional aides who work with smaller groups of students and provide more individualized instruction than regular classroom teachers.

The research describing the impact of pullout programs on the achievement of compensatory education students is less clear. In fact, based on what we know at this time, one would be unable to provide convincing evidence for the effectiveness of either the pullout or in-class approach. Given these mixed results, however, one could and should argue that the widespread use of pullout programs is not justified. Moreover, since there is some evidence to suggest that pullout may result in resegregation, there is further reason to question its wholesale adoption. But that does not mean that pullout programs should be abandoned. Rather, it means that the programs implemented should fit local conditions.

Critics of pullout have suggested that it unnecessarily labels and stigmatizes students, that it reduces communication, cooperation, and coordination between regular and compensatory instructors, that it reduces teacher responsibility for pupil progress, and that valuable content is lost when pullout instruction is received. Despite the importance of these criticisms, counterarguments also appear to have some value. Labeling and stigmatization can occur in in-class settings as well as in pullout settings. Moreover, it may be that it is not the setting itself that aggravates a compensatory education student's feelings of being different, but the sensitivity or insensitivity of teachers operating within the setting (Noddings, 1978). It also appears that even though an in-class program makes it easier and more likely for communication, cooperation, and coordination to occur, it does not guarantee that they will. There is also some evidence to suggest that certain types of teachers are just not able to work together in a single classroom and that joint planning may take place in much the same way in in-class programs as in pullout programs, before school, during recess, during lunch, and after school. Because some teachers may not be able to accommodate another teacher in the same classroom, the issue of teacher autonomy and responsibility for student progress is also not automatically resolved by in-class programs. Perhaps, as suggested by Kennedy (1978), the key to good coordination between compensatory and regular instruction is not the setting for instruction but rather the quality of the joint planning that occurs, the amount of decision-making power given to teachers and specialists by their administrators, and the flexibility in scheduling allowed by the environment.

With regard to the content lost issue, it is clear that some instruction is sacrificed when pullout compensatory instruction is received. It is also clear that valuable instructional time is lost in the process of moving to and from the pullout environment. It is not clear, however, what types of instruction, if any, would be lost if compensatory instruction were delivered in class. It is also not clear whether the interruptions resulting from students being pulled out for instruction are less harmful than the confusion resulting from two teachers working in the same classroom. More research needs to be done on these issues.

Those who favor pullout programs herald the virtues of specialist teachers and aides, smaller class sizes, increased opportunities for individualization, and more effective grouping practices. What do we know about their effectiveness? Surprisingly, we know very little about the impact of instructional specialists and aides on student performance. In fact, this author has been able to uncover only two studies that claim to show that reading specialists have a positive effect on achievement (Flynn, Hass, and Al-Salam, 1976; Kiesling, 1971). Allington (1986) believes there is ample support for the continued use of reading specialists, but his arguments are not particularly convincing. Moreover, he cautions reading specialists that in the future they will be under increasing pressure to justify their positions, particularly to their classroom teacher peers. Regarding classroom aides, Schuetz (1980) reports that quantitative studies lead to no clear conclusions about their effectiveness. She does suggest, however, that some teachers can use them effectively, but that in order for this to occur, teachers must be genuinely receptive to them, the aides must have the necessary literacy and computational skills to perform useful instructional tasks, they must receive intensive training in the tasks they will perform, and effective classroom management plans must be developed to accommodate them.

Despite the paucity of hard, convincing evidence about the effectiveness of instructional specialists and aides, they continue to be used as the primary agents of compensatory instruction. In the early days of Title I, their use was clearly justified given the legal requirements surrounding the allocation of these federal monies. In fact, it has been argued (Archambault, 1986) that these requirements were precisely the reason that pullout programs, with the accompanying specialists and aides, became so popular. At present, however, there are fewer constraints. And yet, even the in-class models that are being implemented use instructional specialists or aides as the service providers. We need more research on their effectiveness; we need more creative approaches to their use.

Turning now to the class size issue, with the exception of the work of Slavin (1984), there seems to be general agreement that class sizes of less than fifteen optimize learning outcomes. Moreover, and as argued by Cooper (1986), the effects are most dramatic in classes containing from one to five students, the size of the group in which the majority of compensatory education students receive their instruction (Archambault and St. Pierre, 1979). Thus it would appear that smaller class sizes are to be favored. But what of the composition of the groups within these classes? Is heterogeneous or homogeneous grouping preferred?

Slavin's (1986) comprehensive review of the effects of instructional grouping strategies offers the best organization of the literature on this subject as well as some of the best insights into what that literature says. Slavin distinguishes within-class and between-class ability grouping, and he considers the effects of each separately. He concludes that homogeneous within-class ability grouping leads to improved student performance in mathematics and that this effect holds for students of all ability levels. This conflicts with the conclusions of Eash (1961), Persell (1977), Wilkinson (1986), and Hallinan (1986) that homogeneous ability grouping is detrimental to students assigned to low groups. One explanation for this difference is that Slavin focused on mathematics, whereas the other reviewers, particularly Wilkinson (1986), focused more on reading. More important that this, however, is the fact that much of the research cited by Wilkinson deals with observations that students in low reading or math groups learn less than students in higher groups, not less than other low-achieving students in contrasting arrangements. Like Reichardt (1979), Slavin argues that when groups are not equivalent preexperimentally (i.e., when there is no random assignment to groups) such comparisons will tend to favor higher achieving groups.

Taken together, then, the research suggests that for mathematics within-class ability grouping should be supported for all students, including low achievers. However, it does not appear reasonable to conclude at this time that either homogeneous or heterogeneous within-class ability grouping is preferred for delivering reading instruction to low-ability students. As suggested by Slavin, such a conclusion can be reached only when experimental comparisons of grouped and ungrouped reading classes have been performed.

Turning now to between-class ability grouping, a wealth of advice is available in the literature. Some reviewers have concluded that no generalizations are possible about the effects of ability grouping (Glass and Smith, 1977), others have concluded that while the performance of students in grouped classes is better than the performance of students in ungrouped classes there appears to be no systematic effect for low-ability students (Kulik and Kulik, 1982), and still others have argued that ability grouping is detrimental for low-ability students (Begle, 1975; Esposito, 1973). Slavin (1986), who looked at the effects of seven types of between-class ability grouping strategies, concluded that research does not support the assignment of students to self-contained classes according to ability, nor does it suggest that ability grouping is harmful for low-ability students. It does suggest, however, that cross-grade tutoring and comprehensive nongraded plans can be effective. It also suggests to Slavin that although the results of regrouping for reading and mathematics are inconclusive, it is still possible that grouping for one or two subjects is instructionally effective.

The last of the practices reviewed in this chapter was individualization. This would appear to be a particular benefit for compensatory education students since the reduced class size in which they receive their compensatory instruction should result in more individual attention. However, Cahen and colleagues (1983) and Harnischfeger (1980) have both concluded that smaller class size does not necessarily lead to increased individualization. Cooley and Leinhardt (1980) have also concluded that there is not any clear evidence for the superiority of individualized instruction over other instructional strategies. Brophy (1986) argues that the problem is not with the conceptual model of individualization, which calls for beginning where students are and moving them along at their own pace. Rather, the problem is that as implemented individualized instruction shifts the responsibility for teaching to the student. This does not work when used over extended periods of time. It can be used effectively, however, in classrooms with small student/teacher ratios, where the teacher is able to provide close supervision and where other types of instructional methods are used in conjunction with individualized instruction, particularly what Brophy calls "active instruction."

What do these results suggest for practice? What advice can we offer to those charged with the implementation of compensatory education programs? Under the best of conditions, the translation of research into practice is a risky business. When the evidence is not clear-cut the perils are even greater. Researchers need to recognize this. They also must recognize that practitioners want and need help and that the practice of schooling cannot wait for unambiguous research results. With this in mind, and with no little amount of trepidation, the following advice is given:

1. *Setting:* Based on what we know at this time, it is safe to conclude that setting is not directly responsible for student outcomes and that the issue of effective practices within settings, and not the setting itself, should be the focus of our attention. This implies that educators can more confidently select a setting based on local conditions, perhaps using pullout approaches in those areas where resegregation would not occur, where teachers are committed to the use of these practices, where coordination and cooperation is possible, and so forth. But, where these and certain other conditions are not met, and perhaps even within the same school district, in-class programs should be used.

2. *Specialists and Aides:* It is clear that classroom teachers need help in meeting the needs of the academically disadvantaged. It is less clear whether that help should be provided by instructional specialists, aides, or some other type of teacher. Since there is so little evidence telling us what combinations of instructors and conditions are likely to maximize student performance, the best advice is that school districts should again feel confident in using whatever combination appears to meet local needs. In certain situations it may be best to have specialists work with students in a pullout setting; in others it may be more effective to introduce a specialist or aide into the regular classroom. If the latter option is chosen, it may be better in some situations for the specialist to work with compensatory education students; in others the skills of the teacher and specialist may dictate that the specialist should work with other students or groups while the classroom teacher concentrates on the needs of the compensatory education student. In determining which option is best, school administrators should honestly assess the competencies of their staff and attempt to match them to the needs of students. They should also consider the needs of teachers and their preferences for and their ability to adapt to the various options. Finally, and no less importantly, they should determine which of the options is likely to deliver the highest-quality instruction to the student. Key issues in this determination should be which program will ensure the greatest amount of engaged time in specific subject areas, the best communication, cooperation, and coordination among the regular and compensatory program, the greatest integration of instruction across these two domains, and the fewest negative consequences such as the stigma attached to receiving compensatory instruction.

3. *Class Size and Grouping:* Smaller class sizes are preferred, particularly when they include fifteen or fewer students. Educationally disadvantaged students benefit from such arrangements, as do other students in the class. Educationally disadvantaged students also benefit from classes that are heterogeneous in ability, and they do so at no expense to the higher-ability students. This does not deny the advantages of within-class ability grouping for certain subjects, particularly reading and mathematics, nor the possibility that cross-grade grouping for certain content would also be beneficial. In fact, both of these practices are to be encouraged.

4. *Individualization:* Individualized instruction can be harmful when used as the sole method of instruction. That is not to say that teachers should not determine the individual needs of students and help them to progress at their own pace. It does mean, however, that teachers should not transfer the responsibility for this progress to students laboring on their own for extended periods of time on worksheets and other published materials. Said in a different way, teachers must take a much more active role in instruction than the practice of individualization has come to imply. Individualization can be used effectively, however, in classrooms with small student/teacher ratios where the teacher is able to provide close supervision.

From a number of quarters and for a number of reasons, effective educational practices are now being emphasized in the literature. Edmonds (1979) and Brookover, Schweitzer, Schneider, Beady, Flood, and Wisenbaker (1978) talk about effective schools, that is, schools in which (1) there is a commitment to particular instructional models and programs, (2) there is agreement on goals and objectives, (3) principals assume a leadership role in the determination of what instruction is to be offered and how it is delivered, (4) administrators and teachers have high expectations for students and communicate these expectations to them, (5) there is frequent monitoring and feedback of student performance, and (6) there is effective teacher training. Leinhardt and Palley (1982), looking more closely at classrooms, call for smaller classes, mastery learning (i.e., clear goal statements and regular monitoring of student progress), more time spent in cognitive activities, reasonably rapid pacing of instruction, using a formal management system that encourages task orientation and successful completion of tasks, and increased teacher instructional time. Brophy (1986), echoing some of Leinhardt and Palley's comments, would use this increased time for instruction for what he calls active teaching. This connotes frequent presentations by the teacher in which she or he develops concepts through lecture and demonstration, follows those up with recitations by students or dialog with them, prepares the students for assignments by giving instructions and going through practice examples, monitors progress on assignments, and follows up with appropriate feedback and reteaching when necessary. There is a great deal of teacher talk, but most of it is academic rather than procedural or managerial, and most of it involves asking questions and giving feedback rather than extended lecturing.

These and other researchers have taught us a great deal about what makes schools and the people within them effective. Nonetheless, we have much more to learn.

REFERENCES

Advanced Technology, Inc. (1983). *Local operation of Title I: A resource book.* Washington, DC: U.S. Department of Education.

Allington, R. L. (1986). Policy constraints and the effective delivery of remedial instruction. In J. Hoffman (Ed.), *Effective teaching of reading: Research and practice.* Newark, DE: International Reading Association.

Archambault, F. X. (1986, June). *Instructional setting: Key issue and bogus concern.* Paper presented at the Office of Educational Research and Improvement sponsored and Research and Evaluation Associates, Inc. conducted Conference on the Effects of Alternative Designs in Compensatory Education, Washington, DC.

Archambault, F. X., and St. Pierre, R. G. (1980). The effect of federal policy on services delivered through ESEA Title I. *Education Evaluation and Policy Analysis, 2,* 33–46.

Atkinson, J. W., and O'Connor, P. (1963). Effects of ability grouping in schools related to individual differences in achievement-related motivation. *Final Report, Cooperative Research Project No. 0E-2-10-024.* Washington, DC: U.S. Department of H.E.W.

Bean, R. T., and Eichelberger, R. T. (1985). Changing the role of reading specialists: From pullout- to in-class programs. *Reading Teacher, 38,(7),* 648–653.

Begle, E. G. (1975). *Ability grouping for mathematics instruction: A review of the empirical literature.* Stanford Mathematics Education Study Group, Stanford Univeristy. (ERIC Document Reproduction Service No. ED 116 938).

Billet, R. O. (1932). *The administration and supervision of homogeneous grouping.* Columbus: The Ohio State University Press.

Bloom, B. S. (1976). *Human characteristics and school learning.* New York: McGraw-Hill.

Breglio, V. J.; Hinckley, R. H.; and Beal, R. S. (1978). *Students' economic and educational status and selection for compensatory education* (Technical Report. No. 2). Santa Monica, CA: System Development Corporation.

Brookover, W. B.; Brady, N. M.; and Warfield, M. (1981). Educational policies and equitable education. A report of studies of two desegregated school systems. In *Procedures and pilot research to develop an agenda for desegregation studies.* East Lansing, MI: Michigan State University, College of Urban Development, Center for Urban Affairs.

Brookover, W. B.; Schweitzer, J. H.; Schneider, J. M.; Beady, C. H.; Flood, P. K.; and Wisenbaker, J. M. (1978). Elementary school social climate and student achievement. *American Educational Research Journal, 15,* 301–308.

Brophy, J. (1986, June). *Research linking teacher behavior to student achievement:*

Potential implications for instruction of Chapter 1 students. Paper presented at the Office of Educational Research and Improvement sponsored and Research and Evaluation Associates, Inc. conducted Conference on the Effects of Alternative Designs in Compensatory Education, Washington, DC.

Cahen, L. S.; Filby, N. N.; McCutcheon, G.; and Kyle, D. W. (1983). *Class size and instruction.* New York: Longman.

Calhoun, G., and Elliott, R. (1977). Self concept and academic achievement of educable retarded and emotionally disturbed pupils. *Exceptional Children, 44,* 379–380.

Carter, L. F. (1984). The sustaining effects study of compensatory and elementary education. *Educational Researcher, 21,* 4–13.

Cohen, E. (1984). Talking and working together: Status, interaction and learning. In P. Peterson, L. C. Wilkinson, and M. Halliman (Eds.), *The social context of instruction: Group organization and group processes.* Orlando, FL: Academic Press, pp. 171–188.

Coleman, J. S.; Campbell, E. Q.; Hobson, C. J.; McPartland, J.; Mood, A. M.; Weinfeld, F. D.; and York, R. L. (1966). *Equality of educational opportunity.* Washington, DC: Government Printing Office.

Cooley, W. W. (1981). Effectiveness in compensatory education. *Educational Leadership, 38,* 298–301.

Cooley, W. W., and Leinhardt, G. (1980). The instructional dimensions study. *Educational Evaluation and Policy Analysis, 2,(1),* 7–25.

Cooper, H. M. (1986, June). *Chapter 1 programs reduce student-to-instructor ratios but do reduced ratios affect achievement?* Paper presented at the Office of Educational Research and Improvement sponsored and Research and Evaluation Associates, Inc. conducted conference on the effects of Alternative Designs in Compensatory Education, Washington, DC.

Cornell, E. L. (1936). Effects of ability grouping determinable from published studies. In G. M. Whipple (Ed.), *The ability grouping of pupils.* NSSE Yearbook, *35,* Part I. Bloomington, IL: Public School Publishing Co., pp. 289–304.

Coulson, J. E.; Ozenne, D. G.; Hanes, S. D.; Bradford, C.; Doherty, W. S.; Duck, G. A.; and Hemenway, J. A. (1977). *The third year of the Emergency School Aid Act (ESAA) implementation.* Santa Monica, CA: System Development Corporation. (ERIC Document Reproduction Service No. ED 154 952).

Crawford, J. (1983). A study of instructional processes in Title I classes: 1981–82. *Journal of Research and Evaluation of the Oklahoma City Public Schools, 12,(1).*

Doss, D., and Holley, F. (1982, April). *A cause for national pause: Title I schoolwide projects.* Paper presented at the Annual meeting of the American Educational Research Association, New York, NY. (ERIC Document Reproduction Service No. ED 214 996).

Dreeban, R. (1984). First-grade reading groups: Their formation and change. In P. Peterson, L. C. Wilkinson, and M. Hallinan (Eds.). *The social context of instruction: Group organization and group processes.* Orlando, FL: Academic Press, pp. 69–84.

Eash, M. S. (1961). Grouping: What have we learned. *Educational Leadership, 18,* 429–434.

Edmonds, R. A. (1979). *A discussion of the literature and issues related to effective schooling*. St. Louis, MO: Central Midwestern Regional Educational Laboratory.

Educational Research Service (1978). *Class size: A summary of research*. Arlington, VA: Educational Research Service.

Ekstrom, R. B. (1961). Experimental studies of homogeneous grouping: A critical review. *School Review, 69,* 216–226.

Esposito, D. (1973). Homogeneous and heterogeneous ability grouping: Principal findings and implications for evaluating and designing more effective educational environments. *Review of Educational Research, 43,* 163–179.

Eyler, J. (1982). *Resegregation: Segregation within desegregated schools*. (ERIC Document Reproduction Service No. ED 216 075).

Fitzgerald, N. B., and Hunt, R. K. (1985, April). *Cost-effectiveness predictors in Chapter 1 programs: The Minnesota example*. Paper presented at the annual meeting of the American Educational Research Association, Chicago, IL.

Floyd, C. (1954). Meeting children's reading needs in the middle grades: A preliminary report. *Elementary School Journal, 55,* 99–103.

Flynn, D. I.; Hass, A. E.; and Al-Salam, N. A. (1976). *An evaluation of the cost effectiveness of alternative compensatory reading programs*. Bethesda, MD: RMC Research Corporation.

Forbes, R. H. (1985). Academic achievement of historically lower-achieving students during the seventies. *Phi Delta Kappan, 66,(8),* 542–544.

Frechtling, J. A., and Hammond, P. A. (1978, March). *Policy implications of the Instructional Dimensions Study*. Paper presented at the annual meeting of the American Educational Research Association, Toronto, Ontario.

Glass, G. V.; McGaw, B.; and Smith, M. L. (1981). *Meta-analysis of social research*. Beverly Hills, CA: Sage.

Glass, G. V., and Smith, M. L. (1977). *'Pull out' in compensatory education*. Boulder, CO: University of Colorado, Laboratory of Educational Research.

Glass, G. V., and Smith, M. L. (1979). Meta-analysis of the research on class size and achievement. *Educational Evaluation and Policy Analysis, 1,* 2–16.

Goldberg, M. L.; Passow, A. H.; and Justman, J. (1966). *The effects of ability grouping*. New York: Teachers College Press, Columbia University.

Goodlad, J. I., and Anderson, R. H. (1963). *The non-graded elementary school*, rev. ed. New York: Harcourt, Brace, and World.

Hallinan, M. T. (1986, June). *Chapter 1 and student achievement: A conceptual model*. Paper presented at the Office of Educational Research and Improvement sponsored and Research and Evaluation Associates, Inc. conducted Conference on the Effects of Alternative Designs in Compensatory Education, Washington, DC.

Harnischfeger, A. (1980). Curricular control and learning time: District policy, teacher strategy, and pupil choice. *Educational Evaluation and Policy Analysis, 2,(6),* 19–30.

Hayes, M. V. (1983). *A survey of teacher attitudes towards in-class versus pull-out compensatory reading programs*. (ERIC Document Reproduction Service No. ED 228 619).

Hedges, L. U., and Stock, W. (1983). The effect of class size: An examination of rival hypotheses. *American Educational Research Journal, 20,* 63–85.

Heyns, B. (1986, June). *Summer programs and compensatory education: The future of an idea*. Paper presented at the Office of Educational Research and Improvement sponsored and Research and Evaluation Associates, Inc. conducted Conference on the Effects of Alternative Designs in Compensatory Education, Washington, DC.

Hinckley, R. H.; Beal, R. S.; and Breglio, V. J. (1978). *Student economic and educational status and receipt of educational services* (Technical Report No. 3). Santa Monica, CA: System Development Corporation.

Kaestle, C. F., and Smith, M. S. (1982). The historical context of the federal role in education. *Harvard Educational Review, 52*, 383–408.

Kennedy, G. C. (1978). School setting and learning. In *Perspectives on the Instructional Dimensions Study: A supplemental report from the National Institute of Education*, pp. 33–39. (ERIC Document Reproduction Service No. ED 174 728).

Kiesling, H. J. (1971). *Input and output in California compensatory education projects*. Santa Monica, CA: Rand Corporation.

Kimbrough, J., and Hill, P. (1981). *The aggregate effects of federal education programs*. Santa Monica, CA: Rand Corporation.

Knight, M. E. (1979a). *Evaluation of diagnostic/prescriptive reading program, Community School District 31, New York City*. (ERIC Document Reproduction Service No. ED 187 792).

Knight, M. E. (1979b). *Evaluation of Title I program, Community School District 31, New York City*. (ERIC Document Reproduction Service No. ED 187 791).

Knight, M. E. (1979c). *Evaluation of Title I program, Community School District 31, New York City*. (ERIC Document Reproduction Service No. ED 186 544).

Kulik, C. C., and Kulik, J. A. (1982). Effects of ability grouping on secondary school students: A meta-analysis of evaluation findings. *American Educational Research Journal, 19,(3)*, 415–428.

Leinhardt, G. (1980). Transition rooms: Promoting maturation or reducing education. *Journal of Educational Psychology, 72*, 55–61.

Leinhardt, G.; Bickel, W.; and Palley, A. (1982). Unlabeled but still entitled: Toward more effective remediation. *Teachers College Record, 84,(2)*, 391–422.

Leinhardt, G., and Palley, A. (1982). Restrictive educational settings: Exile or haven? *Review of Educational Research, 52,(4)*, 557–578.

Levin, H. M.; Glass, G. V.; and Meister, G. R. (1984). *Cost-effectiveness of four educational interventions* (Project Report No. 84-A11). Washington, DC: National Institute of Education.

Levine, D. U., and Stark, J. (1982, April). *Instructional and organizational arrangements and processes for improving academic achievement at inner city elementary schools. A study of the Chicago Mastery Learning Reading Program and other school-wide approaches for improving reading at selected schools in Chicago, Los Angeles, and New York*. Paper presented at the annual meeting of the American Educational Research Association, New York, NY. (ERIC Document Reproduction Service No. ED 213 814).

Ligon, G. D., and Doss, D. A. (1982, April). *Some lessons we have learned from 6,500 hours of classroom observations*. Paper presented at the annual meeting of the American Educational Research Association, Montreal.

Madden, N. A., and Slavin, R. E. (1983). Mainstreaming students with mild handicaps: Academic and social outcomes. *Review of Educational Research, 53,(4),* 519–569.

Madhere, S. (1981). *Issues in program evaluation.* (ERIC Document Reproduction Service No. ED 217 098).

McLaughlin, M. W. (1975). Evaluation and reform. *The Elementary and Secondary Education Act of 1965: Title I.* Cambridge, MA: Ballanger Publishing.

Miller, W. S., and Otto, H. J. (1930). Analysis of experimental studies in homogeneous grouping. *Journal of Educational Research, 21,* 95–102.

National Assessment of Educational Progress (1981). *Has Title I improved education of disadvantaged students? Evidence from three national assessments of reading.* Denver, Colorado.

National Institute of Education (1977). *The effects of services on student development.* Washington, DC: The National Institute of Education, U.S. Department of Health, Education, and Welfare.

National Institute of Education (1978). *Perspectives on the Instructional Dimensions Study.* Washington, DC: The National Institute of Education, U.S. Department of Health, Education, and Welfare.

Nearine, R. J., and Pecheone, R. L. (1984, April). *Multiple assessments of a compensatory reading program over time.* Paper presented at the annual meeting of the American Educational Research Association, New Orleans, LA.

Neumann, T. (1985). In-class remedial instruction. An alternative to the pull-out programs. *Wisconsin State Reading Association Journal, 29,(3),* 26–27.

Noddings, N. (1978). Overview of the Instructional Dimensions Study Conference. In *Perspectives on the Instructional Dimensions Study,* pp. 5–14. (ERIC Document Reproduction Service No. ED 174 728).

Oakes, J. (1985). *Keeping track.* New Haven, CT: Yale University Press.

Persell, C. (1977). *Education and inequality: The roots and results of stratification in America's schools.* New York: Free Press.

Peterson, P.; Wilkinson, L. C.; Spinelli, F.; and Swing, S. (1984). Merging the process-product and the sociolinguistic paradigms: Research on small-group processes. In P. Peterson, L. C. Wilkinson, and M. Hallinan (Eds.), *The social context of instruction: Group organization and group processes.* Orlando, FL: Academic Press, pp. 3–11,

Reichardt, C. S. (1979). The statistical analysis of data from nonequivalent group designs. In T. C. Cook and D. T. Campbell (Eds.), Quasi-experimentation: Design and analysis for field settings. Chicago: Rand McNally, pp. 147–205.

Rosenbaum, J. E. (1980). Social implications of education grouping. *Review of Research in Education, 8,* 361–401.

Schafer, W. E., and Olexa, C. (1971). *Tracking and opportunity.* Scranton, PA: Chandler.

Scheutz, P. (1980). *The instructional effectiveness of classroom aides.* Pittsburgh, PA: University of Pittsburgh Learning Research and Development Center.

Shuy, R. W. (1978). Toward Future Study of the effect of school setting on learning. In *Perspectives on the Instructional Dimensions Study: A supplemental report from the National Institute of Education,* pp. 40–48. (ERIC Document Reproduction Service No. ED 174 728).

Slavin, R. E. (1979). Integrating the desegregated classroom: Actions speak louder than words. *Educational Leadership, 36,* 322–324.

Slavin, R. E. (1980). Cooperative learning. *Review of Educational Research, 50,(2),* 315–342.

Slavin, R. E. (1984). Meta-analysis in education: How has it been used? *Educational Researcher, 13,(8),* 6–15.

Slavin, R. E. (1986a). Best evidence synthesis: An alternative to meta-analysis and traditional reviews. *Educational Researcher, 15,(9),* 5–11.

Slavin, R. E. (1986b). *Ability grouping and student achievement in elementary schools: A best-evidence synthesis, Report No. 1.* Baltimore, MD: Center for Research on Elementary & Middle Schools, The Johns Hopkins University.

Slavin, R. E., and Madden, N. A. (1979). School practices that improve race relations. *American Educational Research Journal, 16,(2),* 169–180.

Smith, M. L., and Glass, G. V. (1980). Meta-analysis of research on class size and its relationship to attitudes and instruction. *American Educational Research Journal, 17,(4).*

Stickney, B. D., and Plunkett, V. R. L. (1982). Has Title I done its job? *Educational Leadership, 64,* 378–383.

Stonehill, R. M., and Anderson, J. I. (1982). *An evaluation of ESEA Title I Program operations and educational effects.* Washington, DC: U.S. Department of Education.

Swing, S., and Peterson, P. (1982). The relationship of student ability and small-group interaction to student achievement. *American Educational Research Journal, 19,* 259–274.

Tobias, S. (1982). When do instructional methods make a difference? *Educational Researcher, 11,(4),* 4–9.

Vanecko, J. J., and Ames, N. L., with Archambault, F. X. (1980). *Who benefits from federal education dollars?* Cambridge, MA: Abt Books.

Vasquez-Nuttal Associates (1983). *Chapter 1 elementary reading programs. Interim evaluation report.* (ERIC Document Reproduction Service No. ED 238 968).

Wang, M. (1980, April). *Evaluating the effectiveness of compensatory education.* Paper presented at the annual meeting of the American Educational Research Association, Boston.

Wang, M. M.; Hoepfner, R.; Zagorski, H.; Hemenway, J. A.; Brown, D. S.; and Bear, M. B. (1978). *The nature and recipients of compensatory education* (Technical Report No. 5). Santa Monica, CA: System Development Corporation.

Wargo, M. J.; Tallmadge, G. K.; Michaels, D. D.; Lipe, D.; and Morris, S. J. (1972). *ESEA Title I: A reanalysis and synthesis of evaluation data from fiscal year 1965 through 1970.* Palo Alto, CA: American Institute for Research.

Webb, N. (1982). Peer interaction and learning in cooperative small groups. *Journal of Educational Psychology, 76,* 33–44.

Webb, N. (1985). Verbal interaction and learning in peer-directed groups. *Theory Into Practice, 24,* 32–39.

Webb, N., and Kenderski, C. (1984). Student interaction and learning in small group and whole-class settings. In P. Peterson, L. S. Wilkinson, and M. Hallinan (Eds.), *The social context of instruction: Group organization and group processes.* Orlando, FL: Academic Press, pp. 153–170.

Wilkinson, L. (1986, June). *Grouping students for instruction*. Paper presented at the Office of Educational Research and Improvement sponsored and Research and Evaluation Associates, Inc. conducted Conference on the Effects of Alternative Designs in Compensatory Education, Washington, DC.

Yap, K. O. (1983). *Effects of instructional setting and approach in compensatory education: A statewide analysis*. (ERIC Document Reproduction Service No. ED 230 645).

Yap, K. O. (1985). *A cost-analytic approach to determining Chapter 1 program impact: Some preliminary findings*. (ERIC Document Reproduction Service No. ED 254 564).

9

INSTRUCTIONAL ACTIVITIES RELATED TO ACHIEVEMENT GAIN IN CHAPTER 1 CLASSES

John Crawford

Planning, Research, and Evaluation Department
Oklahoma City Public Schools

On a Monday morning in March at 8:42, nine students come in for their second-grade reading lesson. They are met by the Learning Center teacher and aide. The setting is a school serving a relatively lower socioeconomic status constituency—more than one-half of the students in the school qualify for free or reduced-payment lunches. The students in the class have qualified for compensatory education with scores below the 40th percentile nationally in reading. The resources for the pullout program teacher, the small class size, the extra materials, and the paraprofessional aide come from the federally funded Title I program (now Chapter 1).

What the observer (also the author of this chapter) did not know at the time was that this teacher would have students with the highest achievement gains of any of the seventy-nine teachers in the study.

The fact that all the students arrived at the same time (and on time) suggests some coordination with the regular classrooms and/or a system whereby student transition time is monitored and minimized.

Within seconds of the students' arrival, the teacher has greeted everyone and has them all on the rug for whole-group activity. For about eight minutes the teacher reads a story to the students and asks comprehension questions of the whole group. Students respond chorally most of the time. The narrative comments for those minutes noted:

> At 8:42, kids come in and sit together to hear Teacher read story on Silly Sam and the Singing Fish.
> Kids very attentive.
> At 8:50, end of story. Kids break out to work individually.

From 8:50 to 9:20 the students worked individually on worksheet-type activities. However, in addition to pencil and paper, the activities for six of the nine students involved some kind of audiovisual equipment (audio cassette, video reels with sound, etc.). During this time of individual work, the teacher and the aide are both quite busy. While students are engaged with their individual tasks, the teacher and aide are circulating to the students. Although all students are contacted, more time is allocated to the students with the greater need for help.

When procedure-related interactions occur (such as helping a student with some of the audiovisual equipment), they are mostly likely to be brief. However, when the teacher initiates an academic contact with a student, it was more likely to be coded as "long" or "very long" (in the coding scheme, "long" was more than a brief phrase or interaction but less than thirty seconds; "very long" was defined as more than thirty seconds with the same student).

Narrative notes indicated that:

From 9:13 on, Teacher with one boy for very long interaction (approximately 2 to 3 minutes).

As the teacher was working with a student individually, the aide was moving around the room to monitor and help other students.

At 9:20, the teacher told the students to begin getting ready to go, and by 9:22 the students were off to their regular classrooms.

More than 90 percent of the available time had been devoted to the academic content. During the forty-minute observation, only two student misbehaviors were coded. Both were "mild" in intensity (not distracting to the whole class), and were efficiently dealt with by a "mild desist" from the teacher. The teacher did not make a disciplinary error (behavior management codes were based on the work of Kounin, 1970).

This teacher placed a high priority on mastery of academic content. Good use was made of the 4.5 to 1 student-to-adult ratio by individual instruction (private one-to-one contacts) for the majority of the lesson. About one-fifth of the time was spent in a nonthreatening whole-group exercise. There was a pleasant affective climate and the students were actively engaged with their reading lessons.

Over the course of the school year, the average gain of this teacher's students was 13 NCE (Normal Curve Equivalent) points on total reading. NCE scores were developed as an equal interval scale for measuring achievement; NCEs agree with percentiles at 1, 50, and 99. Depending on where one starts on the percentile scale, a 13-point NCE gain could result in a 15- to 20-point percentile gain (e.g., a student increasing from the 10th to the 26th percentile, or a student going from the 20th to the 40th percentile).

The above description resulted from low inference coding, time-use description, and narrative records of a particular teacher's class—an elementary lesson in reading. It is of some interest that the teacher with the highest-gaining students displayed integrated coordination of the same complex of behaviors that were found in the full sample to be correlated with greater achievement growth. (See Shulman, 1986 for speculation that process-product research has yielded little evidence that any individual teachers behave in ways that the research indicates is effective.)

This chapter covers currently available information on what works in Chapter 1 compensatory programs. Characteristics of programs labeled "exemplary" will be compiled with research findings into a picture of effective instructional principles for Chapter 1 classes.

IDENTIFICATION OF EFFECTIVE CHAPTER 1 PROGRAMS

The U.S. Department of Education (DOE) recently undertook an effort to identify successful compensatory programs across the nation. The rationale and results are reported in a two-volume sourcebook prepared by Griswold, Cotton, and Hansen (1985). Volume I presents a review of school and teacher effects research and synthesizes the findings into thirteen attributes of effective programs. Volume II presents brief profiles of each of the projects selected as successful.

The identification of compensatory projects worthy of national recognition was modeled after the earlier DOE Secondary School Recognition Program. Nominations were requested from state educational agencies, and following a review panel consideration of program documentation, the final selection of effective projects was completed. The state agencies nominated 334 projects nationwide. Of that number, 118 were selected as most effective and ready for dissemination. Two of the 118 withdrew, so 116 projects are described in the sourcebook.

Projects were selected on the basis of evidence of effectiveness in one or more of three areas of performance: achievement (relatively short-term gains or point-in-time measures), sustained gains (at least three measures of achievement over at least one year), and other outcomes such as attendance, attitude, improvement in discipline, and so on. Almost all (114 of 116) of the cited projects presented evidence of effectiveness in achievement in basic skills. A total of 45 projects reported sustained gains. And 31 of the identified programs documented other (affective) outcomes associated with their projects.

The schooling attributes related to the previously described outcomes were termed *organizational* and *instructional* characteristics of effective programs. The organizational attributes included school and parent/community influences. Instructional attributes referred to materials, grouping methods, use of time, interactive teaching, high expectations, feedback, and reinforcement. Each of the organizational and instructional attributes are described briefly below.

ORGANIZATIONAL ATTRIBUTES OF EFFECTIVE PROGRAMS

Positive Climate

A school with orderly classrooms, high expectations for student achievement and behavior, a pleasant physical environment, and well-established rules is one with a strong positive climate. School effects research (e.g., Brookover, Schweitzer, Schneider, Beady, Flood, and Wisenbaker, 1978; Crawford and Watson, 1985) has consistently shown that high-achieving schools also tend to have a positive climate for learning. For example, successful Chapter 1 programs identified in the sourcebook discussed the process of gaining visibility and a positive image for the program within the school, involvement in a districtwide climate committee, and maintenance of a resource room that is pleasant, well-lighted, and colorful.

Clear Goals and Objectives for the School

The school's goals and objectives should be articulated clearly and should arise from needs identified by parents, staff, and the community. Once set, the goals and objectives are communicated to interested parties. One of the Chapter 1 programs identified as exemplary used a systematic needs assessment where input was sought from civic clubs, the local Chamber of Commerce, parent groups, and school staff. Based on the survey results, program staff set specific objectives for the Chapter 1 project.

Coordination

Many of the successful Chapter 1 projects cited in the sourcebook included as part of their documentation a discussion of how they coordinated their program with the regular classroom instruction or with other special programs. The principal plays a key role in fostering cooperation among programs. At effective schools, principals and other leaders in the school encourage planning groups and provide opportunity for them to work together. Coordination efforts work to align curricula and objectives across programs. Examples from successful Chapter 1 programs included: use of daily log sheets that record Chapter 1 and regular teacher communication (reviewed by coordinators and principals), staff meetings where objectives and instructional activities of the Chapter 1 program and the regular classroom are examined and made to match, and use of information on how well instruction is coordinated with the regular classroom in evaluating Chapter 1 teachers.

Parent/Community Involvement

Although *general* support by parents and community (e.g., PTAs, Adopt-a-School programs) may be only weakly related to program and school effectiveness, the *direct* involvement of parents in their children's learning can be a potent facilitator of student achievement. According to Volume I of the sourcebook "The most effective parent involvement emphasizes providing parents with training to extend the classroom into the home" (p. 31). For example, one Chapter 1 program sent a traveling resource center to schools to allow parents to check out learning materials for use with their children at home. One such course suggested forty ways that parents could work with their children. Parent support was also given by inservice training.

Staff Development and Training

Professional development activities form a portion of the profile of the effective school. Effective principals encourage staff development with opportunity and incentive. One effective Chapter 1 program involved their staff in: the development of inservice activities, focusing of the content of the inservice on research-based effective practices, and evaluation of the inservice in order to plan subsequent training sessions.

Use of Evaluation Results for Program Improvement

Although the norm for Chapter 1 projects may be little use of evaluation results (see David, 1981), many effective programs did indicate that evaluation findings were used to improve the program. Commitment to the use of evaluation as an integral piece of school improvement was an effective attribute. One successful Chapter 1 program (in the Oklahoma City Public Schools—also the source of the process-product relations to be reported later in this chapter) used evaluation results to change student eligibility criteria and to derive content for inservice packets based on local teaching effectiveness studies in Chapter 1 classes. In another program, evaluation results led to the development of a management system to improve coordination between the regular classroom and Chapter 1.

Strong Leadership

One of the more consistent findings from school effects research indicates that effective schools have strong instructional leaders. Instructional leadership (typically by the principal) creates a climate within which student learning is a top priority. Such leadership engenders a focus on school or program goals and motivates teaching staff. Examples of successful programs documented close coordination between a strong principal and project director. Also, the project director may assume the leadership role in fostering a focus on goals.

INSTRUCTIONAL ATTRIBUTES OF EFFECTIVE PROGRAMS

Instructional attributes are those characteristics presumed to occur within *classes* (as opposed to the school-level organizational attributes just discussed). These factors are more under the control of teachers than the organizational attributes.

Appropriate Instructional Materials and Methods

This broadly conceived category actually includes several specific attributes: "interactive" teaching, ability grouping and individualized instruction, mastery learning, adaptive learning environments, cognitive education, and cross-age tutoring.

Interactive teaching, as referred to by the sourcebook, is a combination of direct instruction and active teaching (Brophy, 1979; Good and Grouws, 1979; Rosenshine, 1983). Teachers skilled in this method of teaching follow a sequence of presenting concepts, explaining, providing practice activities, and actively monitoring student learning. They frequently ask questions and provide feedback to students.

Ability grouping in the lower grades is common practice. Some research in regular classes suggests that the lower-ability groups may have lower expectations communicated to them by the kinds of activities in which teachers engage them. For example, the lower group may spend more time with flash cards and less time reading stories, and teachers may emphasize pronunciation rather than meaning when instructing these students. When using ability grouping, these kinds of differentiations should be avoided.

Commonly held opinion is that pullout programs have an undesirable stigma attached and that negative effects on students may occur as a consequence. However, research has not shown pullout programs to be consistently inferior for achievement growth. And some in-class programs amount to pull-out within the regular class (e.g., the resource teacher gathers the low achievers together in the back of the room). The author's personal experience with Chapter 1 students and teachers suggests that in the early grades there may be little or no negative stigma attached to going to the Learning Center, although upper-grade students are surely more aware of the reason that they go and are more concerned about peer attitude.

Instructional programs such as mastery learning and individualized instruction are also discussed in the DOE sourcebook. Mastery learning strategies, as discussed by Bloom (1976), are based on an instructional sequence in which student success on lower-level objectives is required prior to moving on to more advanced objectives. Students are allowed to vary on the amount of time (e.g., the number of trials or attempts) required for mastery; however, the theory is that almost all (95 percent) of the students are able to master the basic skills. Although the term *individualized instruction* is used many different ways, the sourcebook uses the term to refer to implementation of mastery learning by individual pacing, individual diagnosis and prescription, and use of different materials for different students. In Chapter 1 classes where small numbers of students may be present, it could be feasible to individualize effectively, though such individualization should *not* take the form of large amounts of unmonitored seatwork (which would supplant active teaching).

The sourcebook briefly mentions "adaptive learning environments" and "cognitive education." By adaptive learning environments they mean an instructional strategy that combines sequenced mastery learning with individualized instruction. Cognitive education refers to the recent work on teaching students *how* to learn—strategies for organizing, retrieving, and synthesizing information are covered.

The last specific method discussed was cross-age tutoring, where older students (e.g., in grades 4–6) instruct younger students (such as grades 1–3). Research has supported the effectiveness of such tutoring, especially with students who are initially lower achieving. The sourcebook also cites evidence that cross-age tutoring is more effective in math than in reading.

Examples of use of appropriate instructional methods and materials in exemplary Chapter 1 projects include: use of frequent (mastery) unit tests, focus on one or two skills at a time, tutoring, direct instruction models (with maximizing of teacher-student interactions), and use of computer-assisted instruction for individual pacing and increased student motivation.

Maximum Use of Academic Learning Time

The instructional attributes related to use of in-class times were also discussed. The Fisher, Filby, Marliave, Cahen, Dishaw, Moore, and Berliner (1978) Beginning Teacher Evaluation Study (BTES) and results regarding "academic learning time" constituted the primary research evidence. Effective teachers maximized allocated academic time and the amount of time students were engaged with the curriculum content. Also, BTES results suggested that the level of difficulty of in-class work was geared so that students experienced success. Other factors relating to use of available time were management strategies (the better managers had more time available for content) and assignment of homework (best with written comments from the teacher and if feedback on homework is not delayed). Exemplary Chapter 1 programs made effective use of time by careful scheduling of students, monitoring student success rate, training of *students* on how to remain "on task," and parent-monitored homework.

High Expectations

Following the Rosenthal and Jacobsen (1968) study, much attention in the research community has been focused on the phenomenon of teacher expectations. The results have indicated that expectations and belief systems of teachers are often reflected in teaching behavior, and *that* behavior impacts how students respond and perform. Expectations are made visible in the kinds of feedback given to students, the amount of wait time (following a question from the teacher), and the within-class climate regarding learning and discipline. Exemplary Chapter 1 projects focused on specific and appropriate feedback and included encouragement for student effort and attitude (in addition to achievement).

Monitoring

The use of tests, in-class performance assessments, and analysis of verbal responses from students to monitor student progress is positively related to learning. One successful Chapter 1 project diagnosed student needs with frequent criterion-referenced testing.

Feedback and Reinforcement

Verbal praise has been found to be an effective reinforcer if it is genuine, not too frequent, specific, and truly contingent on superior performance. The sourcebook review notes that the impact of teacher praise probably diminishes as the grade of the student increases beyond elementary. The authors indicate that for upper-grade and relatively higher-SES (socioeconomic status) students, *corrective* feedback is an effective strategy—this kind of feedback conveys information about the student's response. Effective Chapter 1 programs have trained teachers to give very specific praise and to avoid reprimands that do not correct the student positively.

Recognition and Reward for Excellence

The teachers who recognize and reward excellent performance from students can be effective users of reinforcement. The rewards may be symbolic or more concrete, such as small amount of free reading time at the end of the period. Effective Chapter 1 programs use a variety of rewards for superior performance: awards, certificates, phone calls or letters to parents, display of student work, special awards from the principal, and ceremonies for students who test out of the program.

SUMMARY OF EFFECTIVE PROJECT PROFILES

Of the 116 projects, 46 were from urban school districts, 27 from suburban districts, 27 from small towns, and 25 from rural areas. (Some projects were classified in more than one category.) The identified effective programs varied in size: 17 served less than 100 students, 49 served 100 to 499 students, 41 served 500 to 2,500 students, and 9 served more than 2,500 students. The majority of the projects were focused on elementary-grade students: 91 of the 116 served kindergarten through grade 3 and 86 projects had students in grades 4 through 6. A total of 35 projects served students in grades 7 through 9, 22 were in grades 10 through 12, and 12 were serving preschool students. Some 94 projects delivered services in reading, 58 in math, 29 in language arts, and 23 in other curriculum areas (63 of the 116 successful programs served students in more than one curriculum area).

Each project was identified by three primary attributes of success, categorized either as organizational or instructional factors. In rank order of frequency of citation:

Instructional attribute	*Number of projects*
Appropriate instruction	66
Monitoring of progress	26
Maximized academic learning time	23
High expectations	20
Feedback/reinforcement	14
Recognition of excellence	7

Organizational attribute	
Coordination	42
Parent/community involvement	41
Professional development	27

Instructional attribute	Number of projects
Clear goals/objectives	25
Strong leadership	20
Use of evaluation	19
Positive climate	18

THE INSTRUCTIONAL DIMENSIONS STUDY

Cooley and Leinhardt (1980) reported a major investigation of regular classroom instruction of educationally disadvantaged students. Their study was designed to identify variation in classroom activities in reading and math (grades 1 and 3) and to relate that variation to learning outcomes. Observations were made of the students while they were in the regular classroom.

The Instructional Dimensions Study (IDS) was framed by a model of classroom processes. The IDS model addresses six classes of variables: initial student performance, opportunity, motivators, instructional events, structure, and criterion performance. Each of these will be described briefly below.

Initial student performance represents skill level or ability of students prior to the educational intervention. In the model, initial performance is hypothesized as a direct influence on the outcome or criterion.

The four constructs representing classroom processes are also presumed to impact criterion performance directly. *Opportunity* refers to the students' opportunity to learn the content assessed as criterion. This construct derives from John Carroll's (1963) model of school learning, which included opportunity to learn. In the IDS, opportunity was measured by how time was spent in classrooms and by the degree of match between the curriculum content and the tests. *Motivators* were assessed by measures relating to interpersonal climate and interactions in the classroom. Indicators included variables such as interest in curriculum material, use of peer tutoring, games and contests, and teacher praise. The *instructional events* measures addressed frequency, content, quality, and duration of teacher-student interactions. For example, management variables, individual/small-group/whole-class measures, and questioning and feedback variables were all recorded. What Cooley and Leinhardt refer to as *structure* is characterized by level of organization of curriculum, specificity of objectives, and the match of student and curriculum. Measures of class structure included how students were placed in the curriculum, use of mastery tests, formation of groups, attention to individual needs, and sequencing.

The criterion performance measure was a standardized achievement test—the Comprehensive Test of Basic Skills. Classrooms were selected for the IDS through a multistage sampling process intended to increase the likelihood of identifying variation in classroom processes. Data collection was carried out in 400 classrooms, in 100 different schools, from fourteen school districts in five different states. The classroom was the unit of analysis—process data and student test scores were aggregated to the class level. Therefore, process-outcome relations reflect among-class covariation. The method of collecting process data was by videotaping classrooms, with subsequent coding of observation variables from the taped records (approximately four hours per teacher). Teachers were also interviewed and curriculum experts generated data on curriculum indicators.

In order to yield a more manageable number of classroom variables, process measures were combined under the framework of the IDS model so that fifteen constructs were represented in the analyses. A total of 200 classes entered the grade 1 analysis and 200 entered the grade 3 analysis. Cooley and Leinhardt indicated a preference for a "conservative" approach to one that would explicitly argue causality. Therefore, they abstained from analysis of formal causal models and proceeded to commonality analysis. They argued that commonality analysis:

> . . . presents separately the confounded portions of effects on outcomes (called commonalities). These confounded portions are not included in estimating the irreducible effects (called uniquenesses) of the separate possible causes. The conservativeness of the method resides in the use of minimum rather than maximum estimates of separate effects (p. 16).

IDS Results

Means and standard deviations are presented in Cooley and Leinhardt (1980). Here, we focus on process-outcome relations. One way to examine the overall effect of classroom processes is to examine the change (increase) in R^2 when process predictors are added to a model that already has pretest as a predictor. (The R^2 for a regression analysis indicates the proportion of outcome variation that is shared with, or can be "accounted for," by predictor variables.) Those results indicated that combined process effects were greater in grade 1 than in grade 3. In grade 1 reading, the R^2 value *with* the process variables in the model was 0.51, compared to 0.25 for the analysis of pretest and outcome. In grade 1 math, the R^2 increased from 0.15 for pretest predicting posttest to 0.43 for pretest and process measures predicting posttest. These data indicate that the process measures (collectively) can account for as much or more outcome variation as the classroom's pretest standing.

The regression results for third grade suggested less potent effects for process measures, although *not* zero effects. In grade 3 reading, the R^2 increased from 0.74 (pretest alone as predictor) to 0.81 when process measures were included—about a 10 percent increase in R^2. In grade 3 math, the R^2 went from 0.61 for pretest only to 0.73 for a model with pretest and classroom process variables—approximately a 20 percent increase in outcome variance accounted for. In the IDS third-grade data, the pre-with-post correlations were around 0.8 or higher; therefore, there was relatively less outcome variation that could potentially be attributed to process variables.

Among the process variables, which specific indicators were most responsible for process covariation with outcomes? This question was addressed by the commonality analysis described above. Cooley and Leinhardt used raw gain as the outcome measure in the commonality analysis. One of the four process constructs—opportunity—correlated significantly positively with gain in all four contexts (reading and math, first and third grades). The opportunity variables included measures of the percent of students on task, the allocated instructional time, absenteeism, and curriculum-with-test overlap. The strongest individual correlations with gain were for measures of curriculum and test content overlap. IDS results did not suggest effects for class size—large classes were just as likely as small classes to have high gains. Also, measures of individualized instruction did *not* indicate that individualization methods were related to greater academic growth.

Another interesting result was that the degree of pullout instruction was *not* related to achievement of students. Apparently, the nature and quality of the instruction was more important for learning than whether (and how many) students were pulled from their regular classroom. The authors summarize their findings by calling attention to the importance of direct instruction in curriculum areas that are tapped by the criterion test (with a call for informed test selection and use, so that test content reflects desired values).

REVIEW OF RESEARCH IMPLICATIONS FOR INSTRUCTION OF CHAPTER 1 STUDENTS

Brophy (1986) recently completed a paper for the Office of Educational Research and Improvement of the DOE. The focus was to synthesize the currently available research results with particular attention to the relevancy of those findings for Chapter 1 instruction. The paper ranges broadly and is quite extensive. This discussion will deal with specific teaching behaviors cited by Brophy and with the need for more research.

Brophy begins by dealing explicitly with the issue of *why* the currently available research is adequate to inform policymakers about effective instruction for Chapter 1 students. This approach is somewhat unique in that he did not *assume* that it would be self-evident that one could generalize earlier research findings to Chapter 1 classes. Brophy cites four reasons for why be believes research in regular classroom instruction has implications for Chapter 1 instruction: (1) reviewers of research have suggested that, in some cases, the *setting* is less important than quality and quantity of instruction; (2) literature such as the aptitude-treatment interaction work has not clearly indicated that qualitatively distinct programs work best with certain types of students; (3) much of the regular classroom research (such as the Follow Through Program evaluations) was carried out in lower-SES schools; and (4) a portion of what little research *was* done in Chapter 1 settings (e.g., the Oklahoma City study to be described later) agreed with results from regular classes.

Brophy's four reasons are due some consideration. One could argue that the near absence of empirical process-product work in Chapter 1 classes is the underlying component of each of the four reasons.

Although quality and quantity of instruction are surely important factors for effective teaching, they may be mediated by the context of the setting—such as small, homogeneous classes working with a teacher, an aide, and a wide variety of materials. In this conception, the context or setting could be more important for student learning than "main effects" for quality or quantity of instruction. For example, the same teaching strategy may be effective or not effective, depending on the setting (teacher contact of individual students fits this pattern).

More aptitude-treatment interaction studies do need to be done in public school classes. Whereas Brophy is correct about the current paucity of evidence, there have been some suggestions of ways of teaching effectively that vary with socioeconomic status of students; the Brophy and Evertson (1976) second- and third-grade study is one example. In addition, the Crawford (1983) study in Chapter 1 classes showed differences in effective teaching according to the grade-level of the students. Even ordinal interactions of teaching strategies and student characteristics can imply different effective profiles for different types of students.

Even though much of the regular classroom research was done in lower-SES schools, that alone does not mean that findings can generalize to Chapter 1 programs. That question—degree of generalization—depends on the *strength* of the Chapter 1 context as a mediator variable (and should be decided empirically). The results of the Oklahoma City studies suggest that context (as defined in that one program) can be a potent mediator. Brophy does include the following caveat near the end of his paper (while arguing in favor of policy implications of regular research for Chapter 1 in the early and middle portions of the paper):

> Most process-outcome findings were based on natural variation observed in traditionally taught classrooms, so that generalization of these data is *limited to such classrooms* (p. 60). (emphasis added)

And although many of the findings of the Chapter 1 process-product research (to be described in detail following the review of the Brophy paper) *did* agree with earlier research, there were also many salient differences in indications of effective teaching in Chapter 1 and regular classes. The global or more "molar" variables (like time-on-task or amount of instruction) do replicate across contexts. The more molecular variables (use of individual contacts, duration of interactions, type of feedback given) may *not* replicate in different settings.

It is easy to agree with Brophy that in the absence of a replicated empirical base generated from Chapter 1 classes, the next best thing would be reasoned extrapolation of regular classroom research results. One could also issue a strong call for more research done *in the Chapter 1 setting*. The results from that research would inform us as to the strength of the Chapter 1 setting as a mediating context variable.

Under the heading of *quantitative* findings, Brophy discusses instructional dimensions concerning how teachers can increase the amount of student engagement with curriculum content. Student opportunity to learn, teacher expectations, engaged time, and active teaching are described as methods for fostering classroom gains. Emphasis is placed on *teacher* delivery of curriculum content (rather than reliance on worksheets, books, supplemental materials, etc.).

Discussion of *qualitative* findings centered on process measures reflecting *how* the teacher delivers content and keeps students on task. Brophy used three categories in synthesizing the research regarding quality of instruction: giving information (structuring), asking questions (soliciting), and providing feedback (reacting).

Giving Information (Structuring)

Brophy cites research evidence that indicates support for teaching strategies that structure or organize the content in such a way as to facilitate student learning. Effective teachers employ advance organizers, use overviews, outline lesson content, signal transitions, call attention to main ideas, and provide for review. In addition, achievement is fostered when the content is sequenced logically and is presented with appropriate redundancy. Clarity of presentation, as indicated by continuity and precision of verbal explanations, has also been a consistent (positive) correlate of achievement (particularly when learning new or difficult material). Teacher enthusiasm probably relates more to student attitude than to learning, but when it has correlated with learning, the relations have been positive.

Questioning Students (Soliciting)

Brophy notes that studies of the optimal difficulty of questions have yielded mixed results. The probable reason for this finding is that the appropriate level of difficulty varies with setting or with type of student. Brophy suggests that the majority of teacher questions (he uses the figure 75 percent) should elicit correct responses. When conducting fast-paced drill activities, he maintains that error rates in student responding should be minimal. However, when dealing with difficult material or trying to get students to synthesize or generalize lesson content, a higher error rate would be appropriate. The Brophy and Evertson (1976) study found *positive* correlations for percent of questions answered correctly and gain in lower-SES classes, but *negative* correlations in their higher-SES classrooms. This pattern suggested that effective teachers in higher-SES classes challenged students with more difficult questions, whereas effective teachers of lower-SES students made greater use of "small steps," higher redundancy, and a high success rate when questioning. These findings will be contrasted with the Oklahoma City results of process-outcome analyses in Chapter 1 classes.

Regarding the cognitive level of questions, Brophy again points to conflict in research results. Certainly all questions should not be higher-order (analysis, synthesis, etc.), since questions requiring lower-level skills like knowledge and comprehension have been shown to relate to student performance (*even on higher-level objectives*). Brophy concludes that teachers should take their lesson goals, curriculum content, and student progress into account when deciding on lower- versus higher-order questions. When questioning, effective teachers also made use of three to five seconds of "wait time"—by asking the question and then waiting before calling on a student to respond.

In the early grades, especially in small-group settings, it is important to use methods that ensure equitable student involvement; some teachers accomplish this by using patterned turns for calling on students. In the upper grades, lesson continuity and pace may be more important than simply engaging all students overtly. Those upper-grade students may have more fully developed skills in learning by modeling (watching and listening to other students).

Providing Feedback to Students (Reacting)

If students respond correctly, effective feedback may consist of only an acknowledgment from the teacher. Use of praise following correct responses has been shown to have only low positive (and sometimes negative) relations with achievement. Ineffectiveness of too much praise may be due to its intrusiveness, or it may embarrass the student being praised (particularly older students), or it may not be "genuine" (if all or nearly all responses are praised). Brophy does recommend that teachers of Chapter 1 students: ". . . probably should praise these students more often than other teachers praise their students . . ." (page 22). However, process-product data that came from Chapter 1 classes showed negative correlations between most measures of praise and achievement. This will be discussed in more detail in the next section.

If a student responds incorrectly, the research has consistently indicated that teachers with high-gaining classes are more likely than others to sustain the interaction by rephrasing or repeating the question, or by providing clues to the student who answered incorrectly. Brophy points out that, in some situations, such sustaining feedback must be constrained so as not to amount to "pointless pumping." Students should probably not be allowed to remain silent or to mumble "I don't know" in response to a question (an incorrect response is better than no answer at all).

When students offer questions and comments during a lesson, effective teachers will discourage such student initiations if they are not relevant to the lesson content. However, if the student verbalization is on-topic, then effective teachers *use* the student idea, incorporating it into his or her lesson in a smoothly flowing manner. In particular, as the grade level of the students increases, it appears to become more important to use and encourage topic-relevant student ideas.

Following his synthesis of the teaching effectiveness results, Brophy discusses qualifications of findings due to interactions with three factors: the grade or developmental level of the students, the subject matter being taught, and student socioeconomic status or ability. Other areas dealt with in the paper are special education settings, cooperative learning, conceptual change teaching in science, the teaching of cognitive or "metacognitive" learning strategies, and mastery learning approaches.

THE OKLAHOMA CITY STUDY: PROCESS-OUTCOME RELATIONS IN CHAPTER 1 CLASSES

In the spring of the 1981–82 school year, process data were collected in the Chapter 1 classes in the Oklahoma City Public Schools. The Crawford (1983) document is the full technical report, and Crawford (in press) focuses on differences and similarities between the Chapter 1 results and process-product results from regular classes.

Participants in the study were the seventy-nine Chapter 1 teachers in the district. Although the low inference coding system did record dyadic interactions between the teachers and individual students, individual student identity was not retained (teachers were the focus of the study and the unit of analysis). Forty-four of the teachers were in elementary grade classes and thirty-five were in fifth-year centers or middle schools. Fifth-year centers were created as part of the district's desegregation plan; those schools provide a transition year from elementary to middle school.

Observers were trained to use the instruments reliably prior to data collection. The low inference system was an adapted version of the Brophy and Evertson (1976) dyadic interaction analysis system. The coding system recorded public response opportunities, private teacher-student contacts (whether initiated by the teacher or the student), behavior management interactions, and public student-initiated questions or comments. High inference measures were completed at the end of each observation. The more global, high inference ratings addressed areas such as the difficulty of seatwork, use of aides, overall attentiveness, and distribution of teacher contacts within the classroom. In addition, time allocation narrative was coded to yield indicators of on-task/off-task minutes and type of grouping patterns in use. Although the classes had paraprofessional aides assisting the teacher, there was little systematic analysis of the aides' activities (one high inference variable and anecdotal notes), since the teacher was the focus of the study.

The data collection sampled three days of teaching between the first week of March and the first week of May. Depending on the grade level of the students, the length of an observation ranged from thirty to thirty-five minutes in the lower grades to fifty to fifty-five minutes in grades 6 through 8. (More *observations* were done in the early grades, but the amount of *time* observing was the same across grades.) Data were obtained for 337 observations and then aggregated to the teacher level.

Student achievement scores were also aggregated to the teacher level, so the outcome measure reflects the average gain for a teacher's students. Therefore, correlations are assessing the covariation among (Chapter 1) teacher measures of process and achievement. The achievement data came from the California Achievement Test (CAT), total reading and total math subtests. Pretest data were taken from the spring, 1981, districtwide testing, and the posttest measures were the end-of-year CAT scores from May of 1982.

The data analysis proceeded by running process-product correlations for the total sample, *and* for elementary (first through fourth grades) and upper grades (fifth through eighth) separately. The reading process data were correlated with reading outcomes, and math processes were related to math achievement. The teacher-level gains entering the analyses included both raw achievement gains and regression-adjusted gains.

Results of Process-Product Analysis

Reading.   Across all grade levels, there were several indications that active, task-oriented teaching was related to greater reading gain in Chapter 1 classes. For example, the total number of minutes allocated for academic activity and the number of academic teacher-student interactions were both significantly positively correlated with gain. In addition, the number of nonacademic contacts per minute (a rate variable) was negatively correlated with gain. A variable that was calculated as the *ratio* of a teacher's academic rate of interacting to his or her nonacademic rate of interacting was a significant correlate of reading gain.

Analysis of data from the full sample also indicated that a number of measures of the quality or nature of interactions were significant predictors of reading gain. The high inference rating of seatwork difficulty was positively related to gains, suggesting that teachers with high-gaining classes made relatively more use of challenging materials. Those same teachers were active monitors, circulating to students who needed help with their seatwork exercises. Across grades, results also suggested that teachers who asked relatively more opinion questions of Chapter 1 students tended to have higher gains.

The proportion of all public response opportunities with teacher praise was correlated negatively with reading gain for the whole sample. The mean indicated that 8.6 percent of all response opportunities in reading were followed by praise. Teachers with rates less than this value tended to have higher gains. The results for criticism were mixed. In private (one-to-one) contacts when the teacher initiated the interaction, the correlations of criticism and gain were negative, whereas criticism following student-initiation of private contacts was positively related to gain. In any case, the means for criticism were very low (from 0.25 to about 1.2 percent of private contacts), so the positive correlation reflects the difference between teachers who *never* used critical feedback and those who use it very rarely. Virtually all of the observed critical feedback instances were work-related ("Billy, you can do a lot better than this") and did not criticize the student as a person. And lastly, the overall analyses in reading suggested that the Chapter 1 teachers with the higher gains avoided redirecting a question to another student after the first student failed to answer correctly. Instead, they were more likely to sustain the interaction with the first student, rephrasing or giving clues to help improve the student's response.

Analyses were also carried out within subsamples defined by grade level: elementary (grades 1 through 4) and upper grades (grade 5 and middle school grades 6 through 8).

Elementary results in reading indicated that high-gaining teachers relied on individualized (teacher and one student at a time) instruction and use of small groups to cover academic content. Keep in mind that these are Chapter 1 pullout classes with a teacher and an aide and a full class size of six to eight students—an adult-to-child ratio of about one to four. As in the total sample, the elementary results support the profile of an active teacher (high numbers of academic contacts) who often sustains interactions when students respond incorrectly, and who uses praise sparingly in a public setting. Student-initiated *questions* in public were positively related to gain, whereas student comments were negatively correlated with reading gains in the elementary grades.

The high inference rating of seatwork difficulty was based on indicators such as how much help the students requested when completing their seatwork assignments. In both the elementary and upper-grade subsamples, that high inference variable was positively related to reading gain, suggesting that the teachers with the higher-gaining students often challenged those students with relatively difficult seatwork. Those same high-gaining teachers, especially in the early grades, also tended to have relatively more private, one-to-one interactions with students.

Upper-grade results showed some differences from elementary grades. High-gaining teachers in grades 5 through 8 made relatively more use of public question-and-answer sessions and were more likely to be spending time with the whole class, rather than with one student at a time. In most observed Chapter 1 contexts, the behavior management variables did not show strong or consistently meaningful relations with gains. Generally, the behavior-related measures showed little variance and had highly skewed distributions. However, in the upper-grade reading results, there was some indication of the effective teacher as a successful behavior manager—high-gaining classes were characterized by few interruptions and high ratings on momentum and "withitness." From Kounin's (1970) work, a "withit" teacher is one who is aware of behavior problems and communicates that awareness to the students.

Math.   Math results were also analyzed for the total sample, and for elementary and upper grades separately. In math, across grades, the number of minutes of small-group academic time and the total number of dyadic contacts were significantly positively related to gains. If the verbal interactions constitute the virtual curriculum of the class, then these teachers are covering content at a brisk pace. In math, as in reading, use of opinion questions was positively related to gain. When effective math teachers did contact students privately, it was more likely to be a brief interaction—suggesting relatively active monitoring. Private social interactions were negatively related to math gains, as was the use of a feedback strategy of redirecting a question to another student (when the first student answered incorrectly). The use of "very long" (more than thirty seconds continuously with one child) private contacts was also negatively related to math gains.

In math in grades 1 through 4, there were negative relations with gain for public, social-procedural interactions, but positive correlations for student-initiated questions or comments. As in reading, public praise was negatively correlated with gain. The proportion of public response opportunities where the students answered incorrectly was positively related to math gains in the early grades. This suggests that teachers who ask more difficult questions tend to have higher-gaining classes. The mean for proportion incorrect (at the elementary level) was 0.23, with a standard deviation of 0.15. Therefore, in this Chapter 1 sample, the higher-gaining teachers may have been eliciting errors on more than one-fourth to one-third of the occasions. Again, the small class size and the ability to provide substantive and nonthreatening feedback may have helped produce this finding. Teacher criticism of student-initiated questions/comments was negatively related to math gains, suggesting a need for encouragement of student involvement in the lesson.

In the upper grades in math, the total amount of time and the total number of academic minutes were positive predictors of gain. Also, the total amount of teacher praise was significantly negatively related to gain. Again, in the upper grades in math, the teachers who elicited relatively fewer correct responses to public questions tended to have higher gains. The mean for grades 5 through 8 on proportion of response opportunities coded as correct was 0.65, with a standard deviation of 0.25. Therefore, some upper-grade math teachers who had high-gaining students were getting more than 50 percent errors when questioning students publicly. These same analyses showed strong negative correlations for redirecting feedback, indicating that effective teachers sustained the interaction with a student when he or she did respond incorrectly. Teacher praise following student questions and comments was positively related to gain, whereas praise in other settings was negatively correlated with math gains. Infrequent use of critical feedback (fewer than 1 out of 100 interactions) was associated with math achievement gains in the upper grades.

SUMMARY OF OKLAHOMA CITY STUDY: SOME CONFIRMATIONS AND SOME SURPRISES

Some of the findings of the Chapter 1 process-product study replicated earlier research in the regular classroom, but many of the results did not agree with regular classroom results. In some instances, the Chapter 1 results differed from earlier research in lower-SES classrooms. If the differences in patterns of effective teaching behavior were to be replicated by other studies, then the evidence would indicate that the context of the Chapter 1 instruction is an important mediator.

Areas of *agreement* between regular classroom research and the Chapter 1 findings included documentation of the effectiveness of active instruction and student engagement with content. The amount learned by students is, at least in part, a function of interactions in class regarding the lesson content. The Chapter 1 study analyzed an "academic ratio" variable that was the ratio of a teacher's academic rate (number of interactions per minute) of interacting to his or her nonacademic rate. That measure correlated positively with reading and math gains, across elementary and upper grades. Several studies done in regular classrooms (e.g., Stallings and Kaskowitz, 1974; Good and Grouws, 1979) found, as in Chapter 1 classes, that teachers who sustain interactions with students tend to have higher gains; also, allowing students to remain silent or say "I don't know" was negatively related to gains.

Both the Chapter 1 study and earlier work by Evertson, Anderson, Anderson, and Brophy (1980) in regular classes indicated that classrooms of junior-high-age students with high gains were often taught by teachers concerned with rapport, as well as with academic achievement. For example, teacher acceptance and encouragement of student-initiated questions or comments and occasional use of brief social interactions were related to greater gains in fifth- to eight-grade Chapter 1 classes. The Evertson junior high study also found that whole-class (public) discussions were effective during math lessons, and this finding also arose in the Chapter 1 results.

Despite some areas of agreement with earlier regular classroom research, the Chapter 1 results also brought forth several notable disagreements.

For example, there were indications in the Chapter 1 results that a degree of challenge in lesson content or in questions from the teacher was related to greater gain. In reading, ratings of seatwork difficulty correlated positively with gain, and in math, public questions that elicited relatively more student errors were associated with achievement growth. This finding seems in contradiction with the BTES results (Fisher et al., 1978) and agrees only with the higher-SES subgroup of results from the Brophy and Evertson (1976) study. The setting of the Chapter 1 classes could account for the discrepancy in results. There may be less anxiety about public responding in Chapter 1 math classes, perhaps facilitating learning through errors in that situation. Also, the small class sizes makes immediate, nonthreatening feedback possible. Relatively greater difficulty in seatwork or in questions may be a part of a complex of behaviors by which teachers communicated high expectations to the Chapter 1 students. Those higher expectations could lead to greater student achievement.

In addition, Burstein (1980) pointed out that the widely referenced Fisher et al. (1978) results regarding the need for a high success rate came from analyses with the *student* as the unit of analysis. When the student is the unit of analysis, in-class error rates constitute a proxy for ability. Therefore, it makes sense that positive correlations with achievement would be found (it has little to do with the teachers' instructional strategies). When the BTES data were reanalyzed with the teacher as the unit of analysis, negative correlations between gain and success rates emerged, which *was* in agreement with the current results. Although results are mixed, there are indications that teachers who make use of a relatively challenging style (coupled with substantive and useful feedback) tend to have higher-gaining classes.

Another area of some disagreement with regular classroom research concerns the use of praise and criticism. The Chapter 1 results showed many negative correlations between measures of praise and gain, and some positive correlations between criticism and gain. The means of measures of praise were in the 10 to 15 percent range (10–15 percent of response opportunities), suggesting that teachers with lower-gaining classes may have been giving praise after every third or fourth question. Such overuse would diminish the effectiveness of praise as a reinforcer and could communicate lower expectations to students. The means on critical feedback were typically less than 1 percent of the interactions. Positive correlations of criticism and gain might be another expression of a teacher's challenging, high-expectations style of teaching (higher-gaining classes had very occasional use of work-related criticism). These Chapter 1 results agree only with the higher-SES findings of Brophy and Evertson (1976), but do agree with some of the results of Stallings and Kaskowitz (1974) from lower-SES Follow-Through classrooms.

One area of disagreement with earlier research concerns the effectiveness of private, one-to-one interactions between the teacher and individual students. Researchers such as Brophy and Stallings found negative correlations with gain, whereas the Chapter 1 results (especially in reading in the early grades) showed positive correlations. Reports of the earlier research included speculation that individualized instruction *per se* was not ineffective, but rather that the rest of the class (of perhaps twenty-five or more students) may not be engaged with lesson content while the teachers works with one student. In Chapter 1 lab-type classes, an adult-to-child ratio of about 1 to 4 probably permits more active teacher (and aide) monitoring of the remainder of the class as the teacher works with an individual student. The aide can assist in monitoring and helping the other students and the teacher can easily maintain awareness of what the entire class is doing.

DISCUSSION

Even *within* a single study (such as McDonald and Elias, 1976; Cooley and Leinhardt, 1980; Crawford, in press), results for process measures are qualified by grade level and subject matter. Many teaching behaviors are effective in reading, but not math (or vice versa), or show different patterns of correlation in different grade levels. So it should not be surprising that some differences *across* studies will emerge as research accrues. Brophy (1986) discussed differences in effective strategies across three mediating variables: subject matter, grade level, and ability/background of the student. A fourth could be added for the *setting* or context of the instruction. Chapter 1 pullout classes look different from regular classrooms in terms of number of classmates, materials and equipment available, and access to the teacher. Additional studies need to be done in order to determine fully the nature of the effects of classroom setting. Other groupings of classes could be analyzed: special education, bilingual, gifted/talented, and fine arts classes could form the focus for studies of each particular setting.

Nevertheless, we do have the beginnings of research-based knowledge about programs that work in compensatory education settings. By pulling together information from the DOE identification of exemplary sites with regular classroom research and Chapter 1 process-product results, it is possible to see several consistent themes regarding impact on the achievement of educationally disadvantaged students. Figure 9–1 shows the major categories of variables. This framework is adapted from Centra and Potter (1980).

School District or Among-School Conditions

Instructional leadership is a primary factor operating among schools. Typically this has been represented as the effect of the principal and his or

FIGURE 9–1.   Model of School and Classroom Effects in Compensatory Education

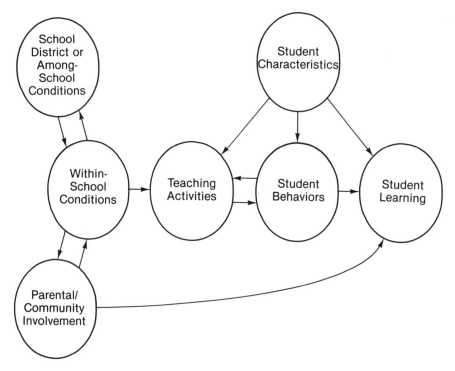

Source: Adapted from J. Centra and D. Potter, "School and teacher effects: An interrelational model," *Review of Educational Research, 50(2).*

her instructional focus. In the context of Chapter 1 instruction, the program director may fill the leadership role. In addition, *physical facilities, books, quantity of schooling, and curriculum focus* are candidates for important among-school factors.

Parental/Community Involvement

The most potent impact can result from extension of learning into the home, with the *parent as teacher*. Other community involvement activities may contribute to a positive climate and therefore indirectly enhance school effectiveness: *PTA activity, adopt-a-school programs, and parent volunteers* in classrooms are examples.

Within-School Conditions

In the context of effective Chapter 1 programs, *coordination* of the remedial and regular classroom instruction is of prime importance. In addition, a positive *climate* has been shown to relate to achievement in the school effects research. Schools where *professional development* is fostered also tend to be more effective than others. The *use of evaluation results* and clear *goals and objectives* for the school are also successful attributes. These within-school factors may be partly outside of the control of Chapter 1 programs, but do contribute to the effectiveness of support programs like Chapter 1.

Teaching Activities

Teaching activities that occur within the compensatory education setting are proposed as having a direct impact on student in-class behaviors (which, in turn, no doubt have some reciprocal effect on those teaching strategies). In Chapter 1 classes, *active instruction* where the teacher transmits the content is an effective approach. Effective Chapter 1 teachers are busy *monitors* of student learning, and they display *high expectations* of students through a concerted pattern of actions (such as assignment of relatively difficult seatwork, asking questions that cause some student mistakes, and focusing of student attention on the academic content to be learned). Effective programs may *recognize excellence* in student performance through symbolic or tangible reward systems. During classroom instruction, effective Chapter 1 teachers *use praise judiciously* (sparingly, only when it is truly called for) and may make very occasional use of work-related critical feedback. Primarily in reading in the early grades, effective teachers in small pullout classes made use of *individual contacts* (one-to-one interactions) with students. In math, *content coverage* and maintenance of a brisk pace seemed more important than individual contacts. Teachers with high gains in reading and in math were more likely to *sustain an interaction* with a student if he or she answered incorrectly (instead of redirecting the question to another student). Encouragement of *student involvement* in the lesson was more important as grade-level increased. Effective teachers also were successful *managers* who found it necessary to devote very little class time to behavior problems.

Student Behaviors

Students who are *actively engaged* with lesson content are more likely to learn that content. Further, *opportunity* to learn is impacted by the manner that teachers allocate class time. The *content overlap* between the classroom curriculum and the criterion test is of considerable importance (and criteria measures should be carefully selected based on desired values of schooling). And when students *learn how to learn*—through metacognitive strategies— greater achievement can result.

Student Characteristics

These *background* characteristics of students do impact student learning; those factors are exogeneous to the model in the sense of not being directly affected by school/classroom factors. Prior characteristics like SES and previous achievement level have a direct impact on students' learning. However, several studies have indicated that, particularly in the early grades, instructional factors may have an impact as great or greater than prior student characteristics. With appropriate instruction, educationally disadvantaged students may gain 15 to 20 (national) percentile points in basic skills achievement over the course of one year.

Student Learning

Exemplary Chapter 1 programs provide evidence of student *achievement* in basic skills, *sustained gains* over time, and increases in student *attitude* and affective outcomes that were related to program activities. Research has indicated strongest effects for compensatory education in the early grades (e.g., see the nationwide study of compensatory education by Carter (1984).

We have the beginnings of a research base regarding effective practices in Chapter 1 instruction. With more studies, it should be possible to observe further gains in knowledge about successful compensatory education.

REFERENCES

Bloom, B. (1976). *Human characteristics and learning.* New York: McGraw-Hill.

Brookover, W.; Schweitzer, J.; Schneider, J.; Beady, C.; Flood, P.; and Wisenbaker, J. (1978). Elementary school social climate and school achievement. *American Educational Research Journal, 15,(2),* 301–318.

Brophy, J. (1979). Teacher behavior and its effects. *Journal of Educational Psychology, 71,(6),* 733–750.

Brophy, J. (1986). *Research linking teacher behavior to student achievement: Potential implications for instruction of Chapter 1 students.* East Lansing, MI: Institute for Research on Teaching, Michigan State University.

Brophy, J., and Evertson, C. (1976). *Learning from teaching: A developmental perspective.* Boston: Allyn and Bacon.

Burstein, L. (1980). Issues in the aggregation of data. *Review of Research in Education, 8,* 158–233.

Carroll, J. (1963). A model of school learning. *Teachers College Record, 64,* 723–733.

Carter, L. (1984). The sustaining effects study of compensatory and elementary education. *Educational Researcher, 13,(7),* 4–13.

Centra, J., and Potter, D. (1980). School and teacher effects: An interrelational model. *Review of Educational Research, 50,(2).*

Cooley, W., and Leinhardt, G. (1980). The instructional dimensions study. *Educational Evaluation and Policy Analysis, 2,(1),* 7–25.

Crawford, J. (1983). A study of instructional processes in Title I classes: 1981–82. *Journal of Research and Evaluation of the Oklahoma City Public Schools, 13.*

Crawford, J. (in press). Teaching effectiveness in Chapter 1 classrooms. *The Elementary School Journal.*

Crawford, J., and Watson, P. (1985). Schools make a difference: Within and between school effects. *Journal of Research and Evaluation of the Oklahoma City Public Schools, 15,(8).*

David, J. (1981). Local uses of Title I evaluations. *Educational Evaluation and Policy Analysis, 3,(1),* 27–39.

Evertson, C.; Anderson, C.; Anderson, L.; and Brophy, J. (1980). Relationships between classroom behaviors and student outcomes in junior high mathematics and English classes. *American Educational Research Journal, 17,* 43–60.

Fisher, C.; Filby, N.; Marliave, R.; Cahen, L.; Dishaw, M.; Moore, J.; and Berliner, D. (1978). *Teaching behaviors, academic learning time, and student achievement: Final report of phase III-B, Beginning Teacher Evaluation Study.* San Francisco: Far West Laboratory for Educational Research and Development.

Good, T., and Grouws, D. (1979). The Missouri mathematics effectiveness project: An experimental study in fourth grade classrooms. *Journal of Educational Psychology, 71,* 355–362.

Griswold, P.; Cotton, K.; and Hansen, J. (1985). *Effective Compensatory Education Sourcebook, Volumes I and II.* Washington, DC: U.S. Department of Education.

Kounin, J. (1970). *Discipline and group management in classrooms.* New York: Holt, Rinehart, and Winston.

McDonald, F., and Elias, P. (1976). *The effects of teaching performance on pupil learning, Beginning Teacher Evaluation Study, phase II, final report: Vol. 1.* Princeton, NJ: Educational Testing Service.

Rosenshine, B. (1983). Teaching functions in instructional programs. *Elementary School Journal, 83,(4),* 335–351.

Rosenthal, R., and Jacobson, L. (1968). *Pygmalian in the classroom.* New York: Holt, Rinehart, and Winston.

Shulman, L. (1986). Paradigms and research programs in the study of teaching: A contemporary perspective. In M. Wittrock (Ed.), *Handbook of research on teaching.* New York: Mcmillan Company.

Stallings, J., and Kaskowitz, D. (1974). *Follow-Through classroom observation evaluation, 1972–73.* Meno Park, CA: SRI International.

10

EFFECTIVE STRATEGIES FOR ACADEMICALLY HANDICAPPED STUDENTS IN THE REGULAR CLASSROOM

Barbara Larrivee

California State University at San Bernardino

During the 1960s and 1970s, the merit of special class placement for handicapped learners came under attack as mounting evidence challenged its positive effect on the achievement and social status of these students. Researchers consistently found that, at best, these special classes brought about academic performance no better than regular class placement (Budoff and Gottlieb, 1976; Calhoun and Elliott, 1977; Carroll, 1967; Goldstein, Moss, and Jordan, 1965; Johnson, 1962; Ritter, 1978; Vacc, 1972). Thus the enactment of the Education for All Handicapped Children Act of 1975 marked the culmination of more than a decade's efforts to promote regular class placement for handicapped students.

However, having lived with mainstreaming for the past decade, educators are now questioning its effectiveness in achieving the goals originally intended. One of the major goals of mainstreaming is the enhancement of social acceptability of handicapped students by their nonhandicapped classmates, yet the outcomes of mainstreaming on this variable have proved disappointing (Asher and Taylor, 1981; Gottlieb, 1981; Gresham, 1981, 1983; Levine, Hummel, and Salzer, 1982). It appears that mainstreaming per se has had little impact on the social status of handicapped students. Likewise, handicapped learners educated in the mainstream have not made the academic progress expected as a result of integration and continue to fall further and further behind. The mere physical integration of handicapped learners with their nonhandicapped peers is clearly insufficient to bring about increased academic progress in the absence of carefully designed instructional strategies to accommodate low achievers. Thus the implementation of mainstreaming is presently occurring in the absence of an empirical data base warranting its continuation as currently practiced.

291

Just as mainstream education is coming under attack as an environment historically unresponsive to the needs of low-achieving students, traditional special education practices are likewise suspect. For example, there is now general acceptance among special educators that little empirical support has accrued to warrant continued endorsement of the contention that perceptual, psycholinguistic, or motoric training or remediation is a necessary prerequisite to the attainment of basic academic skills, or a meaningful educational goal for handicapped learners in and of itself (e.g., Larrivee, 1981a; Meyers, 1980; Tarver and Dawson, 1978).

Similarly, although intuitively attractive to special educators, a priori matching of teaching approaches to particular student characteristics identified through assessment finds little support in the research literature. Despite many efforts over the past two decades to identify aptitude-treatment interactions (ATIs), none have been substantiated to the degree required for direct application to differential instructional treatment of students (e.g., Cronbach and Snow, 1976; Lloyd, 1984; Zigmond and Miller, 1986).

Although research in the area of identification of students with learning disabilities has been exhaustive, the result of this massive effort has been failure to disclose reliable methods of distinguishing the learning disabled from other low achievers (Moran, 1984; Wilson, 1985). In fact, the data serve to continually document overlap in identification profiles, actual classroom performance, and demographic factors (Warner, Alley, Schumaker, Deshler, and Clark, 1980; Ysseldyke, Algozzine, Shinn, and McGue, 1982). This finding has particular significance given the alarming increase in the number of students being identified as learning disabled (Algozzine and Korinek, 1985). Thus there is little research basis for offering instructional programs to learning-disabled children that are different from those for other groups experiencing academic difficulty, such as the educable mentally retarded, emotionally disturbed, or those eligible for Chapter 1 remedial services. In fact, Gardner (1982) concluded that a special education student's categorical label is largely irrelevant for instructional purposes since there is no apparent interaction between diagnosis and teaching program. Further, recent research has shown that students in special education resource rooms with diagnosed reading problems may actually receive less overall instruction in reading than regular students, leading Haynes and Jenkins (1986) to conclude that there is no obvious relationship in practice between student need and amount of assigned resource room time or actual reading instruction. Also, Leinhardt, Zigmond, and Cooley (1981) found that in the self-contained learning disabilities classrooms they studied, teachers spent only an average of sixteen minutes per day actually teaching reading.

Thus it appears that the very core of "special education" is being challenged on several fundamental assumptions of special education, such as the need for specialized instructional programs aimed at remediation of perceptual, psycholinguistic, and motoric deficits; the need to match student-assessed needs with differential instructional treatments (ATI model); the utility of separate special education classifications for instructional purposes; as well as the overall quality of instructional practices in special education settings.

As educators begin to question the appropriateness of both special and regular education instructional practices for students experiencing learning difficulties, a revamping of ongoing instruction programs to make them more responsive to the growing population of children experiencing failure in our schools is needed. This chapter will review what we now know about effective teacher behaviors and classroom practices for students with learning problems who are maintstreamed in regular classrooms for some or all of their academic subjects.

TEACHER EFFECTIVENESS RESEARCH

The emerging teacher effectiveness research base has come to the forefront as a possible means of increasing the effectiveness of school programs, especially in the area of basic skill acquisition. This body of literature has identified a core of specific teaching practices that appear to be reasonably stable across basic skill areas (e.g., reading as well as math), affective as well as academic outcomes, and across many types of students (at least at the elementary grade levels).

Since teaching practices designed to benefit mainstreamed students must also be beneficial for their nonhandicapped peers for such practices to be advocated for use in integrated settings, traditional special education modes of research (e.g., treatment/effect studies, one-to-one tutorial techniques, case studies) are likely to have limited application to the mainstreamed situation in which the special child is educated with normal learners in large-class settings.

A line of research that has rarely been utilized in special education research and that has important implications for the mainstreamed child is process-product research, that is, research conducted in classrooms for the purpose of identifying effective teaching behaviors. In this type of research, teaching behaviors are correlated with student performance measures, generally academic achievement, to identify significant relationships. Researchers engaged in this research over the past two decades have found that certain teaching behaviors consistently correlate with student achievement. Though much of this research has been conducted in classrooms serving disadvantaged students and/or low achievers, research has not been conducted specifically to examine the effect on mildly handicapped students, such as students diagnosed as learning disabled, educable mentally retarded, or behaviorally disordered, and receiving the majority of their education in a mainstreamed setting. A study by this author (Larrivee, 1985) was designed to extend the process-product research findings to the mainstreamed population. This research is summarized in the following section. The underlying premise upon which the research was based is that many of the effective teaching behaviors identified via process-product research in classrooms should also be appropriate for dealing with mainstreamed students placed in regular classrooms.

TEACHER EFFECTIVENESS IN THE MAINSTREAMED CLASSROOM

Research Plan

The procedural plan for the first phase of the research called for development of a comprehensive list of teaching variables for consideration based on the teacher effectiveness literature pertaining to regular elementary classrooms, selection of teachers with a proven record of success with mainstreamed students, and, through observation and other assessment procedures, identification of common characteristics of teachers who are effective with mainstreamed students.

The second phase was a large-scale correlational study to examine the relationship between specific teaching behaviors identified in the first phase and various aspects of mainstreamed student performance. This phase was intended to validate the teaching behaviors previously identified as effective for mainstreaming derived from the study of successful teachers.

Of particular relevance for selecting variables for consideration in this study were those teaching variables identified as especially effective for low-SES and/or low-ability students. Several reviews of the considerable accumulation of process-product research provided by Medley (1977), Brophy (1979), Gage (1978), and Rosenshine (1979) provided the primary basis for establishing an initial set of teaching behaviors to be studied.

These comprehensive reviews suggest a tentative picture of the teacher who is effective in elementary classrooms with low-achieving students. Given modest losses of precision, a descriptive profile of such a teacher will be attempted. The teacher who is especially effective in this type of classroom engages students in more lesson-related activities than the less effective teacher does, with more class time devoted to task-related or academic activities, more structure provided, more student-teacher interactions related to lesson content, and less time in which students are unoccupied. The effective teacher spends more time in group instruction, making the amount of time students spend working independently or in small groups less in the effective teacher's classroom.

In terms of questioning strategies, the effective teacher is most likely to ask a question and then choose a respondent who has not indicated a desire to answer. The questions asked are predominantly factual and elicit responses that are usually correct, seldom meriting further discussion. This teacher is likely to raise a question first and then to indicate who is to answer it, possibly as a way of holding students' attention. The student chosen to respond is likely to get the right answer, since these teachers ask more appropriate questions and have a better sense of the difficulty level their students can handle. Criticism of a pupil's answer is rare, even when it is incorrect. If a student fails to answer or does not know the answer, this teacher is more likely to help out by rewording the question or asking an easier one than to turn to another student. The ratio of student-initiated to teacher-initiated questions and comments also tends to be lower for the effective teacher.

In the area of classroom management, there is less deviant or disruptive student behavior in classes taught by the effective teacher. Teacher rebukes are less frequent and less time is devoted to managing the classroom. The successful teacher controls the class with less criticism and uses a more varied repertory of techniques in doing so. This teacher also uses more praise or positive motivation. Permissive behavior, or giving students freedom to govern their own activities, is consistently found to be less common in the effective teacher's class. In summary, the effective teacher maintains an atmosphere that is supportive and relatively free from disruptive student behavior. This environment is sustained with little obvious effort and without expression of negative affect. Finally, the teacher who is effective with lower-ability students spends more time assisting individual students and checking their individual work, and is more likely to have been the initiator of the contact. When the effective teacher responds to questions related to content, he or she tends to interact longer and pay closer attention to the student than the less effective teacher.

Although the emphasis of the research design in the Larrivee (1985) study was on teacher variables deemed to be important for the academic success of lower-ability students in regular classrooms, the design was supplemented by inclusion of some variables from the affective domain believed to be of particular concern for the special needs child, such as teacher responsiveness, relationship with students, and awareness of feelings. Also incorporated into the overall design were variables derived from advocated special education practices, such as providing opportunities for success and a supportive and highly structured environment. Academic learning time (ALT) was also included as an indication of actual opportunity to learn for the mainstreamed child. Lastly, a series of variables was included to explore specific intervention strategies directed at particular student behaviors characteristic of special needs students, as were several teacher attitudinal variables, since much research is available to support the importance of a favorable attitude toward mainstreaming handicapped children (e.g., Harasymiw and Horne, 1976; Higgs, 1975; Horne, 1979; Larrivee, 1981b).

Ultimately, the final list of variables to be considered in the design consisted of sixty-eight teaching variables and six attitudinal variables. These variables encompass the domains of questioning strategies, teaching style, affective classroom climate, classroom management, academic learning time, and individualization.

During the first phase of the research, the operational plan called for the selection of regular classroom teachers who had demonstrated their effectiveness with special needs students placed in the regular classroom setting. Teachers were selected based on the performance of these students who were assessed on a pre-post basis on academic, behavioral, social, and attitudinal variables. Since all children in schools are affected by mainstreaming, successful mainstreaming practices would necessarily have to be effective for the nonhandicapped child as well. In fact, one would hope that increased attention to individual student needs and greater individualization of instruction would eventually result in improvement in the quality of education for all children. Hence, our definition of teacher effectiveness was influenced by the belief that teachers identified as effective for this study should be effective not only with mildly handicapped learners placed in their classrooms but also with their nonhandicapped classroom peers. Teacher effectiveness was further operationalized to mean producing greater progress than would normally be expected over the duration of the school year on several dimensions deemed as important educational outcomes for both handicapped and nonhandicapped students. This definition required that gains on each of the student performance measures, as well as gain on an overall profile score, be averaged over all children in all classes to provide a standard of comparison. Similar averages among the special needs children in all classes were determined to provide a meaningful comparison for these children in particular.

Considering gains made by the special needs students as well as gains made by the class at large, twelve teachers were identified as outstandingly effective from an original data base of thirty-three elementary classrooms. Subsequently, more than twenty classroom observations were conducted in each of the classrooms of the identified teachers in an effort to isolate characteristic teaching behaviors. Ultimately, forty-two of the teaching variables considered were determined to be characteristic of teachers who are effective with mainstreamed students, as were an additional four attitudinal variables. These variables are designated in Figure 10–1 by one asterisk (*), indicating that the effective teachers engaged in a high amount of the behavior, and by two asterisks (**), indicating a low amount of the behavior to be characteristic of the effective teachers. Variables without asterisks were not found to be significantly correlated with performance gains for mainstreamed students. (For detailed descriptive information on this phase of the study, see Larrivee, 1980, 1982, 1985, and Larrivee and Vacca, 1980.)

Analysis and Results

The design, methodology, analysis, and results of the final phase of the study have been presented in detail elsewhere (see Larrivee, 1985) and will only be summarized here for the purpose of discussing potential ramifications of the research findings.

The large-scale correlational study was based on a sample of 118 classroom teachers and selected mainstreamed students. The sampled mainstreamed students had a primary classification of learning disabled but also included behaviorally disordered and speech and hearing impaired mainstreamed students. The design incorporated teacher characteristics expected to affect performance with mainstreamed students such as highest degree earned, number of courses in special education, years of teaching experience, experience with mainstreamed students, perceived success with mainstreamed students, and attitude toward the practice of mainstreaming special needs students.

For the mainstreamed students, data pertaining to age, sex, prior achievement, type of handicapping condition, length of time mainstreamed, and amount of time spent with specialists were collected. Additionally, grade level, class size, proportion of mainstreamed students in the class, and number of reading groups were included in the design as well as school-level variables such as administrative support and availability of supportive services. The following performance measures for the selected mainstreamed students were considered: reading achievement, social status, self-perception of peer acceptance, overall maladaptive behavior as well as eleven individual behavior scores, off-task rate, difficulty level of learning tasks, student and teacher transition time, waiting-for-help time, and academic learning time (ALT), defined as the time a student spends actively engaged in a content-related task that is of appropriate difficulty.

Thus this massive data set included twenty-one dependent variables assessed for selected mainstreamed students and forty-eight independent variables, including twenty-seven classroom observation variables, each coded on four occasions for 118 classroom teachers.

Of the forty-two teaching behaviors identified as characteristic of teachers effective with mainstreamed students, thirty-four were included in this phase of the study. To determine the degree of relationship between each teaching behavior and the student performance measures, a series of partial correlation analyses was conducted. Grade placement, sex, length of time mainstreamed, and hours of services provided were selected as control

FIGURE 10–1.   Teaching Variables

QUESTIONING STYLE

Volunteer Respondent
Student Selection
Narrow Questions
* Positive Feedback
* Sustaining Feedback

* Content Questions
* Low-Order Questions
* Correct Student Response
** Criticism of Response

CLASSROOM CLIMATE

Movement-Free vs. Restricted
Affective Environment
Physical Environment
Noise Level Appropriateness
Non-Permissiveness
Controlling Behavior
Acceptance of Feelings

Awareness of Feelings
* Warmth
* Teacher Responsiveness
* Teacher Fairness
* Performance Expectation
* Relationship with Students
* Initiation of Student Contact

INDIVIDUALIZATION

Time in Small Groups
Time in Large Groups
Teacher Time with Individuals
Individualization of Work
Grouping for Math

Checking Student Work
* Ad Hoc Grouping
* Instructional Appropriateness
* Grouping for Reading
* Attention to Individual Needs

CLASSROOM MANAGEMENT

Supportive Response to Conduct
   Problems
Supportive Response to High
   Severity Behavior
Teacher Consistency
Use of Praise
* Supportive Response to Learning
   Problems
* Supportive Response to
   Personality Problems
* Supportive Response to Low
   Ability Students
* Effective Use of Time

* Total Supportive Response

* Task Engagement Feedback

* Variety of Interventions
** Need for Discipline
** Total Punitive Response

** Punitive Intervention

** Incidence of Intervention

ACADEMIC LEARNING TIME

Allotted Time
Teacher Directed Time
Student Directed Time
* Easy Difficulty Level
* Engagement Rate
* Academic Learning Time
** Special Individual Work Time

** Unassigned Time
** Teacher Transition TIme
** Student Transition TIme
** Waiting-for-Help Time
** Off-Task TIme
** Hard Difficulty Level

FIGURE 10–1.   (continued)

TEACHING STYLE

Assignment of Tasks   * Clarity
Assignment of Homework   * Academic Feedback
* Teacher Flexibility   * Active Involvement
* Lesson Structure

OPINION AND ATTITUDINAL VARIABLES

Situational Job Satisfaction   * Professional Job Satisfaction
Educational Philosophy   * Scope of Professional
* Positive Attitude Toward   Responsibility
  Mainstreaming   * Teacher Self-Perception of
                                        Competence

* High amount characteristic of effective teachers.
** Low amount characteristic of effective teachers.

variables. Prereading achievement was controlled when postreading was considered. The results to follow are, of course, limited by the fact that the data are only correlational, and thus no causal inferences can be drawn from the data. An alternative plausible explanation is that higher-achieving, more well-behaved classes were observed and the selected covariates undercontrolled for these factors.

It is of interest to note that no significant correlations were found between the number and/or ratio of mainstreamed students within a class and any of the teaching behaviors or any of the mainstreamed student measures. Apparently the number of mainstreamed students in a class did not in itself influence teaching behaviors or mainstreamed student achievement. These results, coupled with the earlier finding that those teachers who were successful with their special-needs students were able to accomplish these gains while simultaneously achieving similar gains for all their students, serve to challenge the generally accepted notion that the extra time required to educate mildly handicapped learners will be to the detriment of the rest of their classmates.

The only student measure that did not correlate significantly with any of the teaching behaviors examined was self-perception of peer acceptance. These results could be interpreted to mean that mainstreamed students' perceptions of their acceptance is unrelated to specific teaching behaviors, and is more influenced by other factors.

Due to the magnitude of the data set, a large number of significant relationships between teaching variables and mainstreamed student performance measures were identified from the analyses. In an effort to summarize the results, Table 10–1 has been organized to include the four categories of performance measures. Included here are all teaching variables that had a minimum of three meaningful significant correlations with the mainstreamed

TABLE 10-1. Significant Correlates of Mainstreamed Student Measures

| | Mainstreamed Student Performance | | | |
Teacher Variable	Reading achievement	Social acceptance	ALT variable*	Behavior variable†
Sustaining Feedback		X	ALT	CI
Positive Feedback	X		ALT, EDL, OTR(−)	
Easy Difficulty Level			EDL, ALT	IW(−)
Correct Student Response			ALT, EDL, ST(−)	T(−), CD(−), DD(−), IR(−), EB(−), IW(−),C
Student Transition Time	X(−)		ALT(−), OTR	CD
Off-Task Rate	X(−)		ALT(−), TT	ER
Incidence of Intervention	X(−)		ALT(−), OTR, TT	ER
Punitive Intervention			ALT(−), EDL(−), TT	
Criticism of Response		X(−)		
Total Punitive Response				T, I, CD, IW, IR, C(−)
Supportive Response to Low-Ability Students	X			T(−), CD(−), I(−), EB(−), AA(−), IW(−), IR(−), C
Supportive Response to Learning Problems			OTR(−)	CD(−), IW(−)
Total Supportive Response			OTR(−)	T(−), CD(−), IW(−), I(−), IR(−), C
Need for Discipline	X(−)		ALT(−), OTR	
Efficient Use of Time	X		ALT, OTR(−)	

* ALT = Academic Learning Time; OTR = Off-Task Rate; EDL = Easy Difficulty Level; ST = Student Transition; TT = Teacher Transition; WHT = Waiting-for-Help Time.

† T = Total Maladaptive Score; CD = Classroom Disturbance; I = Impatience; DD = Disrespect-Defiance; EB = External Blame; AA = Achievement Anxiety; ER = External Reliance; IW = Inattentive-Withdrawn; IR = Irrelevant Responsiveness; C = Comprehension; CI = Creative Initiative.

student performance measures. Since a variety of outcomes are desirable for handicapped students placed in regular classrooms, it was decided to consider only those teaching behaviors correlating with at least three measures of mainstreamed students' classroom performance as effective teaching behaviors for mainstreamed settings. The single exception to this criterion was the variable labeled "criticism of response," correlating significantly with only one of the performance measures—peer acceptance of the mainstreamed student. This variable was retained based on the relative importance of social outcomes for mainstreamed handicapped students.

Ultimately, a total of fifteen teaching behaviors or strategies emerged based on their relationship to several desired outcomes for mainstreamed students. These behaviors are as follows:

1. Frequent positive feedback to students
2. Providing sustaining feedback to students responding incorrectly to questions
3. Supportive, encouraging response to students in general
4. Supportive response to low-ability students in particular
5. Supportive response to problem behaviors indicative of a learning problem (as distinguished from conduct problems)
6. Asking questions that students answer correctly
7. Providing learning tasks that students can accomplish with a high rate of success
8. Using classroom time efficiently
9. Low incidence of teacher intervention
10. Infrequent need to discipline students
11. Limited use of punitive interventions
12. Minimal punitive response to students
13. Rare criticism of student responses
14. Little student transition or noninstructional time
15. Low rate of student off-task time

Discussion

The descriptive profile that emerges for teachers who are effective with mainstreamed students is remarkably similar to that of teachers who are effective for all students, based on an emerging body of teacher effectiveness literature (e.g., Brophy and Good, 1986). The teaching behaviors identified here as effective relative to questioning strategies (i.e., giving positive feedback for correct student responses; using sustaining feedback or attempting to prompt, rephrase, or provide clues for incorrect responses; high correct response rate; and infrequent criticism of student responses) have been well documented as effective teaching practices in classroom settings. The findings for opportunity to learn variables, in particular instructional appropriateness (operationally defined as easy difficulty of tasks, high engagement rate, and little transition time, indicating more instructional time), have also appeared repeatedly as effective teaching behaviors based on a multitude of process-product research findings.

Indicators of effective classroom management skills, specifically low incidence of intervention, lack of need for discipline, and efficient use of time, have likewise consistently appeared on lists of effective teaching behaviors derived from the process-product literature. The remaining identified teaching variables pertain to intervening and responding punitively to students. Here, the data support the common finding that punitiveness is negatively correlated with student performance.

The recommendations for teacher behavior to accommodate mainstreamed students resulting from this research would be that teachers provide positive and encouraging feedback to students responding to questions (75 to 95 percent of the time), give sustaining feedback when students answer incorrectly (for from 60 to 80 percent of incorrect responses), ask questions during instruction that students can answer correctly (correct response rate of from 70 to 90 percent), refrain from criticizing student responses (less than 1 percent), and provide instructional materials and learning tasks that students appropriately engage in (80 percent engagement or better) at a low error rate (80 percent or more correct). Furthermore, it is desirable that teachers working with mainstreamed students provide a supportive classroom environment in which there is little student transitional or noninstructional wait-time (less than 8 percent) and where the need for discipline as well as the actual intervention rates (less than six per hour) are low, and use of punitive interventions is minimal (less than 5 percent).

Whereas the majority of the teaching behaviors recommended for the benefit of mainstreamed students have general applicability for elementary classrooms at large, three teaching behaviors in particular appear to be required with greater frequency for special needs students: providing positive and encouraging feedback, high success rate, and lack of criticism. Mainstreamed students and other low-ability and/or low-SES students apparently require greater amounts of positive and encouraging feedback and higher success rates, especially when working independently. An extremely low level of criticism is likewise beneficial for these types of students, whereas there is some evidence that higher-achieving students benefit from occasional criticism (although even here, criticism should be relatively infrequent).

The results reported here suggest a tentative profile of the teacher who is effective with mainstreamed students. The successful teacher asks factual questions that are most often answered correctly by students. Correct answers receive positive feedback, whereas incorrect answers receive supportive, clarifying feedback. Criticism is hardly ever used. The effective teacher is very responsive to students and holds high expectations for them. In the classrooms of successful teachers, interventions are supportive, student contact is teacher-initiated, and on-task behavior is reinforced. Students work at their own instructional level, are appropriately engaged in learning activities, and seldom need disciplinary interventions.

These research results indicate that the mildly handicapped child can be accommodated by teaching practices that are beneficial to the class as a whole, since teaching strategies that meet the needs of mainstreamed students are also likely to be effective practices for the majority of students.

Since this research did support the position that the identified effective teaching behaviors would likewise have a positive outcome on the academic, social, and behavioral performance of mildly handicapped learners, the findings serve to substantiate further the generalizability of the identified set of teaching behaviors to regular classroom settings serving children with mild learning handicaps.

It is important to consider here that the notion still persists, despite evidence to the contrary, that an academic focus or orientation will necessarily operate to the detriment of affective development. Yet Medley (1977), in comparing pairs of relationships, reported a 72 percent overlap for achievement gains with attitude toward school, and a 75 percent overlap for achievement gains with measures of self-concept. Similarly, in a later phase of the Beginning Teacher Evaluation Study (BTES) that included an ethnographic study of forty elementary classes, academically effective teachers were able to develop a generally positive classroom atmosphere while simultaneously orchestrating an efficient learning environment (e.g., see Berliner and Tikunoff, 1976, 1977). Indeed, the data reported here showed that individual teaching behaviors (i.e., sustaining feedback, off-task rate, student transition time, and incidence of intervention) correlated with as many as three of the four outcome areas considered—achievement, academic learning time, social status, and behavioral adjustment. In fact, nine of the fifteen effective teacher behaviors were associated with positive outcomes in achievement or academic learning time in addition to desired social or behavioral outcomes.

Thus it appears that although teachers may operate somewhat differently—that is, vary their teaching behaviors according to subject matter, grouping structure, lesson format, or their intended outcomes—they frequently are more or less effective across subjects (in particular, reading and math) and produce consistent affective outcomes. This conclusion is supported in the present data, in Medley's review, and in the early Brophy and Evertson data (1974). Moreover, in this study, all of the teachers who were found to be highly successful with mainstreamed students were likewise effective with the total classroom. However, it is important to note that the reciprocal relationship (i.e., those teachers successful with the total classroom crossed with those experiencing success with special-needs students) showed only 47 percent overlap. Apparently, realizing success with the class at large is not predictive of success with the special student, even though the opposite is true.

Nonetheless, as Brophy and Good (1986) have recently pointed out, although it may be possible to optimize student progress along several dimensions concurrently to a certain degree, beyond some point further progress toward one set of goals will come at the expense of progress toward other goals that necessarily compete within the confines of the classroom. No doubt some tradeoffs must be faced because of the rival forces that operate in the typical classroom setting.

The data reported here indicate that different sets of teaching behaviors might be advocated depending on the prioritizing of specific educational outcomes for mainstreamed students. The behaviors identified in this research could be organized into clusters of teaching behaviors that are primarily related to specific types of outcomes for mainstreamed students. For training purposes, the following four category distinctions are offered: (1) Classroom Management and Discipline, (2) Feedback During Instruction, (3) Instructional Appropriateness, and (4) Supportive Environment.

Utilizing this organizational framework, each of the units incorporates several compatible teaching behaviors and classroom practices and is predominantly associated with a specific type of student performance. In the Classroom Management and Discipline cluster, the specific teaching behaviors and classroom conditions recommended are: (1) efficient use of time, (2) low incidence of intervention, (3) minimal use of punitive interventions, (4) lack of need for discipline, (5) infrequent student transition time, and (6) low student off-task rate. In terms of advocated practices, teachers would establish a classroom setting for mainstreamed students that offers a well-organized, highly structured environment in which teacher time is appropriately allocated with little student transitional or noninstructional wait-time or student off-task behavior. Need for discipline as well as actual intervention rate should be low, and use of punitive interventions minimal. These classroom management behaviors correlated significantly with greater academic learning time as well as reading achievement.

The second cluster, Feedback During Instruction, would include: (1) providing positive feedback, (2) giving sustaining feedback, and (3) avoiding criticizing student responses. Recommended classroom practices when giving feedback to students relative to instructional content (not behavior) would be that teachers provide positive feedback to students responding correctly to questions and use sustaining feedback for students answering incorrectly. For example, teachers should ask clarifying or helping followup questions intended to give students a second chance to respond correctly. Furthermore, teachers should refrain as much as possible from criticizing students' incorrect responses. This cluster of teaching behaviors was associated primarily with greater peer acceptance.

In the third cluster, Instructional Appropriateness, the recommended teaching practices are: (1) appropriate difficulty of tasks and (2) high rate of correct student response to teacher questions. Teachers should provide instructional materials and tasks that students appropriately engage in at a low error rate most of the time. Questions asked during instruction should be geared to the target group or individual such that student rate of correct response is high. Both these teaching practices correlated significantly with greater academic learning time and with less inattentive and withdrawn behavior.

The Supportive Environment cluster would include: (1) use of supportive interventions, (2) responding supportively to low-ability students, (3) responding supportively to learning problem behaviors, and (4) infrequent usage of punitive response options. The recommended teaching practices would be that teachers working with mainstreamed students provide a supportive, nonthreatening classroom environment. Accomplishing such an atmosphere would entail greater use of supportive behaviors and intervention strategies directed at specific student behaviors characteristic of special needs students. Employing these teaching strategies correlated significantly with less inappropriate student behavior.

Thus, depending on the outcome of interest, different teaching behaviors could be advocated. These clusters of behaviors might also be implemented successively according to prioritized goals for individuals or groups of mainstreamed students.

ALTERNATIVE CLASSROOM MODELS FOR MAINSTREAMED CLASSROOMS

This chapter has principally discussed effective teacher behaviors within the traditionally organized classroom. However, several groups of researchers have developed and evaluated classroom instructional methods quite different from traditional instructional practices, and have examined their effects on mainstreamed as well as nonhandicapped students. This section discusses such methods.

The Need to Reconsider Current Practice

Several factors are currently contributing to the present reexamination of existing policies regarding education of academically deficient students and are providing impetus for the movement for a coordinated service delivery system to accommodate all at-risk students. This would include students with diagnosed learning handicaps such as the learning disabled, educable mentally retarded, behaviorally disordered, and so on, as well as economically deprived students currently serviced by Chapter 1, students receiving remedial instruction in basic skill areas, as well as all other students falling behind in the acquisition of basic skills. The first factor is the alarming increase in the number of school-age children currently experiencing failure in our school systems. An even greater increase is projected for the years to come as children from low-SES and minority backgrounds become an increasing proportion of the school-age population. As estimated by Will (1986), some 20 to 30 percent of the school-age population (or nearly 8 million) are having difficulty progressing in our public schools. The sheer numbers alone argue for new strategies to enhance the educational success of these students.

The second factor is the increasing failure of our special education system to remediate learning problems or to impact on the cumulative deficit phenomenon. Similarly, recent investigations of instructional practices occurring in special education settings indicate a sparcity of quality practices, such as failure to make use of assessment data (Joyce, 1980; McNair and Joyce, 1979; Potter and Mirkin, 1982), failure to evaluate students' progress regularly (Fuchs, Fuchs, and Warren, 1982), failure to allocate sufficient time to basic skill instruction (Leinhardt and Pallay, 1982), use of slow-paced instruction with few lessons completed and less content material read (Madden and Slavin, 1983), as well as limited direct instruction (Leinhardt, Zigmond, and Cooley, 1981). These findings lead many educators to view special education as not, in reality, special but as potentially inferior to regular education.

The third major factor is the expanding discrepancy between low and normal achievers as they progress through the curriculum content. A corollary issue is the new "great debate" or the "time/achievement/equality debate," with evidence supporting the notion that the gap is ever increasing with initial academic differences in learning rate (or time needed to learn) remaining stable (see Bloom, 1984; Slavin, 1987).

Research evidence is beginning to accumulate to support the notion that the majority of academically deficient students can achieve both academic and social success in heterogeneous class groupings, provided effective teaching is practiced and adaptive, individualized, and/or cooperative learning strategies are implemented. In this section of this chapter, instructional programs and strategies that have been employed successfully with academically handicapped students in regular class settings will be reviewed for the purpose of isolating specific programmatic components as well as identifying those components corresponding to the variables identified in the teacher effectiveness literature. Direct instruction techniques, the Adaptive

Learning Environment Model (ALEM), cooperative learning strategies, peer tutoring, and learning strategies will be addressed, respectively. Although each approach is considered separately, it is important to note that these methods have overlapping components. Furthermore, a thorough discussion is not being offered here since these programs are discussed in other chapters of this book.

Direct Instruction

Direct instruction has recently come to have two meanings. Traditionally, *direct instruction* referred to work primarily done by Engelmann and his colleagues (e.g., Becker, Engelmann, Carnine, and Rhine, 1981); however, more recently the term *direct instruction* often refers to a set of procedures derived from the teacher effectiveness literature and delineated by Rosenshine (1976). Rosenshine and Stevens (1984) concluded that low-achieving students show greater academic achievement when their teachers follow a consistent pattern of demonstration, guided practice, and feedback, irrespective of curriculum.

Though the term generally connotes a form of highly structured, teacher-directed instruction, one way to view direct instruction is as a comprehensive system of instruction encompassing classroom organization and management, quality of teacher-student interactions, and design of curriculum materials (Gersten, Woodward, and Darch, 1986). Direct instruction conceived by Engelmann and colleagues is concerned with rigorous analysis of exactly how curricular materials should be constructed. In direct instruction programs, initial teaching involves explicit instruction on each step in the sequence. Thus direct instruction is an instructional program that meets the conditions as conceived by Rosenshine, yet incorporating additional features. Design components of direct instruction curriculum include mastery learning, carefully designed sequential instruction, flexible skill-level grouping, adequate opportunity for practice, and periodic review of previously learned concepts.

A number of studies have found direct instruction superior to other instructional approaches for academically handicapped students in reading comprehension skills (e.g., Patching, Kameenui, Carnine, Gersten, and Colvin, 1983; Carnine and Kinder, 1985), as well as math and reading achievement (e.g., Gersten, Becker, Heiry, and White, 1984). Similarly, Stein and Goldman (1980), examining the effect of Distar Reading with primary-age learning-disabled students, found appreciable gains in reading achievement.

The Exemplary Center for Reading Instruction (ECRI) is a highly structured, teacher-directed, mastery learning approach, utilizing a demonstration-prompt-practice format relying on the prior establishment of classroom routines, and thus can also be designated as a direct instruction approach. Key instructional features include greater allotted instructional time, positive reinforcement, overt and rapid student response procedures making the levels of student opportunity to respond high, and specific procedures, to maximize actual instruction time. Although the method was developed and validated prior to the more recent effective teacher behavior literature, the approach shares many of the instructional components described by Rosenshine and Berliner (1978) based on summarizing this literature base.

Data regarding the effectiveness of ECRI has shown the method to be effective in significantly increasing student achievement for both regular and special education students (e.g., Linn, 1980; Reid, 1986; Vaux, 1979) as well as for compensatory education and minority students (Garner, 1975; Sloan, 1979).

Thus this approach offers individualized instruction as well as mastery learning while also incorporating several recommendations stemming from the teacher effectiveness literature, namely, increased ALT, positive reinforcement and feedback, and increased opportunity for student response.

Adaptive Learning Environment Model

Adaptive instruction is defined as use of alternative instructional strategies and school resources to provide effective education for all students. One application, the Adaptive Learning Environment Model (ALEM), developed at the University of Pittsburgh R & D Center, combines aspects of prescriptive instruction with aspects of open education for the purpose of basic skill acquisition (Wang, 1980). The five major components of ALEM are: (1) a highly structured, hierarchical basic skills curriculum integrated with exploratory learning activities; (2) an instructional/learning/ management system to maximize class and school resources; (3) family involvement via integration of school and home learning experiences; (4) flexible grouping, team teaching, and peer tutoring to increase the amount of school time available for learning and the amount of time students actually spend on learning; and (5) a data-based staff development program.

Data on the use of ALEM with disadvantaged and learning-handicapped students have shown achievement gains in reading and math (though generally not significant) as well as increased engaged time and enhanced student self-perception of cognitive competence, social competence, and general self-esteem (e.g., Wang and Birch, 1984; Wang and Reynolds, 1985; Wang and Walberg, 1983).

ALEM can thus be described as a program that attempts to enhance use of school time and resources by specifically increasing the time available for instruction and learning. It incorporates individualized instruction, mastery learning, peer tutoring, and teaching variables derived from the teacher effectiveness research relating to efficient use of instructional time.

Cooperative Learning Strategies

Cooperative learning strategies primarily involve a change in the interpersonal reward structure of the classroom from a competitive reward structure to a cooperative one. Most research on the practical application of cooperative learning techniques in a classroom setting has involved four models: Teams-Games-Tournament (TGT); Student Teams-Achievement Divisions (STAD); Jigsaw; and Small-Group Teaching (SGT) (Slavin, 1980).

TGT establishes four- to five-member student teams with instructional tournaments. Students are assigned to teams maximizing heterogeneity. STAD uses identical team membership but replaces tournaments with simple quizzes that students take after studying in their teams. In Jigsaw, team structure is the same as for TGT and STAD but academic material is broken into as many sections as team members. Students study the sections with members from other teams with the same assigned sections and then return to their teams and in turn teach their sections to other team members. Team members are tested but individual student scores contribute to individual grades only, therefore there is no formal group goal. SGT is a general classroom organizational plan in which learning takes place through cooperative group inquiry with students selecting topics and organizing themselves into small groups.

Classroom cooperative learning techniques generally include any combination of the following dimensions: reward interdependence, task interdependence, individual accountability, teacher-imposed structure, and use of group competition. Research results from implementation of cooperative learning strategies approaches show a relatively consistent pattern of positive effects on both student achievement and self-esteem for regular nonhandicapped students (Slavin, 1980).

In more recent work, Slavin, Madden, and Leavey (1982) combined cooperative learning with individualized instruction to form Team-Assisted Individualized (TAI). Focusing on outcomes for mainstreamed students in particular, they found that TAI did positively affect the social status of mainstreamed students as well as teacher ratings of their classroom behavior and self-confidence. Similar positive results were not found for math achievement in a preliminary eight-week study; however, in a longer twenty-four-week intervention, significantly positive effects on the math achievement of mainstreamed academically handicapped students were found (Slavin, Madden, and Leavey, 1984). Most recently, using a combined program of mixed-ability, cooperative work groups and skill-based reading groups (Cooperative Integrated Reading and Composition—CIRC), Stevens, Madden, Slavin, and Farnish (1987) found positive effects for mainstreamed academically handicapped students in both reading comprehension and vocabulary.

Similarly, considerable evidence exists that cooperative learning experiences are more effective in promoting positive relationships between handicapped and nonhandicapped students than competitive and individualistic ones (Johnson and Johnson, 1975, 1978, 1983, 1984, 1985; Johnson, Johnson, and Maruyama, 1983).

Although cooperative learning experiences have generally been found to result in higher achievement than competitive strategies for overall student achievement, the evidence in terms of academically handicapped students in particular is somewhat less apparent (e.g., Cosden, Pearl, and Bryan, 1985; Johnson, Johnson, and Maruyama, 1983; Talmage, Pascarella, and Ford, 1984), with the exception of the work by Slavin and his colleagues which combines cooperative learning with other instructional features.

Peer Tutoring

The results of a meta-analysis of findings from sixty-five studies of school tutoring programs showed that peer tutoring has positive effects on the academic performance and attitudes of those tutored (Cohen, Kulik, and Kulik, 1982). Although both structured and unstructured tutoring produced measurable effects, effects from structured programs were stronger, and effects were stronger for math than for reading. In delineating specific components required for successful peer tutoring, Jenkins and Jenkins (1985) noted the following: highly structured and carefully prescribed lessons, content based on the classroom curriculum and immediate teacher goals; requiring mastery to be demonstrated; a continuous program of moderate duration (fifteen to thirty minutes daily); and providing specific tutor training for giving clear directions, encouraging and praising, confirming correct responses, correcting errors in a nonpunitive fashion, and avoiding overprompting.

Concerning handicapped students in particular, one study using trained high school students to tutor elementary special education students who failed to master regular education curriculum objectives found that the tutored students made appreciable academic gains (Armstrong, Conlon, Pierson, and Stahlbrand, 1979)

On application of peer tutoring, labeled the Classwide Peer Tutoring System (CPT), was developed to improve instruction for minority, disadvantaged, and/or learning-disabled students by increasing their opportunities to respond and their active engagement in lessons (see Delquadri, Greenwood, Whorton, Carta, and Hall, 1986). The method is predicated on selection of skill activities for tutoring as closely aligned as possible with teacher outcome criteria. The system also includes behavior analysis principles for providing reinforcement for correct responding, such as individual and group contingencies, as well as social and token reinforcement. The program is structured to require systematic teacher review to provide reinforcement based on student progress. Also included are peer-mediated contingencies, implemented by establishing teams that earn points and compete for "team of the week.'' A third component consists of daily and weekly posting and feedback.

Use of these techniques has been found to improve considerably the rate of active student responding (Elliott, Hughes, and Delquadri, 1984), substantially reduce spelling errors for students with high prior error rates (Hall, Delquadri, Greenwood, and Thurston, 1982; Delquadri, Greenwood, Stretton, and Hall, 1983), and increase the number of words read correctly for learning-disabled students (Greenwood, Delquadri, and Hall, 1984).

This approach basically increases direct teaching time while providing increased opportunity for active responding and a motivational system. Again, these components are features primarily derived from the teacher effectiveness research.

Learning Strategies Approaches

Although several labels have been applied to approaches that attempt to teach students how to learn (e.g., cognitive-behavioral training, metacognitive strategies, and, most commonly, learning strategies), all are "learning to learn" strategies and include two levels: (1) teaching specific learning strategies and routines, followed by (2) gradually relinquishing the application to students.

Basically, learning strategies are techniques, principles, or rules that enable students to learn, solve problems, and complete tasks independently (Deshler and Schumaker, 1984). The ultimate goal of the approach is to enable students to analyze and solve novel problems while requiring students to accept major responsibility for their learning and progress. The Learning Strategies Curriculum (e.g., Deshler and Schumaker, 1986) is organized into three major strands corresponding to the demands of the secondary curriculum: (1) acquisition of information from written material, (2) identification and storage of important information, and (3) strategies for facilitating written expression. Students exposed to this approach have shown marked gains in reading comprehension and reduced number of errors in written material (e.g., Clark, Deshler, Schumaker, and Alley, 1984; Schumaker, Deshler, Alley, and Warner, 1983). Deshler and Schumaker note, however, that it is essential to provide careful staff development to bring about student progress since little change in student behavior has been noted in the absence of such training.

Metacognitive strategies instruction, as described by Palincsar (1986), are techniques designed to teach students to plan, implement, and evaluate strategic approaches to learning and problem solving. Palincsar has developed a procedure labeled *reciprocal teaching* defined as ''dialogue between teachers and students for the purpose of jointly constructing the meaning of text.'' The four activities include summarizing, question generating, clarifying, and predicting. The research on reciprocal teaching for remedial reading students' results indicates that these students make substantial progress in accuracy of answering comprehension questions from memory as well as on tests of reading comprehension in subject areas, indicating generalization to these settings (Brown and Palincsar, 1982; Palincsar and Brown, 1984).

Although learning strategies approaches were originally designed for mildly handicapped adolescents, the developers are currently attempting to determine if and how students in upper elementary grades can benefit from these interventions to prepare them better for the transition into secondary school. There has been some evidence regarding the possibility of training strategic use of both cognitive and metacognitive processes for younger students. Recent studies have shown that even primary grade students are able to abandon ineffective strategies and use appropriate strategies more effectively during deliberate memory tasks as a result of being trained to monitor and evaluate the utility of task strategies (e.g., Ghatala, Levin, Pressley, and Lodico, 1985).

Gerber (1986) has recently suggested that the tendency to dismiss cognitive-behavioral techniques (CBT) with younger students because of assumptions about their cognitive immaturity and lack of basic knowledge is unwarranted. He defines CBT as a means for facilitating the organization of previous knowledge or behaviors into more efficacious problem-solving routines, and advocates that training begin in the elementary grades and be systematically developed to parallel the basic skills curriculum.

SUMMARY

It appears that the approaches that attempt to incorporate several features that jointly impact on the learner and the teaching process, as well as instructional delivery, have greater promise for increasing the achievement of academically handicapped students. Further evidence of this reasoning has been offered by Bloom (1984). He contended that two or more alterable variables used together would contribute more to learning than any one alone. Considering the direct object of the intervention (i.e., the learner), the instructional materials, the home environment/peer group, and the teacher and teaching process, Bloom speculated that two variables involving different objects of the change process (teacher, student, materials, learning environment) may, in some instances, be additive, whereas two variables involving the same target of the change process would be less likely to be additive.

For improving the academic performance of handicapped students in the mainstream, a three-tier structure may be necessary, incorporating not only change in teaching behaviors and instructional method or materials, but altering the learner variables as well. The first level would call for establishing a learning environment most conducive to learning for academically handicapped children (and in fact all students). To operate such an efficient learning environment, teachers would teach students expected behaviors by using demonstration and modeling of the expected behaviors until they performed the new procedures automatically. They would maintain an effective surveillance system during instruction, attending to all students within and outside the lesson. Furthermore, they would maximize learning time by sustaining high levels of academic responding or practice and keeping students engaged in learning tasks. Lastly, they would arrange their grouping schedule to avoid long periods of seatwork and increase the percentage of students involved in direct instruction.

The second level would involve using instructional methods and materials that are so economical and potent that reliable gains can be achieved independently of individual differences (e.g., direct instruction, phonics instruction). These methods serve to organize information more efficiently than low-achieving students can on their own by increasing the probability of correct responding and reducing response uncertainty.

The third level would be the teaching of specific learning strategies to empower students to become more efficient learners, which may be the only strategy with the ultimate potential of reducing the time needed to master important skills in an instructional sequence.

Although this strategy basically extends Bloom's approach of varying two dimensions of the learning process to varying three components, it represents the ideal situation—which may not be feasible in practice. However, clearly establishing any one of the three levels is likely to positively effect the academic progress of mildly handicapped learners, whereas any combination promises to be a more powerful intervention, with a three-way merging, in all probability, being the most potent for enhancing the performance of low achievers.

REFERENCES

Algozzine, B., and Korinek, L. (1985). Where is special education for students with high prevalence handicaps going? *Exceptional Children, 51,(5)*, 388–394.

Armstrong, S. B.; Conlon, M. F.; Pierson, P. M., and Stahlbrand, K. (1979). The cost effectiveness of peer and cross-age tutoring. Paper presented at the annual meeting of the Council for Exceptional Children, Dallas, TX.

Asher, S. R., and Taylor, A. R. (1981). The social outcomes of mainstreaming: Sociometric assessment and beyond. *Exceptional Education Quarterly, 1*, 13–30.

Becker, W. C.; Engelmann, S.; Carnine, D. W.; and Rhine, R. (1981). The Direct Instruction Model. In R. Rhine (Ed.), *Encouraging change in America's schools: A decade of experimentation*. New York: Academic Press.

Berliner, D., and Tikunoff, W. (1976). The California Beginning Teacher Evaluation

Study: Overview of the ethnographic study. *Journal of Teacher Education, 27,(1),* 24–30.

Berliner, D., and Tikunoff, W. (1977). *Ethnography in the appraisal of teaching: Concepts and process.* Reading, MA: Addison-Wesley.

Bloom, B. S. (1984). The 2 sigma problem: The search for methods of group instruction as effective as one-to-one tutoring. *Educational Researcher, 13,* 4–16.

Brophy, J. (1979). Teacher behavior and its effects. *Journal of Educational Psychology, 71,* 733–750.

Brophy, J. and Evertson, C. (1974). *Process-product correlations in the Texas Teacher Effectiveness Study: Final Report* (Research Report No. 74-4). Austin: University of Texas, Research and Development Center for Teacher Education. (ERIC ED 091 094).

Brophy, J., and Good, T. L. (1986). Teacher behavior and student achievement. In M. C. Wittrock (Ed.), *Handbook of research on teaching,* 3rd ed. New York: Macmillan, pp. 328–375.

Brown, A. L., and Palincsar, A. S. (1982). Inducing strategic learning from text by means of informed, self-control training. *Topics in Learning and Learning Disabilities, 2,* 1–17.

Budoff, M., and Gottlieb, J. (1976). Special class EMR students mainstreamed: A study of an aptitude (learning potential) x treatment interaction. *American Journal of Mental Deficiency, 81,* 1–11.

Calhoun, G., and Elliott, R. (1977). Self-concept and academic achievement of educable retarded and emotionally disturbed pupils. *Exceptional Children, 44,* 379–380.

Carnine, D., and Kinder, D. (1985). Teaching low performing students to apply generative and schema strategies to narrative and expository material. *Remedial and Special Education, 6,(1),* 20–30.

Carroll, A. W. (1967). The effects of segregated and partially integrated school programs on self-concept and academic achievement of educable mental retardates. *Exceptional Children, 34,* 93–99.

Clark, F. L.; Deshler, D. D.; Schumaker, J. B.; and Alley, G. R. (1984). Visual imagery and self-questioning: Strategies to improve comprehension of written materials. *Journal of Learning Disabilities, 17,(3),* 145–149.

Cohen, P. A.; Kulik, J. A.; and Kulik, C. L. C. (1982). Educational outcomes of tutoring: A meta-analysis of findings. *American Educational Research Journal, 19,(2),* 237–248.

Cosden, M.; Pearl, R.; and Bryan, T. H. (1985). The effects of cooperative and individual goal structures on learning disabled and nondisabled students. *Exceptional Children, 52,(2),* 103–114.

Cotten, J. L., and Cook, M. S. (1982). Meta-analysis and the effects of various reward systems: Some different conclusions from Johnson et al. *Psychological Bulletin, 92,(1),* 176–183.

Cronbach, L. J., and Snow, R. B. (1976). *Aptitude and instructional methods.* New York: Irvington.

Delquadri, J.; Greenwood, C. R.; Stretton, K.; and Hall, R. V. (1983). The peer tutoring game: A classroom procedure for increasing opportunity to respond and spelling performance. *Education and Treatment of Children, 6,* 225–239.

Delquadri, J.; Greenwood, C. R.; Whorton, D.; Carta, J. J.; and Hall, R. V. (1986). Classwide peer tutoring. *Exceptional Children, 52,(6),* 535–542.

Deshler, D. D., and Schumaker, J. B. (1984). *Strategies instruction: A new way to teach.* Salt Lake City: Worldwide Media, Inc.

Deshler, D. D., and Schumaker, J. B. (1986). Learning strategies: An instructional alternative for low-achieving adolescents. *Exceptional Children, 52,(6),* 583–590.

Elliott, M.; Hughes, V.; and Delquadri, J. (1984, May). Experimental validation and field testing of instructional packages that increase "opportunity to respond." In J. Delquadri, *Applications of behavioral instruction models: Issues influencing adoption and use in public schools.* Symposium presented at the Tenth Annual Convention of the Association for Behavior Analysis, Nashville, TN.

Fuchs, L. S.; Fuchs, D.; and Warren, L. M. (1982). *Special education practice in evaluating student progress toward goals* (Research Report No. 81). Minneapolis: University of Minnesota, Institute for Research on Learning Disabilities.

Gage, N. (1978). *The scientific basis of the art of teaching.* New York: Teachers College Press, Columbia University.

Gardner, W. I. (1982). Why do we persist? *Education and Treatment of Children, 5,* 369–378.

Garner, W. L. (1975). Excerpt from a letter to Gerald M. Hogan, Haverford Township School District, PA, March 4.

Gerber, M. M. (1986). Cognitive-behavioral training in the curriculum: Time, slow learners, and basic skills. *Focus on Exceptional Children, 18,(6),* 1–12.

Gersten, R.; Becker, W. C.; Heiry, T. J.; and White, W. A. T. (1984). Entry IQ and yearly academic growth of children in direct instruction programs: A longitudinal study of low SES children. *Educational Evaluation & Policy Analysis, 6,(2),* 109–121.

Gersten, R.; Woodward, J.; and Darch, C. (1986). Direct instruction: A research-based approach to curriculum design and teaching. *Exceptional Children, 53,(1),* 17–31.

Ghatala, E.; Levin, J. R.; Pressley, M.; and Lodico, M. G. (1985). Training cognitive strategy monitoring in children. *American Educational Research Journal, 22,(2),* 199–215.

Goldstein, H.; Moss, J.; and Jordan, J. (1965). *The efficacy of special class training on the development of mentally retarded children* (Cooperative Research Project No. 619). Washington, DC: U.S. Office of Education.

Gottlieb, J. (1981). Mainstreaming: Fulfilling the promise. *American Journal of Mental Deficiency, 86,* 115–126.

Greenwood, C. R.; Delquadri, J.; and Hall, R. V. (1984). Opportunity to respond and student academic performance. In W. L. Heward, T. E. Heron, J. Trap-Porter, and D. S. Hill (Eds.), *Focus on behavior analysis in education.* Columbus, OH: Charles Merrill, pp. 58–88.

Gresham, F. M. (1981). Social skills training with handicapped children: A review. *Review of Educational Research, 51,* 139–176.

Gresham, F. M. (1983). Social skills assessment as a component of mainstreaming placement decisions. *Exceptional Children, 49,* 331–336.

Hall, R. V.; Delquadri, J.; Greenwood, C. R.; and Thurston, L. (1982). The importance of opportunity to respond in children's academic success. In E. Edgar, N. Haring, J. Jenkins, and C. Pious (Eds.), *Mentally handicapped children: Education and training*. Baltimore, MD: University Park Press, pp. 107–140.

Harasymiw, S., and Horne, M. (1976). Teachers attitudes toward handicapped children and regular class integration. *Journal of Special Education, 10,* 393–400.

Haynes, M. C., and Jenkins, J. R. (1986). Reading instruction in special education resource rooms. *American Educational Research Journal, 23,(2),* 161–190.

Higgs, R. W. (1975). Attitude formation—Contact or information? *Exceptional Children, 41,* 496–497.

Horne, M. (1979). Attitudes and mainstreaming: A literature review for school psychologists. *Psychology in the Schools, 16,* 61–67.

Jenkins, J., and Jenkins, L. (1985). Peer tutoring in elementary and secondary programs. *Focus on Exceptional Children, 17,(6),* 1–12.

Johnson, D. W., and Johnson, R. (1975). *Learning together and alone*. Englewood Cliffs, NJ: Prentice-Hall.

Johnson, D. W., and Johnson, R. (1978). Cooperative, competitive, and individualistic learning. *Journal of Research and Development in Education, 12,* 3–15.

Johnson, D. W., and Johnson, R. (1983). The socialization and achievement crisis: Are cooperative learning experiences the solution? In L. Bickman (Ed.), *Applied social psychology annual 4.* Beverly Hills, CA: Sage Publications.

Johnson, D. W., and Johnson, R. (1984). The effects of intergroup cooperation and intergroup competition on ingroup and outgroup cross-handicap relationships. *Journal of Social Psychology, 134,* 85–94.

Johnson, D. W., and Johnson, R. (1985). Mainstreaming hearing-impaired students: The effects of effort in communicating on cooperation. *Journal of Psychology, 119,* 31–44.

Johnson, D. W., Johnson, R.; and Maruyama, G. (1983). Interdependence and interpersonal attraction among heterogeneous and homogeneous individuals: A theoretical formulation and meta-analysis of the research. *Review of Educational Research, 53,* 5–54.

Johnson, D. W.; Maruyama, G.; Johnson, R.; Nelson, D.; and Skon, L. (1981). The effects of cooperative, competitive, and individualistic goal structures on achievement: A meta-analysis. *Psychological Bulletin, 89,(1),* 47–62.

Johnson, G. (1962). Special education for the mentally handicapped—A paradox. *Exceptional Children, 29,* 62–69.

Joyce, B. (1980). *Toward a theory of information processing in teaching* (Research Series No. 76). East Lansing: Michigan State University, The Institute for Research on Teaching.

Larrivee, B. (1980). Assessing the impact of an intensive inservice training model on regular teachers and mainstreamed students. *Teacher Education and Special Education, 3,* 39–48.

Larrivee, B. (1981a). Modality preference as a model for differentiating beginning reading instruction: A review of the issues. *Learning Disability Quarterly, 4,(2),* 180–188.

Larrivee, B. (1981b). The effect of intensity of inservice training on teachers' attitude toward mainstreaming, *Exceptional Children, 48,* 34–41.

Larrivee, B. (1982). Factors underlying regular classroom teachers' attitude toward mainstreaming. *Psychology in the Schools, 19,* 386–391.

Larrivee, B. (1985). *Effective teaching for successful mainstreaming.* New York: Longman.

Larrivee, B., and Vacca, J. (1980). A comparison of academic learning time (ALT) for mainstreamed, low, average, and high ability students. Paper presented at the annual meeting of the American Educational Research Association.

Leinhardt, G., and Pallay, A. (1982). Restrictive educational settings: Exile or haven? *Review of Educational Research, 52,* 557–578.

Leinhardt, G.; Zigmond, N.; and Cooley, W. (1981). Reading instruction and its effects. *American Educational Research Journal, 18,(3),* 343–361.

Levine, M.; Hummel, J. W.; Salzer, R. T. (1982). Mainstreaming requires something more: The person-environment fit. *Clinical Psychology Review, 2,* 1–25.

Linn, W. (1980, Dec.). ECRI everywhere. *ECRI Newsletter,* p. 3.

Lloyd, J. (1984). How shall we individualize instruction—Or should we? *Remedial and Special Education, 5,* 7–15.

Madden, N., and Slavin, R. E. (1983). Mainstreaming students with mild handicaps: Academic and social outcomes, *Review of Educational Research, 53,* 519–569.

McNair, P. K., and Joyce, B. (1979). *Teacher's thoughts while teaching: The South Bay study, Part II* (Research Series No. 58). East Lansing: Michigan State University, The Institute for Research on Teaching.

Medley, D. (1977). *Teacher competency and teacher effectiveness: A review of process-product research.* Washington, DC: American Association of Colleges for Teacher Education.

Meyers, M. J. (1980). The significance of learning modalities, modes of instruction, and verbal feedback for learning to recognize written words. *Learning Disability Quarterly, 3,* 62–69.

Moran, M. R. (1984). Excellence at the cost of instructional equity? The potential impact of recommended reforms upon low achieving students. *Focus on Exceptional Children, 16,(7),* 1–12.

Palincsar, A. S. (1986). Metacognitive strategy instruction. *Exceptional Children, 53,(2),* 118–124.

Palincsar, A. S., and Brown, A. L. (1984). The reciprocal teaching of comprehension fostering and comprehension monitoring activities. *Cognition and Instruction, 1,* 117–175.

Patching, W.; Kameenui, E.; Carnine, D.; Gersten, R.; and Colvin, G. (1983). Direct instruction in critical reading. *Reading Research Quarterly, 18,* 406–418.

Potter, M., and Mirkin, P. (1982). *Instructional planning and implementation practices of elementary and secondary resource room teachers: Is there a difference?* (Research Report No. 65). Minneapolis: University of Minnesota, Institute for Research on Learning Disabilities.

Reid, E. R. (1986). Practicing effective instruction: The Exemplary Center for Reading Instruction approach. *Exceptional Children, 52,* 510–519.

Ritter, P. (1978). Surviving in the regular classroom: A follow-up of mainstreamed children with learning disabilities. *Journal of School Psychology, 16,* 253–256.

Rosenshine, B. (1976). Classroom instruction. In N. L. Gage (Ed.), *The psychology of teaching methods: The seventy-fifth yearbook of the National Society for the Study of Education.* Chicago: University of Chicago Press.

Rosenshine, B. (1979). Content, time, and direct instruction, In P. Peterson and H.

Walberg (Eds.), *Research on teaching: Concepts, findings, and implications.* Berkeley, CA: McCutchan.

Rosenshine, B., and Berliner, D. C. (1978). Academic engaged time. *British Journal of Teacher Education, 4,* 3–15.

Rosenshine, B., and Stevens, R. (1984). Classroom instruction in reading. In D. Pearson (Ed.), *Handbook of research on teaching.* New York: Longman.

Schumaker, J. B.; Deshler, D. D.; Alley, G. R.; and Warner, M. M. (1983). Toward the development of an intervention model for learning disabled adolescents. *Exceptional Education Quarterly, 3,(4),* 45–50.

Slavin, R. E. (1980). Cooperative learning. *Review of Educational Research, 50,(2),* 315–342.

Slavin, R. E. (1987). Mastery learning reconsidered. *Review of Educational Research, 57,(2),* 175–213.

Slavin, R. E.; Madden, N. A.; and Leavey, M. (1982). Combining cooperative learning and individualized instruction: Effects on the social acceptance, achievement and behavior of mainstreamed students. Paper presented at the annual meeting of the American Educational Research Association.

Slavin, R. E.; Madden, N. A.; and Leavey, M. (1984). Effects of team-assisted individualization on the mathematics achievement of academically handicapped and nonhandicapped students. *Journal of Educational Psychology, 76,* 813–819.

Sloan, T. M. (1979, March). ECRI system aids in language development. *ECRI Newsletter,* pp. 2–3.

Stein, C., and Goldman, J. (1980). Beginning reading instruction for children with minimal brain dysfunction. *Journal of Learning Disabilities, 13,* 219–222.

Stevens, R. J.; Madden, N. A.; Slavin, R. E.; and Farnish, A. M. (1987). Cooperative Integrated Reading and Composition: Two field experiments. *Reading Research Quarterly, 22,* 433–454.

Talmage, H.; Pascarella, E. T.; and Ford, S. (1984). The influence of cooperative learning strategies on teacher practices, student perceptions of the learning environment, and academic achievement. *American Educational Research Journal, 21,(1),* 163–179.

Tarver, S. G., and Dawson, M. M. (1978). Modality preference and the teaching of reading: A review. *Journal of Learning Disabilities, 11,* 5–7.

Vacc, N. (1972). Long-term effects of special class intervention for emotionally disturbed children. *Exceptional Children, 39,* 15–22.

Vaux, I. (1979, Dec.). ECRI works in Clarion, Iowa. *The Reader (ECRI Newsletter),* p. 2.

Wang, M. C. (1980). Adaptive instruction: Building on diversity. *Theory into Practice, 19,(2),* 122–128.

Wang, M. C., and Birch, J. W. (1984). Comparison of a full-time mainstreaming program and a resource room approach. *Exceptional Children, 51,(1),* 33–40.

Wang, M. C., and Reynolds, M. C. (1985). Avoiding the "Catch 22" in special education reform. *Exceptional Children, 51,(6),* 497–502.

Wang, M. C., and Walberg, H. J. (1983). Adaptive instruction and classroom time. *American Educational Research Journal, 20,(4),* 601–626.

Warner, M. M.; Alley, G. R.; Schumaker, J. B.; Deshler, D. D.; and Clark, F. L. (1980). *An epidemiological study of learning disabled adolescents in secondary schools* (Research Report No. 13). Lawrence: KS: Institute for Research in Learning Disabilities.

Will, M. C. (1986). Educating children with learning problems: A shared responsibility. *Exceptional Children, 52,(5),* 411–415.

Wilson, L. R. (1985). Large-scale LD identification: The reprieve of a concept. *Exceptional Children, 52,(1),* 44–51.

Ysseldyke, J. E.; Algozzine, B.; Shinn, M. R.; and McGue, M. (1982). Similarities and differences between low achievers and students classified learning disabled. *Journal of Special Education, 16,* 73–85.

Zigmond, N., and Miller, S. E. (1986). Assessment for instructional planning. *Exceptional Children, 52,(6),* 501–509.

11

COORDINATION, COLLABORATION, AND CONSISTENCY: THE REDESIGN OF COMPENSATORY AND SPECIAL EDUCATION INTERVENTIONS

Richard L. Allington

Peter Johnston

State University of New York at Albany
School of Education
Department of Reading

Children who are having academic learning difficulties become eligible for various extra-instructional support programs under Chapter 1 (remedial reading), PL 94–142 (special education services), migrant education tutorials, and so forth. Over the course of a day these children move back and forth among these programs and their regular classroom program—instructional programs that may or may not relate to each other in any discernible way. In this chapter we will focus on the coordination among these programs. We think this coordination is important to study for several reasons. First, studies of remedial programs have found coordination to be a characteristic of more effective programs (e.g., Griswold, Cotton, and Hansen, 1986; Venezky and Winfield, 1977). Second, researchers who have looked for coordination between programs have rarely found it (e.g., Johnston, Allington, and Afflerbach, 1985; Kimbrough and Hill, 1981). Third, there is a pervasive belief among teachers and administrators that children should have remedial reading programs that are entirely different from their classroom programs, which are obviously not working (Allington, 1986; Johnston, Allington, and Afflerbach, 1985). Some believe this because of particular views about learners and some because they believe regulations require it. Fourth, a most common feature of at-risk learners is a low level of tolerance for variations in instructional quality (Bloom, 1976, 1984). However, the at-risk learner, the child who exhibits the most "cognitive confusion" (Vernon, 1958), is the learner most likely to be confronted with an uncoordinated and inconsistent set of curricular approaches and instructional experiences (Allington, Stuetzel, Shake, and Lamarche, 1986; Moore, Hyde, Blair, and Weitzman, 1981; Kimbrough and Hill, 1981; Lee, Rowan, Allington, Anderson, Bossert, Harnischfeger, and Stallings, 1986).

In this chapter, then, we discuss studies that support these findings in an attempt to understand why extra-instructional support programs so seldom evidence coordination with each other or with the regular education programs and why coordination might be a critical feature of such programs. Our focus is primarily on efforts designed to promote literacy in at-risk learners, since, in our view, most instructional support programs were originally developed in response to learners' difficulties in acquiring literacy skills.

We will discuss consistency at three levels of curriculum. The first is that which appears in print, in state or district curriculum plans, scope and sequence charts, in analyses of instructional materials (such as basal reader series), and so on. A second level lies in the manner with which the teacher organizes the classroom, interacts with children, and presents the curriculum materials selected. The third is the curriculum as experienced by the learner. This is the most important level of curriculum and our discussion revolves primarily around the consistency of the curricular experiences of at-risk learners. Whereas state or district curriculum plans (or lack thereof) influence the experienced curriculum in many subtle, and not so subtle, ways, we discuss those only briefly here. We focus on consistency in the experienced curriculum and on coordination of instructional efforts of the various personnel who instruct the at-risk learner in the course of the school day. In our view, consistency in the experienced curriculum is unlikely without an effort to coordinate the instructional activities of all personnel working with a given child. This coordination would involve collaboration between regular education and instructional support personnel. Collaboration in the design and delivery of instruction is a necessary beginning to move toward curricular consistency.

PROGRAM COORDINATION

School Systems

In an earlier study we found evidence of curricular consistency in few schools. Most often, classroom teachers and support instruction teachers had little knowledge of the instruction offered to an at-risk learner by the other (Johnston, Allington, and Afflerbach, 1985). Our analysis of their reports of curriculum materials used with the at-risk learner suggested that, more often than not, these learners were experiencing curriculum conflict. That is, the curricula experienced in the regular classroom reading instruction and that experienced in the support instruction program were dissimilar in nature and philosophically incompatible. The few instances of curricula consistency were generally found in schools where key administrators believed such consistency was important and where classroom and support teachers communicated and collaborated with one another in planning the instructional intervention. Similar findings are noted by Moore and his colleagues (1981), Birman (1981), and Kimbrough and Hill (1981), suggesting that district-level administrators and districtwide policies can have substantial influence on whether curricular consistency, coordination of efforts, and instructional collaboration will occur in schools. However, as Kimbrough and Hill (1981) note, few districts (or states) "appear to make serious attempts at coordination" (p. 42). Bogdan (1983) argued that the lack of coordination was evidenced by a lack of clarity in who was responsible for ensuring the appropriateness of instruction for handicapped learners. That is, it was unclear in many districts whether the special education director or building principal was responsible for ensuring appropriate instruction was offered in the mainstream classroom. Similar confusion often existed between the mainstream teacher and the resource room teacher. The point here is that in the absence of any district-level plan for achieving curricular consistency and instructional collaboration, one should probably not be suprised by the absence of such consistency and collaboration in the instruction experienced by at-risk learners.

School Level

When there is little district-level activity to enhance coordination, attempts at coordination will fall to building-level administrators or the instructional staff of the core and support programs. Perhaps because of the autonomy afforded many school-level administrators, coordination efforts at this level, in various forms, seem more common than district-level plans and policies, yet these activities still occur infrequently (Hannifin and Barrett, 1983).

We have argued that at-risk learners need larger quantities of high-quality instruction, and yet Ligon and Doss (1982), Archambault and St. Pierre (1980), and Kimbrough and Hill (1981) all report that participation in support programs often serves to replace core curriculum instruction. Students served by various support programs actually ended up with less instructional time than students not served. In comparing schools with Chapter 1 programs to schools without such programs, others also report that students in Chapter 1 schools received less academic instructional time than students in non-Chapter 1 schools (Stanley and Greenwood, 1983). Similar results are reported for handicapped students attending resource room programs from mainstream classroom placements (Haynes and Jenkins, 1986; Ysseldyke, Thurlow, Mecklenburg, and Graden, 1984). Thus the available evidence suggests that coordinating support program instruction with core curriculum instruction in order to provide targeted students with a consistent curricular approach and additional amounts of academic instructional time is not particularly common. Indeed, it seems that the lack of coordination often results in reduced services to the students.

If coordination demands communication between the core and support instructional staff, the evidence is also less than encouraging. Cohen, Intilli, and Robbins (1978) report a survey of teachers in forty-six elementary schools in which they found that more than half of the classroom teachers reported that reading resource teachers rarely or never offered instructional information, suggestions, or materials. Bogdan (1983) reports that core program teachers and special education teachers indicated substantial confusion about who was responsible for instructional planning and delivery. His report parallels some of the situations discussed by Moore and colleagues (1981) in which both the support program teacher and the core program teacher thought the other was responsible for reading instruction.

In an interview study conducted in ten school districts in two states, we found that nearly one-third of core program and support program teachers could not remember when they had last had either an informal or formal discussion of remedial students' needs, progress, or concerns (Johnston, Allington, and Afflerbach, 1985). In addition, there was wide variability between the pairs of respondents in terms of these meetings. Support teachers reported more frequent and longer contacts with students than did the classroom teachers with whose students they worked. When queried on instructional needs and goals for specific remedial students, there was little agreement between the responses of the classroom and remedial teachers. In a further assessment of communication, we asked classroom and remedial teachers about the curricular materials used in each instructional setting (regular classroom and support instruction). Two of every three support program teachers were unable to identify the reading instructional material the remedial student used in the core classroom reading context. Fewer than one in ten core classroom teachers could name the material that remedial students from their classrooms used during support program instruction. Similar results were obtained in interviews conducted with participating teachers in two observational studies (Allington and McGill-Franzen, 1989; Rowan, Guthrie, Lee, and Guthrie, 1986).

Several studies have sought to assess coordination between the core and support instruction offered students. These studies reported observational analyses of the consistency of instruction in classroom and remedial reading contexts. Allington and associates (1986) observed students enrolled in remedial programs, though the observations included both core curriculum and support program instruction. The qualitative field notes were examined for several types of potential instructional consistency or congruence. However, inconsistency of the experienced curriculum was found most frequently. The types of tasks, the specific skills emphasized, and the nature of the instructional materials more often differed than matched. In short, the instruction received by the remedial students in the two settings seemed generally independent of each other. This occurred even in an in-class remediation design in which support program personnel offered remediation in the core curriculum classroom. Similarly, Rowan and colleagues (1986) reported little evidence of instructional coordination between Chapter 1 and classroom instruction in schools in six states. Where coordination was observed, however, it was typically planned in the district- or school-level design.

Pike (1985) reports on Chapter 1 programs in four elementary schools in a district where coordination was emphasized. This study of primary-grade students indicated a fairly high degree of congruence between the decoding skills taught in the core curriculum classroom and in the support program. The district provided a management checklist indicating the scope and sequence for decoding skills in the adopted basal reader series and remedial teachers were to use this as a guide for instructional intervention. Most did, and although the remediation tended to focus only on this narrow band of reading behaviors, it was generally consistent. However, the teacher interviews did not support the suggestion that communication between core and support staff was frequent. Coordination was less evident in some schools than in others, seemingly a result of support staff personality characteristics and professional beliefs.

The Haynes and Jenkins (1986) study, noted earlier, indicated little evidence of coordination among core and support program instruction for elementary special education students. They also noted wide variability in the amount and nature of both core and support program reading instruction offered to students who had seemingly similar instructional needs. Licopoli (1984) offers one of the rare observational studies of high school support programs. He noted few instances of coordination and suggested that participation in special education resource rooms offered little in the way of preparing handicapped students for participation in mainstream classes. Here, however, there seemed to be little agreement in the school about the fundamental purpose of the resource room support program, with quite divergent views offered by school-level administrators, resource room support staff, and core curriculum instructional staff.

The incidence of school-level coordination seems low and the level of coordination is quite variable in the available reports. Moore, Goertz, Hartle, Winslow, David, Sjogren, Turnbull, Coley, and Holland (1983) seem to characterize best the current situation in this area by noting that "program coordination both in the sense of deliberate steps to dovetail instructional efforts and in the sense of less deliberate actions to make programs somehow fit into the school setting almost invariably fall to those actually delivering services to students . . ." (p. 100). Thus, although some have pointed to the principal as a key factor in achieving school-level coordination (Moore et al., 1981), more often that not such leadership seems to be lacking. In most instances, neither district-level nor building-level administrators seem to provide adequate leadership for achieving either coordination between core curriculum programs and support programs or among the various support programs delivering services to at-risk students.

However, we need to return to the evidence that curricular coordination does occur, though not frequently. Too rarely did coordination appear as a result of general program design or district-level administrative planning. Often, these instances of coordination were the result of "teacher deals" (Biklen, 1985). That is, a support teacher (e.g., remedial reading, learning disability, or speech/language specialist), through his or her own efforts and on the strength of acknowledged professional expertise and personal style, managed to collaborate with some or many of the core curriculum classroom teachers whose children were served. As Biklen notes, this coordination is often unnoticed, or if noticed not recognized, by key administrators. In addition, we agree with Biklen when he notes that although intervention programs for at-risk children ultimately depend on the expertise of the teachers providing the services, programs should not be hinged on teacher effort alone. That is, Allington and colleagues (1986) note that much well-intentioned instructional effort was unleashed in the compensatory education classes they observed. But, at the same time, the lack of leadership at higher levels left the support teachers primarily to their own resources and, at times, denied them even that. Biklen (1985), like others, noted that support of the school principal was important to successful mainstreaming of handicapped children. Mainstreaming might ensue without active support but only on a limited and uneven basis. However, any resistance by the principal spelled doom for the effort. We think there is a parallel for the development of coordinated education programs for all at-risk learners. Ideally, principals would provide the leadership for such redesign but at the least they would not impede development of such efforts.

THE EFFECTS OF SCHOOL-LEVEL
PROGRAM COORDINATION

School-Level Coordination

Although program coordination at the school level is reported as uncommon, there does exist some evidence to indicate not only that such coordination can be achieved but that these efforts can enhance student achievement. For instance, a report by the New York State Office of Education Performance Review (1974) noted that schools that were considered successful had greater amounts of interaction between classroom teachers and support program teachers combined with an emphasis on instructional continuity. Likewise,

Venezky and Winfield (1979) found that more effective schools were more likely to have integrated support services. In their review of effective compensatory education practices, Griswold, Cotton, and Hansen (1986) noted that coordination of the regular program with other support programs was one of the seven organizational attributes of successful Chapter 1 projects. Gezi (1986) also notes that coordination of compensatory instruction with core curriculum was one feature of leadership provided in successful compensatory education schools.

Nonetheless, we have argued elsewhere (Allington and Shake, 1986; Johnston, Allington, and Afflerbach, 1985) that as attractive as coordination among programs appears, we still have little understanding of the effects of coordination of any of the several types discussed and similarly impoverished notions of how such coordination can be routinely achieved. There is some reason to believe that coordination in terms of more appropriate scheduling of services could result in greater amounts of basic skill instruction being delivered to target students. Whereas expanding the quantity of instruction seems likely to affect achievement favorably (Cooley and Leinhardt, 1980; Greenwood, Delquadri, Stanley, Sasso, Wharton, and Schulte, 1981; Kiesling, 1978) and would rectify the current situation reported in schools in which support program participation seems to decrease quantity of instruction, such efforts seem minimal and still insufficient. In a similar vein, we suppose that coordination that attempts to link the content of instruction will result in enhanced achievement. Here, however, we have few reports to buttress the argument. Winfield (1987) assessed the achievement of Chapter 1 participants on reading skills that were emphasized by both the Chapter 1 teachers and the classroom teachers against those skills emphasized by one set of teachers or the other. She reports that the dual emphasis skills were more likely to be mastered than the single emphasis skills, suggesting that the coordinated effort produced better learning and retention. However, in her data it was only lower-level reading skills (simple decoding tasks) that received the dual emphasis, and the evidence suggests that these skills are relatively easier to master than some of the more complex skills that were not emphasized (e.g., drawing inferences from text). Thus, although supportive, these data cannot provide an adequate base for recommending curricular coordination. This is not to argue that achieving curricular coordination has little to recommend it, but simply that we currently lack any substantial empirical evidence. Indeed, later we will argue on theoretical grounds that curricular coordination is critical.

Federal, State, District, and Local Policies

Currently there is much opinion but little hard evidence to support any conclusion about the effects of policies developed at any level, except that policymaking begets policymaking. Our analysis of the various reports indicates that two views exist about the effects of federal policies concerning the development and delivery of support program instruction. In one view, federal policies are the root of all of our problems. Moore and associates (1983) argued that the federal goal of isolating federal monies from state and local funds contributed to the administrative separation of the various support programs and that the full federal funding of Chapter 1 produced only minimal state bases for support of compensatory education. Cohen (1982) suggests that "specialization at the lower level parallels developments higher up; it also impedes coordination of activities within schools and districts . . ." (p. 481). Ginsburg and Turnbull (1981) echo this view with their statement that "federal fiscal controls have also unintentionally encouraged schools to isolate federal programs from each other and from the regular school program" (p. 36). This view is also offered by Kaestle and Smith (1982).

The common theme in these analyses is that much, if not most, of the current fragmentation can be attributed to the rather patchwork development of federal policies concerning the various laws, regulations, and programs intended to guarantee or enhance the education of target populations. This fragmented development has been coupled with continuously shifting regulations within programs and shifting interpretations of the same regulations (NIE, 1977). On the other hand, the analysis by Moore and colleagues (1981) of implementation at the local level led them to conclude that state and federal regulations had slight impact in the decisions made by district- or building-level personnel. In addition, they note that they found little evidence that any comparable level of effort to meet the needs of at-risk students would have existed in the absence of federal policies. Similarly, McLaughlin (1982) notes that "federal policies cannot, by themselves, cause particular outcomes; they must be implemented within and through existing institutional arrangements . . ." (p. 567).

As a result of our analysis of the various reports, we have adopted what might be considered an *interactionist* perspective. Like Leinhardt, Bickel, and Pallay (1982) and Stainback and Stainback (1984), we see much of the existing federal policy structure as unnecessarily duplicative, unwieldy, and influential in producing the fragmentation so often noted. However, the development of federal policy has often followed shifting social beliefs about the nature of school failure and responded to political pressure brought to bear by different interest groups (Johnston, McGill-Franzen, and Allington, 1985). Federal policy has as often reflected professional wisdom and social beliefs as it has nurtured or refined them. For example, the development of the pullout model, which has been so widely adopted in compensatory and special education, seemed to follow the professional wisdom of a previous era as much as a desire of the federal agencies to develop clear audit trails. The small-group clinical model adopted by Chapter 1 teachers and special education teachers mirrored the clinical model so prevalent in university-based clinics where these support teachers received specialized training. The use of separate and different curricular materials to meet the presumed special instructional needs of special populations is likewise part of the professional wisdom (Cook and Earlly, 1979; Dechant, 1981; Gilliland, 1974). An example is the "differential teaching" model that has dominated compensatory and special education training for so long (Johnston, Allington, and Afflerbach, 1985), and also fits very nicely into some misinterpretations of the "supplement, not supplant" provision of Chapter 1.

It seems undoubtedly true that the pullout model of instructional delivery has contributed to the fragmentation of the instruction received by at-risk students. However, it seems unlikely that federal policies can be wholly blamed for the institutionalization of the model. On the other hand, local administrators who prefer a safe bet in anticipation of a compliance audit might be edged away from other designs by the widespread understanding that federal policies have cast the pullout design in a favorable light. Likewise, state and district administrative organizational structures may have been refined by federal policies, but rarely does it seem that they were created by such policies. We feel we can argue this simply because of the wide variability in existing administrative structure one can currently find. Conventional wisdom and special interest influences largely drove federal policy and thus the patchwork quality of much of the federal effort (McGill-Franzen, 1987). But without federal programs and policies, many of the current efforts to alleviate school failure in at-risk children would be nonexistent (Moore et al., 1981).

ASSUMPTIONS AND THEIR CONSEQUENCES

A number of assumptions seem to have guided federal policymaking in the past twenty years, the era when the federal role expanded significantly. These assumptions were generally not the result of the federal policies but rather preceded them. The first, and probably most critical, assumption is that there exist several identifiable categories of at-risk children. Implicit in this assumption are the notions that (1) children in these several categories have different instructional needs, (2) these categories are reliably different from one another, and (3) we can identify children that fit in each category. Unfortunately, as has been argued elsewhere (Algozzine and Ysseldyke, 1983; Johnston, McGill-Franzen, and Allington, 1985; Leinhardt, Bickel, and Pallay, 1982; Stainback and Stainback, 1984), there is little theoretical or empirical evidence to support any of these assumptions. These assumptions were not created by the federal policymaking but rather made their way into policy that has maintained and strengthened them.

The influences that have led to the fragmentation of support instruction services have fed and nurtured each other. As educators, sociologists, psychologists, economists, and others have created their various rationales for explaining school failure, a variety of beliefs about the etiology of school failure have arisen and have affected federal policy. In her analysis of explanations for school failure, McGill-Franzen (1987) traces the evolution of economic disadvantagedness as a primary rationale and the resultant development of the Federal Title I programs designed to compensate for such disadvantagedness. The number of publications in professional journals with both reading and disadvantagedness as key descriptors rose steadily for better than a decade but then gave way to another developing belief system.

This shift was evidenced in the rise in the number of professional journal publications using the key descriptors "reading and learning disability." In the past decade the number of such articles has risen tenfold and ten years ago replaced the previous standard of "reading and disadvantagedness." In fact, articles on reading failure are now more frequent in journals published for special education and learning disabilities professionals than in journals published for reading professionals (McGill-Franzen, 1987). These trends in publishing seem to mirror the categorical identification of students and the expenditure of funds for providing support instruction. That is, the recent rise in the numbers of children identified as learning disabled, and the related rise in expenditures for the services provided, parallels the increase in publication with a brief time lag. However, there is little evidence that the passage of PL 94–142 created this trend since the number of articles on reading and learning disability had reached significant proportions before the enactment of the legislation. On the other hand, the legitimization of the category through the development of federal policy seems to have had an enormous effect. Prior to inclusion of learning disability as a fiscally reimbursable category, relatively few school districts had any significant number of students so classified. Now the situation has changed dramatically (McGill-Franzen, 1987; Ysseldyke and Algozzine, 1982).

Even though the number of children living at the "poverty level" has risen above earlier levels, the number of disadvantaged children served by Chapter 1 programs continues to decline (McGill-Franzen, 1987). We see the trends as reflections of shifting social beliefs about reading failure—beliefs not born in federal policymaking but nurtured by it. To reiterate our earlier point, however, there is little evidence to support the notion that children identified as learning disabled exhibit any substantial psychometric or educational differences from economically disadvantaged children who experience school failure (Algozzine and Ysseldyke, 1983). Rather than new populations with newly discovered etiological bases for reading failure, what we have is shifting or developing social belief systems that attribute reading failure to an ever increasing array of etiologies—etiologies most commonly located in the learner. A common feature of these developing social beliefs and resultant intervention programs is the lack of concern for the possible deficiencies in the original educational environment in which the deficits were nurtured (Bogdan, 1983; Gelzheiser, 1987; Stainback and Stainback, 1984). When children fail to learn to read competently after some schooling we rush to identify them categorically with one program or another, but regardless of categorical identification, there seems little evidence of concern for adopting or improving the original educational program from whence they came. This "fix-it" mentality works against collaborative efforts to remedy reading failure because it presumes the etiology is centered in a deficit in the learner, not in the educational program. Although it may be less distressing to the educational system to blame the victim, it is unlikely that wholehearted efforts for coordinated instructional planning will ensue until this belief system is modified.

Although not as popular in the current debates, the same could be said of differences between migrant populations and either learning disabled or other economically disadvantaged nonmigrant children, but there is a separate federal program for that population also. The key qualities of effective support programs seem generally similar regardless of student classification (Leinhardt and Pallay, 1982). Federal policy, then, has influenced the design of state and local programs by providing the various categorical programs, but the policies seem to have mirrored emerging social belief systems. The development of the policies strengthened these social beliefs, and categorical separation became even more evident and entrenched.

The problem has been compounded by the interpretation—or misinterpretation—of federal policy at the local level. The most obvious example is the "supplement, not supplant" provision of Chapter 1. There are numerous references in the literature to the misinterpretation of this regulation, suggesting commonly that the misinterpretation led to the widespread use of the pullout model for delivery of compensatory instruction (NIE, 1977; Shulman, 1983). As Allington (1986) reports, this aspect of the regulation still seems widely misunderstood, since better than one of three compensatory education administrators surveyed viewed the provision as disallowing both in-class designs and the shared use of curricular materials in both settings. Nonetheless, we noted earlier that the pullout design also mirrored the most common organization for remedial services delivered in the university-based reading clinics that trained the reading specialists who organized the remedial services in schools. Thus the small group, in a small room, with a specially trained teacher, using specialized curricular materials and methods fit well into both the professional belief system and the federal policy. This design is being perpetuated in programs for the learning disabled even though no similar federal policy exists (Junkala and Mooney, 1986).

Federal policy under PL 94–142 requires placement of handicapped learners in the least restrictive environment as a matter of course. However, the design of support services for the learning disabled leans heavily toward pullout from the least restrictive environment for services delivered in separate resource rooms. Undoubtedly, there are a variety of reasons why the pullout design has evolved as the most popular and some of these are related to federal policies, but other reasons also exist (Bogdan, 1983; Lortie,

1976; Milofsky, 1976). We do not wish to argue that in-class programs are inherently superior—they have their own set of problems—but congruence between instructional programs may be less likely in pullout programs.

Regulations that presume categorical identification and identifiable instructional needs based upon the categorical label will obviously shape the policies made at lower levels, especially if fiscal incentives are present (McGill-Franzen, 1987). However, as Leinhardt, Bickel, and Pallay (1982) argue, the established professional beliefs and alliances sustain and refine the policies made at the service delivery level. The separate federal programs administered from different federal offices often present a maze of conflicting information. This maze is often further complicated by state laws and regulations and state level interpretations of federal policies. By the time the bundle reaches the local district, much less the local school building, the task of coordinating may seem unmanageable (McLaughlin, 1982; McLaughlin, Shields, and Rezabek, 1985). Although more attention to the coordination of support services at the federal level would certainly help, that simply will not ensure that services at the local level provide coordinated and coherent instructional environments for the children served. Our pessimism should not deter any attempts at clarifying federal policies, but we believe that it will take a major reconceptualization of both reading failure and support program design to undo what has already been so unfortunately achieved.

Alternative Assumptions and Practices

Instructional Congruence.   We have reviewed a number of studies that have stressed the importance of coordination between instructional programs. Few of these reports have described the features of such programs. Some have discussed the coordination in terms of the congruence between the curricula in the two contexts (Allington and Shake, 1986; Johnston, Allington, and Afflerbach, 1985). However, exactly what it means for instruction to be congruent has not been made clear. For example, we cannot see a remedial reading teacher bound to replicate a classroom reading program that is narrowly defined or in other ways unsatisfactory. Also, we would not like to see a basal reader approach in a classroom program prevent the use of other materials, such as trade books or predictable language texts, in the support program. Thus we need to clarify the notion of instructional coordination so that it is not interpreted simply as "more of the same."

Perhaps we should explain our notion of what would be appropriate before addressing what we feel would be inappropriate. We view literacy development in terms of broad concepts about communication and social and personal development. Within these higher-level concepts lies a substantial variety of conceptual and procedural knowledge that individuals integrate in the pursuit of various goals in various circumstances. The individual skills, unorganized and unintegrated, are of limited help. Similarly, they are of little help if they are not automated or if they are used inflexibly. Optimally, children will develop within a balanced language arts program. By balanced, we mean a program that emphasizes a variety of means of controlling the difficulty of text, such as predictable language, familiar content, prereading, rereading, word frequency, meaning unit repetition, interest level, recency, and so on, integrated with a writing program. Through a careful balance of such means of controlling difficulty, children can develop their weaknesses while being allowed success through the support of their strengths. For example, in the language experience side of a program a child is supported by his or her personal knowledge, syntax, vocabulary, and the personalized nature of the text, while he or she works on developing an understanding of graphophonic relationships through writing. Patterned language reading materials, on the other hand, support the child through the predictability of the language, while introducing new vocabulary, new syntax, and new experiences. It is not difficult to tell whether children are involved in a literacy-related task. However, it is hard for researchers or administrators who do not understand children's literacy learning to distinguish a balanced literacy program from an uncoordinated one and a coordinated one from a rigid, unbalanced program.

There are several major elements in this coordination issue. First, there is congruence between curricula—what is to be taught, in what order, and using which materials. Second, there is the method of instruction—the actual techniques that teachers use to help children learn the curriculum. Conflicts arise in the following sets of circumstances, which we have encountered all too frequently in school settings (Johnston, Allington, and Afflerbach, 1985):

1. The strategies used to control text difficulty in the materials in the two settings are radically different, as when word frequency and natural language rule in the one setting but extreme orthographic regularity reigns entirely in the other setting. In such a situation, the reading strategies that are learned and practiced in one setting will be extremely inefficient in the other situation. One might see such conflict in a school where at-risk learners receive reading instruction from a core curriculum based on the Scott Foresman Reading Systems (1971), an approach emphasizing predictable and natural language text, and from a support program (offered in remedial or special education resource rooms) that uses the DISTAR curriculum (Engelmann and Bruner, 1975).

2. The assumed hierarchy of learning in the two settings conflicts, such as when one setting focuses strongly on comprehension yet the other setting emphasizes decoding as the essence of reading. In one case, the development of prediction will be encouraged, whereas in the other setting it will be discouraged. One might see such a conflict in a school where the Houghton-Mifflin (Durr, 1981) basal is the source of core curriculum reading instruction

and the Merrill Linguistic Readers (Wilson, 1980) is the curriculum of support programs.

3. The strategies to be learned differ from one setting to the other. For example, long division can be taught in terms of borrowing or through conceptually quite different procedures.

4. Instructional strategies differ radically in the two settings, as when one setting depends entirely on teacher-directed instruction and the other setting depends on learner-directed instruction. In such a case the latter setting will stress self-monitoring and self-correction, whereas the former will prevent them.

5. The terminology and metaphors differ in the two settings, causing the child to become confused about some of the concepts. For instance, when use of a word family (e.g., *ake, ame*) approach to decoding is coupled with a synthetic phonics approach (or when word families of the classroom become phonetic keys in the support setting).

If the two parts of a program could easily be seen operating within a coherent classroom program, then they are likely to be more or less congruent. There is the risk that with widely divergent approaches the children will be unable to integrate what they are being taught and will develop confused notions of the nature and purpose of reading. "Cognitive confusion" was the term Vernon (1958) used to describe the problem, and some of its consequences have been documented by Johnston (1985). Thus if two parts of a program are necessarily separate, then some part of the program needs to be devoted to making clear how the parts fit together. Otherwise, the integration—the tough bit—is left up to the children. It also seems likely that conflicts stemming from programmatic differences will be intensified with factors such as anxiety, which are often quite severe for failing learners. It is probably more efficient to ensure coordination from the ouset.

We feel that the major aspect that affects these dimensions of instruction is the teacher's expertise. If we can consider both classroom and support teachers as experts, then presumably the support teacher is more expert than the classroom teacher in a specific area such as reading or mathematics curriculum and instruction. Of course, there are exceptions to this, and too often poorly trained teachers' aides provide the remedial instruction. Experts differ from novices in three major ways. They differ in terms of the extent of their knowledge, the structure of their knowledge, and the flexible use of their knowledge (Chi, Glaser, and Rees, 1982). It is their knowledge of teaching of a specific domain like reading, and how children learn, that makes them choose materials and techniques (to the extent that they perceive that they have choice in each area). The structure of teachers' knowledge becomes apparent when they teach and when they choose materials, and the differences can be substantial (DeFord, 1985). Unfortunately, these ideological differences are most pronounced at the beginning stages of reading and, as Carter (1984) and Clay (1982, 1985) have pointed out, the earlier remedial programs begin, the greater the likelihood of success. Cordination is most critical where it is least likely.

In some sense, then, there are essentially three curricula involved. One is the explicit curriculum formally expressed by the school curriculum. The second is the implicit curriculum held in the knowledge structures of the teachers and expressed in their interactions with the children. The third curriculum is that experienced by the child. Program planning decisions can be made on the basis of the explicit curriculum, but the moment-to-moment decisions must be automatic or intuitive, and will be made on the basis of the implicit curriculum. Neither of these decribes the curriculum actually experienced by a given child. When the coordination issue is viewed this way, the clarity and coherence of the overall school curriculum becomes important. There should be a clear, explicit reading curriculum, including the philosophical underpinnings of the curriculum, and it should encompass descriptions of how instruction for students with special needs should differ from that of regular students needs if it is indeed felt that it should differ in some way. However, ongoing discussions and observations between teachers in the context of day-to-day instruction are more likely to induce congruence between the written and expressed curricula. Only close monitoring of the child's development will provide information on the child's experienced curriculum.

If a school seriously adopts a basal series, there is likely to be some coherence in the overall reading instruction provided. Indeed, some evidence suggests that effective schools are more likely to have a schoolwide adoption than are less effective schools (Clark and McCarthy, 1983). This may be because the basal curriculum, while constraining decisions, does provide a more coherent schoolwide curriculum than an "every teacher for himself/herself" situation in which no common basal or other unified curriculum exists. However, a unified curriculum, whether or not achieved through a basal series, does not ensure compatibility of the curricula implicit in the teachers' knowledge structures, which is a much more difficult congruence to attain and infinitely more important. For example, with respect to reading instruction, the training undertaken by teachers preparing to serve learning-disabled students is generally substantially different from that undertaken by teachers training specifically to serve students with special needs in reading. This difference is ideological and influences how students' behaviors are interpreted and how they are seen as different from other students (Ysseldyke and Algozzine, 1982).

The effects of teachers' ideological differences might be minimized through a clear curriculum, cooperative planning of that curriculum, coordinated inservice programs, and constant opportunity for and encouragement to engage in dialogue. Many schools' curricula are defined by the basal series adopted, and serious schoolwide adoption constrains some dimensions of classroom instruction. For example, each basal series opts for particular forms of text difficulty control. It would not be easy for a teacher to stress prediction and self-monitoring if the basal program selected and enforced were the Merrill Linguistic Series, for which unpredictable text has deliberately been constructed, difficulty control being through restriction of the letter-sound relationships. In the same way, a developmental reading program based on reading trade books stressing self-monitoring and self-correction in the classroom would seriously conflict with a direct instruction program such as DISTAR (Engelmann and Bruner, 1975) in the support program, which stresses immediate feedback by the teacher where errors occur.

To illustrate, we provide samples of beginning reading texts from commercial programs with quite different forms of text difficulty controls (see Figure 11–1). "The Bus Ride" excerpt is an example of a patterned language text where the repetition and common topic all serve to ease the difficulty for the beginning reader (as does the rather limited vocabulary and accompanying artwork). The code-emphasis excerpts, on the other hand, attempt to control text difficulty by restricting the range of word families encountered, but in so doing create text with unnatural syntax and rather nonsensical form (and no traditional story structure). Children experiencing difficulty in either curricular material may well be further confounded when presented with both. The appropriate strategies for reading either text are simply quite divergent from the other.

To return to the question of balance, then, an expert support teacher might observe the classroom teacher's reading program and decide that it is a balanced program, but that within the program, a certain student requires special attention in a specific area. Such instruction would include the broader framework particularly by highlighting how the focal points fitted into the broader program. For example, the student may require additional attention to hearing sequences of sounds in words. This can be difficult for some children to pick up in a group setting. The support teacher could work on that in the context of writing and/or reading real stories. On the other hand, observation of the classroom instruction might reveal an unbalanced program. For example, suppose a classroom teacher's program consisted almost entirely of completing skill sheets emphasizing phonic analysis. Difficulty control in such a program is accomplished by constraining the letter-sound relationships, and success is defined by accurate pronunciation of words in isolation. A support teacher could decide to work with the classroom teacher or try to shape up the balance independently. The former involves extensive communication, which currently seems lacking. The latter requires not simply teaching the untaught skills, but teaching in such a way that the instruction ensures the integration of skills learned in the regular program with those learned in the remedial program. Again, this

FIGURE 11–1.   Examples of Reading Material Using Different Approaches for Controlling Text Difficulty

> The fox is on a log.
> The fox is by the sty.
> Can Red get Pub?
> Yes, the fox has the pig by a leg . . .

Source: Excerpted from *The Fox and the Cat*, Behavioral Research Labs, Palo Alto, CA, 1967.

> The man had the log on sand and the log got hot. The log had
> tag fog. The log got hot and the cod got hot . . .

Source: Excerpted from P. J. McInnis and S. K. Curtis (1982). *The Cursive Approach to Readiness and Reading.* Hammondsport, NY: M/C Publications.

The Bus Ride

> A girl got on the bus.
> Then the bus went fast.
> A boy got on the bus.
> Then the bus went fast.
> A fox got on the bus.
> Then the bus went fast.
> A hippopotomus got on the bus.
> Then the bus went fast . . .
> A bee got on the bus.
> Then . . .
> The hippopotomus got off the bus.
> The fox got off the bus.
> The boy got off the bus.
> The girl got off the bus.
> Then they all ran fast.

Source: Reprinted with permission of Scott, Foresman Co.

requires knowledge of the other program, which implies some form of communication.

The important issue here is that the individual responsible for program coordination must have extensive knowledge of how readers develop and of frameworks of instruction. It is not possible to attend to the relationship between the learning in two programs if one is aware only of the activity in one of the programs, as is frequently the case (Johnston, Allington, and Afflerbach, 1985). There needs to be extensive investigation of ways in which cooperative instructional programs can be developed. This raises the issues of communication and awareness of other teachers' approaches, as well as that of compatibility of knowledge structures. It seems likely that the more congruent teachers' knowledge structures are, the less time is likely to be involved in communicating and coordinating programs, and the more congruent the programs are likely to be in the first place. Similarly, when two teachers have an extensive knowledge of how the other teaches, even if their knowledge structures differ, they are more likely to be able to build bridges between each others' programs.

Current "cellular organization" (Lortie, 1976) of classrooms tends to isolate teachers from one another so that they do not acquire knowledge of each others' teaching approaches. The use of in-class approaches for support program instruction may foster a greater knowledge of program compatibility, but because of ego defense may actually reduce the likelihood of cooperation unless the arrangement is self-induced. Various contextual factors seem likely to influence the probability of teachers cooperating. For example, competitive organizational structures such as those set up in some career ladder systems seem less conducive to coordination than do cooperative organizational structures (Ames and Ames, 1984).

Pugach and Johnson (1987) have shown that training teachers to be "peer collaborators" can be an effective way to solve the instructional problems of students with mild learning and behavior problems. Their approach has involved helping teachers to structure and focus their conferences around particular children or groups of children. The dialogues are initiated by a teacher who has an instructional problem to solve and feels he or she needs support. The success of such a program must surely rest on the non-ego-threatening response of the cooperating teacher. These teachers are trained to respond to the initiator in a similar way to the reponse of the writing teacher in a process writing class. Perhaps the facts that such meetings are expected and the timing is intended to be preventive (suggesting that the problem is not yet serious) help to allow the teachers to seek help. However, the collaborations they report were between regular classroom teachers. Whether or not they could operate between a regular classroom teacher and a specialist teacher without the differential power status fouling it up is an unanswered question.

Opportunity to Learn.   Although support for the notion of differential instruction for differential categories of students has been seriously undermined (Marston, 1987; Reynolds, Wang, and Walberg, 1987; Stainback and Stainback, 1984), the residual effects of the approach are still evident in the training of many specialists and teachers, and it remains implicit in the structure of many federal and state policies. In some respects this situation almost guarantees a lack of congruence between instructional programs. We believe that there is reasonable evidence that this situation deserves to be remedied. On the basis of the lack of support for differential instruction, and the rather extensive evidence that sheer opportunity to learn is a powerful explanatory variable (Leinhardt and Pallay, 1982), we think it would be better to begin planning support instruction with the assumption that the difference between the at-risk and other students resides largely in the need for differential opportunities to learn (Good, 1983; Crawford, Kimball, and Patrick, 1984; Hiebert, 1983; Kiesling, 1978). Currently, participation in instructional support programs seems to more often reduce the at-risk learner's exposure to instruction (Allington, 1986; Haynes and Jenkins, 1986; Zigmond, Vallecorsa, and Leinhardt, 1980). Simply put, we argue that some learners will, at times, require larger amounts of higher-quality literacy instruction in order to facilitate progress in literacy development. The instructional support we propose for at-risk learners would not, then, necessarily involve any alternative curricular approach, but would, instead, provide at-risk learners with access to more, and better, instruction.

Acceptance of this alternative assumption provides a reason to coordinate instruction—so that program effects are cumulative rather than fragmented. Whereas coordinated instructional efforts would enhance learning, we argue that at-risk learners will often need increased opportunities to learn. Although we are advocating the position that the at-risk learner needs more time to learn, we do not advocate this in a permanent, trait-like way. With Clay (1985), we argue that with optimal instruction and more of it in the early stages, these students will become able to learn as fast as the other students. Thus the extra-instructional time requirement will disappear ultimately.

Supplement, Not Supplant.   A major provision of Chapter 1 has been that remedial assistance should supplement and not supplant the regular instructional efforts (unfortunately, this has not been a tenet of special education services). The intent was to prevent schools from simply using federal money to fund existing instructional efforts, but interpretations of this regulatory language have produced aberrant instructional situations. For example, some believe that it prohibits in-class programs and others believe that it insists on different instructional methods and materials (Allington, 1986; Johnston, Allington, and Afflerbach, 1985; NIE, 1977). However, the basic problem is that within a given school day, unless the school day is extended for at-risk children, something must be supplanted in order to provide remedial support. Thus the notion of supplementation needs to be examined in terms of the alternatives open to school systems.

One approach to this is to stagger the school day to allow some students to arrive and leave before others. This allows for reduced pupil-teacher ratios during parts of the day. Such an approach has been used successfully in Sweden (Clay, 1985). Similarly, it has been shown that using Chapter 1 money to reduce substantially the pupil-teacher ratio across the board can produce gains for the low-achieving students (Doss and Holly, 1982), primarily by increasing the amount of teacher-student contact. However, staggering to reduce pupil-teacher ratio does not, in itself, result in consistent achievement gains (Balow, 1969; Filby, Barnett, and Bossert, 1983; Cahen, Filby, McCutcheon, and Kyle, 1983). Leinhardt (1980) notes some of the potential problems with this approach. First, smaller, more homogeneous classes may result in classroom teachers having lowered expectations for achievement. In her study of transition rooms, teachers with small classes often offered less reading instruction than regular classroom teachers—a result unlikely to enhance children's reading achievement. Second, unless the quality of instruction is improved, there would be little reason to predict greater achievement gains even if the opportunity to learn remained constant. In short, any strategy that has little positive effect on the quantity or quality of instruction offered, or both, seems unlikely to enhance achievement. For teachers who know what they are doing, and who increase the opportunity to learn, this seems to be an option well worth exploring. We are not yet convinced that this approach will make a difference for teachers with limited expertise, however. The teacher with limited expertise and thirty pupils still has limited expertise when assigned only fifteen pupils.

Within a fixed-length school day, it seems possible to supplant regular instruction somewhat, provided the displacement is of such high quality that it is relatively short-lived. The critical features have to do with the fact that these students must learn substantially faster in this situation than the regular classroom program. The faster they learn, the briefer the supplantation. The conditions that produce this accelerated learning seem to include efficient, effective instruction focusing on independence, low pupil-teacher ratio (particularly one-on-one), and early intervention (Carter, 1984; Clay, 1985). For example, under these conditions, Clay (1982, 1985) and Pinnell (1987) have shown that for the children making the least progress in literacy development, one-on-one instruction for thirty minutes per day, four days a week, can bring most of them to levels comparable to the average group of students within six to twenty weeks. In addition, by and large, these students have needed no further support throughout elementary school. It is important to note that this approach took place within a context of highly comparable teacher knowledge structures, extensive cooperative arrangements between teachers to release one another for parts of the school day, and considerable administrative support. However, with respect to the present discussion, the important point is that if regular instruction, in whole or in part, is temporarily and partially replaced with highly effective individual instruction, the problem of congruence is substantially reduced, except for the problem of reintegration into the regular curriculum, which is, of course, the goal of the program and remains critical. The reintegration means, first, that instruction must be directed toward independence. This is most critical because the effects of nonindependence focused instruction (highly teacher directed) will leave the child without flexible problem-solving strategies and more at the mercy of exactly the strategies that are taught. This will be most problematic in the classroom in independent work and will likely result in backsliding. Second, it means that the instruction should emphasize, and allocate most time to, the reading of connected text, which is what will generally be required in the regular classroom.

Currently, the likelihood of such intensive, preventive approaches being implemented seems minimal. The notion of prevention appears to require resource investment where there is not yet (and may never be) a problem. In times of shrinking resources such as the present, this does not seem likely to gain favor. Although individualized instruction has received bad press in some of the literature on the grounds that small group instruction is more efficient (e.g., see Rosenshine and Stevens, 1984), it appears that it may be inappropriate to generalize from classroom studies. The work of Bloom (1984), Clay (1982, 1985), and Pinnell (1987) strongly favors early, intensive, individualized one-on-one-tutoring, and the Chapter 1 evaluation work of Carter (1984), Crawford, Kimball, and Patrick (1984), and Guthrie, Seifert, and Kline (1978) provides additional support for low teacher-pupil ratios, preferably one-on-one.

Unfortunately, such early intervention is not encouraged by current assessment practices (Johnston, 1984) or by funding policies and practices, but such intervention has some clear advantages. Given approximately equivalent amounts of instruction, less able readers normally progress more slowly than do other students. Each year they fall increasingly further behind. This means that even with accelerated learning, later intervention will require longer intervention in order for students to catch up. In addition, the secondary characteristics that such students develop as a consequence of continued failure extend even further the necessary length of the intervention program (Johnston, 1985; Johnston and Winograd, 1985). Associated with this, support teachers currently have to deal with up to ten children at once, and because of scheduling problems, frequently the children range over several grades in performance level. The size and heterogeneity of the instructional groups scheduled for support teachers makes faster learning impossible. Each of these factors simply compounds and prolongs the coordination problem, thus we suggest that along with consideration of program coordination, additional assumptions that impact on the length and likelihood of coordination should be reexamined.

CASE STUDIES

How School Districts Have Improved Coordination

The development of a well-coordinated approach to literacy instruction for at-risk students involves far more than an administrative mandate that instruction will be coordinated. We have observed such attempts. In one case, in-class support program instruction was simply mandated districtwide. Little thought had evidently gone into this mandate since a previous mandate concerning use of separate and philosophically distinct curricula in the classroom and support program instruction was left intact. Thus there was literally nothing for teachers to plan collaboratively—each was supposed to follow a different packaged curriculum. It is perhaps not surprising, then, that we found little communication or coordination between classroom and support teachers, even though they taught in the same classroom. Likewise, it is not surprising that teacher resentment was high and efforts to sabotage or simply ignore the mandate were frequent.

Similarly, another district simply mandated daily teaching logs be exchanged between classroom and support teachers with an accompanying monthly ten-minute joint planning session. Here again, the classroom and support program teachers were mandated to use separate and philsophically distinct curricular approaches. Our observations of instruction and the planning conferences again indicated little coordination or communication about instructional issues.

One might say that coordination cannot be wished, mandated, or legislated into existence. We offer several descriptions of school district efforts to attain instructional programs for at-risk students that, at least, involve the development of a coordinated effort and, in some, have produced programs we find hard to improve upon. Each of these programs is described briefly, followed by a discussion of the implementation process.

North Warren Project.   The North Warren, New York, school district is small and located in a very rural and economically depressed region. The effort in this district has been to redesign the reading and language arts program in the single elementary school. The effort was initiated when a new Chapter 1 teacher and new district superintendent were employed. The Chapter 1 teacher organized a literature-based remedial effort in an attempt to involve at-risk learners in enhanced amounts of text reading with an emphasis on understanding. Her initiative, with support from the superintendent, has developed into a redesign of the classroom reading and language arts curriculum along with an integrated approach to support instruction for at-risk learners. A similar spreading effect has been reported in the Ohio Reading Recovery Project (Pinnell, 1987).

The North Warren redesign was guided by three principles (Walmsley, 1986):

> [First,] if genuine reading and composing are to be the primary language arts activities, they should occupy the largest portion of the language arts curriculum. . . . Second, . . . the notion of "skills first, application later" has been replaced with the principle of skills through application. . . . Finally, . . . rather than offer [poor readers] a separate language arts curriculum . . . they engage in the same reading and writing activities as their classmates, but we

offer them help both in the classroom, and in the remedial reading room, where the books they have been reading in class are the primary vehicle for remedial reading, and what they have been writing in class becomes the major vehicle for remedial writing . . . (p. 5).

To put these principles into practice, the program uses primarily trade books, supplemented by shorter pieces of literature (fiction and nonfiction) drawn from basal reading series, magazines, newspapers, and elsewhere. The teaching staff, both classroom and suppport teachers, collaboratively select a theme and generate a list of books, articles, and excerpts on that theme. Each theme is studied for about a month, with literary, science, and social studies themes developed to this point. The list of texts on the topic varies in difficulty with some materials below and others above grade level. All teachers read all books and then discuss them and collaboratively develop lessons and instructional activities. The skills of reading, such as "main idea," are developed in the context of reading full-length literature rather than through skill sheets or separate lessons. In addition to reading activities of various sorts, writing activities of several kinds are developed. These usually include at least short-answer writing to test comprehension, extended writing related to the reading theme, and writing of the students' choice related to the theme. Here again, the skills of editing, such as grammar, spelling, and handwriting, are developed in the context of the students' writing rather than through separate exercises.

The classroom program is organized for ninety-minute daily sessions with remedial assistance for at-risk learners being offered both during their regular classroom instructional time and also during pull-out sessions in the remedial reading room. Walmsley (1986) notes:

> This project was originally designed for remedial readers, and it is in the approach to remediation of reading and writing difficulties that the greatest departure from traditional methods is evident. The philosophy of remediation is quite simple. Poor readers and writers need as much exposure to and practice in reading full-length literature as their better reading counterparts, but they will need more than ordinary assistance if they are to tackle this extended reading (p. 6).

However, Walmsley (1986) notes that the difficulty in developing and implementing this approach should not be underestimated. Much planning and staff development time was expended during the three-year implementation process. This approach requires that teachers develop compatible knowledge structures about reading instruction, classroom teachers become secure enough to allow support teachers into the classroom, and support teachers acquire the instructional and social skills needed for a collaborative effort. In addition, the support of the key district administrator seems critical for any number of reasons, but perhaps especially with fiscal support for the development and implementation activities. However, dramatic improvement of at-risk learners' literacy skills has been a central result (though literacy levels of achieving students also improved) at North Warren.

Reading Recovery Program.   The Reading Recovery Program is a highly effective early intervention program that was originated in New Zealand by Marie Clay (1985). It has since been replicated in several parts of the United States, most notably Columbus, Ohio (Pinnell, 1987; Short, 1987). There are several noteworthy characteristics of the program that make it unique. First, it begins early, after one year of instruction in New Zealand, or early in first grade in the United States. This is done in order to prevent the child from building a history of failure and the characteristics associated with that failure (e.g., Johnston and Winograd, 1985; Johnston, 1985). Second, through one-on-one intensive daily instruction, the performance of the lowest group of children is raised quickly (average of thirteen weeks) to the average level of the remainder of the children in the regular class. These children are then discontinued from the program and replaced by the next lowest children. Discontinued children, even at long-term followup, do not need further assistance (Clay, 1985; Pinnell, 1987). Third, the central component of the program is an expert teacher who knows how to observe and record children's literacy development and to tailor instruction specifically to the child's needs.

The instructional activities themselves are characterized best by a whole language philosophy. Virtually all of the daily thirty-minute session is spent reading and writing. A child will read or reread about three books each session. There is a balance of reading and writing activity with a focus on those aspects of the conceptual, procedural, and conditional knowledge involved in independent reading and writing activity. Independence is seen as critical in order to prevent regression when children are returned to the classroom, thus self-correction rather than teacher correction is emphasized. The instructional session is also characterized by a high pace while maintaining the wait-time necessary to develop independence. This is made possible because of the teacher's expertise in matching the child and the task so that the error rate is optimal. There is a larger amount of easy reading to develop automatic responses. Interestingly there is little direct instruction or direct phonics instruction.

Coordination between regular and remedial instruction is not the focus of this program. Indeed, the remedial teacher has first choice of when to schedule which children, and the program is individually tailored regardless of the nature of the classroom program. The Columbus experience has shown that the program is effective even when classroom practices conflict with it (Pinnell, 1987). What can account for this apparent paradox? We have several possibilities that need further investigation. The first possibility has to do with the nature of the teacher expertise, which is the center of—or even the entire—program. Teachers are trained to monitor children's development and tailor instruction specifically to the individual child's response. Thus a balancing procedure is built into the program. If a child tends to overpredict in his reading, the tutor gives feedback aimed at focusing his attention on monitoring the print detail. If a child focuses too much on print detail, losing the meaning, the tutor's feedback focuses her attention on the meaning of the text. In other words, there is an attempt to base instruction on the curriculum as experienced by the child.

Second, the whole language principles upon which Reading Recovery are based may be in essence a more "healing" program since whatever pieces (or "skills") of literacy the learner brings, the program places them within a context of natural language functioning. Indeed, if such a program produces a clearer understanding of what it means to be literate, perhaps the children are able to place classroom skills instruction into a more sensible context. The detailed monitoring of each child's development prevents the development of inappropriate concepts about print and literacy while involving the child continually in reading genuine text for meaning.

Third, the program focuses on flexible use of the various strategies in reading. Thus diversity of response is emphasized, which may help to undo any rigidity that is built into the regular classroom program. At the same time, the sheer volume of reading done during the sessions ensures automatic responses in the context of "real" reading.

Nonetheless, those who are directing the program are greatly concerned about ensuring the compatibility of the classroom and remedial programs, and have taken steps to ensure the development of this compatibility. In particular, they have encouraged classroom teachers to collect particular types of information about children's reading development. Teachers' views of the children and how to teach them tend to revolve around how they "know" the child (Johnston, 1987). Thus if teachers view the child in a similar way, they are likely to teach in more compatible ways and to have more grounds for discussion, which is likely to produce program convergence. Initial results suggest that more congruent teacher pairs produce more powerful effects (Pinnell, 1987).

Westwood Project.   Although it shares some features with the North Warren project, the Westwood (New York) project is historically older and evolved quite differently (Lee et al., 1986). The use of trade book reading and composition as primary support instruction activities, a mixed in-class and pullout model, and a well-developed district philosophy for the integrated teaching of the language arts are similarities that first come to view. However, the impetus for coordination, the building-level special services team, seems to stem from a board of education decision that each resident child in this sprawling suburban district would have adequate and appropriate educational opportunities available. This decision led to the creation of a districtwide plan for instruction of at-risk learners.

In order to provide better for appropriate educational services, the special services team, comprised of classroom and support teachers, was created. Its function is to review, with the classroom teacher, the issues involved when any child experiences learning difficulties. This building-level team decides on appropriate interventions, which range from assistance for the classroom teacher to remedial reading, mathematics, or writing services, a variety of special education services, and instructional planning assistance. The district uses multiple categories of funds to pay support teachers, so a reading teacher might be paid in part from Chapter 1, state compensatory, local, and, perhaps, special education funds. Thus there is little quibble about who can work with whom. However, categorical identification of students is rare, or at least knowledge of categorical identification is rare. We found that only the central office administrator had reliable records on which students "belonged" to which categorical program. The classroom teachers, reading teachers, special education teachers, and principal had no reliable knowledge of the categorical identification of the students with whom they worked. What each individual knew was that Jimmy needed additional instruction in reading, Buffy in math, and Wanda needed strategies to control her emotional outbursts.

In short, the district philosophy was one of providing whatever instructional support was needed without worrying about categorical identification. Thus reading teachers worked with identified learning-disabled children, a special education teacher worked with Chapter 1 children, and both worked with children who needed support but were not eligible for any categorical program. The use of multiple funding sources to employ the support teachers blurred categorical differences. The addition of local funds to support the effort ensured that all children who needed assistance received it, whether or not they qualified for any categorical program. The general attitude in the district was simply to provide whatever instructional support was deemed appropriate by the special services team and ignore categorical eligibility.

The district has a long history of ongoing staff development and each elementary school has a building language arts coordinator. The language arts coordinator is a full-time teacher who works with children, develops instruction with teachers, offers model teaching lessons in classrooms, orders all materials, and directs all assessments of student learning. This position is the building-level liason to the district language arts cabinet that plans all staff development, curriculum revision, and materials purchases, although other teachers in the building will also serve on this cabinet. The cabinet, language arts coordinators, and teachers are guided by an explicit and written district philosophy of literacy development.

However, unlike the North Warren project, support teachers do not necessarily provide additional instruction on the curricular materials used in the classroom. Rather, while they focus on increasing the amount of genuine reading and composition activities for at-risk learners, they select materials from a wide array of potential resources. Thus while these at-risk students receive greater opportunities to engage in assisted contextual reading and writing, the coordination is more often at the skill or strategy level. By analyzing the classroom curricular materials and instruction, the support teachers work to create the "balance" we noted earlier. Collaboration between the support teachers is prevalent but not as prevalent as in North Warren. Nonetheless, the resultant instructional support for at-risk learners enhances opportunities to engage in genuine reading and writing activities and provides additional instructional support for acquiring control over skills and strategies necessary for success in the classroom reading and language arts curriculum.

Here again, we saw the influence of a districtwide administrator on the development and implementation of a coordinated program. In addition, principals are involved in a variety of ways but are most obviously involved in working out scheduling difficulties. This could be a serious problem since the district also adheres to a plan whereby all students in need of any support services are scheduled out of the room during the same one-hour block of time. Thus in some rooms the at-risk learners leave from 9:00 to 10:00, while in other rooms they are absent between 1:00 and 2:00. Although difficult to schedule (but not impossible, principals assure us), since a dozen support teachers' schedules need to be considered, this plan assures classroom teachers and all learners of a largely uninterrupted instructional day.

Aurora Project.   A variety of concerns about instructional support programs led to the redesign of Chapter 1 programs in the Aurora, Colorado, schools (Rickert, Ripple, and Coleman, 1985). These concerns included the fragmentation of the school day for at-risk students who were pulled out of classroom instructional settings for special services, lack of appropriate separate instructional spaces with growing school enrollments, and the underutilization of support teacher expertise in enhancing classroom reading and language arts instruction. District and school administrators, as well as board of education members, felt that the lack of coordination between instructional programs hindered the educational development of at-risk learners (Rickert, 1987). Thus a district task force was created to study and recommend methods for enhancing the coordination between instructional support programs and the regular education program.

The proposed primary shift was to move from a pullout program to an in-class instructional support design. In the first year of the project, support teachers were to implement the in-class design with at least one classroom teacher and were to begin to meet twice monthly with all classroom teachers whose children were served. These meetings were to be sketched on a monthly reporting form that was then submitted to the central office. The support teachers were to find ways that their instruction could be coordinated with the classroom program, and a variety of such strategies were developed.

However, there were significant implementation problems that year. Among those most common were: the difficulty of finding common free periods to meet twice each month, the refusal of some classroom teachers to meet for cooperative planning, philosophical differences about how reading is best taught, personality conflicts between the teachers, the difficulty some classroom teachers had accepting another teacher in the room, and, finally, the difficulty in establishing two-way communication, primarily getting classroom teachers to participate actively in the planning, as opposed to a passive listening participation. As a result of these difficulties a variety of staff development programs were offered, including programs that provided support instruction teachers with improved interpersonal skills necessary for collaboration, programs on the philosophy of coordinated instruction and in-class models, and opportunities for teachers to visit classrooms where in-class models were working well. Over time, the in-class component and the collaborative planning have been well integrated into the school system and teacher acceptance, although not universal, is substantial.

There were several building-level features and options that enhanced acceptance of the redesign. First, when building administrator support was clearly available, the transition was more easily accomplished. When building administrators assisted in planning meeting times and instructional interventions, implementation went more smoothly. Provisions that allowed teachers to decide who would work together also seemed important. Whenever two teachers who did not want to work together were forced to do so, little communication, coordination, or collaboration was evident, even though meetings were held as required and instruction was delivered in the mainstream classroom.

Currently, observations of instruction suggest coordination is most generally evident. Even in those cases where the pullout model is used, the communication between teachers has enhanced the coordination of instruction. In the in-class efforts, coordination is also easily evident and is higher than in the early stages. However, it seems that communication between teachers is the primary factor, not necessarily the location where instructional support is offered (Rickert, 1987). In both the elementary and middle schools, teacher acceptance of collaboration and in-class support instruction is high. As both sets of teachers have become more experienced and knowledgeable about collaborative planning, the process has improved and gained support (Reed, 1987).

The Aurora experience again indicates the need to consider program redesign as a long-term and ongoing process. The success can be traced to the administrative support for the effort, from both district- and school-level administrators. Staff development, flexibility, and experience all worked to facilitate implementation over the three-year period.

SUMMARY AND CONCLUSIONS

We have reviewed the available research on instructional coordination and tried to clarify what coordination is, what it does, and what is likely to maximize its occurrence. Our particular focus in this chapter has been on the lowest level of coordination—classroom and support program instruction—that which impacts the individual student's learning directly. We have examined coordination as it influences the quality of instruction delivered to students. We have argued that current evidence suggests many at-risk learners do not currently have access to instructional settings that offer larger amounts of high-quality literacy instruction driven by a consistent curricular approach. Rather, the least able students are those most likely to participate in instructional settings that offer reduced amounts of instruction generally and a fragmented curricular experience frequently. Those who need the most carefully organized instruction receive, instead, a virtually incoherent mixture of competing curricular approaches and emphases. Such need not be the case, as indicated by the brief case studies of well-planned support programs.

Our experience suggests that coordinated efforts are not easily achieved, and most difficult may be obtaining shifts in the content of instruction offered in support of regular programs, in order to produce an integrated program of instruction for the individual student. Studies that have examined coordination among regular and various support programs, regardless of definition, have invariably found it rare, but where evident, important to children's learning. However, we have found that there is little clear description of exactly what coordinated instruction would look like. Although we have made an attempt, there are currently substantial ideological differences concerning methods of reading instruction, and thus we see a need for research directed toward clarifying these issues. However, whatever the ideology, it does not seem unreasonable that within a given school, for a given pupil, the instruction be coherently articulated.

The major issue really comes down to coordination of the curricula as they are experienced by the student. That is, the objective is to set up a situation in which students find that support instruction makes it easier to make sense of the regular instruction.

We feel that curricular coordination may be further encouraged at the local level through some of the following:

1. Explicit and cooperatively developed curricula with similarly explicit rationales would seem likely to enhance instructional congruence.
2. Explicit curricula would help, but these would certainly not guarantee coherently articulated instructional services. A serious stumbling block remains in the form of teachers' knowledge structures, or what might be termed the "implicit curriculum." This implicates teacher training and programmatic teacher inservice development. Teacher training initially

develops these knowledge structures, and subsequent teacher isolation, issues of "turf," and the other institutional and policy issues discussed perpetuate the differences.

3. Communication among teachers, both regular and support, might be fostered in a variety of ways, including requiring regular conferences between teachers involved with specific special needs children. Time must be specifically allocated to this activity but time allocation is not enough. All teachers will have to acquire a sense of ownership of the targeted student and his or her instruction. Cooperative planning may not be easily accomplished but it must begin.

4. Observation of at-risk student performance in another instructional setting is likely to provide better knowledge of different components of the child's actual curriculum, and concrete grounds for discussions between teachers.

5. Continuous process records of children's development may be very helpful in inducing curricular alignment. For example, such records might contain samples of the child's writing, and running records of reading behaviors (Clay, 1985) over time. If teachers are required to keep such records and are provided with the expertise to do so with minimal additional effort, the nature of the files will focus on instruction, and the data within the files will give a more concrete foundation for teachers' discussions of students' progress and difficulties.

We have argued that, in addition to attempts to improve coordination, it would be helpful to have concurrent progress toward reducing the demands on coordination. In particular, we have stressed the need for:

1. Explicit district policies supporting coordination
2. Early attention to learning difficulties with an emphasis on prevention
3. Intensive intervention in order to eliminate the need for support services as quickly as possible
4. Low teacher-pupil ratios, particularly in the early stages, and even one-to-one support instruction where possible
5. Support programs that focus on student independence so that students might return to the regular instruction and maintain progress
6. Support programs that focus on service quality more than categorical identification and regulatory compliance.

Achieving the type of support instruction we envision is not an easy task. Simple mandates to coordinate do not work. Simple accountability measures, such as a written log of planning conferences, do not work. In order to achieve the current level of coordination observed, our case study districts invariably worked over extended periods of time to develop expertise in both classroom and support teachers and to develop a local design that worked with the particular features of that district. The impetus for the redesign in each case, however, was concern for the academic experience of the individual at-risk student.

REFERENCES

Algozzine, B., and Ysseldyke, J.E. (1983). Learning disabilities as a subset of school failure: The oversophistication of a concept. *Exceptional Children, 50,* 242–246.

Allington, R.L. (1986). Policy constraints and the effective delivery of remedial instruction. In J. Hoffman (Ed.), *Effective teaching of reading: Research and practice.* Newark, DE: International Reading Association.

Allington, R.L., and McGill-Franzen, A. (1989). Different programs, indifferent instruction. In A. Gardner and D. Lipsky (Eds.), *Beyond separate education.* New York: Brookes.

Allington, R.L., and Shake, M. (1986). Remedial reading: Achieving curricular congruence in classroom and clinic. *Reading Teacher, 39,* 648–654.

Allington, R.L.; Stuetzel, H.; Shake, M.; and Lamarche, S. (1986). What is remedial reading? A descriptive study. *Reading Research and Instruction, 24,* 15–30.

Ames, C., and Ames, R. (1984). Goal structures and motivation. *The Elementary School Journal, 85(1),* 39–52.

Archambault, F.X., and St. Pierre, R.G. (1980). The effect of federal policy on services delivered through ESEA Title I. *Education Evaluation and Policy Analysis, 2,* 33–46.

Balow, I. (1969). A longitudinal evaluation of reading achievement in small classes. *Elementary English, 46,* 184–187.

Barrozo, A. (1986). *Instruction: Are compensatory education students shortchanged?* Paper presented at the annual meeting of the American Educational Research Association, San Francisco, CA.

Biklen, D. (1985). *Achieving the complete school: Strategies for effective mainstreaming.* New York: Teachers College Press.

Birman, B.F. (1981). Problems of overlap between Title I and P.L. 94–142: Implications for the federal role in education. *Educational Evaluation and Policy Analysis, 3,* 5–19.

Bloom, B. (1976). *Human characteristics and school learning.* New York: McGraw-Hill.

Bloom, B. S. (1984). The 2 sigma problem: The search for methods of group instruction as effective as one-to-one tutoring. *Educational Researcher, 13(6),* 4–17.

Bogdan, R. (1983). A closer look at mainstreaming. *Educational Forum, 47,* 425–434.

Cahen, L.S.; Filby, N.; McCutcheon, G.; and Kyle, D.W. (1983). *Class size and instruction.* New York: Longman.

Carter, L.F. (1984). The sustaining effects study of compensatory and elementary education. *Educational Researcher, 13,* 4–13.

Chi, M.; Glaser, R.; and Rees, E. (1982). Expertise in problem solving. In R.

Sternberg (Ed.), *Advances in the psychology of human intelligence*. Hillsdale, NY: Erlbaum Associates, pp. 7–75.

Clark, T.A., and McCarthy, D.P. (1983). School improvement in New York City: The evolution of a project. *Educational Researcher, 12,* 17–24.

Clay, M.M. (1982). Reading recovery: A follow-up study. In *Observing young readers: Selected papers*. Portsmouth, NH: Heinemann.

Clay, M.M. (1985). *The early detection of reading difficulties*, 3rd ed. Portsmouth, NH: Heineman.

Cohen, D.K. (1982). Policy and organization: The impact of state and federal education policy on school governance. *Harvard Educational Review, 52,* 474–499.

Cohen, E.G.; Intilli, J.K.; and Robbins, S. H. (1978). Teacher and reading specialists: Cooperation or isolation? *Reading Teacher, 32,* 281–287.

Cook, J.E., and Eardly, E.C. (1979). *Remediating reading disabilities*. Germantown, MD: Aspen.

Cooley, W.W., and Leinhardt, G. (1980). The instructional dimensions study. *Educational Evaluation and Policy Analysis, 2,* 7–25.

Crawford, J.; Kimball, G.H.; and Patrick, A. (1984). *Differences and similarities in teaching effectiveness findings between regular classroom instruction and Chapter 1 compensatory instruction*. Paper presented at the AERA annual meeting, New Orleans, April.

Dechant, E. (1981). *Dignosis and remediation of reading disabilities*. Englewood Cliffs, NJ: Prentice-Hall.

DeFord, D. (1985). Validating the construct of theoretical orientation in reading instruction. *Reading Research Quarterly, 20,* 351–367.

Doss, D.A., and Holley, F. (1982). *A cause for national pause: Title I schoolwide projects*. Paper presented at the American Educational Research Association, New York.

Durr, W. (1981). *Houghton-Mifflin Reading Series*. Boston: Houghton-Mifflin Co.

Engleman, S., and Bruner, E.C. (1975). *DISTAR*. Chicago, IL: Science Research Associates.

Filby, N.; Barnett, B.; and Bossert, S. (1983). *Grouping for reading instruction*. San Francisco: Far West Laboratory for Educational Research and Development.

Gelzheiser, L.M. (1987). Reducing the number of students identified as learning disabled: A question of practice, philosophy or policy? *Exceptional Children, 54,* 145–150.

Gezi, K. (1986). *The role of leadership in compensatory schools*. Paper presented at the annual meeting of the American Educational Research Association, San Francisco, CA.

Gilliland, H. (1974). *A practical guide to remedial reading*. Columbus, OH: Merrill.

Ginsburg, A.L., and Turnbull, B.J. (1981). Local program coordination: An alternative for federal aid to schools. *Education Evaluation and Policy Analysis, 3,* 33–42.

Good, T. (1983). Research on classroom teaching. In L.S. Shulman and G. Sykes (Eds.), *Handbook of teaching and policy*. New York: Longmans, pp. 42–80.

Greenwood, C.R.; Delquadri, J.C.; Stanley, S.; Sasso, G.; Wharton, D.; and Schulte, D. (1981). Locating opportunity to learn as basis for academic remediation: A developing model for teaching. In R.B. Rutherford, Jr., A.G. Prieto, and J.E. McGlothlin (Eds.), *Severe behavior disorders of children and youth: Monograph in behavioral disorders*. Reston, VA: Council for Exceptional Children.

Griswold, P.A.; Cotton, K.J.; and Hansen, J.B. (1986). *Effective compensatory education sourcebook: A review of effective educational practices,* vol. 1. Washington, DC: U.S. Department of Education.

Guthrie, J.T.; Seifert, M.; and Kline, L. W. (1978). Clues from research on programs for poor readers. In S. Jay Samuels (Ed.), *What research has to say about instruction.* Newark, DE: International Reading Association.

Hannifin, M.J., and Barrett, B.K. (1983). Preparing for educational change: Incorporating the support curriculum into the basic curriculum. *American Education, 7,* 32–37.

Haynes, M.C., and Jenkins, J.R. (1986). Reading instruction in special education resource rooms. *American Educational Research Journal, 23,* 161–190.

Hiebert, E.H. (1983). An examination of ability grouping for reading instruction. *Reading Research Quarterly, 18,* 231–255.

Johnston, P. (1984). Assessment in reading: The emperor has no clothes. In P.D. Pearson (Ed.), *Handbook of reading research.* New York: Longman.

Johnston, P. (1985). Understanding reading disability: A case study approach. *Harvard Educational Review, 55,* 153–177.

Johnston, P. (1987). Assessing the process, and the process of assessment, in the language arts. In J.R. Squire (Ed.), *The dynamics of language learning: Research in reading and English.* National Conference on Research in English. Urbana, IL.

Johnston, P.H.; Allington, R.L.; and Afflerbach, P. (1985). The congruence of classroom and remedial reading instruction. *Elementary School Journal, 85,* 465–478.

Johnston, P.; McGill-Franzen, A.; and Allington, R.L. (1985). *Obstructions to an integrated understanding of reading difficulty.* Paper presented at the annual meeting of the American Educational Research Association, Chicago, IL.

Johnston, P., and Winograd, P. (1985). Passive failure in reading. *Journal of Reading Behavior, 17,* 279–301.

Junkala, J., and Mooney, J.F. (1986). Special education students in regular classes: What happened to the pyramid? *Journal of Learning Disabilities, 19,* 218–241.

Kaestle, C.F., and Smith, M.S. (1982). The historical context of the federal role in education. *Harvard Educational Review, 52,* 383–408.

Kiesling, H. (1978). Productivity of instructional time by mode of instruction for students at varying levels of reading skill. *Reading Research Quarterly, 13,* 554–582.

Kimbrough, J., and Hill, P.T. (1981). *The aggregate effects of federal education programs.* Santa Monica, CA: Rand Corportation.

Lee, G.; Rowan, B.; Allington, R.; Anderson, L.; Bossert, S.; Harnischfeger, A.; and Stallings, J. (1986). *The management and delivery of instructional services to Chapter 1 students: Case studies of twelve schools.* Final report to the U.S. Office of Educational Research and Improvement, Department of Education (Proj. 400-85-1015), Far West Laboratory for Educational Research and Development.

Leinhardt, G. (1980). Transition rooms: Promoting maturation or reducing education? *Journal of Educational Psychology, 72,* 55–61.

Leinhardt, G.; Bickel, W.; and Pallay, A. (1982). Unlabelled but still entitled: Toward more effective remediation. *Teachers College Record, 84,* 391–422.

Leinhardt, G., and Pallay, A. (1982). Restrictive educational settings: Exile or haven? *Review of Educational Research, 52*, 557–578.

Licopoli, L. (1984). The resource room and mainstreaming handicapped students: A case study. *Topics in Learning and Learning Disabilities, 3*, 1–15.

Ligon, G.D., and Doss, D.A. (1982). *Some lessons we have learned from 6500 hours of classroom observations.* Pub. No. 81.56. Office of Research and Evaluation, Austin Independent School District, Austin, TX.

Lortie, D.C. (1976). Discussion (of integration of the handicapped child into regular schools by E. Martin). *Minnesota Education, 2*, 16–20.

Marston, D. (1987). Does categorical teacher certification benefit the mildly handicapped child? *Exceptional Children, 53*, 423–431.

McGill-Franzen, A.M. (1987). Failure to learn to read: Formulating a policy problem. *Reading Research Quarterly, 22*, 475–490.

McLaughlin, M.W. (1982). States and the new Federalism. *Harvard Educational Review, 52*, 564–583.

McLaughlin, M.W.; Shields, P.M.; and Rezabek, D.J. (1985). *State and local response to Chapter 1 of the Educational Consolidation and Improvement Act, 1981.* Report No. 85-A6. Institute for Research on Educational Finance and Governance, Stanford University.

Milofsky, C.D. (1976). *Special education: A sociological study of California programs.* New York: Praeger.

Moore, D.R.; Hyde, A.A.; Blair, K.A.; and Weitzman, S.M. (1981). *Student classification and the right to read.* Chicago: Designs for Change.

Moore, M.T.; Goertz, M.E.; Hartle, T.W.; Winslow, H.R.; David, J.L.; Sjogren, J.; Turnbull, B.; Coley, R.J.; and Holland, R.P. (1983). *The interaction of federal and related state education programs,* vol. 1. Princeton, NJ: Educational Testing Services.

National Institute of Education (1977). *Administration of compensatory education.* Washington, DC: U.S. Department of Health, Education and Welfare.

New York State Office of Education Performance Review (1974). *School factors influencing reading achievement: A performance review.* Albany, NY.

Pike, K. (1985). The content of reading instruction in pullout compensatory education classes and its relationship to regular classroom instruction. Unpublished dissertation, State University of New York at Albany.

Pinnell, G. (1987). *Studies of early intervention: The Ohio Reading Recovery Project.* Symposium presented at the annual meeting of the American Educational Research Association, Washington, DC.

Pugach, M.C., and Johnson, L.J. (1987, April). *Systematic teacher dialogue as a prereferral intervention: self-appraisal through peer collaboration.* Paper presented at the annual meeting of the American Educational Research Association, Washington, DC.

Reed, S.L. (1987). Treasure Island: Treasured Literature. *Reading Teacher, 40*, 480–481.

Reynolds, H.; Wang, M.; and Walberg, H. (1987). The necessary restructuring of special and regular education. *Exceptional Children, 53*, 391–398.

Rickert, C. (1987). The process used to improve coordination of Chapter 1 and regular education instruction in Aurora Public Schools. Unpublished paper, Aurora Public Schools, Aurora, CO.

Rickert, C.; Ripple, J.; and Coleman, P. (1985). *Linking Chapter 1 with the classroom reading program*. Paper presented at the annual meeting of the International Reading Association, New Orleans, LA.

Rosenshine, B., and Stevens, R. (1984). Classroom instruction in reading. In P.D. Pearson (Ed.), *Handbook of reading research*. New York: Longman.

Rowan, B.; Guthrie L.; Lee, G.; and Guthrie, G. (1986). *The design and implementation of Chapter 1 instructional services: A study of 24 schools*. Final report to U.S. Office of Educational Research and Improvement, Department of Education (Proj. #400-85-1015). Far West Laboratory for Educational Research and Development.

Scott, Foresman Co. (1971). *Reading systems*. Glenview, IL.

Short, K. (1987). *Reading recovery: Developing strategies for reading*. Paper presented at the annual meeting of the American Educational Research Association, Washington, DC.

Shulman, L.L. (1983). Autonomy and obligation: The remote control of teaching. In L.S. Shulman and G. Sykes (Eds.), *Handbook of teaching and policy*. New York: Longman.

Stainback, W., and Stainback, S. (1984). A rationale for the merger of special and regular education. *Exceptional Children, 51*, 102–111.

Stanley, S.O., and Greenwood, C.R. (1983). How much "opportunity to respond" does the minority disadvantaged student receive in school? *Exceptional Children*, 370–373.

Venezky, R.L., and Winfield, L.F. (1979). *Schools that succeed beyond expectations in teaching reading*. Newark, DE: University of Delaware. (ERIC Doc # : Ed 071 181).

Vernon, M.D. (1958). *Backwardness in reading*. New York: Cambridge University Press.

Walmsley, S. (1986). Toward an integrated language arts program: The North Warren Project. Unpublished paper, Department of Reading State University of New York at Albany.

Wilson, R. (1980). *Merrill linguistic readers*. Columbus, OH: Merrill.

Winfield, L.F. (1987). Teachers' estimates of test content covered in class on first grade students' reading achievement. *Elementary School Journal, 87*, 437–454.

Ysseldyke, J.E., and Algozzine, B. (1982). *Critical issues in special and remedial education*. Boston: Houghton Mifflin.

Ysseldyke, J.E.; Thurlow, M.L.; Mecklenburg, C.; and Graden, J. (1984). Opportunity to learn for regular and special education students during reading instruction. *Remedial and Special Education, 5*, 29–37.

Zigmond, N.; Vallecorsa, A.; Leinhardt, G. (1980). Reading instruction for students with learning disabilities. *Topics in Language Disorders, 1*, 89–98.

12

EFFECTIVE PROGRAMS FOR STUDENTS AT RISK: CONCLUSIONS FOR PRACTICE AND POLICY

Robert E. Slavin

Nancy A. Madden

Nancy L. Karweit

Center for Research on Elementary and Middle Schools
Johns Hopkins University

Each of the chapters in this volume reviews a considerable portion of the research on effective programs for students at risk of school failure, and among them hundreds of conclusions are drawn. However, there is a small set of themes that runs through these numerous conclusions and that have the greatest importance for practice and policy. These are as follows:

1. The *setting* within which remedial or special education services are provided makes little difference. What does matter is the quality of the *programs* implemented in the setting.

2. Prevention and early intervention are much more promising than waiting for learning deficits to accumulate and only then providing remedial or special education services.

3. Effective classroom and pullout programs for students at risk tend to accommodate instruction to individual needs while maximizing direct instruction. They frequently assess student progress through a structured hierarchy of skills, and adapt instructional strategies to the results of these assessments. Highly effective and cost-effective classroom programs include continuous-progress and cooperative learning models. When pullout programs are used, they should be intensive (e.g., one-to-one tutoring or computer-assisted instruction), brief, and designed to quickly catch students up with the rest of the class, not to support them indefinitely.

4. Preschool and extended-day kindergarten programs can contribute to the cognitive and social development of children from low-SES backgrounds. Effective preschool programs tend to emphasize exploration, language development, and play, not academics. Effective kingergarten programs build language and prereading skills using structured, well-organized, comprehensive approaches.

5. Remedial and special education services are too often poorly integrated with the regular education program, and therefore burden at-risk students with the task of accommodating very different approaches. Collaboration and consistency between regular, remedial, and special education are essential.

6. Teacher behaviors associated with outstanding achievement gains for students in Chapter 1 pullout programs and for mainstreamed academically handicapped students in regular classrooms tend to be similar to behaviors found to be effective with all students. This and other research tends to suggest that effective practices for students at risk tend not to be qualitatively different from the best practices of general education.

SUCCESS FOR ALL: A COMPREHENSIVE DESIGN FOR REFORM OF REMEDIAL AND SPECIAL EDUCATION

In addition to the specific conclusions just outlined, three more general conclusions should be abundantly clear from the preceding chapters. First, the remedial and special education programs now in widespread use are not doing enough to overcome the problems of students at risk for school failure. Second, we know enough about effective programs and practices for students at risk to increase substantially the number of students who leave the elementary school with a firm basis in the basic skills. Third, we still have a long way to go in translating research on effective practices for students at risk into replicable models and in learning how to successfully disseminate and implement such models on a broad scale.

Major changes are needed in our approach to education of students at risk for school failure. Although many improvements can and should be made within the programs most typically seen today, we believe that to make a marked difference in the chance that at-risk students will succeed in school and in life, fundamental changes are needed in the basic organization of the elementary school.

In this section, we propose a model of elementary school organization that incorporates much of what we have learned about effective programs for students at risk. This model, which we call Success for All, was piloted and evaluated at one Baltimore City elementary school during the 1987–88 school year, and is being expanded to additional schools during the 1988–89 school year. The program elements are being introduced gradually over time, and many of the objectives of the model could be accomplished differently in different schools, so the model is described here both in its complete conception and as it exists at this writing.

The Pilot School

The Success for All model is currently being implemented at Abbottston Elementary School, a pre-K to 5 school with approximately 440 students. Almost all students are black; 76 percent receive free lunch. The school was selected from among the category of schools that receive the most intensive Chapter 1 resources in the city of Baltimore. In addition, the school had to meet a set of criteria specifying lack of other major programs, adequate space, location near Johns Hopkins University, and manageable size. In spring 1987, the principal and school staff were given an opportunity to serve as the Success for All pilot site, and they voted unanimously to do so. The intention in the selection process was to locate a school that served a typical inner-city population with a staff that was typical of Baltimore City elementary school teachers but willing and able to work with our staff to refine and implement the model. The program at Abbottston Elementary is being compared to a matched control school.

Program Design

The main organizing principle behind the Success for All design is that no child is permitted to fall behind in basic skills. Resources are concentrated in the early grades to attempt to ensure that every child is successful.

Three essential ideas about school and classroom improvement are central to the design of Success for All. The first premise is that the best place to work on ensuring success for all students is in the classroom and its instructional program. Further, it is assumed that research-based *programmatic* efforts will have the highest chance for achieving the important goal of ensuring success for all. That is, rather than focusing on single variables, such as learning time, parent involvement, or reading methods, the improvement efforts must be focused on implementation of strategies that successfully address *all* major components of learning in classrooms.

The second essential idea is the importance of responsiveness to students' needs for corrective instruction. When students experience difficulties, they must receive specifically targeted assistance right away, not weeks or months later when small deficits have accumulated into large ones. The timing of remedial efforts as well as the integration of these efforts with regular instruction is seen as a critical factor in ensuring success for all students. Incorporation of specific structures for tutoring students who are not keeping up with their classmates and for frequent assessment, feedback, and correction, address the need to catch problems early.

The third essential idea is the need for the flexible use of school resources, in particular time and personnel. In most schools, a set level of resources is provided to students, and student success is allowed to vary. In Success for All, success is seen as an entitlement for all students, and it is the resources needed to ensure success that are allowed to vary. Student learning deficits can first be addressed by the reading teacher. If this is not enough, the student may be assigned to a reading tutor. If the student's problem is due to a problem at home, a family support team is available to work with families and social agencies. If health or psychological services are needed, they are provided. Few if any students will be assigned to special education, and few if any will be retained. It is seen as the responsibility of the school to see that every child succeeds in the regular program, no matter what their needs may be.

Program Elements

Reading Tutors.   One of the most important elements of the Success for All model is the use of tutors to support students' success in reading. Tutors replace Chapter 1 and special education resource teachers; research on class size suggests that one-to-one instruction is far more effective than instruction given to small groups (see Glass, Cahen, Smith, and Filby, 1982; Slavin, in press). The tutors are certified teachers with experience in teaching Chapter 1, special education, and/or primary reading. Tutors work one-on-one with students who are having difficulties keeping up with their reading groups. Students are taken from their homeroom classes by the tutors for twenty-minute sessions during times other than reading or math periods. In general, tutors support students' success in the regular reading curriculum, rather than teaching different objectives. For example, if the regular reading teacher is working on long vowels, so does the tutor. However, tutors seek to identify learning deficits and use different strategies to teach the same skills.

During daily ninety-minute reading periods, tutors serve as additional reading teachers to reduce class size for reading. Information on students' specific deficits and needs pass between reading teachers and tutors on brief forms, and reading teachers and tutors are given regular times to meet for purposes of coordinating their approaches with individual children.

Initial placements in tutoring are made based on informal reading inventories administered at the beginning of the school year. Subsequently, decisions about who receives tutoring are made based on eight-week assessments, which include teachers' judgments as well as more formal assessments. First graders receive first priority for tutoring, on the assumption that the primary function of the tutors is to help all students be successful in reading the first time, before they become remedial readers.

Part of the role of the tutors is to identify effective teaching strategies that the regular classroom reading teachers may apply. Many students receive tutoring for one eight-week block and then remain with their class the next eight weeks to see if the regular teacher can keep the child on track without tutoring.

At Abbottston Elementary, a total of six tutors are being provided for grades K through 3, a total of approximately 300 students. They each work with a total of eleven students per day, so about 22 percent of all students in grades K through 3 are receiving tutoring at any given time. However, since tutoring services are concentrated on first graders, approximately 40 percent of first graders are receiving tutoring. Since homeroom classes are reduced to twenty-five students in grades 1 through 3, use of tutors as reading teachers reduces reading class sizes to about fifteen.

A Program Facilitator (see below) supervises the tutors' activities, sitting in with tutors to observe tutoring sessions, suggesting or modeling alternative approaches for specific students, and so on.

Program Facilitator.   A Program Facilitator works at the school full time to oversee (with the principal) the operation of the Success for All model. The Facilitator helps plan the Success for All program, helps the principal with scheduling, and visits classes and tutoring sessions frequently to help teachers and tutors with individual problems. The Program Facilitator may work with individual children having particular difficulties to find successful strategies for teaching them, and then return the children to the tutors or teachers. She or he helps teachers and tutors deal with any behavior problems or other special problems, and coordinates the activities of the Family Support Team with those of the instructional staff.

Reading Program.   Students in grades 1 through 5 are regrouped for reading. That is, students are assigned to heterogeneous, age-grouped classes with class sizes of about twenty-five most of the day, but during a regular ninety-minute reading period they are regrouped according to reading performance levels into reading classes of about fifteen students all at one level. For example, a 2–1 reading class might contain first, second, and third grade students all reading at the same level. Beginning at midyear, kindergarten students are regrouped in the same way. Initial placements in reading classes are made on the basis of individually administered informal reading inventories, but placements are revised every eight weeks on the basis of assessments of progress through the reading curriculum.

The idea behind regrouping is to allow teachers to teach the whole reading class without using reading groups within the class. This greatly reduces the time needed for seatwork and increases direct instruction time.

This regrouping plan is a form of the Joplin Plan, which has been found to increase student achievement in reading (see Slavin, 1987).

The reading program itself (Madden, Slavin, Karweit, Livermon, and Stevens, 1987) has been designed to take full advantage of having ninety minutes of direct instruction. The reading program emphasizes development of basic language skills, auditory discrimination, and sound and letter recognition skills in kindergarten, and uses an approach based on sound blending and synthetic phonics starting in first grade (although kindergarten students who show readiness are accelerated into the first grade program). Peabody Language Development kits are used in grades pre-K, K, and 1 to help students build language concepts. The reading program emphasizes oral reading to partners as well as to the teacher, instruction in story structure and specific comprehension skills (especially in grades 2 and 3), and integration of reading and writing. At the kindergarten and first grade reading levels, students use phonetic mini-books. When they reach the 2–1 reading level, students begin to use the district's Macmillan basal series. The program for grades 2 through 5 is essentially Cooperative Integrated Reading and Composition or CIRC (Stevens, Madden, Slavin, and Farnish, 1987), which as been found to increase student reading achievement in two field experiments.

Language Arts/Writing.   Language arts and writing instruction are given in the homeroom class. The emphasis of the language arts/writing program is on development of oral language skills in preschool and kindergarten, and development of creative and expository writing skills in grades 1 through 5. Students are taught to write using a writing process model in which they plan, draft, revise, edit, and ultimately publish compositions. In the early grades, students are encouraged to use invented spelling, applying letter sounds and phonics skills they have learned in their reading program. Language mechanics instruction (e.g., capitalization, punctuation) is provided in the context of students' writing and in specific lessons provided based on students' needs. Spelling and handwriting instruction is also being provided in the language arts/writing period. The language arts/writing program is adapted from Cooperative Integrated Reading and Composition (Stevens et al., 1987).

Mathematics.   Although implementation of the mathematics component of Success for All has not yet begun at the pilot school, plans call for a mathematics program emphasizing manipulatives, diagrams, and other means of making mathematical concepts real to students, and problem solving, estimation, and use of calculators. Beginning in grade 3, students will be regrouped for mathematics, and will begin to use a form of cooperative learning based on Team Assisted Individualization (Slavin, 1985).

Eight-Week Reading Assessments and Individual Academic Plans.   Every eight weeks, reading teachers assess student progress through the reading program. Any students who seem to be having difficulties keeping up or who may be candidates for acceleration into a higher reading group are referred to the tutors for individual assessments on Informal Reading Inventories (IRIs). The results of the assessments are used to determine who is to receive tutoring, to suggest other adaptations in students' programs, and to identify students who need other types of assistance, such as family interventions, vision/hearing screening, or (in extreme cases) referral for special education evaluation. On the basis of the eight-week assessments, Individual Academic Plans (IAPs) are developed for each student indicating areas of weakness to be addressed by classroom teachers and/or tutors.

Class Size.   Class sizes in the Success for All school are held to twenty-five in grades 1 through 3, twenty in kindergarten, and fifteen in pre-K.

Preschool.   The Success for All school provides a half-day preschool for all eligible students. Class size for preschool is held to fifteen students, with one teacher and one aide. The focus of the preschool is on providing a balanced and developmentally appropriate learning experience for four-year-olds. The curriculum places a heavy emphasis on the development and use of language. Specific structured approaches to language development with demonstrated effectiveness are being integrated into the curriculum.

The curriculum itself follows a thematic approach, integrating various prereadiness activities. A curriculum manual with specific suggested activities has been written and forms the basis for teacher training. One important element of the program emphasizes structured story telling and retelling, which is designed to enhance students' comprehension as well as expressive and receptive language skills. Peabody Language Development kits are used to build students' language concepts and oral expression.

Kindergarten.   The kindergarten program is a full-day program with class sizes of no more than twenty children, with one teacher and one aide in each class. The major focus of the program is on providing a balanced curriculum of academic readiness and nonacademic activities of music, art, and movement.

Continuing the approach in the preschool, a major emphasis in the kindergarten is on language use and development. Strategies for stressing language as a critical part of prereading readiness are incorporated into the curriculum. These include the story telling and retelling program begun in preschool and use of the Peabody Language Development kits, as well as training teachers to use every available opportunity to promote students' use of elaborated, descriptive language. Prereading instruction in the kindergarten emphasizes reading to students, teaching concepts about print, auditory discrimination training, and letter sounds and sound blending.

All students entering kindergarten spend the first half of the year in their regular kindergarten classroom with their regular teacher. This half year allows for settling in to the routine of a full day at school and to the routine of academic activities. At the start of the second half of the year, those kindergarteners who are ready to do so move into the reading program itself, while others continue with the readiness program in their regular classroom.

The afternoon program in the kindergarten is not focused directly on academics. There is a period, however, where additional help might be given to students who did not understand the morning's lessons. This is not a one-on-one tutoring session, but a small group session where the teacher or aide goes over specific material with a group of students.

Family Support Team.   A Family Support Team consisting of at least one social worker and one paraprofessional parent liaison works full-time in the school. The Family Support Team provides parenting education and works to involve parents in support of their children's success in school, both in setting up a home reading program in which students read to their parents and in establishing opportunities for parents to volunteer within the school. Also, family support staff are called on to provide assistance when there are indications that students are not working up to their full potential because of problems at home; for example, families of students who are not receiving adequate sleep or nutrition, are not attending school regularly, or are exhibiting serious behavior problems receive family support assistance.

Special Education.   Every effort is being made to deal with students' learning problems within the context of the regular classroom, as supplemented by tutors. Students who would have ordinarily been referred to special education resource programs are instead retained in class and helped by tutoring and family support services. A self-contained special education program is still provided, but very few referrals are made to the program.

Advisory and Steering Committees.   An advisory committee composed of the building principal, Program Facilitator, teacher representatives, and Johns Hopkins staff meets weekly to review the progress of the program and to identify and solve any problems that arise. In addition, a steering committee composed of Baltimore City administrators, the principal, Facilitator, and Johns Hopkins staff meet monthly to resolve any system-level concerns and to keep the administration up-to-date on the progress of the program.

Costs.   In its full form, the Success for All program can be expensive. However, in disadvantaged schools receiving high levels of Chapter 1 funds (such as Abbottston), the costs can be little or no more than those already provided by Chapter 1 and special education programs, because the Success for All model replaces existing Chapter 1 and special education pullout services. The most expensive single element is the provision of preschool education; in Baltimore, the cost of providing a teacher and an aide to a half-day class of fifteen is more than $1,850 per student per year in salaries alone. The extended-day kindergarten progarm is also very expensive. If these can be provided by other funds, the other elements of Success for All can typically be implemented with current levels of Chapter 1 and special education monies, as long as legal requirements regulating use of these funds are satisfied.

Evaluation Results

Implementation of Success for All at Abbottston Elementary began in September 1987. The program is expected to remain at the school for at least five years. The program evaluation compares Abbottston students to those in a nearby school matched on socioeconomic status and historical achievement level. Then individual children were matched on the basis of standardized test scores. Fall Boehms and Metropolitans were used to match preschool and kindergarten students, respectively, and spring CATs were used to match students in grades 1–3.

For more details on the research procedures and findings, see Madden, Slavin, Karweit, Livermon, and Dolan, 1988.

Preschool and Kindergarten. Preschool results indicated that Success for All children scored significantly higher than control on the Test of Language Development (TOLD) Picture Vocabulary and Sentence Imitation Scales, and on the Merrill Language Screening Test's Comprehension scale, with effect sizes ranging from 0.44 to 0.66. Success for All kindergarteners outscored control students on the TOLD Sentence Imitation and Grammatic Completion scales, the Woodcock Letter-Word Test and Word Attack scales, and the Merrill Language Screening Test. Effect sizes ranged from 0.47 to 0.71 except for Word Attack, which had an effect size of 3.74.

First Grade. Across five scales taken from the individually administered Woodcock and Durrell reading inventories, first graders scored at an average grade equivalent of 2.0 (50th percentile), in comparison to 1.5 in the control group (28th percentile). Effect sizes ranged from 0.34 to 1.39. Among students who scored in the lowest 25 percent on the pretests, Success for All students scored at the 32nd percentile, in comparison to the 8th percentile for similar control students. These results are depicted in Figure 12–1. As the figure shows, the lowest 25 percent of the Success for All first graders outscored the *average* control students.

FIGURE 12–1.   Mean Reading Scores for Success for All and Control Schools

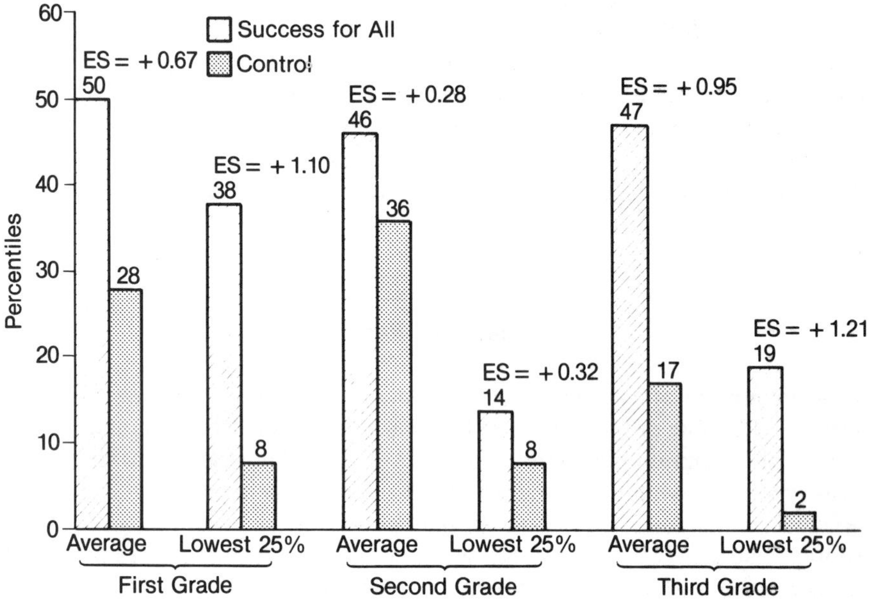

Source: N. A. Madden, R. E. Slavin, N. L. Karweit, and B. J. Livermon, "Success for All: Restructuring the urban elementary school," *Educational Leadership* (in press).

Second Grade.   At the second grade level, Success for All students significantly outscored control on the Woodcock Letter-Word Identification and Word Attack scales, but not on the Durrell scales. Similar results were obtained for the lowest 25 percent of students.

Third Grade.   The strongest effects of all were seen at the third grade level. Success for All third graders averaged 3.6 grade equivalents (47th percentile), in comparison to their counterparts in the control school, who averaged 2.4 (17th percentile). Effect sizes ranged from 0.71 to 1.42. As in the first grade, the lowest 25 percent of third graders in Success for All outscored the *average* in the control school. The lowest-scoring 25 percent of Success for All students scored at the 19th percentile, in comparison to their matched counterparts who scored at the 2nd percentile.

Retentions and Special Education Referrals.   Some of the most important effects of Success for All do not appear in the standardized test scores, but in the ability of the school to maintain students in the regular program. At Abbottston, approximately 12 percent of students in grades 1–3 were retained the year before the program began. At the end of the first program year, only one student was retained. In the previous year, thirty students were referred to special education and eighteen were accepted. Currently, two students diagnosed as retarded were the only ones assigned to special education for a learning problem. As noted earlier, Abbottston lost its special education resource teacher because of the program.

In the first year, Success for All brought the average scores for children at all grade levels to almost the 50th percentile (the control school averaged at about the 28th). This is good, but it does not yet fulfill the commitment to bring *every* child to grade level in the basic skills. Not until the current preschoolers have reached the third grade can this commitment be assessed. Also, long-term effects of the program must be determined to see if early success does in fact eliminate or greatly reduce the need for continuing remedial or special education services.

If, however, Success for All is ultimately found to meet its promise to provide all children with adequate skills, the implications for compensatory and special education could be dramatic. If it could be shown that high rates of learning problems are not inevitable consequences of poverty but could be prevented by the schools, the political calculus surrounding compensatory education would be greatly altered. Withholding proven, effective interventions from students at risk might be seen as tantamount to withholding effective medications from children with curable diseases. Special education could get out of the extremely expensive and largely ineffective business of serving large numbers of students categorized as "learning disabled" and instead concentrate its efforts on the truly handicapped.

The success and widespread adoption of Success for All could also have many less immediately apparent consequences. First, it would reverse the growth of special education programs for the learning disabled. All but the most disabled (or behaviorally disordered) students could be served within the regular classroom setting, supplemented by tutoring. This would allow most students with learning disabilities to receive appropriate and effective services without the expensive and cumbersome special education assessment and referral processes now in use. Special education could return to a focus on truly "special" cases, where a child would come to the attention of the special education process only after appropriate placement in reading and mathematics, optimal classroom instruction, tutoring, family support interventions, and other interventions within the regular education program had been tried and had failed.

The impact of Success for All on remedial and compensatory education would be equally profound. Pullouts for remedial services would be brief and intensive. Tutoring sessions and decisions about who should receive tutoring would be made every six weeks. In this way, few students would receive remedial services every day for even a whole year—much less year after year, as so often happens under current practices. Chapter 1 would no longer be a separate program housed within the school, but would become an integral part of the school's attempts to provide all students with an adequate level of basic skills. Every teacher in the elementary building, Chapter 1-funded or not, would teach reading, so that all teachers would have a common language and experience base from which to work together to ensure student success. This use of Chapter 1 funds is permitted under the recently passed Chapter 1 reauthorization for schools with at least 75 percent of their students receiving free lunch, and could be adapted to work within less disadvantaged schools.

Widespread adoption of Success for All models could also have important effects on regular education. Even students who never received a day of tutoring or other services would benefit from a school organization plan that freed the teacher from constantly having to deal with students who lack basic skills and removed the constant disruptions inherent to remedial and special education pullouts. The opportunity for bright students to be grouped with older students for reading and mathematics would allow for vertical acceleration in these subjects without the drawbacks of comprehensive tracking or separate gifted programs.

Finally, if Success for All is, in fact, successful, this could pose an important challenge to the political and legal status quo. Imagine that it could be demonstrated that virtually all students could, in principle, be successful in school, given a level of resources greater than that which is now available but within a range that local, state, or federal governments could provide. In this circumstance, withholding proven, effective services capable of preventing educational failure could be perceived as similar to withholding effective antibiotics from children with bacterial diseases. At present, it is difficult to prove convincingly that per-pupil expenditures are strongly related to achievement, and because of this, court cases challenging school finance policies are typically unable to establish that gross disparities between suburban and inner-city schools result in educational disadvantages for the latter. If it could be shown that money spent on ensuring the success of every child in the elementary grades could have a substantial and lasting impact, then there may arise political and legal pressures to provide every child with enough services to bring them to an acceptable level of basic skills.

POLICY RECOMMENDATIONS

How can programs for students at risk of school failure be reformed to make a substantially greater impact on student achievement? The chapters in this book have identified critical changes in practice at many levels, from changes in teacher behaviors to changes in school and classroom organization to changes in instructional programs to changes in legal and political systems. The preceding section described a model elementary school program that operationalizes many of these changes. However, beyond the particular reforms suggested in the chapters, there are broader policy changes that are needed at the federal, state, and local levels to bring about lasting changes in the ability of remedial and special education programs to meet the needs of at-risk students.

These policy changes flow from two observations about the current status of programs for students at risk. First, there is much more we need to know about how to ensure success for low-achieving students. Second, that which we do know is having little effect on current practice in remedial and special education, and there are few mechanisms in place for translating research into practice.

The remainder of this chapter lays out a set of actions which, if successfully undertaken, would result in a major improvement in the effectiveness of remedial and special education.

Establish National Program Evaluation Centers

One of the most vexing problems in translation of research into practice is that it is difficult for practitioners or policymakers to assess the adequacy of program evaluations. All programs that are disseminated claim to be effective, but it is often difficult to determine the validity of these claims. The Joint Dissemination Review Panel (JDRP), an ad hoc group within the U.S. Department of Education, does examine evaluation data and passes programs that appear to be effective. However, the quality of research designs required to pass JDRP is very low. For example, most programs claiming effects on achievement used fall-to-spring NCE or percentile gains or other pre-to-post gains as the criterion for effectiveness, and these designs have been found to produce greatly inflated estimates of program effects (see Chapters 1 and 2). Also, the JDRP has no way to determine whether or not it is seeing *all* evaluations of a given program. A program might fail in nine sites and succeed in one, and the program could be approved based on the one site. At present, there is no requirement that all evaluations be submitted to JDRP.

Although reforming JDRP rules would be helpful, the JDRP system is fundamentally incapable of identifying programs that could be counted on to produce positive achievement effects. There are just too many ways that a program developer evaluating his or her own program can, in all good faith, bias the results in favor of program success. For example, developers can key their program to the limited set of objectives assessed on the criterion measures; they can choose measures particularly likely to favor their curriculum; they can use as control groups schools or teachers that refused the program and can therefore be assumed to be less motivated; they can devote extraordinary amounts of staff time in a small number of classrooms to ensure that the program will work; and so on.

If we are to expect federal, state, and local educational agencies to invest seriously in reforming programs for students at risk, we must have the utmost confidence that we have a set of programs which, if properly implemented, will make a significant difference in the achievement of students at risk. This state of affairs will only come about when we have independent, rigorous, and widely recognized program evaluations, much as the Food and Drug Administration oversees independent evaluations of new drugs or *Consumer Reports* evaluates consumer goods.

We propose that the Department of Education establish one or more independent evaluation centers to evaluate programs that could be used under Chapter 1 or special education funding. These centers would select programs that had already been shown to be successful by their developers (e.g., programs that had already passed JDRP) for independent evaluation. They would locate some number of school districts willing to evaluate the programs. Each district would make available two or more similar schools whose principals and staffs had volunteered to use the program, and the evaluation center would randomly select one set of schools to use the program and one set to serve as a control group. The program developer would receive funding to train teachers, local support staff, and so on, to work in the experimental schools. Students in the experimental and control schools would be pre- and posttested on measures specially designed or adapted by the evaluation center. Although program developers would know what objectives the measures assessed, they would not have access to the measures themselves (to keep them from gearing their program to the tests). These measures would assess achievement broadly, and need not be restricted to paper-and-pencil assessments. For example, individually administered reading assessments are essential in this area; a subset of students could be given such assessments. In mathematics, higher-order problem-solving and estimation skills might be assessed using nontraditional formats, along with more traditional measures of computations and simple applications. Matrix sampling procedures might be used to achieve broad-scale assessment without taking too much time for testing. For example, in assessing a writing program, one-third of the students might be randomly assigned to write a personal narrative, one-third an expository essay, and one-third a mystery story.

Based on recommendations of the program developer, the evaluation center would prepare observation forms to assess degree of implementation and would send trained observers into project classrooms (and control classes) to characterize the degree to which the program was being implemented and the differences between experimental and control classrooms. Also, evaluation center staff would carefully monitor the costs of implementing the program in order to compute cost-effectiveness ratios at the end of the evaluation process.

In most cases, program evaluations would be continued for two school years, to examine (in the second year) the program's effects when it is fully implemented and no longer novel.

Clearly, the evaluations conducted by the independent evaluation center(s) would have immediate national visibility. Programs that held up under the stringent conditions likely to be applied by these centers could be counted on to make a difference with students, and this fact could have a considerable impact on policy and practice. For example, Chapter 1 and Title I legislation have always specified that school districts applying for funds must satisfy their state departments of education that their programs are "of a sufficient size, scope, and quality to give reasonable promise of substantial progress toward meeting the educational needs of the children being served." The national average effect of Chapter 1 on reading and mathematics achievement is on the order of two to three percentile points at most (see Chapter 1 of this book)—hardly "substantial progress." If there were programs known to be capable of providing "substantial progress," then there may be a legal basis for requiring that school districts invest in such programs or demonstrate that their existing programs are more effective. In any case, having a set of proven, effective programs would certainly provide a basis for federal, state, and local dissemination efforts focused on students at risk.

Obviously, it makes most sense to have independent evaluation centers funded by the federal government, as their findings would apply throughout the country. However, states or even large districts could establish smaller-scale evaluation centers of their own to systematically locate promising programs and then rigorously evaluate them within the state or district. We have established a center of this type at Johns Hopkins University to serve the Baltimore City Schools. This center, called the Baltimore Public Education Institute, is funded by the Abell Foundation, a local private foundation, and has as one of its functions the task of bringing promising programs into the Baltimore City Public Schools and evaluating them.

Fund Research and Development of New Programs

Most of the effective programs discussed in Chapters 2 through 4 are very old, having been developed in the 1960s and 1970s. Some are no longer in existence. One reason that few comprehensive programs have been developed in recent years is that since the Nixon administration, there has been very little federal support for the kinds of systematic development and evaluation of instructional programs that have the greatest promise for making substantial differences in the achievement of at-risk students. If we are serious in our undertaking to replace current remedial and special education programs with proven, research-based alternatives, we must have a wide range of alternatives from which districts may choose, both to allow for adaptations to local circumstances or needs and to avoid putting governments in the uncomfortable position of promoting a small number of programs. As the earlier chapters in this book demonstrate, we have learned a great deal in the past twenty years, but little of what we have learned has been translated into practical, comprehensive, and replicable programs. For example, it is ironic that much of the debate about the use of systematic direct instruction models to teach reading and mathematics to disadvantaged students still revolves around Distar, a program that is now older than many of the teachers using it. After three decades of advances in research on cognitive psychology, reading and mathematics education, and classroom organization and management, we can surely do better, yet the funds to undertake systematic development work on the scale that would be required are nowhere on the horizon.

A major federal commitment is needed to fund promising development efforts specifically directed toward the needs of students at risk. It is not enough to state that we know "what works." We also need to know how to establish and maintain that which "works" in real classrooms. University- and school-based developers could be funded over a period of years to develop, pilot test, refine, and evaluate programs that would ultimately be evaluated by the independent evaluation centers. Of course, not all programs would have to start from scratch; many promising programs now exist that are further along in the development-evaluation process. The idea would be to get the best minds in education (and related fields) working to solve a very well-defined objective of enormous importance—the prevention and remediation of learning problems among students at risk.

One requirement for the development effort would be that developers could be exempted from certain Chapter 1 or special education regulations, as long as they operate within rules that could, *in principle,* be enacted. For example, there was a recent debate in Congress about extending the opportunity for high-poverty schools to opt for schoolwide projects, in which Chapter 1 funds could be used to benefit all students. The problem is that there were few examples of schoolwide projects, fewer coherent models appropriate for use within schoolwide projects, and almost no rigorous evaluations of such models. The discussions of changes in the legislation would have been greatly enriched if research on coherent schoolwide models could have been under way before the legislative changes were considered.

In addition to providing major funding for researchers to develop and evaluate programs, it would be a good idea to provide smaller amounts of funding and perhaps waivers of certain regulations to school districts that are implementing innovative programs. In order to receive this funding, the districts could be required to set up an adequate experimental design, perhaps with the assistance or under the supervision of an independent evaluation center.

Again, although the federal government is the logical source for funding of development and evaluation activities, state, local, and private foundation funds may also be appropriate for this purpose.

Resources to Help Districts Adopt Effective Programs

Once we have a set of proven, effective models for students at risk, it will next be necessary to provide a mechanism for implementing these programs successfully under Chapter 1 or special education funding. These implementation issues must be taken very seriously; research on dissemination of externally developed innovations finds that implementation must be planned for and executed on a classroom-by-classroom basis. At a minimum, local districts (or intermediate districts, when appropriate) would need to have "circuit-riders" or even building-level coaches who are experts in a given program and have full-time responsibility to ensure that the new program is being adequately implemented by, among other things, visiting classes constantly to respond to teachers' concerns and see that teachers are adequately implementing the program. Providing release time for training, followup, and preparation of materials is also critical.

For most types of innovations, it is important to involve teachers in selecting the innovation and in participating in planning the phasing in of the program. For example, schools whose Chapter 1 programs have been ineffective in the past may be compelled to select a different program, but *which* program is selected should be left up to a free and informed choice of the professional staff. When appropriate, teachers may be allowed to choose different programs within the same building, or the program may be phased in over time, with volunteers serving as the first wave of implementers.

Providing training and support for staff developers at the local level could be done in many ways. State or regional Chapter 1 or special education effectiveness centers might be established. These centers would employ experts in the validated models who also are experts in dissemination of innovations. Alternatively, the developers themselves might be funded to provide training and followup to staff developers located within adopting districts.

The role of staff development in this conception would be vastly different from current practice. The emphasis would be on sustained training and on-site followup in a relatively small number of proven programs, not the one-day workshops in larger numbers of programs which characterize much of current staff development.

Dissemination of effective programs could be funded by federal, state, or local education agencies. One model for this might be the National Diffusion Network (NDN), a federal program that funds developers to refine and disseminate programs passed by JDRP. The NDN also funds a system of state facilitators who work to bring these programs into their states. However, adoption of the programs themselves is paid for by the districts. The NDN system itself might be expanded to permit it to focus on effective programs for students at risk, or a similar system might be developed within

Chapter 1 and/or special education. In addition, some proportion of Chapter 1 or special education funds could be set aside to pay the costs of bringing in and maintaining validated programs.

At present, both Chapter 1 and special education funding are as secure as they have ever been. For example, the vote reauthorizing Chapter 1 was nearly unanimous in both the House and the Senate. Certainly, efforts to maintain and expand funding for these programs must continue, but we must also turn our attention to ensuring that the programs purchased by these funds are the best they can be. We must undertake a major commitment to expand the knowledge base underlying effective programs for students at risk, to develop and evaluate new programs, and to set up dissemination procedures to ensure high-quality implementation of effective programs at the school and classroom level. Without such a commitment, it is certain that remedial and special education programs will continue to produce the mediocre results they produce now. We can do much better. The tragic waste of the learning potential of so many of our children is needless and cannot be allowed to continue. A long road lies ahead to make the needed changes, but at the end of that road is a chance to transform the elementary school into an institution that guarantees all students an adequate level of basic skills.

REFERENCES

Glass, G.; Cahen, L.; Smith, M.L.; and Filby, N. (1982). *School class size*. Beverly Hills, CA: Sage.

Madden, N.A.; Slavin, R.E.; Karweit, N.L.; and Livermon, B.J. (in press). Success for All: Restructuring the urban elementary school. *Educational Leadership*.

Madden, N.A.; Slavin, R.E.; Karweit, N.L.; Livermon, B.J.; and Dolan, L. (1988). *Success for All: Effects on student achievement, retentions, and special education referrals*. Baltimore, MD: Johns Hopkins University, Center for Research on Elementary and Middle Schools.

Madden, N.A.; Slavin, R.E.; Karweit, N.L.; Livermon, B.; and Stevens, R.J. (1987). *Success for All: Teacher's manual for reading*. Baltimore, MD: Johns Hopkins University, Center for Research on Elementary and Middle Schools.

Slavin, R.E. (1985). Team-assisted individualization: Combining cooperative learning and individualized instruction in mathematics. In R.E. Slavin, S. Sharan, S. Kagan, R. Hertz-Lazarowitz, C. Webb, and R. Schmuck (Eds.), *Learning to cooperate, cooperating to learn*. New York: Plenum, pp. 177–209.

Slavin, R.E. (1987). Ability grouping and student achievement in elementary schools: A best-evidence synthesis. *Review of Educational Research, 57*, 293–336.

Slavin, R.E. (in press). Class size and student achievement: Small effects of small classes. *Educational Psychologist*.

Stevens, R.J.; Madden, N.A.; Slavin, R.E.; and Farnish, A.M. (1987). Cooperative integrated reading and composition: Two field experiments. *Reading Research Quarterly, 22*, 433–454.

INDEX